YOUR *babycare* BIBLE

2013

YOUR
babycare
BIBLE

general editor
Dr. Harold S. Raucher

weldon**owen**

Weldon Owen Inc.
415 Jackson Street, San Francisco, CA 94111
www.weldonowen.com

President, CEO **Terry Newell**
VP, Publisher **Roger Shaw**
Executive Editor **Elizabeth Dougherty**
Assistant Editor **Katharine Moore**
Creative Director **Kelly Booth**
Designer **Michel Gadwa**
Production Director **Chris Hemesath**
Production Manager **Michelle Duggan**

Adapted from the book originally produced by
Carroll & Brown Limited
20 Lonsdale Road, Queen's Park
London NW6 6RD
All rights reserved.

Managing Art Editor **Emily Cook**
Photography **Jules Selmes**

ISBN: 978-1-61628-148-9
Library of Congress Control Number: 2011936813

Printed by 1010 Printing International Limited in China

10 9 8 7 6 5 4 3 2 1
2011   2012   2013   2014

Contents

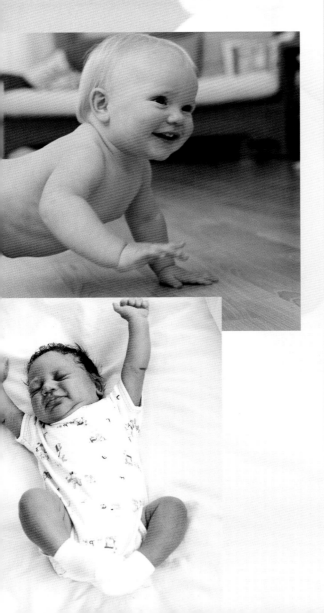

GENERAL EDITOR

Harold S. Raucher, MD, is an associate clinical professor of pediatrics at the Mount Sinai School of Medicine in New York, where he received his medical training and has been teaching for nearly 20 years. A member of the American Academy of Pediatrics, Dr. Raucher is board certified in general pediatrics and in pediatric infectious diseases, and maintains a private practice in both areas. In addition to his clinical and teaching work, he has published numerous peer-reviewed articles on pediatric diseases. A father of two daughters, Dr. Raucher lives with his wife, who is also a physician, in Englewood Cliffs, New Jersey.

OTHER CONTRIBUTORS

A.J.R. Waterston MD, FRCP, FRCPCH, DRCOG,DCH
Penny Preston MD, ChB, MRCP
Clare Meynell, RM
Alison Blenkinsop, RM DipHE IBCLC
June Thompson, RGN, RM, RHV
Nicola Graimes

Introduction

"The days are long, but the years fly by," parents often say. This book is about providing you with relevant information, practical advice, and reassuring support to make those days as easy and enjoyable as possible. Being a parent is a new and sometimes intimidating experience, unlike anything else you will embark upon. You are responsible for keeping your baby fed, clean, and happy, and safe from danger and ill health—often without much preparation. It's natural to feel overwhelmed, anxious, or out-and-out exhausted at times. Rest assured, you can do it!

From establishing feeding to ensuring timely immunizations, you are on the front lines managing your baby's daily care. Don't be surprised when you develop a sixth sense about when everything is okay or when something is just not right with your baby. You will recognize when there may be a problem that needs medical attention, you need to change your behavior, or it's just one of those stages. Whatever you encounter, *Your Babycare Bible* is a resource you can turn to again and again for a wide range of topics.

Your Babycare Bible collects the most up-to-date and important information on all aspects of babycare for newborns to toddlers. The comprehensive chapters explain how to ensure your baby feeds and sleeps successfully and safely, and how you should interpret and respond to his or her crying. Special sections make it easy to master the essentials of newborn care and emergency first-aid procedures. There is also in-depth coverage on keeping your baby safe and healthy, and what to expect if your baby is born a twin, is premature, or has special needs. A month-by-month guide gives an overview of what to expect as your newborn grows into a baby and then a toddler, and an entire chapter is dedicated to your child's development and how you, as a parent, can promote positive growth. Finally, there is specific help given to new moms and dads—advice on how to prepare for your new arrival and how to be the best parent you can be.

Dr. Harold S. Raucher

PREPARING FOR YOUR BABY

Readying your home

Preparing your home will make it much easier to get through the first hectic days of caring for your new baby. By taking care of all the little details ahead of time, you'll have more time and energy to enjoy getting to know your baby.

Many parents-to-be want to paint, remodel, or make repairs around the house before bringing their baby home. If you want to tackle any home projects, try to finish everything at least a month before your due date—earlier is even better. You don't want to come home to a messy, disorganized, and noisy scene while you're recovering from the birth and getting to know your little one.

Keep in mind that pregnant women and newborns should avoid exposure to the dust, commotion, and paint fumes that go along with home improvements, so it would be a good idea to have your partner or professionals do the work.

Your baby's room

Whether you have a separate nursery for your baby or are setting her up in a shared room, it's important to arrange furniture and storage spaces as conveniently as you can. You'll want to make it easy to get your baby into and out of her crib, change her diapers, get her dressed, and rock her to sleep.

Place the crib against a wall where your baby won't be able to reach a window, a curtain, a window-blind cord, or other furniture. A good rule of thumb: Make sure items are an adult arm's length away from all sides of the crib. Avoid placing the crib against a wall shared with a noisy room or in a spot where direct sunlight would fall on your baby in the morning hours or during afternoon naps.

The changing table also should be against a wall and away from any windows. Make sure there's a spot under the table or next to it to store diapers, wipes, and diaper creams or ointments. You'll want to be able to reach all your supplies while standing at the table during a diaper change—never leave your baby unattended on the table, not even for a

moment. Buy a changing pad with a safety strap. Place the diaper pail next to the table.

A comfortable rocking chair or glider will come in handy; you may spend hours at a time there, nursing or rocking your newborn to sleep. Set up a lamp to provide soft lighting so you can read or use it as a night-light. You might want a radio or music player to listen to while you feed or soothe your baby. Position a clock so you can keep an eye on it from the rocking chair.

If you plan to pump breast milk, set up storage for your supplies near the chair. Keep together the pump, accessories, and books or magazines to read while expressing milk.

In fact, storage is essential in a nursery. Use dressers, chests, cabinets, shelves, crates, or baskets to organize clothing, toys, and books.

Preparing for multiples

Expecting more than one baby can be both exciting and daunting. You'll find advice on caring for multiples throughout this book, but here's how you can get your home and nursery ready for twins.

Most important, get an early start! Twins are frequently born before their due date, and they are more likely than singletons to be born prematurely. Twins are also more likely to be delivered surgically, by cesarean section—and that would mean a longer postpartum recovery for you.

Multiples mean double (or more) the gear, such as cribs and car seats. Buy cribs and car seats new to ensure that they meet current safety standards—you can save money elsewhere. Newborns can sleep in bassinets or Moses baskets, both of which have their advantages. Moses baskets are more portable than

bassinets, as they have two handles for easy lifting; however, they are not elevated. Bassinets take up less floor space, making it easier to have your babies in your room at night; you will need one for each baby.

Fortunately, you don't need to duplicate all of the furniture. The changing table and storage, such as bookshelves and dressers, can be shared.

You also don't need two sets of outfits—your twins can share. If your twins are the same sex, this is easy. If one is a boy and the other is a girl, opt for unisex fashions and colors.

Expenses can add up quickly when you're shopping for twins. You can save some cash by borrowing gently used equipment and clothing from friends or relatives or by buying secondhand items. Check to make sure that any secondhand equipment you purchase is in good condition and meets current safety standards.

The layette

Stores and websites selling infant clothing have lists of what they think you should buy. These are useful guidelines, but you'll have to use your own judgment. How much you really need depends on how much of a stickler you are for cleanliness, how often you expect—or are able—to do laundry, and how messy your baby is.

You really don't need to change your baby into fresh clothing for small amounts of spit-up or other little spills, although you may feel more comfortable doing so. If you change his outfit every time he gets a bit of spit-up on his clothes, or if you plan to wait 3 or 4 days between loads of laundry, you'll need to have more outfits on hand. However, if you do laundry every day, you can get away with fewer items of clothing.

So how many outfits do you need? Use this formula for indoor clothing. Let's assume that you'll do laundry every other day and you'll change his snapped T-shirt only when there's a moderate amount of spit-up on it. Multiply the average number of outfits used each day (3) by the number of days between washes (2), or 3 x 2 = 6. Always add an extra day's supply—so your total would be 9.

You most likely don't need extra outerwear, such as a snowsuit, because these items get less use and require less washing. Your baby is more likely to outgrow outerwear than to wear it out.

WHAT YOU NEED FOR 1 DAY

Diapers 8–12
T-shirts with wide neck openings; most have snaps at the crotch 2–3
Pants or leggings 1–2
Socks or booties 2
Pajamas or sleepers 2
Blanket sleeper 2
Receiving blankets 1–2
Crib sheets 1–2
Bibs or burp cloths 2
Washcloths 1–2
Hooded baby towel 1

OUTDOOR CLOTHES

Warm hats 2
Sweaters or jackets 2
Snowsuit or fleece outfit 1
Brimmed sun hat 1

Furnishing your baby's room

Whatever your decorating style, safety is the top priority. (See Chapter 12, "Keeping your baby healthy," for more on keeping a safe home.) It's also smart to look for products that are easy to clean.

Some items—such as dressers and storage units—don't have to be designed for babies; standard-size items can cater to your child's needs for many years. To make the most of your space, look for multipurpose furniture, such as a crib with drawers underneath or a changing table that is also a dresser. Also look for unused areas for storage, such as the back of a door, where you can hang a multipocket container for small items. Wall pegs can provide hanging space. You can consider putting the dresser in the closet if floor space is at a premium.

Diaper pail

Babies go through diapers rapidly. Have on hand a week's worth of diapers—about 75—when you bring your baby home. Most parents like to have a covered container to limit unpleasant diaper odors. You can use a simple lined wastebasket or a more modern version, a disposal unit with plastic bags stored inside that makes it easy to remove and discard disposable diapers. A foot-pedal control makes a diaper pail easier to open while your hands are full. If you'll be emptying the pail often, a small container will work. If you'll be emptying the pail less often or using cloth diapers, you'll probably want a larger container.

Changing table

You'll change a lot of diapers, so if you get a changing table, make sure that it is the right height for you—you don't want to lean over to change your newborn. If changing tables are too low, using the top of a dresser for changes is an option. Either way, look for furniture that has storage shelves or drawers.

A soft changing mat or pad should cover the entire surface. Look for one with a safety strap and a washable, removable cover.

Safety is an important consideration. Some babies protest having their diapers changed, and older babies can squirm and roll over, putting them at risk for falling. Use the safety strap and offer your baby a distracting book or toy. You can also put a changing pad on the floor. Always keep a hand on your baby, and never leave her unattended on a changing table, not even for a moment.

Accessories

Running a fan may help prevent sudden infant death syndrome (SIDS). The white noise it makes can soothe babies, too.

A room thermometer lets you check that the nursery is not overheated, another SIDS risk factor. The recommended temperature range is 68–72°F.

Lights and lamps with low-wattage bulbs or dimmers will provide enough light for you to check on your baby at night without waking her. Position one near your nursing chair.

A mobile will entertain your young baby. If you install one above the crib or changing table, place it high enough so it's out of baby's reach and remove it when your baby can push up on hands and knees.

Crib

Safety is of the utmost importance when choosing a crib and mattress. It's best to buy a new crib. See page 156 for specific advice. Always buy a new, firm mattress. Used mattresses have been linked to SIDS.

Babycare basics

You'll want to have these basic items on hand.
- Hand sanitizer
- Infant acetaminophen (such as Tylenol)
- Saline nasal spray
- Nasal bulb syringe/aspirator
- Moisturizing skin lotion*
- Thermometer (a digital, rectal one is the most accurate)
- Diaper cream or ointment*
- Infant bathtub
- Soap*
- Shampoo*
- Baby safety scissors, nail clippers, or emery board*
- Cotton balls or wipes (unscented, alcohol-free)*

*See Chapter 2, "Caring for your newborn," for advice on buying these.

Storage

For such tiny creatures, babies can amass an astonishing amount of stuff. Clothes, toys, toiletries, and bulky equipment, such as bathtubs and diaper bags, need to be easily accessible but out of the way.

Most of your baby's clothes can be folded and stored in drawers. Bins or baskets can hold everyday items, such as shoes. You'll also need a hamper or laundry bag for dirty clothes.

You could hang a diaper bag on the wall near your changing area to keep diapers nearby. Wipes and creams should be within reach during diaper changes but beyond your baby's grasp. Toys can go on shelves, in bins, or in hanging pockets.

Rocking chair or glider

You'll spend many hours feeding and rocking your baby, so choose a chair that's comfortable and offers good support. Some chairs recline as well as rock or glide, and some have a matching ottoman. Make sure the fabric is easy to wipe clean.

Baby equipment

Car seat

You'll need a car seat suitable for newborns to take your baby home from the hospital or birthing center. Never use secondhand car seats. Look for a rear-facing one with a five-point safety harness and install it in a seat without an air bag. Set it up in the backseat of your car (never in the front) before your due date—car seats can be hard to install, and you may want to have a professional inspection to make sure it's done correctly. You can learn more about car seats on pages 97 and 321. For current information, consult the National Highway Traffic Safety Administration (www.nhtsa.gov) and the American Academy of Pediatrics (www.healthychildren.org).

Swing

An infant swing is a wonderful invention. It can be especially good at calming your baby during fussy spells and can help keep him happy and quiet long enough for you to eat dinner. Swings may be operated manually or with batteries. Make sure your swing has safety straps to keep your baby from sliding out; a washable, removable seat cover that is secured with strong stitching and heavy-duty snaps; and a padded, reclining seat. Never leave your baby unattended in a swing.

Infant seat/bouncer

If you need your hands free but want to be sure your baby is nearby and safe, you may want an infant seat or bouncer. It will recline and gently rock your baby, and some also will support him in a more upright position. If you live in a multi-story home, you might want an extra seat. That way, you can have one in a convenient spot on each floor, and you'll only have to carry your baby up and down the stairs as you move around the house. Never leave your baby unattended in a bouncer.

Bassinet, bedside sleeper, or Moses basket

A bedside bassinet, a Moses basket, or a sleeper that attaches to your bed can make nighttime feedings easier. You can take a portable basket with you if you travel with your baby. Some come with supporting stands and canopies. The downside of these little beds is their small size; your baby will quickly outgrow his. Some bassinets and bedside sleepers can be converted into changing tables or playpens.

Stroller and baby carrier

You have a tremendous range of choices in strollers—and you might want more than one; for example, a heavy-duty one you keep by your front door for daily outings, and a lightweight one you store in your car for short jaunts. Make sure whatever you buy meets safety standards.

At first, you need a stroller that reclines to hold a prone baby or that is designed to accommodate your infant car seat. Popular models are sturdy, foldable, and have padded, comfortable seats that can be adjusted so babies can lie flat. Options include folding canopies, storage baskets, cup holders, and adjustable handle heights. Specialty strollers are available for multiples or for children with physical disabilities (see page 370).

Test-drive a stroller before taking it home. Load it with a few items to see how it handles, and make sure the push-and-fold mechanism is easy to manage one-handed. Fold it up.

You also might want a baby carrier. Slings, wraps, and carriers hold your baby to your chest, back, or hip. Keep in mind an infant must face inward and have good support for his head. Again, it's wise to try it before you buy it. Read more about carriers on page 45.

Monitor

A baby monitor lets you hear your baby when he isn't in the room with you. It's a good idea to have one if you won't be able to hear his cries from your bedroom or when you're in another part of your home. There are also models with video monitors so you can keep an eye on him as he sleeps.

If you can easily hear your baby from where you sleep, you might not need a monitor. Babies are surprisingly noisy sleepers: They whimper and grunt, and they frequently wake briefly and move about. Monitors transmit all these normal little nighttime noises, disrupting your sleep and tempting you—as long as you're awake anyway—to go check on him. This disturbs both your rest and your baby's.

Whether or not you decide to use a baby monitor, don't worry: You'll be able to hear his loud, persistent cries, which will signal to you that he's hungry or uncomfortable and needs your help.

Feeding equipment

Whether you breastfeed or bottle-feed, it's good to have on hand bottles and nipples—extra if you'll be exclusively bottle-feeding. If you're going to express milk, you'll need an electric breast pump and bags and bottles for milk storage. See Chapter 3, "Feeding your young baby," for details.

Key decisions

Before your baby is born, you'll need to make important decisions that can affect both you and your baby, including what type of birth you'd like to have, whether you plan to breastfeed, your baby's name, who will help you look after him, and, if it's a boy, whether he'll be circumcised.

The birth

Although giving birth is a natural part of life, not all births are the same. You may want to think about what kind of birth experience you hope to have, but keep in mind that the event rarely goes as planned. Fortunately, most births go smoothly with no major complications. However, it's important to understand potential risks and complications.

Childbirth without anesthesia or medicinal pain relief, often called natural childbirth, avoids any risk of side effects for you or your baby from pain medications. You should be more alert after a natural delivery and better able to breastfeed.

Epidurals are commonly used to provide pain relief during delivery. Be aware that epidurals are associated with the greater likelihood that forceps or vacuum could be needed during delivery. A more common complication is a strong headache, which could require a second spinal tap. In very rare cases, an infection may develop at the site where the needle was inserted. There are many options for pain relief during childbirth. Discuss your options, as well as the advantages and disadvantages of each, with your physician before the birth.

You may also want to discuss the option of giving birth in a birthing center or at home instead of in a hospital. Giving birth in a birthing center or in your home is an option if you have a low-risk pregnancy. You would probably be attended by a midwife. If complications arise, however, you would need to be taken to a hospital.

In a hospital, you benefit from having specialists and equipment readily available in case you or your

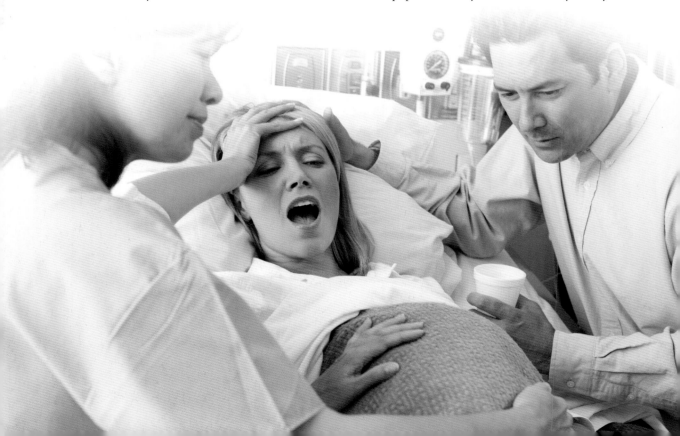

Hospital checks on babies

After birth, your baby will be checked by hospital staff or a pediatrician.

Apgar test

Healthcare providers will perform the Apgar test twice, at 1 and 5 minutes after your baby's birth. Developed by Dr. Virginia Apgar, this test quickly assesses a newborn's health.

The word "Apgar" also stands for the signs caregivers are checking: appearance, pulse, grimace, activity, and respiration. For each of these, your baby will get a score of 0, 1, or 2 (see box, below). Babies rarely receive a total score of 10, but a 1-minute Apgar score above 7 is usually fine. A low score is not an indicator of a baby's future health; it simply means she needs some temporary medical help and monitoring.

Full physical examination

Within the first few days, your baby's features, heart, lungs, spine, anus, fingers, and toes will be checked; her hips will be assessed for proper movement and placement. She'll be weighed, and her head size and length will be measured.

Heel prick test

After the first 24 hours, a nurse will prick your baby's heel to take a blood sample, used to check thyroid function and test for a rare metabolic disorder called phenylketonuria (PKU). Caregivers will also test your baby's hearing, check for jaundice, and conduct other tests required by law (this varies from state to state). To find out what tests are being given to your child, talk with her doctor.

Preventive treatments

Newborns usually receive an injection or oral dose of vitamin K because they often have low levels of this vitamin, which is necessary for normal blood clotting. Further doses may be given in subsequent weeks. Newborns may also receive antibiotic eye drops as well as the hepatitis B vaccine to prevent an infection of the liver.

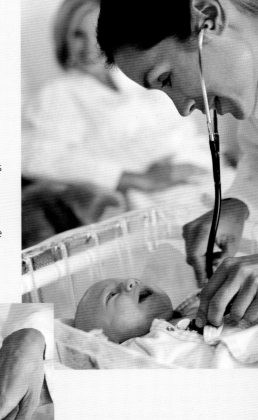

SIGN	POINTS		
	0	1	2
Appearance	Pale or blue	Body pink, extremities blue	Pink
Pulse (heart rate)	Not detectable	Below 100	Over 100
Grimace (reflexes)	No response to stimulation	Grimace	Cry, cough, or sneeze
Activity (muscle tone)	Flaccid (no or weak activity)	Some movement of extremities	A lot of activity
Respiration	None	Slow, irregular	Good, crying

baby need it. In addition to your obstetrician, you would have access to an anesthesiologist if you choose to have an epidural or need a consultation. Sophisticated services, such as sonogram machines or laboratory tests, also are available. If your delivery doesn't go as planned, the hospital is equipped to perform an emergency cesarean.

You might have a planned cesarean delivery, or c-section, if you have a high-risk pregnancy. Planned cesareans are common if you are expecting twins or more, have had a previous c-section, are carrying a very large baby, or have a complicating condition. A cesarean is an invasive surgery usually done using epidural or spinal anesthesia, but in emergencies performed under general anesthesia, and recovery is more difficult. You probably will be hospitalized longer and may have some difficulty handling your baby comfortably. There's a chance your baby may temporarily have breathing problems and be slow to feed at first.

Circumcision

Removing the foreskin—the skin at the end of the shaft of the penis that covers the glans, or head of the penis—has been practiced since ancient times. Religious Jews traditionally have the procedure performed when a boy is 8 days old. Many Muslims circumcise their boys at an older age. Families have many reasons for choosing whether to circumcise their boys.

Studies have shown that boys who have been circumcised have a slightly lower chance of getting a urinary tract infection. Circumcised males also have a lower risk of HIV infection following intercourse with an unprotected, HIV-positive partner, have lower rates of other sexually transmitted diseases, and are less likely to develop cancer of the head of the penis. Circumcision also makes it easier to clean and care for the glans and avoids the discomfort of phimosis, when the undersurface of the foreskin sticks to the glans.

On the other hand, some people believe circumcision is a painful and unnecessary practice. Urinary tract infections are already uncommon in boys, and cancer of the glans is very rare. It isn't

hard to clean the glans on an uncircumcised penis— the foreskin will readily retract by the time a boy is 2 or 3 years old. Phimosis is not very common and is easily treated. In rare cases, circumcision can result in bleeding and infection. Some parents simply don't feel it's their place to choose this elective procedure for their child.

Ultimately, whether to circumcise your boy is a personal decision. You may want to for religious reasons, or perhaps you're concerned about taking care of the glans and reducing the risk of contracting infections and diseases. Or you might want to avoid causing your son any discomfort or chancing any serious complications. The advantages and disadvantages are closely balanced, and you should do what seems best to you.

Storing cord blood

The blood from the placenta and umbilical cord contains stem cells, which have the potential to differentiate into many kinds of blood cells or organ tissues (muscle, liver, etc.). Stem cells can be grown in cell culture artificially or can be frozen and stored for later use. Cord blood has been used to treat scores of diseases, including leukemia. It's collected after delivery and doesn't affect either mother or baby. You may have the option of donating cord blood to a public bank, or you can pay to have it stored for private use.

Public banks store donated blood for free for use by patients anywhere in the world who need a transplant. If you donate your child's blood, you won't have special access to it later. But as more people donate their infant's cord blood to a public bank, it becomes more likely that if your child ever needs stem cells, there will be matching cells available for her. If you're interested in donating, you'll need to see if the hospital where you plan to deliver works with a public cord bank.

Private banks are for-profit organizations; for a fee, they store cord blood for possible future use by an individual's family. The initial fee is considerable and there is a yearly fee that is paid as long as the blood is stored. If you pay for private banking, your baby's cord blood is saved for your use, if ever needed for your child or another family member. If she should ever need a bone marrow transplant, for example, her stem cells would be a perfect match; there would be no risk of rejection by her body's immune system. For private storage, you'll need to obtain a collection kit weeks before your due date.

Cord blood is collected after the umbilical cord is cut. Your doctor or midwife will insert a needle into the umbilical vein and withdraw blood. The blood comes from the detached cord and placenta; it is not taken from you or your baby. Cord blood that is not stored or donated is discarded.

Once the specimen arrives at the cord blood bank, red blood cells and other cells are removed, leaving the stem cells for freezing in liquid nitrogen. Blood samples from both the mother and the umbilical cord are tested for a number of infections to make sure the collected cells are viable.

The American Academy of Pediatrics encourages families to donate cord blood to a public bank, but advises against paying for private storage unless a family has an older child with a medical condition

that might be helped by a cord-blood transplant. Very few families ever use privately banked cord blood. In fact, most stem cells can't be used by the donor child because the genetic coding for her medical problem is also present in her stem cells. Some children who develop leukemia, for example, already have pre-leukemic cells in their cord blood, which could reinfect them.

Breastfeeding or bottle-feeding

There are many health benefits to breastfeeding (see box, page 20) and very few medical reasons not to do so. You can successfully breastfeed twins (see page 76) and a premature baby (see page 92).

Breastfeeding is a natural process, but it isn't always easy. You can get help and support by talking with your doctor or midwife, checking in with a lactation consultant, or contacting a support group.

In a few cases, however, you will be advised *not* to breastfeed: if you have an infection that could be transmitted to your baby in breast milk, such as HIV; if you have shingles or herpes on your breast near the nipple; or if you are taking a medication that passes into breast milk and could harm your baby, such as sedatives, aspirin, or amphetamines.

If you're unsure whether you want to breastfeed, try it for a week or so and then decide. If you decide breastfeeding isn't right for you and your child, you might feel pressured to change your mind. Try not to let it bother you. Breast milk may be the best nutritional food for your baby, but formula is a very good alternative. It's a perfectly adequate source of nourishment, and you and your baby will still enjoy bonding during feedings.

Support team

While your pediatrician will be an invaluable resource, you also might want some practical help at home taking care of your baby, getting chores done, or giving you a little time off. A baby nurse or postpartum doula can provide you with professional, high-quality child care, even living with your family for a few weeks.

Less-expensive options include hiring a mother's helper or babysitter. This could be a professional helper or a competent teenager who could do some chores or hold your baby for a little bit, so you can rest or take a shower.

Baby nurse or doula

Although not always trained nurses, baby nurses or postpartum doulas are experienced in caring for babies. They can help you in the early weeks at home with your baby. Before hiring someone, thoroughly check her qualifications and references.

A baby nurse usually arrives when you bring your newborn home and helps your family for a week or two, up to a few months. The baby nurse should be able to help with all aspects of daily care (including giving night feedings if you're bottle-feeding or using expressed breast milk), keeping up with the baby's laundry, and calming her down when she's fussy.

Baby nurses can be a tremendous support, helping you save time and energy and giving you a chance to rest. Be careful not to rely too heavily on a baby nurse or doula, or you might not build the confidence you need to care for your baby yourself. Ideally, a baby nurse should do less and less babycare as the days go by. By the time she departs, you should be comfortable and confident in your own ability to manage daily care. If you and your baby nurse disagree, you have the final say. If you find yourself resenting her role, or you feel she isn't building your skills and confidence, you may need to reconsider the arrangement.

Your baby's doctor

Choosing a pediatrician may be a simple task if you live in a small town and have few choices. But if you have more options, ask other parents and your ob-gyn about their experiences. Find out what they like and what they don't like about their doctors. Ask about their doctor's bedside manner, if her office

7 benefits of breastfeeding your baby

1 Breast milk is the best nutritional milk for humans; formulas strive to be as close as possible to mother's milk but will never be identical to it.

2 Breast milk contains antibodies, immune system cells, and antimicrobial factors to help protect your baby from infection.

3 Breastfeeding your baby creates a special bond between you and your baby.

4 Breastfeeding is much cheaper than formula and can be done easily wherever you and your baby go.

5 Breastfeeding may lower your baby's chances of developing allergies or eczema.

6 Breastfeeding may boost your baby's IQ by 2–3 points.

7 Breastfed babies, on average, have a lower incidence of obesity.

runs smoothly, what kind of coverage is available on weekends and holidays, and how easy it is to make appointments and get questions answered. Also consider the doctor's location (is the office close to your home?) and insurance coverage.

Be sure to choose a pediatrician well before your due date. If you can, meet with your child's doctor in person to start building a relationship. When you visit a potential pediatrician's office, take note of the details: the receptionist's demeanor; the cleanliness of the waiting area; hand-sanitizer dispensers; the presence of toys, books, and small furniture for children; and posted info about topics such as immunization, disease prevention, and parenting classes. In your conversation with the doctor, ask about her experience, hours, and availability; how the office runs; how she keeps up with new developments in the field; and how emergencies or routine calls are handled. Bring up issues that are especially important to you, such as the use of vaccines or antibiotics: Do you agree? If you don't, will your views be respected?

It's important for you to have a doctor you trust and who you feel is responsive and respectful. There's no limit to the questions you could ask before choosing a doctor, but in the end, you should trust your instincts.

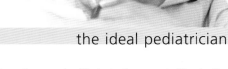

MORE **ABOUT**　　　　　　　　　　　the ideal pediatrician

The ideal pediatrician is kind and gentle, knowledgeable about the care of children, readily available, and not in a rush. She has an efficiently run office with friendly, helpful staff. There are office hours on holidays and weekends for sick children, and the doctors who cover for her when she's away are nice as well as competent. You're seen promptly when you go to her office, and she forms a personal relationship with you and your child. She participates in your health plan, is thorough and conscientious, and offers anticipatory guidance to prepare you ahead of time for what you're likely to face next. She isn't afraid to say she doesn't know the answer to your question, and will find out the answer and promptly get back to you. Her use of medications is judicious and appropriate. She takes time to talk about developmental issues that aren't strictly medical concerns, such as sleeping problems, tantrums, sibling jealousy, etc. She is a patient listener and is willing to discuss concerns you might raise. She returns your phone calls in a reasonable amount of time and respects your opinions when the two of you disagree.

Choosing a name

Coming up with a name for your baby is an important decision and usually a lot of fun! Many families choose a name for their baby before delivery. But if you don't know your baby's sex beforehand, you can pick a name for each gender. There are so many names to consider! You might want to browse the many books listing names along with their derivations and meanings.

Some families have special customs or traditions for naming children, such as naming babies after a deceased relative or a boy after his father.

You may be fortunate and find that you and your partner quickly agree on a name. Sometimes, though, it's hard to agree. Compromise may be necessary. One way to try to reach agreement is the matching-list method: Both parents write down names they like, starting with their favorites. Then they swap lists, crossing off any names they object to. Finally, they look for names they both wrote down. The highest-ranked name that appears on both lists is a likely winner.

Word of advice: Consider choosing the name with your partner and not discussing it with others. Otherwise, everyone may have an opinion—some of which are better left unheard.

For inspiration, here are the most popular names in the United States in 2010, according to the Social Security Administration.

POPULAR GIRLS' NAMES	
1	Isabella
2	Sophia
3	Emma
4	Olivia
5	Ava
6	Emily
7	Abigail
8	Madison
9	Chloe
10	Mia
11	Addison
12	Elizabeth
13	Ella
14	Natalie
15	Samantha
16	Alexis
17	Lily
18	Grace
19	Hailey
20	Alyssa
21	Lillian
22	Hannah
23	Avery
24	Leah
25	Nevaeh
26	Sofia
27	Ashley
28	Anna
29	Brianna
30	Sarah
31	Zoe
32	Victoria
33	Gabriella
34	Brooklyn
35	Kaylee
36	Taylor
37	Layla
38	Allison
39	Evelyn
40	Riley

POPULAR BOYS' NAMES	
1	Jacob
2	Ethan
3	Michael
4	Jayden
5	William
6	Alexander
7	Noah
8	Daniel
9	Aiden
10	Anthony
11	Joshua
12	Mason
13	Christopher
14	Andrew
15	David
16	Matthew
17	Logan
18	Elijah
19	James
20	Joseph
21	Gabriel
22	Benjamin
23	Ryan
24	Samuel
25	Jackson
26	John
27	Nathan
28	Jonathan
29	Christian
30	Liam
31	Dylan
32	Landon
33	Caleb
34	Tyler
35	Lucas
36	Evan
37	Gavin
38	Nicholas
39	Isaac
40	Brayden

CARING FOR YOUR NEWBORN

First reactions

After months of anticipation, your precious baby has arrived. You and your partner have been through a lot—even an "easy," complication-free vaginal delivery is physically exhausting, and longer labors and those ending with cesarean delivery are even more draining. But now your baby is here.

This chapter focuses on the first weeks after a healthy child's birth. If your baby was born prematurely or has medical problems, you might want to go right to Chapter 4 ("Caring for your premature infant") or Chapter 13 ("Addressing health issues").

New parents

Biology has programmed mothers to want to nourish and protect their newborns; you may be astonished by the intensity of your love for this tiny creature. Many women feel tremendous joy and an immediate, strong emotional attachment to their babies—although some new moms won't feel this bond for quite some time.

In the days after delivery, you may feel you're on an emotional roller-coaster ride. You could swing rapidly from soaring happiness to deep melancholy and anxiety, with seemingly little reason. Even if you're generally a levelheaded, practical sort of person, you might find your emotions holding sway over reason for a while.

Keep in mind that your body is going through tremendous changes. The elevated hormones from pregnancy drop abruptly, triggering what's often called the baby blues. It's important to have someone who's patient, understanding, and supportive by your side—your partner, a parent or sibling, or a good friend. This emotional upheaval shouldn't last long. (If it does, talk to your doctor to rule out postpartum depression, a common, treatable problem.)

Fathers and partners, though spared the personal hormonal drama, also share in the happiness and excitement. They often feel deepened love and connection to the mother of their baby. When your partner first holds the baby, any initial feelings of awkwardness usually give way to thankfulness and wonder. Your partner may feel a powerful sense of responsibility, a need to protect and support you and your newborn.

The spotlight will be squarely on the baby and mom, and it's not unusual for partners to feel left out or pushed aside. They might feel relegated to handling logistical tasks such as running errands or even feel in competition with grandparents or other relatives for a chance to hold the baby. On the other hand, some partners are relieved to find themselves in the background—it's normal to feel uncomfortable or unqualified as a parent at first.

You both may be overwhelmed by a feeling of responsibility for your baby's well-being—and unsure whether you're up to the task. New parents—and experienced ones!—frequently doubt themselves and worry whether they're doing their best. Try not to worry. You'll learn surprisingly quickly!

It's normal for parents to experience a range of emotions. Be sure to set aside time to enjoy being a family together and talk about your new roles. An open-minded, loving conversation during which you express appreciation for each other can go a long way toward preventing misunderstandings and resentment, and can bring you closer together.

The baby

Your newborn knows only two states of mind—contentment or unhappiness. To be content, his basic needs must be met. If he feels secure, warm, sated, and comfortable, life is good, but if any one of those wants is lacking, your baby will scream loudly to protest.

Life on the outside is new and exciting. Tasting milk for the first time, taking a deep breath, and letting out a scream—they all seem to happen without much intention, but still, what a change it is from lying confined in the dark womb!

Your newborn's appearance

When your child is born, he'll be covered with a mixture of mother's blood and amniotic fluid. A thick, white, cream cheese–like substance, vernix caseosa, may remain in his groin creases or in his ears. If he has much hair, it will be matted against his scalp. His head might be molded into a conical shape if he was delivered vaginally; fairly round if born by cesarean; or stretched a bit from front to back if he was in a breech position. Once he's been given a quick bath, he'll start to look more like the baby you were expecting.

Don't be surprised if the bottom three-quarters of his fingernails are purplish, and from time to time his hands and feet are cold and bluish. Circulation is sluggish at first in the extremities farthest from the heart. Tiny white dots called milia on his face are clogged skin pores and will soon disappear. He might have bruises from the delivery.

Most of the time, your baby's eyes will be closed. His eyelids will be puffy. When your infant tries to open his eyes, sometimes only one might open. Both eyes might cross briefly or turn in when open—this is normal in the first month or two. He might not

MORE ABOUT   your baby's belly button

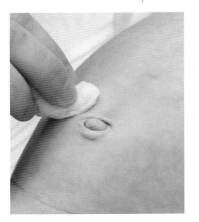

The kind of belly button your baby will have depends upon the amount of force exerted by the pull of the umbilical cord while your baby was in utero. If the cord was short, or if a longer cord was twisted around him while in the womb, the cord would have pulled more strongly on the umbilicus, and he'll have a protruding belly button or an "outie." If there wasn't much cord tension before birth, the button will be recessed—an "innie." If the tension was moderate, his belly button will be even with the surrounding skin on his abdomen. If your baby's umbilicus sticks out, be patient; many outies eventually sink and become innies.

have eyebrows or eyelashes yet. Don't worry, they will soon grow in.

The posture he assumes will reflect the way he was squeezed into the small space of the uterus. His legs will be bowed, and often both feet turn inward (though other poses, such as turning out his feet or bending them fully back at the ankle, also are common). His hands will be tightly clenched, but if you open one and place your finger across his palm, he will hold on to it with surprising strength, demonstrating the grasp reflex.

The skin of the scrotal sack typically will appear swollen on a newborn boy and may have a pink or a darkly pigmented hue. A newborn girl's external labia, the outer lips of her vagina, may be swollen and pink.

In the hours after birth, the stump where the umbilical cord was attached is yellowish-white and soft, with a clip at the end to prevent any blood loss. In another day or two, it will shrink, become darker, and harden, and the clip won't be needed.

Your baby's skin

Your newborn has spent months submerged in water, surrounded by amniotic fluid in the uterus. Shortly after birth, your baby's skin may start to peel and flake, especially at the wrists, ankles, and groin creases. It is as if he's shedding his underwater skin. The next layer of skin will be the soft, moist, smooth skin that is characteristic of older babies.

Birthmarks

Babies are frequently born with birthmarks, which come in many sizes, shapes, and colors. They are rarely of major concern. (For more details, see box on opposite page.)

Newborn rash

Known medically by the name *erythema toxicum neonatorum*, newborn rash is recognizable as red splotches the size of a nickel or dime with a small white- or yellow-headed pimple in the middle, resembling insect bites. The blotches and pimples are fleeting; each spot fades away in just a few minutes or hours. The cause of newborn rash is unknown, but no treatment is necessary: It will go away by itself in a week or two.

Hormonal effects

Shortly before birth, a baby is exposed to high levels of his mother's female hormones. These hormones can cause breast swellings in boys and girls. Hormonal stimulation of the breasts may even prompt your baby to produce a small amount of milk. Don't squeeze the breasts or try to express the milk. The swelling, along with any milk production, peaks at 2 to 3 weeks of age and then goes away.

If you have a girl, you might notice a small amount of a thick, stringy, white or yellow mucous discharge from her vagina in the first days of life. This is harmless. Simply wipe the discharge away when you change her diaper. As the level of maternal hormones in your baby's body decreases, a few drops of blood or even a clump of red blood cells may be seen coming from her vagina. This, too, is normal.

Colored spots in the diaper

You might notice a brownish or salmon-pink stain in a wet diaper. This is common and nothing to worry about. The brownish shading is caused by concentrated urine, while the pinkish-red stain is due to high levels of uric acid crystals excreted in newborn urine. (For information about the color of your baby's bowel movements, see box, page 30.)

Birthmarks

Hemangiomas are composed of many small blood vessels clustered in a localized area. These extra vessels are present at birth, but you may not recognize them as a birthmark until your baby (and the blood vessels) begin to grow.

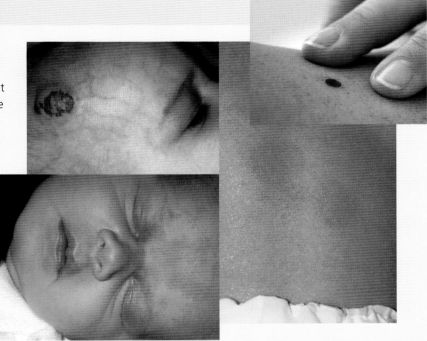

At birth, hemangiomas are flat, well defined, and often pale-purplish in color. In your baby's first months of life, they grow larger, redder, and raised. At this stage, they're often called "strawberries."

A hemangioma continues growing for the first 6 to 9 months of a baby's life and then slowly begins to shrink and lose its color. Most of them, even very large ones, disappear completely within a couple of years after birth.

Rarely, a large hemangioma can become a problem if it's located near the eyes, nose, or mouth, or in another area that is easily irritated, such as on one of your baby's hands or in the diaper area.

There are a few ways to shrink hemangiomas, such as cortisone injections and laser treatments. But since most hemangiomas disappear eventually without intervention, treatment is usually limited to the most potentially problematic ones.

A nevus flammeus is also a localized area with extra blood vessels in the skin, but unlike a hemangioma, a nevus flammeus is visible at birth and doesn't grow. Flat and pinkish-red, these are typically found on the nape of the neck ("stork bite"), on the upper eyelids ("angel's kiss"), on the nose or just above it, and on the forehead.

These birthmarks gradually lighten and usually disappear over time. However, when your baby cries or strains to have a bowel movement, a nevus flammeus will momentarily flush red.

Pigmented spots are large, flat, grayish-black colored spots that may be up to a few inches across. They can look a lot like bruises. Pigmented spots have no medical significance.

Commonly called "Mongolian spots," they're usually on the lower back and upper buttocks and have a capsule-like shape. Pigmented spots also can be found on the back side of the hands, the upper back, and on the shoulders.

They're especially common among black and Asian infants. Pigmented spots become much less noticeable with age and usually fade away completely.

A nevus (plural is nevi) is a black birthmark that may be flat or raised. Like hemangiomas, nevi also may not be visible at birth but appear later on.

Many are small and look like the moles on older children and adults. Sometimes they're larger. They don't grow in size or disappear, and only rarely are they linked to skin cancer (melanoma).

What your newborn can do

Once your baby arrives, you will have a lot to do—holding, feeding, burping, bathing, comforting, changing, and dressing him, for starters.

Meanwhile, your baby won't seem to do much at all—and what he does do is driven by biological necessity and reflex.

Newborns are usually very tired and spend most of their first days sleeping. When he's hungry or wants a hug, your baby will automatically cry. When the breast or bottle is placed in his mouth, he will start to suck. And when he's full, he will stop feeding. Right after he eats, his intestinal tract will increase its activity and frequently, reflexively, this will result in a bowel movement. A sudden movement or noise will startle him. And when you hold your baby in your arms, he will enjoy hearing your heartbeat and being close to you.

A newborn is a master at getting a parent's attention. Within a few weeks he'll prefer his parents' faces to those of others, track them briefly with his eyes, and smile. And from there, it keeps getting better!

4 surprisingly normal behaviors

Newborns are full of surprises. These newborn behaviors are common but often unexpected by parents.

1 **Hiccups** Your baby may spend minutes at a time hiccupping. Usually, she isn't bothered by it at all, and you don't need to do anything to try to stop them.

2 **Snorting and sneezing** Your baby may sometimes breathe loudly and make a snorting noise from the back of her nose. Sneezing is common; it's a reflex to help her clean out her nose.

3 **Tremors** From time to time, your infant's arm or leg may repetitively and rhythmically shake, resembling the shuddering of an older person with a chill. This is a sign of neurological immaturity. It's an even, back-and-forth quivering motion; in a convulsion, the arm or leg moves with much sharper, jerkier motions. Unlike a seizure, which these tremors vaguely resemble, the shaking is easily stopped by gently taking hold of the arm or leg with your hand.

4 **Startle reaction** After a sudden noise, vibration, or movement, your newborn may wrinkle her forehead, squeeze her eyes shut, and quickly move her arms up and out until they're straight at the elbow. This series of motions is called a Moro reflex and will be present for weeks or months.

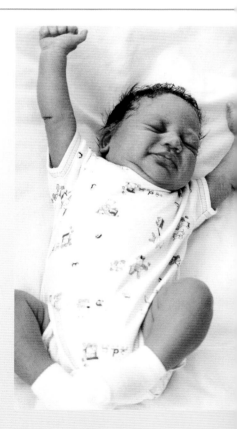

Sleeping

After a few hours of being awake and alert right after birth, your newborn probably will be very sleepy for the next 2 to 3 days. Sleeping 18 hours (not in a row!) a day or more is typical.

Preventing a misshapen head

Parents are strongly urged to place babies on their backs while sleeping to lower the risk of sudden infant death syndrome, or SIDS (see page 63). SIDS is rare, and placing babies on their backs greatly reduces the risk of it.

This practice, however, commonly contributes to uneven shaping of a baby's head. Many babies develop a strong preference for holding their heads to only one side while lying on their backs. If your baby always turns his head to the right when he is laid down on his back, you might see the back of his skull on the right side become slightly flattened. His head is putting weight on his growing skull, which begins conforming to the flat mattress. Without intervention, this flattening could become more pronounced, and his right ear could appear more forwardly placed than the left ear.

To avoid skull misshaping, called plagiocephaly (see page 331), encourage your baby to alternate sides. If he prefers to turn his head toward the right, try to coax him to look in the other direction by giving him something interesting to look at— your face, a window, or a light bulb could do the trick. You can simply turn him around in his crib, reversing the placement of his feet and his head, to redirect his attention.

Feeding

During the first few days, your baby might not seem very hungry. This is perfectly normal. Your breast milk won't fully come in until the third or fourth day after delivery; this is exactly when your infant will become more awake and much more eager to nurse or take a bottle. Some newborns skip this sleepy phase and are always eager to be fed, but most are far more interested in napping than in eating.

This 2- or 3-day period helpfully gives you some time to rest and recover from delivery, but you

BLOCKED TEAR DUCT

Babies begin to produce tears at about 2 to 3 weeks of age. A blocked tear duct is a common, minor problem that usually resolves by itself without medical intervention.

If your baby develops a blocked tear duct, the affected eye will tear up more than the other one. This is because the tears aren't draining to the back of the nose via the internal tear duct, and instead are draining forward, out of the eye.

Repeated bouts of conjunctivitis (see page 349) with mucus in the eye are another sign of a blocked tear duct. Because the germs that are supposed to be washed away down the tear duct instead linger in the eye, babies can get mild infections.

Blocked tear ducts almost always become unblocked on their own; this can happen any time during the first year of life.

While waiting for this spontaneous cure, wipe away the crusts and small amounts of mucus that accumulate due to low-grade conjunctivitis. If the amount of mucus gets very heavy and recurs often after being wiped away, your pediatrician may prescribe a brief course of antibiotic eye drops.

Massaging the area over the tear duct with your finger can help promote drainage, but don't try this without first having your doctor show you how to do it correctly.

In the rare case of a tear duct that doesn't fix itself naturally, a pediatric ophthalmologist can open it by passing a thin wire probe from the inner corner of the eye down the length of the tear duct.

might feel anxious and fret over whether your baby is getting enough to eat. Emotion often trumps reason at this time, and it can be hard not to worry. Try to relax. Within a few days, most babies will want to eat every 2 to 3 hours. If you continue to worry, check in with your pediatrician. You certainly won't be the first parent seeking reassurance about a sleepy newborn!

Weight loss

Your baby was born overstocked with water, perhaps to cushion him during the hard journey of delivery or to provide extra fluids to see him through the early sleepy days. He was also born with fecal matter in his intestines. In the first few days, he'll urinate and pass feces frequently. Since he won't be eating much, he'll lose weight at first.

This is normal and expected. He isn't starving or suffering malnourishment: There's simply more going out (urine and stool) than going in (breast milk or formula). Newborns typically lose up to 10 percent of their initial weight, but they soon begin putting on weight.

Again, it's difficult not to be anxious and concerned to see your new baby's weight dropping. Keep in mind that this is normal and temporary, and try not to obsess over his weight. If he doesn't start gaining weight after a few days, your doctor will help you make sure he's off to a healthy start.

Meconium and bowel movements

Before birth, your baby's intestines already are functioning, producing feces in the form of meconium.

Meconium is blackish-green, thick, and sticky. Your baby will pass quite a bit of meconium in her first 2 to 3 days. Once she's excreted all the meconium, her bowel movements will become yellow, green, or brown, and will be soft and mushy.

A newborn typically has 6 to 10 bowel movements every day. Sometimes stool can be squirted out forcefully. If you're breastfeeding, your baby's stools will be very watery with small solid specks mixed throughout—and they will occur frequently. If you're bottle-feeding, his stools may be greenish and more solid.

MORE **ABOUT** | the color of your baby's bowel movements

Formula is white, and breast milk is usually whitish-gray, but your baby's bowel movements are often more colorful. Here's why.

After milk or formula leaves the stomach, it enters the small intestine, where bile from the liver and bile duct is added. Bile is green, and this colors everything passing through the intestine. Bacteria living in your baby's intestine— particularly the colon, or lower intestine— metabolize components of bile. The first steps in this breakdown of bile result in molecules with a yellow hue. Further digestion by bacteria may turn everything brown.

The faster the intestine propels its contents along the many feet of the alimentary tract, the less time there is for bacteria to metabolize the

green fluid. Green stools are produced when food waste travels swiftly through the intestines, with little time to break down bile components. Iron in formula can also give stools a green tint.

If everything moves more slowly and the bacteria do a better job of breaking down bile, the stool will appear yellow. Breastfed babies, in particular, typically have mustardy-yellow stools.

And if the passage through the intestines is even slower and bacteria more fully metabolize bile, you'll see brown bowel movements.

You'll see more colors once your older baby eats solid foods, such as green vegetables.

However, if your baby's stools are chalky white or have traces of red (blood), you should contact your pediatrician. These could be signs of illness.

Bonding

As you spend time together—holding, feeding, soothing, and diapering your baby—your love and desire to protect this little person can grow and deepen into a very powerful attachment. The development of this strong connection between you and your newborn is known as bonding, and most parents experience these strong feelings from the moment of birth—and some even earlier.

Shortly after she's born, your newborn is alert and ready to nurse. Her eyes will be open when you hold her and will meet your gaze. Interestingly, this initial state usually lasts only an hour or so (see page 73), but it allows both mother and father to experience the first joys of parenting. Interacting with your newborn triggers a loving response in you.

At birth, however, your infant doesn't yet feel the same attachment to you. She is completely dependent on you, and her earliest behavior is designed to deepen your attachment to her.

As she gets older, though, she'll get to know you, become attached to you, and prefer you to all others. The bond she feels with her mother is especially intense, and by the time she's 9 to 10 months old, she will most likely be very upset to be away from you—this is known as separation anxiety.

If you have any older children, you'll see bonding blossom between your newborn and her siblings. Older brothers or sisters may sometimes ignore or be jealous of all the attention given to a newborn sibling, but there's also an innate mechanism to encourage attachment between siblings.

When your newborn is only a few months old, your older child will discover that he has a unique ability to calm and entertain his younger sibling. Your baby will find her older sibling amusing and will respond with laughter and howls of delight—which helps make her older sibling feel warmly about a younger sister.

In a few more months, your baby will seem to worship her older sibling, no matter how nicely or poorly she's sometimes treated. A baby's behavior seems to be designed to win over siblings.

You may not feel close to your baby right away, but warm feelings of attachment should grow during the first days and weeks. If you're concerned about feeling detached from your baby, talk to your doctor or pediatrician. You might be suffering from postpartum depression or another ailment.

PICKING UP

1 Slide one hand under your baby's neck, supporting his head, and the other hand beneath his bottom. Take his weight in your hands and slowly pick him up. If he's awake, talking quietly will help keep him calm as you lift.

2 Keep your baby's head slightly above the rest of his body. Draw him toward your body. If he's awake, look into his eyes as you move him.

HOLDING AND CARRYING

Resting against your shoulder

This is the most intimate way to hold your baby. As with lifting, you need to support his bottom with one hand and upper back and neck with the other. Your baby can nestle close against the skin of your neck and may be comforted by the sound of your heartbeat.

Facedown in your arms

This hold can provide rest for your arms and a change of view for your infant. It may be good for colic. Support your baby's upper chest along your forearm with his head near the crook of your elbow. Slide your other arm between his legs and support his stomach with your hand.

3 Bring your baby in close to your chest. Move the arm supporting his neck down his body so it meets your lower hand near the middle of his back, and support his head and neck.

4 From a cradle hold, slide your upper arm back along your baby's body until it supports his neck, with your lower hand supporting his bottom. Gently move him away from your body and lower him onto a flat surface. Support his neck the entire time, gently removing your hand so his head rests on the surface.

Cradled in your arms

Rest one hand over the other to support his upper back and bottom so that his head rests in the crook of your elbow. This is a convenient way to carry your baby and protect him from accidental bumps.

SWADDLING

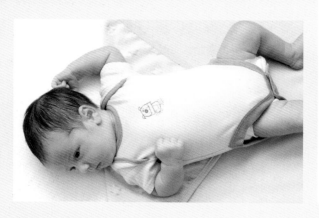

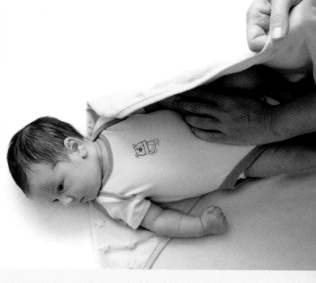

1 Swaddling often comforts newborns. Place a soft blanket on a flat surface. Fold down one corner and place your baby so his head is above the fold.

2 Gently hold one of your baby's arms by his side and pull that corner of the blanket across his body. Tuck it under the opposite side of his body.

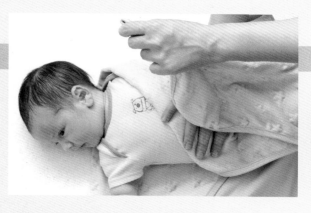

3 Bring up the bottom corner of the blanket, leaving room for your baby's legs to move freely. If you'd like, hold his other arm by his side inside the swaddle.

4 Stretch the other corner over your baby and under his backside, and tuck it at the top fold, optionally leaving space so that one of his hands is free.

SPONGE BATHS

Eyes and ears Wet a cotton ball or a clean washcloth with warm water and wipe one eye, from the inner to the outer corner. Wipe the other eye with a clean ball or cloth. Clean around and behind (but not inside) her ears.

Neck Wipe clean with a wet cotton pad or washcloth and pat dry with a soft cloth.

Hands Unclench your baby's hands to check for dirt between her fingers and underneath her nails. Wipe and pat dry.

Feet Clean the top and bottom of your baby's feet, gently easing her toes apart, where necessary. Pat dry with a towel.

Stomach and legs Wipe her tummy with a washcloth, then clean the folds where her legs meet her torso. Wipe down along the creases and away from her body to avoid spreading infections to the genital area—this is particularly important for a girl. Pat her dry with a towel, checking that no moisture is trapped in the folds.

It is often recommended that soap not be used on the face (so none gets in the eyes), but warm soapy water (from a small basin or bowl) can be used over the entire body.

Care of the umbilical stump

Expose the stump to air
The umbilical stump will dry and heal much faster if you expose it to air as much as possible. Fold down the front of newborn diapers to avoid covering or irritating it. If the stump gets wet, dry it thoroughly.

Caring for the stump
Traditionally, pediatricians have recommended that the base of the cord be cleaned daily with an alcohol pad. However, an approach called "dry care" suggests that the umbilical area be left alone and not cleaned. Studies have shown that this method also works. Ask your pediatrician which technique he prefers (see page 52).

After the stump has fallen off
Gently clean off any blood, mucus or crusting with an alcohol wipe or a cotton ball soaked with alcohol and let air dry daily until it is completely healed.

CHANGING A DIAPER

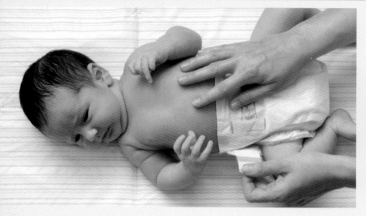

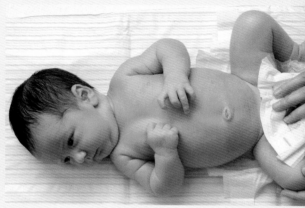

1 Have all the supplies you'll need—diapers, wipes or cotton balls, water, and diaper cream or ointment (if needed)—by the changing mat. Pick up your baby and place him on the mat on his back. If he's dressed, strip his lower half down to just his diaper. Unfasten the tabs, Velcro, or snaps of the diaper.

2 Slide the dirty diaper away, using an unsoiled area to give a first wipe. If your baby is a boy, the cooler air may make him urinate as his diaper is removed. Drape a tissue over the penis to deflect the flow, or, if the diaper is only wet, hold it over his penis briefly in case he urinates.

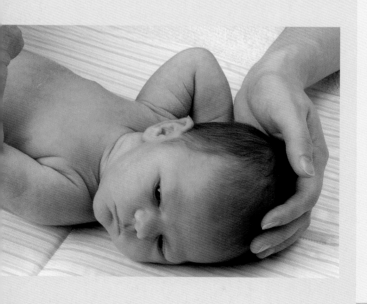

Cleaning a girl

Using a fresh, moistened cotton ball or washcloth, clean inside the outer lips of her vagina. Always wipe downward, using a fresh cotton ball or a clean area of your washcloth for each swipe. Hold both her ankles with one hand and gently lift her bottom to clean her anal area, buttocks, and back thighs. Pat the whole area thoroughly dry.

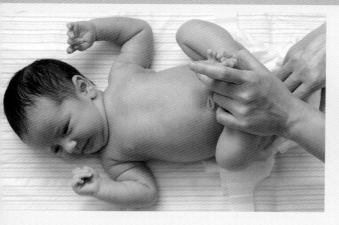

3 Gently grasp your baby's ankles with one hand and lift his bottom just off the mat. With your other hand, roll up the diaper and place it where your baby can't kick it. Carefully clean the genital region, including all the skin folds (see below). Pat dry, particularly in the folds where redness or irritation can develop.

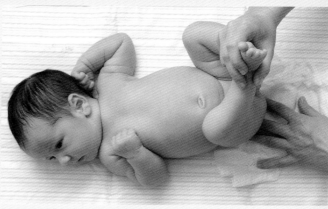

4 Spread out a fresh diaper. Lift your baby's legs and slide the diaper under his bottom. Bring the front of the diaper up between his legs. If your baby is a boy, tuck his penis downward so he doesn't urinate into the waistband or out of the diaper.

Cleaning a boy

Using a fresh, moistened cotton ball or washcloth, wipe his penis using a downward motion. If he is uncircumcised, do not pull the foreskin back. In circumcised boys, after healing is complete, also clean the groove between the head of the penis and the skin of the shaft to remove debris and mucus. Clean around the scrotum as well. Use a fresh cotton ball or washcloth for each wipe. Hold both your baby's ankles with one hand and gently lift his bottom to clean his anal area, buttocks, and back thighs. Pat the whole area thoroughly dry.

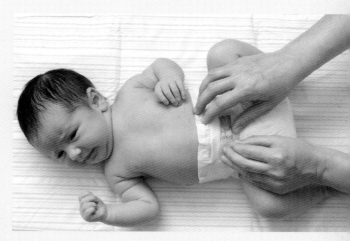

5 Secure the diaper at the sides and tuck in the top edge neatly. Once your baby is dressed, take care of the dirty diaper: Throw away a disposable diaper, or put a soiled cloth diaper into a diaper pail.

PUTTING ON AN UNDERSHIRT

1 Lay your baby on a changing mat. Gather the material together at the neck of the undershirt with both hands. Slip the undershirt behind your baby's head, stretching the opening wide. Gently raise her head. Position the opening over the crown of her head and gently pull the undershirt over her head and neck.

2 Straighten the fabric around her neck. Gather up the material from one sleeve in your hand and hold it with your thumb inside the arm opening. With your other hand, gently guide your baby's wrist through the opening, easing the sleeve over her hand and arm. Repeat with the other sleeve.

Gently smooth the fabric down over her front. If there are crotch snaps, lift your baby's bottom slightly to slide the tail of the undershirt underneath and up between her legs. Fasten any snaps.

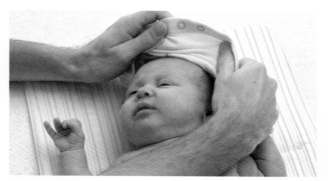

PUTTING ON A SLEEPER

1 Open all the snaps and spread the sleeper out on your baby's changing mat. Lay your baby on top of it. Begin by putting on the sleeves. For each sleeve, gather up the material and gently slide the sleeve over your baby's wrist, taking care that her fingers or nails are not caught up in the process. If the wrist openings are tight, you may need to stretch the material to fit her hands through.

2 Taking each leg in turn, gather up the material and slide in her foot until her toes reach the end. Then gently pull the material fully over her legs.

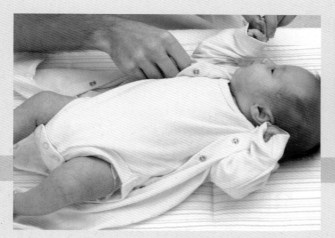

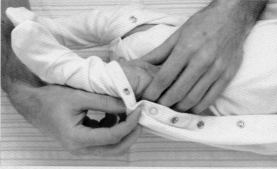

TAKING OFF AN UNDERSHIRT

A clean undershirt With your baby on her mat, undo any snaps. Slide the undershirt up her body. Gather a sleeve in one hand and use your other hand to gently guide her arm out of it. Repeat with the other sleeve. Gather up the undershirt at your baby's neck, stretching the opening as wide as possible to avoid dragging the material over her face. Pull the undershirt over her face to the crown of her head in one smooth motion. Gently lift her head to remove the undershirt.

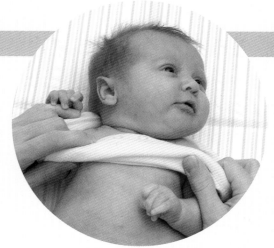

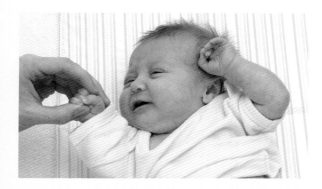

A dirty undershirt Remove the soiled diaper and clean your baby's bottom. Gently lift up her head. If neckline allows, stretch it out over both shoulders. Lay her back down and slide the neck opening down her body, stretching as needed. Gather up the shirt material and slide it down her legs, being careful to avoid further soiling. If the neckline won't stretch enough, slide the gathered undershirt upward, taking care to keep any soiled material as far from her body as possible.

TAKING OFF A SLEEPER

3 Line up the two sides of the sleeper on your baby's front and fasten the snaps from the top down to the crotch. This is the easiest part of the suit to fasten and stops your baby from wriggling out while you attend to the legs. Fasten the leg snaps from the ankle up to the crotch, and then do the other leg, again starting from the ankle.

Undo all the snaps. Support each knee as you ease her legs and feet out of the leg material. Raise your baby's bottom and slide the lower half of the suit up her back. Support her elbow and, without tugging, remove her arm from the sleeve; repeat with the other arm. If the bottom half is soiled, you may want to start with her arms and work downward.

BATHING

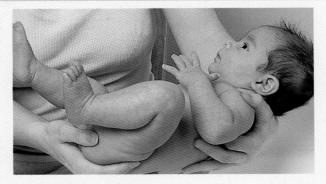

1 Before you pick up your baby, make sure all your cleaning supplies, such as bath soap and clean washcloths, are within an arm's reach. Lay out a clean towel on the floor. Support your baby's bottom with one hand and her back and head with the other. Kneeling close to the baby bathtub, lower her into shallow warm water. Never leave your baby unattended in the bath, not even for a few seconds.

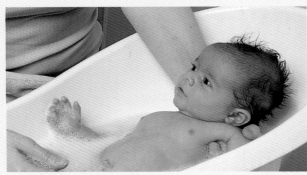

2 Holding her securely under one arm, support her head and shoulders. Use your other hand to wash her neck, chest, and tummy, working out to her arms, hands, legs, and feet. Be sure to wash skin folds, such as the front of the neck and under her arms, and between digits.

3 Sit your baby up; support her chest with one hand. Be careful to keep your hand securely in front of her. Wash the back of her neck and upper back. Wash behind and around, but not in, her ears.

4 Tip her a bit farther forward to wash her lower back. Wash and rinse her hair. Finish with a front to back wipe of her genitals. (See pages 36–37.)

5 Using the same supporting grip you used to lower her into the bath, transfer her to the clean towel on the floor. Use a clean, wet washcloth to wipe your baby's eyes from the inner to outer corner. Pat her dry. Optionally, apply lotion.

BABY MASSAGE

Gentle massage is a great way to bond with your baby. You can do this with your baby laid over your knees or when she's lying flat on a soft, warm towel or mat in a warm, quiet location. You can start off with her fully dressed if she seems ill at ease. Gently stroke your baby over her back and up and down the length of her spine and limbs. When she's about 2 months old, you can try a full-body routine with an appropriate oil. Don't massage her, however, if she's tired, hungry, or has just been fed.

Back, arms, and legs

Lie down on your left side, with your baby lying on her right side and facing you. Stroke your baby with your right hand, from the back of her neck to the base of her spine—in the same way you would stroke a kitten or a puppy. Continue for about a minute.

Using a circular movement, gently massage around your baby's upper back and then down the length of her back to the base of her spine. Continue for about a minute.

Next, slowly stroke one of her

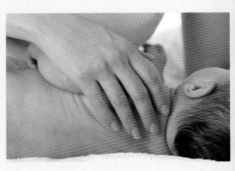

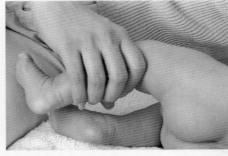

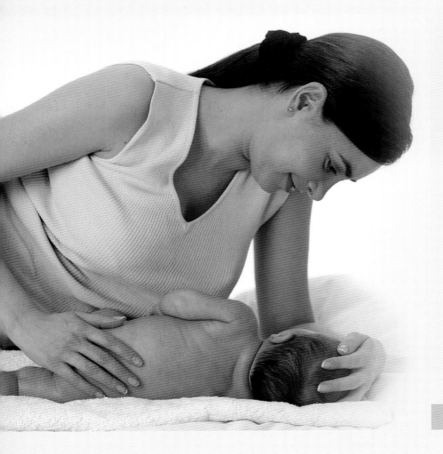

arms; keep your touch gentle and relaxed as you take the stroke from her shoulder to her hand. Continue for about a minute. Repeat with her other arm.

Move your hand to the top of one of your baby's legs and stroke down from her hip to her foot with your palm. You can give her leg a very gentle little shake to loosen it up and help her to relax. Continue for about a minute. Repeat with her other leg.

UNCONSCIOUSNESS

Less than 1 year old

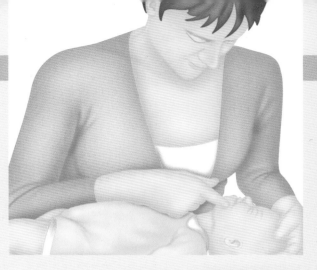

1 If your baby isn't responsive—he doesn't react to you calling his name—lay him on his back on a flat surface. Place one hand on his forehead, gently tilt his head back, and lift his chin. Remove any visible obstructions from his mouth and nose with your finger.

2 Check if he's breathing by looking, listening, and feeling for breath on your cheek for up to 10 seconds. If he isn't breathing normally, follow steps 3 and 4 for 1 minute and then call 911. If another person is present, ask him to call 911 immediately.

3 Take a breath and place your mouth over your baby's mouth and nose. Blow gently and steadily for at least a second, pause, and repeat. You should see your infant's chest rise with each breath.

4 Perform CPR by placing two fingers in the middle of his chest and press down one-third to half the depth of his chest. Give 30 chest compressions at a rate of 100 per minute, then give two breaths as you did in step 3. Continue with cycles of 30 chest compressions and two breaths until emergency help arrives.

Recovery position for babies

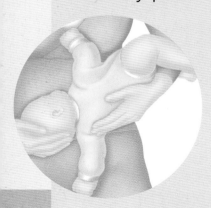

If your baby is unconscious but breathing, hold him on his side, head tilted, as if you were giving him a cuddle, with his head lower than his tummy.

CHOKING

Up to 1 year old

If your baby is able to breathe, cry, or cough, this is a minor situation and the obstruction probably will clear on its own. Keep a close eye on your baby and make sure his condition doesn't deteriorate. If it does, or if he isn't breathing initially, you should:

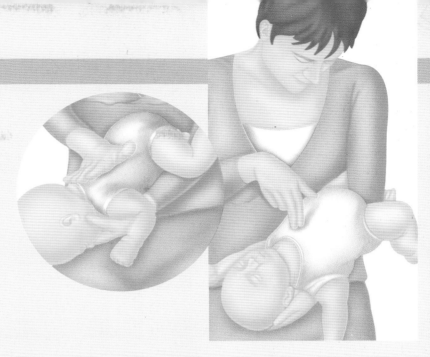

1 Lay your baby facedown along your forearm, with his head held low. Using the heel of your hand, give up to five back blows between his shoulder blades. Check his mouth quickly after each one and remove any obvious obstruction. If the obstruction is still present, go to step 2.

2 Turn your baby onto his back and give up to five chest thrusts. Using two fingers, push inward and upward in the middle of his chest. Check his mouth quickly after each thrust. If the obstruction does not clear after three cycles of back blows and chest thrusts, call 911. Continue cycles of back blows and chest thrusts until help arrives, and resuscitate if necessary.

You must seek medical advice for any child who has been given abdominal thrusts.

Age 1 and older

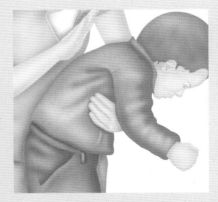

1 Lean your child forward, and using the heel of your hand, give up to five back blows between his shoulder blades. Check his mouth quickly after each blow and remove any obvious obstruction. If the obstruction is still present, go to step 2.

2 Give up to five abdominal thrusts. Place your clenched fist between his navel and the bottom of his breastbone and pull inward and upward. Check his mouth quickly after each one. If the obstruction does not clear after three cycles of back blows and abdominal thrusts, call 911. Continue cycles of back blows and abdominal thrusts until help arrives and resuscitate if necessary.

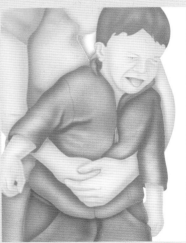

Holding and handling

You'll be handling your baby a lot—picking him up to feed, putting him down to sleep, and holding him when he cries—so it's important to do it right. A young baby's head will flop backward or forward if not supported, so one of your hands should support his neck while your other supports his bottom until he's securely in your arms or has his head on your shoulder (see pages 32–33). Maintaining eye contact will help build attachment.

Your baby will enjoy being held close to your body, particularly if he can hear your heartbeat. Swaddling (see page 34), wrapping him in a blanket so that his limbs are held close to his body, is usually very soothing, as it closely mimics the confined space in the womb. When you're bathing or dressing your baby, try not to expose him to the air any more than necessary—many babies are very unhappy to be naked. But when you're breastfeeding, skin-to-skin contact is enjoyable for both mother and baby.

It's easy to recognize a nervous parent who's new to picking up a baby. With a tense look on her face, she puts both hands beneath her baby, one hand supporting his head, the other under his buttocks. She bends her elbows at stiff 90-degree angles and keeps them that way, even as she slowly and tentatively lifts him up.

But when a baby's grandmother takes him from his crib, she swiftly picks him up without a trace of concern that he may break. With a little practice, you too will feel at ease with your baby, able to lift and carry him almost as easily as you would a kitten, puppy, or football.

Practicing the right approach now will help prevent backaches later on when he's much heavier. It's easier to lift a baby who's lying on his back. If he's on his stomach, gently roll him onto his back with his feet pointing toward you. Standing with your legs slightly apart, bend your knees and keep your back straight as you lift him close to you. Keep the same stance when you lay him back down.

When you hold your baby in your arms, pay attention to the position of his head. Make sure his

head is supported and protected: Tuck his head into your body or keep a hand gently over the top and back of his head while you walk with your baby in your arms, particularly when you pass through doorways and hallways or go near objects that could bump his head.

Carriers and slings

Baby carriers and slings give busy parents the freedom to move around easily and use their hands while still holding their babies. Some parents use them so their hands can be free to do other things, while others prefer them simply because they make it easy to keep their baby close.

Carriers are like backpacks, but you carry the load on your chest and abdomen instead of your back. (Some models convert for use on your back when your baby is older.) Two openings for your baby's legs at the bottom of the carrying pouch help him stay upright against your chest. Straps over each shoulder and one around your midsection hold your baby close to you. A newborn or young baby should be positioned facing you, while an older infant who can support his head may face outward, giving him

CARRIERS

- ◆ A carrier works well for longer outings because it distributes your baby's weight across both your shoulders, which is more comfortable.
- ◆ Adjusting the shoulder and waist straps can be time-consuming. If you and your partner are different sizes and you share the same carrier, you'll have to readjust the straps each time the other one uses it. An alternative is to buy two carriers, adjusting one to fit each of you.
- ◆ Be sure to adjust the size of the leg openings so they're small enough to prevent your baby from falling through.
- ◆ Always read and follow the manufacturer's instructions.

SLINGS

- ◆ Be vigilant about checking your baby while she's in a sling.
- ◆ Make sure your infant's face is not covered and is visible at all times.
- ◆ If you nurse your baby while she's in a sling, afterward change her position so her head is facing up and is clear of the sling and of your body.
- ◆ The weight of your infant is borne by only one shoulder. This can be tiring if he's in the sling for long. You can switch the sling to the other shoulder or use a wrap, which spreads the weight across your shoulders.
- ◆ Babies younger than 4 months are at risk of suffocating in a sling that is not used correctly, the U.S. Consumer Product Safety Commission warns. Always read and follow the manufacturer's instructions.

a better view of what's going on around him.

Slings go over one shoulder and around your waist, and offer more flexibility for positioning your baby. A ring sling holds your baby in an upright position snug against your chest. Use a ring sling for younger or lower-weight babies, who have a higher suffocation risk if a sling is not used correctly. A bag or duffle sling holds your older baby at hip level. This style is not recommended for younger or lower-weight babies because it can cause an infant's chin to rest on his chest, compromising his breathing.

When you're dressing your baby (see page 57), count the carrier or sling as an added layer of clothing. It can get very warm in the pouch, snuggled against someone.

Safety

The Consumer Product Safety Commission urges extra caution if using a sling with any baby younger than 4 months old, citing a risk of suffocation.

A sling could restrict a younger baby's breathing if the fabric presses against his nose and mouth, or if the sling pushes his head to his chest. Always follow the manufacturer's instructions, especially the weight guidelines, carefully—your baby's safety depends on it. Many slings and carriers are not intended for newborns or premature babies, although there are models for babies as small as 3½ pounds.

Don't use the carrier or sling if you can't see your baby's face while he's in it. This is especially important for smaller babies in carriers.

When your baby is carried on your chest in a sling or carrier, his weight will pull you forward. You'll have to compensate by leaning backward. As your baby grows, you'll eventually feel the strain in your back and shoulder muscles. If your baby can hold his head up well while sitting, you can move on to a backpack-style carrier or backpack with a seat (see page 213).

Comforting

Your role as a parent is to care for and soothe your baby, and it's helpful to have different techniques to accomplish this. Some babies find carriers and slings comforting. Holding your baby in your arms, a sling, or a carrier; gentle rocking; and swaddling are all time-tested soothing techniques, often going hand in hand with music, singing, and speaking gently and softly.

How and when to respond to your infant's cries is covered in detail in Chapter 8, but feel free to soothe your newborn whenever he needs you. Don't ever worry about spoiling him. It's not possible to spoil a newborn with too much attention.

Diapering

You'll change a tremendous number of diapers, since your baby will urinate and defecate frequently throughout the day and night. The average baby goes through an estimated 6,000 diapers between birth and toilet training!

Diapers

You can choose disposable diapers, washable cloth diapers, or a mix of both. Since diapers will play such a big role in your day-to-day life for the next few years, it's important to choose the type that best fits your lifestyle.

Disposable diapers are more absorbent, will keep your baby drier longer, and are more convenient. But they are more expensive in the long term than cloth diapers. They need to be disposed of properly, and they generate a significant amount of trash.

Cloth diapers require some investment up front, but because they're reusable, they will save you money over time. However, they must be thoroughly washed and dried. You can get diapers that include a waterproof outer layer or buy separate liners to contain wetness. If you're interested in using cloth diapers but less keen on washing them, check to see if there is a cloth diaper service in your area to do the washing for you. If you use cloth diapers, it's a good idea to wash them before putting them on your baby for the first time. If you wash them yourself, skip the fabric softener, which can make diapers less absorbent; instead, add ½ cup white vinegar to the final rinse. You can even sew your own diapers, if you want to save money.

Some parents like to use a combination of cloth diapers and disposables. A newborn generally needs as many as 12 diapers a day, although this will drop to about 7 per day during the first year and then 5 as he gets older.

Changing a diaper

For illustrated step-by-step instructions on changing a disposable or shaped fabric diaper, see pages 36–37. For how to change a flat or prefolded fabric diaper, see pages 50–51.

Cleaning your baby is the same, no matter what type of diaper you choose. Use cotton balls, a soft, moist washcloth, or wipes to clean away any stool or urine from the skin. If you use a diaper cream or ointment, apply it to areas that come directly in contact with the diaper.

WHICH IS GREENER?

Proponents of cloth diapers often argue that they're a more environmentally friendly choice, generating less garbage and requiring less energy to produce. Backers of disposable diapers, however, counter that cloth diapers also have significant environmental costs, including the water and energy needed to clean them.

It isn't clear which is truly greener, but eco-conscious parents at least have a growing number of options to consider. Flushable diapers offer the convenience of disposables with less waste going into the trash. Biodegradable diapers are somewhat misleading—nothing fully biodegrades in a landfill. You also can buy compostable diapers, but you need to consider what to do with them after they're used. Very few municipalities accept them for composting, and the diaper manufacturers advise against trying to compost them at home.

Similar environmental arguments are made for and against commercial baby wipes. Wipes are convenient and easy to use, and reactions to chemicals in wipes are rare. You can buy alcohol- and fragrance-free wipes, or you can simply use washcloths to clean your baby.

If you're changing a girl's diaper, you need to be careful to wipe front to back. With your baby lying on her back, start cleaning from the lowest part of the abdomen over the genital area and proceed back toward her anus to minimize the risk of spreading fecal bacteria to the vaginal area. Once a cloth or wipe has feces on it or has been near the anus, it shouldn't be used to clean near the vagina. In older girls, improper wiping technique has been shown to increase the risk of urinary tract infections, which are usually caused by germs originating in feces.

But be aware that no matter how careful you are to wipe her properly, you'll frequently find her in a soiled diaper with feces all over her vaginal area.

The front-to-back technique isn't as necessary for boys. They have different anatomy, and there's more distance between the anus and the urethral opening. But still be careful: When your baby boy's diaper is removed, the exposure to the air may prompt him to urinate—and you could get squirted! Hold a clean area of the diaper over his penis for a few moments or drop a clean washcloth over it to catch any urine.

Diaper creams, ointments, powders

Diaper creams and ointments applied to your baby's skin create a barrier against irritants that cause diaper rash. It sounds like a good idea, but there's no evidence that any particular product works any better than another. Note that many common diaper creams and ointments are not meant for use with cloth diapers. These creams and ointments contain substances that will break down cloth diapers and reduce their absorbency. A quick Internet search will tell you which diaper creams and ointments are safe to use with cloth diapers.

There are two schools of thought about using barrier creams. About half of families regularly apply ointment or cream, hoping to prevent rashes. If your baby does get a rash, try switching to a different type of ointment or cream until the rash heals, and then return to the product you used before. Other families don't use a barrier cream routinely. If you don't use diaper cream, and your baby gets a diaper rash, apply cream or ointment until it's fully healed, and then you can stop using it.

There's no compelling evidence that one approach is better than the other. Try whichever approach you prefer, provided it works for your baby. Avoid talc baby powder, however. It doesn't work as a barrier and isn't effective in reducing moisture. Furthermore, inhaling the baby powder that inevitably gets into the air could be harmful to you or your baby.

Diaper rashes

Although diaper rashes are common, what's more remarkable is how often your baby will sit in a wet or dirty diaper *without* getting a rash! No doubt this is a tribute to the innate properties of an infant's skin. Diaper rashes are primarily caused by irritation from urine and feces.

Wetness from urine irritates the skin and breaks

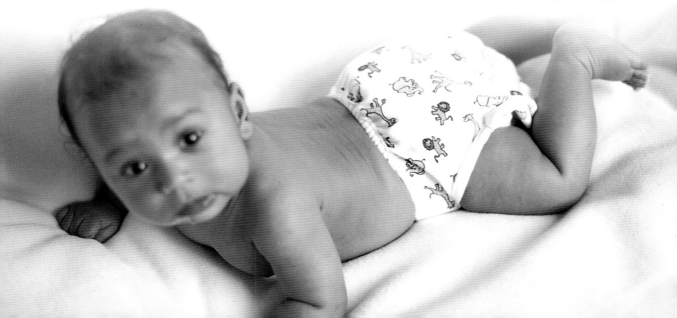

down the skin's barrier to other irritants. Highly absorbent disposable diapers are very good at keeping your baby's skin dry—some studies have shown that babies who wear disposable diapers get fewer rashes than babies in cloth diapers.

Friction between your baby's skin and a diaper can breach his skin's outer protective layer. The repeated rubbing of a clean diaper against skin can cause irritation rashes, but they're more commonly caused by friction from a wet or soiled diaper. Rashes occur most commonly in areas where your baby's skin is in close contact with the diaper, and are less common on the thighs or in creases.

Waste products in feces can damage your baby's skin as well. Feces contain bile elements (called bile salts) and digestive enzymes that can harm skin when they come in contact with it.

Skin barriers work best in an acidic, or low pH, environment. Urine, however, frequently is alkaline, with a higher pH. Diarrhea, which commonly leads to rashes, also has an alkaline pH. To make matters worse, digestive enzymes in stools are activated at alkaline pH.

The role of bacteria and yeasts in causing irritant diaper rashes is poorly documented, but they certainly may be a component in a rash's origin. Candida, a yeast, grows best in a moist environment and often infects already irritated skin.

Preventing and treating diaper rashes involves minimizing exposure to all these irritants (see box).

Stubborn diaper rashes

You may have followed all the prevention and treatment steps described in the boxes above and your baby's rash still didn't get better. There are two likely causes.

First, your baby might still be exposed to factors contributing to diaper rash. Skin exposed to persistent diarrhea, for example, will have a difficult time healing. Or perhaps your baby is sleeping through the night but spends long periods at night in a wet diaper. As long as the irritation continues to occur, it will be difficult to cure the rash.

A second cause of persistent diaper rash is a candida infection. This yeast lives in the intestinal tract and reaches the diaper area through feces.

HOW TO PREVENT DIAPER RASHES

- Change your baby's diaper often.
- Use highly absorbent disposables. Avoid diapers that are too tight; they increase friction between the diaper and skin.
- Try using an ointment or cream to act as a barrier to irritation and moisture, though this isn't always effective.

HOW TO TREAT DIAPER RASHES

- Change your baby's diaper often.
- Clean the skin gently with water and a soft washcloth or an alcohol-free wipe.
- Expose your baby's skin to air. Letting her go about with no diaper is ideal (but risky). As an alternative, you can try holding her in your lap with an open, clean diaper beneath her.
- Use a barrier ointment or cream, such as zinc oxide or petroleum jelly.
- If these measures don't work, see *Stubborn diaper rashes* (left).

Candida thrives when your baby takes an oral antibiotic—higher levels of yeast combined with diarrhea, a likely side effect of the antibiotic, make your child much more susceptible to diaper rash.

Usually, a yeast infection occurs in skin that's already irritated. You may be treating an irritant diaper rash at first, but over time candida can cause a secondary infection.

If you suspect your child has a candida rash, call your pediatrician. Although treatment varies, the medications clotrimazole or terbinafine are commonly effective against yeasts. Your pediatrician may also recommend using hydrocortisone cream to treat the underlying irritant rash.

Flat and fitted cloth diapers

There's a tremendous range of options for cloth diapers: A wide choice of materials and improved designs make the best of a sometimes unpleasant task.

Fitted diapers

These fit your baby's bottom like clothing, so you don't have to fold them or use pins or fasteners. Most have elastic waists and legs, along with snaps or Velcro tabs. All-in-ones come with a waterproof cover sewn on, while others require a separate cover to contain moisture. Disposable diaper liners make cleanup easier.

Fitted diapers wash just like flat diapers, but you should check the care label for specific instructions.

Flats and prefolds

Flats are simply square or rectangular pieces of fabric that you fold around your baby's bottom and secure in place with pins, snaps, or fasteners. Prefolds usually have a reinforced center strip for added absorbency. You'll need to use a separate waterproof cover with flat diapers.

Cleaning soiled diapers

Cleaning diapers requires time and effort, so you might want to consider using a diaper service.

It's important to completely remove ammonia and bacteria to reduce the risk of diaper rash or infection. But using too much detergent can irritate your baby's skin. Carefully measure detergent, using a little less than you might for a load of clothing, and rinse diapers twice. A few drops of tea tree oil or baking soda in the wash and distilled white vinegar added to the rinse cycle can eliminate odors. Do not use bleach, fabric softeners, or some harsh detergents, which can break down the diapers and make them less absorbent over time.

Wash soiled diapers on a hot cycle and rinse with cold water. To be sure they're fully sterilized, line-dry them—the sun is a natural sanitizer—or run them in the dryer for at least an hour.

When you change your baby's cloth diaper, scrape or rinse as

TO PUT ON AND REMOVE A CLOTH DIAPER

1 Fold the diaper, if necessary, to form a rectangle. If using a cover, lay it out on the changing pad, then place the open, clean diaper over it. Lower your baby onto the open diaper.

2 Your baby's waist should be lined up with the top of the diaper. Now gather the bottom corners of the diaper in your hands and pull the fabric up between her legs, smoothing the front over her stomach.

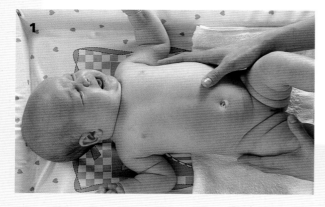

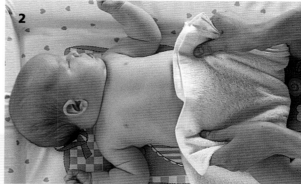

much excrement as you can into the toilet and then rinse the diaper. (This job is easier if you use biodegradable liners, but if you choose to use cloth liners, a sprayer attachment for your toilet makes the job much easier!)

Until you're ready to wash the used diapers, you can toss them into a dry bucket, or you can collect them in a water-filled bucket, which can reduce staining. Sprinkle in some baking soda to reduce odors before washing day. Or try wet bags—these reusable liners fit a garbage pail, and keep odor and wetness in. You can toss the wet bag in the wash with the diapers, cleaning everything at once.

3 If using a fitted diaper, secure the side tabs or snaps. For a flat diaper, keep your hand between the fabric and your baby's skin and pin or fasten one side. Adjust the fit and then fasten another pin on the other side. Bring the front of the waterproof cover up between her legs. Make sure the diaper is securely tucked inside the cover and secure the sides.

4 To remove, unfasten tabs or carefully unpin each side, setting the pins beyond your baby's reach. If there's any mess, hold your baby's ankles with one hand to raise her bottom and wipe away any excrement with the front, clean edge of the fabric. Fold the sides of the diaper into the middle and slide the diaper out from underneath her bottom, rolling it up as you remove it.

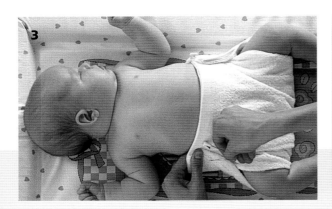

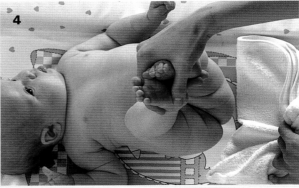

Care of the umbilical stump

Shortly after birth, the umbilical cord is clamped, and its attachment to the placenta is cut. The remaining stump soon shrivels and grows hard. Usually this remnant of the cord falls off in a week or two, but it could linger for up to a month.

Just before or after the stump falls off, you might notice a few blood spots or clumps of thick yellow or green mucus around the base of the cord, where the stump is attached to your baby's body, or within the umbilicus if the cord has already separated. This is a normal part of the healing process and not a sign of an infection.

Health experts recommend keeping the umbilical area dry to speed up healing at the site. When you put a fresh diaper on your baby, fold down the top front edge so the wet diaper won't cover the stump. Until the stump falls off, stick to sponge baths (see page 35); don't immerse your baby in water until after the cord area has completely healed. Thoroughly dry around the navel area after baths and diaper changes.

In the past, pediatricians commonly recommended cleaning the base of the umbilical stump every day with rubbing alcohol. Now physicians are divided on its use, since research has shown that simply leaving the stump alone and skipping the alcohol is as effective in keeping the area infection-free. Ask your pediatrician if he or she recommends "dry care" or rubbing alcohol.

If you see blood, mucus, or crusts in the umbilicus just before or after the stump falls off, use a cotton ball soaked with rubbing alcohol or an alcohol pad to gently clean the navel, being sure to remove any crusts or other debris.

Umbilical granuloma

Any mucous discharge or crusting after the cord separates should last only a few days. If it continues much longer, the problem might be an umbilical granuloma. A granuloma is a small bit of the umbilical cord that remains attached to the baby when the rest of the cord falls off. The oozing probably is coming from this small bit of cord tissue. You can leave it alone to heal, just as you did with the stump, or continue cleaning with rubbing alcohol. Alternatively, your pediatrician can usually remove it by applying silver nitrate.

Umbilical infection

Again, you don't need to be concerned about mucous discharge or spots of blood from the healing navel. This is perfectly normal. But if the skin surrounding the belly button becomes pinkish-red, you should call your pediatrician promptly—this could indicate a bacterial infection.

Umbilical hernia

All babies are born with a weakness or defect in the muscle layer of the abdominal wall. The muscles stretching from the ribs to the pubic bones on each side of the midline form around the umbilical cord as it enters the body of the fetus, which means that there is no muscle layer beneath the belly button. After birth, the muscles gradually grow together and repair over the defect.

If your baby develops an umbilical hernia, his navel will bulge or stick up when pressure increases in the abdominal cavity—such as when your baby cries or strains. The size of the hernia is determined by the diameter of the area lacking muscle; how high up the navel bulges out has nothing to do with the size of the hernia.

Umbilical hernias usually aren't cause for concern. They typically close slowly by themselves and rarely require surgery.

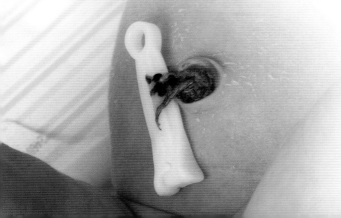

Care of the circumcision

If you choose to have your son circumcised (see page 18), the procedure is done either in the hospital or soon after your arrival at home, most commonly on the eighth day of life.

After the procedure, your son's penis may be wrapped with a gauze bandage saturated with petroleum jelly. You can probably remove this the next day, but you might be instructed to wait longer. To remove the gauze, first moisten it with water and then slowly and gently unwind it. The gauze might stick a bit to your baby's skin, and he might cry a little.

Don't be alarmed if you see a few drops of blood when the dressing is removed. Hold a clean piece of gauze over the bleeding spot for a minute or two. If you see more than a few drops of blood, take another clean gauze square and hold it on the bleeding spot with firm, continuous pressure for 2 to 3 minutes. If the bleeding persists, repeat the procedure again. If this fails to stop the bleeding, continue applying direct pressure while you call your pediatrician for advice.

Once the dressing is off, you can apply ointment onto a single gauze square and then place the gauze onto the head of the penis. Alternatively, you can put a bit of ointment on the head of the penis with your clean finger before putting on a fresh diaper.

Your doctor may recommend an antibiotic ointment, such as Bacitracin or Neosporin, or petroleum jelly to protect the sensitive skin of the head of the penis from irritants in the diaper.

After the circumcision, the entire head of the penis will be fire-engine red. As it heals, you might see small patches of yellow or green crusts on the skin. You also might notice a few drops of blood in his diaper, near the penis, or see a couple of drops of blood when you clean his penis.

Once you've removed the original dressing, you can clean the circumcised area during diaper changes. Moisten a cotton ball with warm water and gently dab the head of the penis. Remove any crusty material if it comes off easily. Let the penis air-dry. Then apply ointment to the penis with your finger or gauze. You can clean the rest of the diaper area with a washcloth or wipe, but don't use either on the circumcision.

When you put on a diaper, make sure it fits snugly against the penis. This seems as if it might be uncomfortable for your son, but the opposite is true: A snug diaper prevents the penis from moving around in the diaper, which is much more irritating.

Acute discomfort lasts only about a day, and even then babies seem to be very good at ignoring it. For the first day or two after the circumcision, keep in mind that besides the usual causes of crying, your baby's cries may mean he's sore or in pain—he might be telling you he's wet and uncomfortable at the site of the circumcision, so change his diaper regularly. It will be some time before the circumcised penis looks normal, but it is essentially healed within a week or two.

Pay attention to cleaning the groove where the head of the penis meets the shaft. Skin glands there produce thick, white mucous secretions that can cause the skin at the end of the shaft to stick to the adjacent skin of the head of the penis and fuse together. Remove the secretions during diaper changes and baths.

Circumcision rarely results in infection, but if your newborn develops a fever and is especially fussy, there might be an infection. The shaft of the penis, which isn't involved in the circumcision, should retain its normal color; reddened skin on the shaft close to the head of the penis could indicate infection. If you're concerned, call your pediatrician immediately—an infection in this area has the potential to become very serious.

Washing and bathing

A newborn doesn't have much opportunity to get dirty, aside from her diaper area. Sponge baths (see page 35) are the best way to keep her clean and ensure the umbilical cord stump stays dry.

Sponge bath

To give your baby a sponge bath, get all your supplies together first and then set her on a dry towel on the counter next to the sink. Stay with her at all times so she doesn't roll off. Using a small basin of warm, soapy water, wipe your baby with cotton balls or a washcloth, rinse with fresh warm water, and promptly dry her off with a second towel (see page 35).

Baby bath

Once you and your baby are ready for a real bath, you'll need a tub with a secure, nonslip base—though some parents make do washing their babies in a clean kitchen sink basin. Your baby should use this until she can sit unsupported, at about 6 months of age. Fill the bath with only 2 to 3 inches of water. Start with cold water and then add warm water. The water should be pleasantly warm but not hot, about 85°F. You can test it with your elbow or use a bath thermometer. Water that's too hot can burn your baby's skin; too cold will be chilly and uncomfortable. Make sure the room is warm and that the tub is securely supported on a waterproof surface away from any drafts.

Have everything you will need within arm's reach before undressing your baby—you don't want to leave her alone for a moment. You'll need a soft, clean washcloth; a fresh, clean towel for drying her off; a clean diaper and clothes to dress her in after the bath; and soap, which you can also use to wash her scalp instead of shampoo.

Follow the procedure described on page 40 and be quick—newborns and young infants can easily get cold and don't like to be naked. She might cry the entire time, so you'll want to move through the process quickly. Start by washing the cleanest parts of your baby first and finish with the dirtiest. This way, you reduce the risk of spreading germs from one area to another.

As soon as you take your baby out of the bath, wrap her up in a towel, being careful not to cover her face. Gently pat her dry, paying particular attention to the skin creases around her legs, the diaper area, under her arms, and around her neck. Put on her diaper and clothes, keeping exposed parts of her body covered with the towel.

Some parents feel babies should have daily baths, but this is more tradition than necessity. Babies only get dirty from soiled diapers and sometimes getting spit-up on themselves. Some babies sweat when they sleep, but this doesn't really make them dirty. A bath every 2 or 3 days is just fine. But if you enjoy the bath ritual or want to make it part of your baby's going-to-bed routine, there's no harm in giving her a bath every day.

BABY BATH FLOAT

If you need to wash your baby in a full-size tub, a float will help support your baby and keep her from slipping into the water. If you use a float, be sure to stay with your baby at all times.

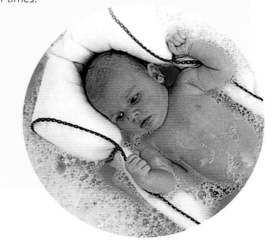

FONTANELLES

When your baby is born, the eight bones of her skull aren't fully fused together. This leaves small soft patches between neighboring bones on the top of her head known as the fontanelles. You should be mindful of them, because your baby's brain is more vulnerable at these spots. But they're covered with a tough protective membrane, so there is no need to be fearful or avoid them altogether. Simply wash and dry the fontanelles gently, as you would the rest of your baby's skin. The skull bones won't knit together completely until your baby is about 2 years old.

Washing the hair

You can wash your newborn's scalp while she's in the bath, but it might be easier to do once she's out of the tub and dried.

Wrap her in her towel and hold her under your arm, supporting her head. Hold her head over the baby bath and wet her head; then gently lather in the soap or shampoo. Rinse with more water (see box, below).

Cradle cap

Cradle cap, otherwise known as infant seborrhea, is a condition marked by excessive flakiness of the scalp (see also *Seborrheic dermatitis*, page 358). When these flakes fall on the forehead, face, ears, or neck and irritate the skin, they cause small pimples. This rash is often mistaken for neonatal acne.

The scalp flakes and pimples don't cause any harm, and treatment is optional. If you want to intervene, getting rid of the scalp flakes will clear up the facial rash. Rub baby or olive oil into your baby's scalp and leave it there for a few minutes; then shampoo and gently massage and scrub her scalp with your fingertips. Shampoo daily to prevent accumulation of flakes. Be aware that on the first day or two of treatment, the rash on her face will probably get worse before getting much better.

Rough, dry patches of eczema sometimes appear on a newborn's scalp, though eczema is more common on a baby's face and neck. See page 357 for more about eczema.

MORE **ABOUT**   shampoos and soaps

Most parents wash their infants' skin with special baby soap and use baby shampoo on their hair, believing they're a better choice because they're "milder" or "gentler." Is this true? Actually . . . no. There's no advantage to using baby soaps over adult soaps when cleaning the skin. In fact, many doctors recommend adult soaps with moisturizers, such as Dove, for bathing babies. The only significant benefit of a baby shampoo is that it won't sting as much if it gets into your baby's eyes. There isn't any evidence that adult shampoos can harm your baby or be too "rough." Some parents, however, who are concerned about exposing their babies to certain common chemicals in personal-care products, choose soaps and shampoos that don't use these chemicals.

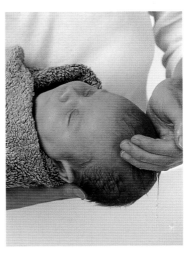

Care of hair and nails

Some babies are born with a full head of hair, while others have a sparse covering. Thick or thin, newborn hair may shed after a couple of weeks—often a cause of concern for parents, but it's normal. Your baby also may be covered with downy body hair, known as lanugo; this, too, will fall out within a few weeks or months.

Your newborn's hair needs only very simple care at first: Wipe it down with a damp cloth or sponge and brush it through with a soft baby brush. Your young baby's head is particularly sensitive due to the soft areas known as the fontanelles (see box, page 55). Don't be afraid of handling his head, however—just be gentle and careful as you wash and brush his hair.

Gently washing and brushing your baby's hair can also guard against cradle cap (see page 55).

Nails

Babies are often born with long nails. Trim them every 3 or 4 days—it can be easier when she's asleep—so she won't accidentally hurt herself. You'll know it's time to trim them when she starts scratching herself (or you) with them. None of the

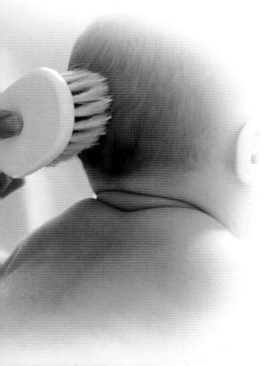

INFANTS' NAILS
You can cover your young baby's hands with a pair of soft mittens to prevent her from scratching herself or irritating any dry skin.

techniques for cutting nails is easy or foolproof. Biting off the tips of nails with your teeth is not recommended, as infection may occur if skin is accidently bitten into. When baby nail clippers are used, it is hard to visualize exactly what you are cutting, and you can easily remove fingertip skin with the nail. Using an emery board is labor intensive and requires much more time. Many pediatricians recommend baby safety scissors (one arm of the scissors has a dull edge).

Luckily for parents, toenails grow more slowly than fingernails, but excess skin often encroaches onto the nail bed, making toenails difficult to trim. To avoid catching your baby's skin, keep the toenails a little longer than the fingernails. If you do draw some blood from the skin surrounding a nail, hold a gauze pad against it until bleeding stops and then dab antiseptic ointment onto the area. When cutting either toe- or fingernails, cut straight across the nail.

Dressing

Baby clothes are irresistibly cute, making it fun to dress your newborn. Just remember that you don't need to spend a lot of money on baby clothes; your baby has no idea what he looks like and will outgrow them quickly!

Dressing your newborn

As a rule, babies don't care whether they're dressed or undressed—but they frequently don't like the feeling of air on their skin and having fabric pulled over their heads. You can make dressing a more enjoyable time for your baby with nuzzling and kisses, but be careful to be gentle. Also, make it easy on yourself and your baby by having everything within reach. Never leave your baby alone on a raised surface.

What to put on

You're aiming for a happy medium when you dress your infant, neither too much nor too little clothing. He shouldn't be too hot or too cold, but should remain "just right." Your baby can withstand cold weather—babies have been born in frigid climates for millennia, remember—or very warm weather, if dressed appropriately.

As a rule of thumb, dress your baby in the same number of layers you need to wear to be comfortable, plus one more light one. Premature infants who are still less than 6 pounds should wear two extra layers. If you're using an infant carrier, remember to count the carrier as a layer of clothing.

When you take your baby outside in very cold weather, he'll usually need an additional layer—but avoid overbundling him. To check whether he's warm enough, place your warm hand under his clothing and touch his chest or back: He should feel just a bit warmer than your hand. In hot weather, he might need only an undershirt or a T-shirt and a diaper, or even just a diaper. For how to put on and take off a undershirt or sleeper, see pages 38–39.

Clothes

Choose clothes that are soft and gentle on your baby's skin. Natural fabrics such as cotton and soft wools will be warm and will allow your baby's skin to breathe. Avoid synthetic fabrics that feel scratchy.

Check all garments for raised seams and scratchy labels. Irritating labels can be trimmed away, but raised seams will annoy your baby.

Your baby's clothes can get dirty and stained quickly, particularly around the diaper area and neckline. Buy colorfast, machine-washable clothes that are suitable for tumble-drying. Avoid anything that needs to be washed by hand or ironed.

Short-sleeved cotton undershirts or T-shirts with snap bottoms keep your baby warm and don't ride up like standard T-shirts. Choose ones with wide, stretchy neck openings; these are easier to pull over your newborn's head. Long-sleeved T-shirts with snap bottoms or sleepers are warm and easy to wear without restricting your baby's movement. Make sure there's always plenty of growing room in the legs. Some parents like to use sleeping gowns—long gowns with elastic or drawstring bottoms—for newborns. For advice on sleepwear, see page 157.

Hats

Your baby will wear a hat for a few hours after birth, but after that he won't need one indoors unless it's colder than 68°F. When outdoors in cool weather, your baby needs a hat whenever your head feels a little cold, too. In the summer, it's important that he wear a wide-brimmed sun hat to protect him from the sun's rays.

Washing clothes

There's no need to buy special laundry detergent formulated for babies (unless you're using cloth diapers), or wash your baby's clothes separately from the rest of the family's laundry. Some babies are sensitive to certain additives in detergent, but this can occur with any brand. If your baby has sensitive skin, try using laundry detergent that is free of added fragrances or colors.

It is a good idea, however, to wash baby clothes before he wears them for the first time.

Visitors and going out

Shortly after your delivery, relatives and friends may want to visit you in the hospital and, later, at home. They come with well wishes, hoping to meet your newborn and perhaps hold her. You'll also want to see your close friends and family, but too many visitors can quickly become overwhelming.

Keep visits short and don't be shy about saying you're tired or uncomfortable, so guests will leave you alone to relax. Your partner can help by paying attention to your energy level and serving as a gatekeeper when you need to take some time to rest.

If you're nursing, you might be unsure about breastfeeding when other people are around. But don't let visitors interfere with feeding your baby: You can cover yourself with a light blanket or ask your visitors for privacy.

Germ prevention

Despite their best intentions, visitors can bring germs that they might share with your newborn.

Parents want to protect their children from feeling poorly, of course, but there are other good reasons to try to keep your newborn healthy. Young babies are more susceptible to severe bacterial infections than older children and adults, and if such an illness occurs, it can progress rapidly. It's also harder to distinguish a milder illness from the start of a potentially serious bacterial infection in newborns and young infants (see box, page 60).

Luckily, bacterial infections in young babies are rare—colds and viruses are far more common. In fact, any germs visitors might share with your baby almost always result in a viral illness. But since these illnesses can resemble the beginning of a bacterial infection, your doctor might want to start treating your baby for a bacterial infection just in case.

It's worth making an effort to protect your baby from getting sick. Not only would you be preventing her from the discomfort of illness, you may be able to avoid the worry and invasive procedures

3 ways to avoid illness

1   **Postpone visits from anyone who isn't feeling healthy.** Tell people with coughs and colds to put off visiting until they are well.

2   **Limit the number of people who hold your baby.** Allow only close family and friends to hold your baby— and only after they wash their hands. Have overly curious visitors touch her feet rather than try to hold her hands.

3   **Keep hand sanitizers close by.** Set out alcohol-based sanitizer near your baby and carry a small, portable bottle of sanitizer in your diaper bag when you go out.

really up to you whether you want to stay home for a few weeks or take your baby out and about.

While it is true that your baby may not be able to regulate her body temperature very well in the first few hours after she's born, this is a short-lived problem (unless your child was born prematurely; see page 94). Dressed properly, your baby can handle varying temperatures just as you can. Make sure she has a hat in cold weather and isn't exposed to direct sunshine. If you feel uncomfortably cold or hot, assume your baby feels the same way and find a more comfortable location.

It's very important to give yourself a chance to rest and recover from your labor and delivery—this is something that many mothers fail to appreciate. You shouldn't take your baby for long outings until you've first taken care of yourself. A brief walk outdoors, however, could help your recovery and be enjoyable for both you and your baby.

Most infections are spread by face-to-face, close contact between a germ "donor" and your baby, so it's a good idea to avoid cramped, closed-in spaces, such as a busy store or crowded restaurant. But there's no danger in going to more open spaces, such as the park, a mall, or the sidewalk for a walk with your baby in the stroller.

that result if your child ends up needing to be hospitalized.

Most infections spread by close contact and touching. Handwashing and limiting contact can go a long way toward minimizing exposure, along with other precautions (see box, page 59). Hopefully your visitors will understand and appreciate your caution. If anyone thinks you're being unreasonable or "neurotic," hold firm. Feel free to place the blame for restrictions on your pediatrician.

Going out

Your family or friends might advise you to keep your baby at home for the first 2 to 4 weeks— so she won't be exposed to the weather, so you can rest and recover, and so your baby won't be exposed to germs. But it's

MORE **ABOUT** | bacterial infections

If your baby develops a fever and seems fussy in the first 2 to 3 months, she should be checked by a doctor. If your pediatrician cannot rule out the possibility that your baby has a bacterial infection, she might admit your child to the hospital for blood tests and evaluation of urine and spinal fluid to detect any bloodstream or urinary tract infections (see page 350) or meningitis (see page 348). Your baby will begin receiving intravenous antibiotics as a precaution: Cultures for bacteria may not be ready for 2 or 3 days. If all the tests come back negative and your baby doesn't have a bacterial infection, she'll be discharged. It's an unpleasant ordeal, and one you can try to avoid by doing your best to limit your baby's exposure to germs.

Common worries

Parents often fret over every little problem with their new babies—and even things that aren't problems at all! Mothers might seem programmed to fret more, but your partner probably will also be concerned about anything that seems unusual.

Establishing feeding

New parents frequently worry whether their baby is getting enough to eat. Mothers who are breastfeeding, in particular, may struggle with feeding at first. Parents who give their babies formula in a bottle have two big advantages: They can see exactly how much milk their child drinks at each feeding, and they don't have to worry about the adequacy of their supply of milk. Although it's easy to tell if your baby is thriving (see page 68), you may second-guess yourself until your milk supply is fully in and your baby is sucking strongly and often at the breast.

Most mothers assume that breastfeeding will go smoothly from the start. It's a natural process, so how hard can it be? But for many new mothers, it doesn't come so easily. About 10 to 20 percent of breastfeeding mothers have difficulty with breastfeeding at first (see also page 77). If you're struggling, follow the advice in the next chapter, give yourself plenty of rest, and seek out the support of your partner, your family, your pediatrician, other moms, and perhaps a lactation consultant.

Demand or schedule?

Breast- and bottle-feeding your newborn is covered in great detail in Chapter 3. Whichever method you use, ideally you'll be able to read cues from your

KNOWING WHEN TO FEED

If your baby wakes about every 2 to 3 hours or so, follow his lead and feed on demand. When he has a long stretch of sleeping, often in the afternoon, it's okay to let him sleep a little longer—a long interval like this between feedings most likely will be balanced later on with a cluster of feedings closer together.

If you're confident that your child is getting enough milk and feedings are progressing successfully, there's no reason to wake him frequently for feeds. If you're worried, you can always have your pediatrician's office check your baby's weight.

If your pediatrician is concerned that your baby is gaining weight too slowly, feed him about every 3 hours if he doesn't wake on his own to demand a feeding.

newborn and feed him only when he shows you he's hungry—this is called feeding on demand.

An alternative philosophy of feeding espouses waking newborns every 2 hours or so, feeding him even if he doesn't seem hungry. Putting him on a schedule might make it easier to fit your baby into your family's patterns and routines.

If your baby is very mellow and doesn't convey his hunger regularly, offering scheduled feedings makes sense. But most babies are very good at making it clear when they're hungry. If your baby seems to have very strong opinions about when he wants to be fed, crying loudly and persistently, you do not want to keep him waiting.

Thrush

Because a newborn's immune system isn't yet fully developed, yeasts such as *Candida albicans* can take hold in the oral cavity.

Candida rarely causes any harm, disease, or discomfort. It appears as a white coating on the tongue that can't be scraped off easily and white, cottage cheese–like patches on the inside of the cheeks, gums, and roof of the mouth. The white coating and patches are called thrush. Very rarely, thrush at the back of the throat can cause discomfort with swallowing. As the yeast travels through the intestinal tract, it can show up in stools and contribute to diaper rashes (see page 49); these can be treated with antifungal creams.

If you're breastfeeding, thrush in your baby's mouth occasionally can spread the yeast infection to your nipples or breasts. If this happens, your nipples will become pink and sore. Keep them as dry as possible between feedings. Consult your physician, who may recommend using an antifungal topical cream on your breast.

To treat your baby's thrush, your pediatrician may prescribe an antifungal liquid medication such as fluconazole, nystatin, or miconazole. Another option is to do nothing: Thrush seldom causes babies any discomfort and, if left alone, will disappear in a month or two when your baby's maturing immune system is able to fight it off.

Lack of sleep

There's no getting around it: The first months with a newborn are utterly exhausting. You might be worried about making sure your baby develops good sleep habits. Eventually, you'll want him to settle into his bed at the same time every night and fall asleep in his crib. But that's usually too much to expect in these early months.

Newborns have erratic sleep rhythms; their longest periods of sleep often come during the afternoon. Their ability to differentiate between day and night begins to improve at about 2 to 3 months of age, when, thankfully, your baby generally will begin sleeping for longer stretches at night. But young infants need to wake up and eat every few hours at night, just as they do during the day. And if your baby has fussy spells of colic in the evening, it's more important to help him through these difficult periods than to try to train him in good sleep habits.

Chronic exhaustion makes these first months some of the hardest for parents. Because your baby hasn't developed day-night rhythms, he'll probably wake often during the night—and he'll need you to be up with him some of the time. If your baby readily cooperates with your efforts to help him establish good sleep habits, then go for it. But if he doesn't seem to be getting the hang of it, don't push that right now. It's more important that you get some sleep whenever you can.

Don't worry about instilling bad habits—you can turn things around later, when your baby is ready and able to sleep through the night. (See Chapter 7, "Sleep matters," for advice.) Do whatever works for your newborn. So if your baby falls asleep best while being rocked, then rock him to sleep. If he falls asleep best in the swing or car seat, that's okay, too. Have him sleep in a bassinet or Moses basket next to you so it's easier to pick him up when he cries at night. Whenever and wherever you lay your baby down to go to sleep, remember that the safest position is on his back, facing up.

As much as you may worry about your baby's sleep habits, it's important that you don't neglect your own sleep. You'll feel worse, be grouchier, and have much less patience for your partner and baby when you're overtired. Resist the urge to fold dirty laundry or wash dishes during your baby's daytime naps—lie down yourself and catch a few minutes of rest.

Share night duties with your partner. If you use bottles, have some prepared formula ready to go so you can minimize nighttime disruptions. If you're breastfeeding, you'll still need to do most of the nighttime work. But your partner can bring the baby for feeding, change his diaper afterward, and settle him back to sleep. If you're using bottles of formula or expressed milk, your partner can take over a nighttime feeding or two.

MORE **ABOUT** | sudden infant death syndrome

SIDS (sudden infant death syndrome) is the sudden death of a baby less than a year old, where no specific cause can be found despite a detailed investigation. Babies who die from SIDS appear to die painlessly in their sleep. It usually happens when a baby is asleep in his crib, but it can happen any time a baby is sleeping, even in a stroller or a parent's arms. SIDS can happen to any baby, but premature babies, low-birth-weight babies, and boys are at greater risk. SIDS is more likely to occur at night, between midnight and 9 a.m.

Although the specific cause is unknown, researchers believe a combination of factors play a role in SIDS. Suspected factors include breathing failures or problems in the medulla oblongata, the part of the brain that controls breathing; irregular heartbeats; allergies; bacterial toxins; and genetic abnormalities—but nothing has been proven. Although little is known about what causes SIDS, there is a great deal of proven information on how parents can reduce the risk for their baby (see pages 156–158).

SIDS

Many parents worry about sudden infant death syndrome, or SIDS (see box at left). It's very rare, but just the thought of it prompts many parents to frequently check their sleeping baby both day and night. You can take steps to minimize your baby's risk—lay your baby on his back when he goes to sleep, and don't smoke—but unfortunately there's no way to guarantee your baby's safety. If you find yourself fretting about SIDS, remind yourself that you're doing everything you can to keep your baby safe and healthy—and then try to set these fears aside.

Work commitments

Parents who work may feel additional stress. They may be worried about how they'll provide for a new baby and possibly a stay-at-home partner, and they may feel torn between the wish to spend time at home as a family and the desire to thrive at work and help support their family. Mothers who plan to return to work might fret over how they'll manage both roles. And single mothers might worry about how they'll be able to do it all.

Take a deep breath and try to focus on enjoying your baby and finding your family's new rhythm. It can take time to figure out how you'll juggle all these responsibilities and desires. Look at your household budget, consider what kind of support you can rely on, and, most important, give yourself time to figure out what you want.

Twins

Twin pregnancies have increased dramatically in recent years, mostly due to the success of in vitro fertilization and other techniques to improve a woman's chance of becoming pregnant, as well as better nutrition.

When an embryo of only a handful of cells splits in two and each half becomes a separate fetus, identical twins result. Each fetus develops from the same fertilized egg, so they share the same genetic makeup. When the two identical embryos implant in the uterus, they usually are enclosed in a single amniotic sac.

If two separate and unrelated fertilized eggs reach the uterus, fraternal, nonidentical twins result. They don't share the same genetic code because they developed from separate eggs. Like all brothers and sisters, they share many genes, but they don't resemble each other as much as identical twins do.

The challenge with twins, of course, is that there are two of them! You'll need to choose two names instead of just one, you'll need two car seats to get them home from the hospital—and you'll have to be able to tell them apart. This is easier if you have fraternal twins, but it can be very difficult if they're identical. As you get to know your babies, their uniqueness will become obvious to you. But in the beginning, you'll need to look for identifying clues: a birthmark, head shape, the amount of hair, their belly buttons. To ensure certainty, you can leave

IDENTICAL OR FRATERNAL TWINS?

You might not be able to tell whether your newborn twins are identical or fraternal. Identical twins can be born with different weights and sizes, and, due to different positions within the uterus, their heads may be shaped differently. Proof of whether your twins are identical or fraternal comes after careful study of the placenta. You could also find the answer with genetic testing, but this usually isn't necessary. Here are some clues to figuring out whether your twins are identical.

◆ If your twins are different sexes, they cannot be identical. Same-sex twins, however, can be either identical or fraternal.

◆ If a single placenta was found at delivery, the twins probably are identical. Fraternal twins typically have separate placentas or, if the two placentas are conjoined, the single placenta is much larger than usual.

◆ Twins occurring after in vitro fertilization are usually fraternal, since many fertilized eggs are placed in the uterus at the same time to increase the chance of at least one embryo implanting.

◆ Identical twins have the same blood type. Fraternal twins may have either the same or different blood types.

the hospital identification bands on their wrists or ankles, or you can make an ID bracelet of your own.

Twins require twice as much work: You have twice as many diapers to change, twice as many baths to give, twice as much laundry to do, and twice as much comforting to give in response to twice as much crying. When they're older, you'll have two mischievous toddlers to chase after, double the amount of cleaning up to tackle, and plenty of sibling squabbles to settle. And yes, you'll probably be twice as exhausted as other parents. Look to your partner, family, friends, or babysitters and nannies for help.

It may be difficult to feed both babies at the same time, especially if you're breastfeeding (see page 76). If you want to exclusively breastfeed your twins, you may need to breastfeed them quite frequently, which can be exhausting. To give yourself some relief, you might want to ask your partner to give a twin an occasional bottle of formula. This takes some of the pressure off you, and if done infrequently there is little chance that one or both of your twins could come to prefer the bottle to the breast.

Facing unexpected problems

Even minor things can be distressing to anxious new parents. A birthmark (see page 27), a bumpy start to feedings, or a touch of jaundice (see page 363) can seem like monumental problems. Your pediatrician, family, and friends can help give you the information you need to deal with these issues in their proper context.

On rare occasions, babies are born with a serious illness or malformation (see Chapter 13, "Addressing health issues"). If this happens, your baby probably will be sent straight to the neonatal intensive care unit (NICU). You might feel shocked, distraught, and helpless. (For more about what you'll experience in the NICU, see Chapter 4.) You'll desperately need two things: knowledge and support.

Your pediatrician and other specialists treating your baby are usually the best sources of information

for you. You'll need to understand what's wrong, how it happened, how it can be treated, and how it could affect your baby and your family. Although you can learn a lot from books or on the Internet, these sources can be misleading (see box below). In this book, we've made great efforts to avoid errors commonly encountered in other sources.

Having a sick newborn or a baby with serious medical issues is very stressful for parents. You and your partner may be overwhelmed and overwrought. Helping each other get through this difficult time will benefit you both. Other relatives and friends can provide great comfort just by being there for you.

5 dangers of consulting books and the Internet

1 **You may find wrong information.** Books and websites can have significant factual errors. You may not know whether a book has been critically assessed by an informed reviewer. And on the Internet, free speech rules: People can say anything they want, with no regard for truth and accuracy.

2 **What you find may not be right for your baby.** Different medical conditions can have very similar symptoms. You may find a disease that fits many of your child's symptoms, but that doesn't mean it's the right diagnosis. You could wrongly interpret possible outcomes or misjudge your child's chances of being at risk for a particular condition.

3 **Information is usually generalized.** Books and websites offer information to a broad audience, providing advice and information for many different children. They may recommend extra precautions because they don't know the specifics of your child's case and they don't want to miss a rare, serious complication. But in medicine, a one-size-fits-all approach doesn't work. Each baby's case should be considered in context.

4 **Data may be unreliable.** Many information sources present data in a skewed manner. They include only selected facts to support their perspective, so you don't get a balanced view.

5 **You may face information overload.** You may find out more than you want to. Your pediatrician may have told you, "Your baby has an excellent chance of a full recovery." Do you really want to know about the 0.1 percent of children with the same condition who have a much more serious outcome?

FEEDING YOUR
YOUNG BABY

Feeding basics

Feeding your newborn will at first take up much of your time with her, whether you breastfeed or give her bottles of formula or expressed milk. It can often take a few weeks to settle into a comfortable feeding routine. While you're getting the hang of it, seek out support at home, from a professional, or in a support group. If you're worried your baby isn't getting enough to eat, talk to your pediatrician.

The American Academy of Pediatrics recommends that mothers exclusively breastfeed their babies for the first 6 months, when solids are gradually introduced, and continue breastfeeding for at least the first year. For personal, medical, or practical reasons, you may choose not to breastfeed, to supplement with formula, or to wean your baby earlier. This is a highly personal decision.

Breastfeeding has many positives. Breast milk supplies babies with vital nutrients and helps protect them against diseases and conditions, including diarrhea, type 1 and type 2 diabetes, childhood obesity, and respiratory, ear, and urinary tract infections. Moms who breastfeed have a lower risk of getting breast or ovarian cancer and return to their pre-pregnancy weight more quickly. Breastfeeding also helps moms bond with their babies. Compared to formula-fed babies or those who were weaned early, breastfed babies also have fewer trips to the doctor and pharmacy.

If you're unsure about breastfeeding, keep in mind that human milk is a natural and uniquely superior first food for babies. Try it and see how it goes. Your body can adjust to different feeding schedules; for example, if you go back to work, you can continue to nurse in the morning and evening. Any amount of breastfeeding has benefits for you and your baby.

5 ways to tell your baby is thriving

1   **She is relaxed during feeding.** Your baby sucks and swallows fairly slowly, with occasional pauses.

2   **She's content** and sleeps well between most feedings.

3   **Her poop changes quickly from sticky black to golden yellow** in the first 5 days, and it's always soft (runny if breast-fed, firmer if bottle-fed).

4   **She has plenty of heavy, wet diapers**.

5   **She's alert and usually happy when she's awake,** and she's filling out and feeling heavier.

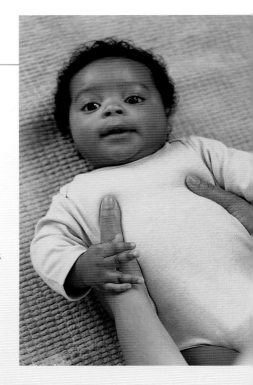

If you're having a hard time with breastfeeding, it's important to get help right away. Feeding issues can often be resolved with some expert guidance (see page 81 for resources). Women have always breastfed their babies, but women in industrialized countries may have some difficulty getting started. As formula has become more popular, women have become less familiar with breastfeeding and sometimes find they have a lot to learn. And while modern medical interventions can make labor and delivery safer and less painful, some can also make it more difficult to establish breastfeeding. For example, Demerol and other pain-relief medications used during labor can cause babies to be very sleepy after delivery, making it more difficult to get a good start with feeding.

Not all new moms can or want to breastfeed. For example, some take medications or have a condition that might interfere with breastfeeding. Whatever your reason for choosing to use formula, it's important that you feel confident and secure that you're making the right decision for your family. Rest assured, your baby will still receive excellent nutrition, and you can bond with your baby while giving her a bottle and enjoying other time together.

How often to feed

Like adults, babies have varying eating habits. All infants need to eat often, especially at first, but they can have different patterns. Some are hungry every few hours, others feed more randomly, and some are so regular you could set your watch by them!

Crying is a late sign of hunger. Early signs of hunger include increased alertness, physical activity, mouthing, or rooting. With a little experience, you'll come to recognize exactly when your baby is hungry.

At first, your baby may seem to want to eat very frequently. Her tummy is tiny and can't hold much more than a couple of ounces at a time. In the first few weeks, a bottle-fed baby usually wants to be fed every 3 to 4 hours, while a breastfed baby typically wants to nurse every 2 to 3 hours, day and night. Babies naturally wake to be fed once or twice a night until they're about 3 months old and may continue to do so after that point, because it has become part of their habitual feeding pattern.

Frequent breastfeeding helps to establish a good supply of breast milk, which is important as your growing baby needs more to eat. If you find yourself tired of serving as an all-hours snack bar, try to remind yourself that you're giving her the best possible nutrition; feedings are a good opportunity to enjoy some calm, relaxing time with your baby; and that this, too, shall pass. Your baby won't always need to eat every 2 to 3 hours.

Breast milk is low in protein and high in milk sugar, and babies need to eat little but often to grow well. Feed your baby whenever she seems hungry, whether you're breastfeeding or using bottles. Most normal-weight babies can go a maximum of 6 hours without a meal—though many will want to eat much more often. This lengthy break usually develops during daytime, but it indicates that your baby is learning to sleep for longer periods. Before long, she may shift that 6-hour break to nighttime.

During the first few days, some newborns don't wake up often and ask to be fed. They may be sleepy from birth medications or uncomfortable after the birth and want to be left alone. Many experts recommend that if your baby has slept for 3 or 4 hours without waking, you should wake her gently and offer her a feeding right away. Others believe in an on-demand feeding schedule, in which healthy babies are allowed to sleep as long as they wish, being fed only when they wake up or seem hungry.

How much to give

Just like adults, babies have both small meals and bigger meals. If you're breastfeeding, your baby probably will want to feed from the first breast for as long as she can. You can offer a break for a burp or a diaper change, and then put her onto the other breast for a second helping. Just as each baby has a different personality and a different suck, each breast has its own capacity and works individually. Frequent feeding will help build your milk supply in the first few weeks.

As a rough guide, a bottle-fed baby will need 2 to 2½ ounces of formula for each pound she weighs. A baby who weighs 7 pounds, for example, should drink about 14 to 17 ounces of formula in a 24-hour period. Since babies take in only about 2 ounces at a feeding, she'll probably need 6 to 8 bottle feedings a day until she weighs about 12 pounds. But this is just an approximation. Just let your baby take as much from the bottle as she wants—she will stop when she has had enough. And you won't need to count ounces because she can be trusted to take the right amount.

There's no need to give your baby water, even in very hot weather, because she'll get plenty of liquid with her small, frequent feedings. Water offers no nourishment. Besides, the main ingredient of milk is water. If she drinks enough to satisfy her hunger, your child will get all the water she needs even on the hottest days. If your baby is bottle-fed, take care to prepare formula with the recommended amount of water; formula prepared with too little or too much water can harm your baby.

Growth

Just when you feel you've established a good feeding pattern, your baby may suddenly want to eat more often: He's probably going through a growth spurt. These usually occur at about 2 weeks, 4 weeks, 6 weeks, and 3 months. Your baby is trying to boost your milk supply to help him grow. If you are formula feeding, the portion size will increase. If you are nursing, he does this by feeding more often,

Helping your baby burp

Several positions will help your baby get rid of painful gas in his tummy. Holding him with his head over your shoulder, support his bottom with one hand and use the other to gently rub or pat his back. Or you can hold your baby in a sitting position on your lap: Prop him up with one hand (support your baby's head if he cannot yet hold it up); use the other to gently rub or pat his upper back. Another option is to lay your baby down so that his stomach rests on one of your knees and his chest is on your bent arm. His head should face away from you with nothing obstructing his mouth. Gently rub or pat his back.

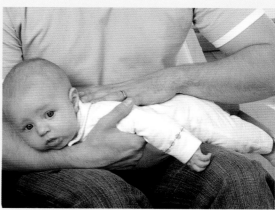

which prompts your body to produce more milk. When you're producing enough milk to keep him sated, he'll settle back into a more normal feeding pattern until the next growth spurt.

Passing the days with a fretful, hungry baby can seem hard, but remind yourself that it's only temporary. Some breastfeeding mothers call these days, when you're spending hours with your baby, "sofa days." That may sound more idyllic than it really is. If you're having a hard time, don't go it alone. Invite a friend to visit, or seek out support in a group for new parents—check with your pediatrician or inquire at your local hospital for information.

If you're breastfeeding and your baby seems fussy much of the time, don't hesitate to seek advice from someone knowledgeable. You can get support and practical advice from your pediatrician, a lactation consultant, or a midwife (see page 81). To determine how much breast milk your baby is taking in, a healthcare professional can weigh your baby before and after a feeding.

Discuss any questions about your baby's growth with your pediatrician, who will track your baby's height and weight at checkups. You also can refer to the growth chart in the back of this book, which plots babies' weights against national averages. Keep in mind that babies range in size. As long as your baby is growing steadily and your pediatrician is happy with his growth, you don't need to worry. Weighing your baby weekly will only make you more anxious, as babies don't grow at steady rates.

Gas
Most of the gas in your baby's intestines is air swallowed with feedings or while crying. As your baby consumes more milk, however, she also ingests more milk sugar. This ferments and produces a little gas as well. Letting go of gas will make your baby feel better. She can release it from her bottom or with a burp.

If your bottle-fed baby suffers from a lot of gas,

| HEALTHFIRST | crying and spitting up |

Crying at feeding time can have several causes (see pages 170–172). Frequent spitting up is common (see below) but can be part of a medical condition such as gastroesophageal reflux or, rarely, an intestinal blockage. If your baby cries often during feedings or spits up frequently or forcefully, report this to your pediatrician.

you'll know because she'll seem unsettled. Check that the nipple flow is correct (see page 83). If the formula flow is slower than recommended, the hole is too small. This forces your baby to suck harder, and she can take in too much air along with the formula. On the other hand, if your baby tends to gulp during feedings, check that the nipple flow isn't too fast. Remember to tilt the bottle during feedings. Liquid should always completely cover the top of the bottle and fill the nipple.

It's difficult for a baby to swallow air, but she may gulp and take in more air if she isn't fully attached to the breast or if the bottle nipple is too big. Most babies get very indignant if you try to interrupt a steady flow of milk to burp them. Imagine how you'd feel if your drink was removed just when you were starting to enjoy it! If your baby tends to be very gassy, try to burp her when she takes a natural pause (see box, opposite page).

You don't need to spend more than a few minutes trying to burp your baby. She can expel gas just as well with a nice cuddle during or after her feeding.

Spitting up
The back of the throat and the top of the stomach are close to each other. Also, the narrowing at the point where the stomach and esophagus meet in newborns is not very effective at preventing stomach contents from being pushed upward into the esophagus (or higher) when the stomach contracts. As a result, some babies regurgitate a little milk along with a big burp (or without one). Some babies spit up after every feeding. This is normal for most infants. If she spits up very often or very forcefully, check in with your pediatrician.

Breastfeeding

Regardless of whether you planned to breastfeed or bottle-feed, during pregnancy your body began to prepare your breasts for nursing. You grew more mammary tissue, and your breasts became larger.

Only a very small percentage of women are medically unable to breastfeed their babies; they may have had breast surgery or have injured breast tissue, or they may have hormonal or endocrine problems. Women in the United States who are HIV-positive are advised against breastfeeding. Much more commonly, women struggle with nursing because they lack the confidence to breastfeed or don't get enough (or the right kind of) help when they encounter problems. Most babies are instinctively able to feed shortly after birth, given the right opportunity and environment. If you hold your baby skin-to-skin during the "golden hour" (see opposite page), he'll probably show natural feeding responses.

Ensuring a good milk supply

Just as your body nourished your baby in the womb throughout pregnancy, you can continue to nourish him naturally with your milk. The key is establishing and keeping a good milk supply. Your breasts have developed a large network of special cells to make milk; when they release it for your baby to drink, they automatically make more. The more milk your baby takes, the more your breasts will produce.

As soon as your baby is born, colostrum—a highly nutritious early form of milk already in your breasts—starts to flow. It's important to begin breastfeeding immediately to give your baby colostrum and to stimulate more milk production. If no milk is released, your milk supply will dry up within a few days.

By the third or fourth day after delivery, your breasts should begin producing much larger amounts of sweet milk. You may find you have far more than you need for a few days, but this shows that your breasts can produce plenty for your baby—or babies! The process is designed to match your baby's needs: The more your baby nurses, the more milk you produce. Conversely, the less she drinks, the less your body produces. Any milk left in your breasts after your baby has finished feeding will signal your body to slow down the supply. If you're having trouble with

 ways to build up a good milk supply

1   **Encourage your baby to nurse within the first few hours of birth** or, if he can't feed right away, start expressing your milk.

2   **Make sure your baby is fully attached to your breast at each feeding;** get help immediately if this is difficult.

3   **Encourage frequent feedings,** day and night, for the first few weeks. Sleep in the same room as your baby, and consider using a sling or wrap to carry him around.

4   **Get lots of help and support from your pediatrician, family, and friends;** your job is to heal and be with your baby.

breastfeeding and very little milk is taken out, your supply could go down too much.

If you find that you don't seem to have enough milk, or that your supply appears to be diminishing, immediately seek professional help to boost your supply. You may be advised to introduce a bottle, an easy solution with a big potential drawback: It sets up a cycle in which your baby drinks formula, is sated, and then nurses less frequently—when you really need your baby to breastfeed more often to stimulate milk production. That said, if you've tried multiple strategies to boost your milk production, and your pediatrician is concerned that your baby is still losing too much weight, do not feel guilty about supplementing breastfeeding with formula feedings. Continue to nurse as much as you can; any breast milk has benefits.

You'll have an easier time of it if you get sufficient food, drink, and rest while you're breastfeeding. Looking after a young baby is tiring, and when you're stressed, your milk may not flow well—the let-down reflex works best when you're relaxed. You might enlist family and friends to take care of household tasks so you can enjoy feeding; the hormones released when you feed your baby will help you relax.

If your baby is fretting after feedings, don't assume she's still hungry or unsatisfied. She might just want to be held close to you. Holding her or carrying her in a soft sling should help soothe her.

It's normal if your breasts start to feel soft after a few weeks; it doesn't mean you aren't producing enough milk. If your baby seems to be thriving (see box on page 68), you have plenty.

Your baby may go through phases of more frequent feedings. This is normal and not a sign that you should worry about your supply. He might be going through a growth spurt, signaling your body to produce more milk. Or he may simply be seeking comfort as he learns to deal with the world around him.

The golden hour
If your medical situation allows it, uninterrupted skin-to-skin contact between a baby and mother during the time immediately after birth—sometimes called the "golden hour"—has been shown to improve bonding, improve breastfeeding success, and give a baby a very good start in life. If you are not able to immediately be with your baby, for example, if you deliver via cesarean section, skip the guilt and come together as soon as you can.

Skin-to-skin contact provides your newborn with warmth, safety, and access to food at a time when she's most receptive and interested in feeding. It allows mothers to share with their babies beneficial skin bacteria for populating the newborn's intestinal tract. Breastfeeding mothers are also able to pass along endorphins, so-called "feel-good" chemicals, to their babies to help soothe them after the stresses of childbirth.

EXPRESSING MILK
If your baby cannot breastfeed right away, your partner is taking a turn at feeding, or you're going to be away from your baby, you may want to express breast milk. Using an electric, dual pump is the quickest and easiest way to do this. A pump is essential if you want a regular supply of expressed milk; for instance, if you return to work. (See page 80 for tips.) A manual pump will do on an occasional basis (see page 79). In some cases a doctor or lactation consultant will recommend that you rent a hospital-grade pump.

You express milk straight into a sterile bottle, plastic container, or breast-milk freezer bag. Store the milk in the refrigerator for up to 48 hours or freeze it for up to 6 months.

Expressing milk by hand can be tricky to learn, but it's a handy skill if you're away from your baby and become engorged. To do it, stimulate your milk flow by gently stroking downward from the top of your breast toward the areola. Then place your thumbs above the areola and your fingers below. Begin rhythmically squeezing the lower part of your breast while pressing toward your breastbone.

Breastfeeding routine

You'll be most relaxed if you try to breastfeed in a calm environment. You might want to turn off your cell phone or close the door so you won't be disturbed. Have a glass of water or juice nearby—nursing can make you very thirsty. Make sure both you and your baby are comfortable. If you're sitting upright, you can support his back and shoulders on your forearm with a nursing pillow or with your free hand. His head should be at the same level as your nipple, and he should be able to reach your breast without any effort. Hold him so that his entire body is facing your breast.

GETTING COMFORTABLE

A comfortable position can be the key to successful breastfeeding, so try a few techniques to see which works best. Always hold your baby firmly close to you with his whole body facing your breast and his chest next to yours. You should be able to bring him easily to your breast.

Most women sit upright to nurse, often with their feet raised and a pillow supporting their arms, but you can try other positions as well. You can get a specially designed nursing pillow to help.

Try lying on your side if you're tired or find it uncomfortable to sit—perhaps if you've had an episiotomy. Make sure you have plenty of pillows to support you. Hold your baby close to you with his mouth in line with your breast. If you've had a cesarean or if your baby wriggles or arches his back, bend your knees and support your back with a pillow.

Offering the breast

You may find it helpful to cup your breast with your hand or support it by placing your fingers against your ribs just underneath it. Try not to place two fingers in a "scissors grip" around your nipple, as doing so can prevent your baby from feeding properly. You also don't need to press your

breast away from his nose so he can breathe—his nostrils are flared to allow him to breathe and feed simultaneously.

Your baby may instinctively start to suck as soon as he feels your breast against his cheek. If he doesn't, brush his lips against your nipple or stroke his cheek with your finger to trigger his

rooting reflex. Once he opens his mouth, draw him quickly to your breast.

Latching on

Your baby's mouth needs to be wide open so he can take in part of your breast as well as your nipple. His tongue needs to come well forward so he can hold on

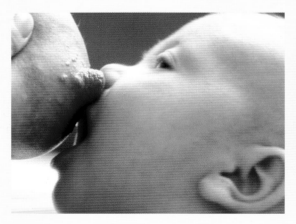

to your breast comfortably while feeding and express the milk from your breast behind your nipple. When he is fully on your breast, your nipple will be near the soft part on the roof of his mouth, and every section of your breast will release milk equally. When the milk flows, he'll drink it slowly and steadily, and you may hear him swallowing.

If your nipple hurts or you don't think he's latched on properly, you can break the suction by inserting your little finger in the corner of his mouth and then repositioning him. Latch problems are a common source of nipple pain. Seek help from a lactation consultant if your baby persistently has trouble latching.

Drinking his fill

Your baby's sucking pattern will change while he feeds, from short sucks to longer bursts, with pauses in between. He'll let you know when your breast is empty by playing with it, falling asleep, or letting your nipple slide out of his mouth. You can then offer the other breast. When you need to remove him from your breast, break the suction with your finger. Don't worry if he refuses the second breast, but start with it at the next feeding. It's important for all areas of your breasts to drain evenly, to prevent blockages and continue stimulating milk production.

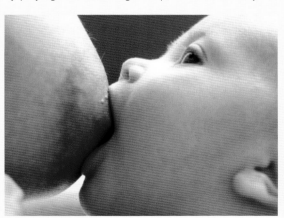

Breastfeeding twins

Breast milk may be even more important for twin babies than it is for singletons. For twins born prematurely, breast milk will provide the nutrients they would have received if they'd gone to term in the womb, including nutrients necessary for brain growth and protecting against infection.

The mechanics of milk supply and latching on (see pages 74–75) are the same for twins as for other babies. With twins, however, it's easier to maintain a good milk supply: If one twin becomes ill or is a poor feeder, the other can keep the supply going.

Feeding together or separately

Breastfeeding both babies simultaneously will be quicker and easier than bottle-feeding, and you'll have two calmed and satisfied babies. But it can take time and some experimenting to figure out the best ways to manage it. You'll probably be most successful if your babies are slower feeders.

Feeding your twins separately will give you a chance to get to know each baby as an individual. It will be easier to manage if your babies have very different feeding patterns—for example, if one wants to feed more frequently or more vigorously than the other. Sometimes twins have to feed separately—if there is a medical problem, for example—in which case you can express milk while you feed the healthy one. However, breastfeeding separately is definitely more time-consuming, and you'll probably want to feed both babies together at least some of the time. This will also make it easier for you to get necessary and sufficient rest.

It's easiest to establish a routine when twins are similarly sized and have similar feeding patterns. Even if you begin by feeding separately on demand, you can make things easier by feeding the first baby who wakes and settling him back down before his twin wakes up and nurses. Then begin modifying this by waking the second when the first one wakes and feeding both together. It can take weeks to establish a routine, but it can be worth the effort.

Helpful positions

It's important that each baby latches on correctly. Get one baby started before you start trying to feed the other.

One useful way to position young babies is in a "V" position with both babies' feet toward each other (see picture).

Another option is the football hold: Both babies are placed on pillows so their heads are level with your nipples, with their bodies lying on your forearms and their legs tucked under your upper arm and behind you. In the cross-cradle hold, both babies lie parallel across your chest in the same direction. Using pillows to support the babies' bodies, place one baby at your right breast, cupping his head with your right hand, and hold the second one, tucked under your arm, at your left breast, holding his head with your left hand (see page 93 for both positions).

Whichever position you use, make sure you are sitting upright, your back is well supported, and you feel comfortable.

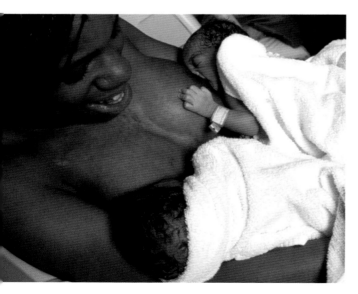

Overcoming difficulties

Your baby was born to breastfeed, but that doesn't mean it always goes well right from the start. Be assured that breast milk will meet all your baby's nutritional needs in the first 6 months. When complementary solid foods are introduced around this time, your baby will still receive half or more of her nutrients from breast milk until she's about 1 (and about one-third of her nutritional needs beyond a year). Breastfeeding keeps you both as healthy as possible. It also will give you a break from menstrual periods for several months. Breastfeeding can reduce the chance of becoming pregnant while your baby still needs a lot of attention. This is not foolproof, however, so use contraception if you want to delay or avoid becoming pregnant. Talk to your doctor about your options while nursing.

Most mothers initiate breastfeeding, but many encounter problems and stop long before they had planned. The most common reasons for stopping are:

- Baby rejected the breast.
- Breastfeeding was painful.
- The milk supply seemed low.

If you find yourself in any of these situations, don't despair. While breastfeeding is a natural act, it's also a learned behavior. Extra support is available (see page 81). The more you understand about why breastfeeding is important and how it works, the easier it may be for you to gain the necessary confidence and overcome any initial difficulties.

If you had a routine delivery and were able to hold your baby right after delivery, you're probably off to a good start. If your baby appears to reject your breast, it's important to find out the reason and address it. You might feel as if your baby is rejecting *you* and consider switching to a bottle. But your baby isn't saying, "I don't want to breastfeed"—she's telling you, "I'm not able to do this yet." Initial problems are usually related to the birth.

ways to boost your baby's interest in breastfeeding

1 **Keep her in close contact.** Hold your baby skin-to-skin or wear lightweight clothing; your familiar scent, your voice, and your heartbeat will soothe her.

2 **Maintain peace and quiet.** Keep the room quiet and dimly lit, and handle your baby gently. Hum or play music that you enjoyed in pregnancy—she'll recognize it!

3 **Try indirect feeding.** Offer small feedings of expressed milk by syringe or cup every couple of hours.

4 **Share a warm bath.** Put your baby facedown on your chest with her tummy on your tummy as you scoop water over her back. Have someone help you—wet babies can be slippery!

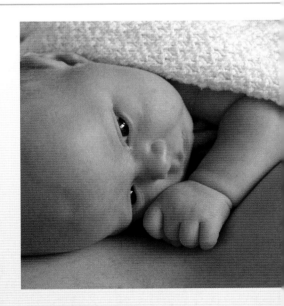

Baby doesn't seem interested

Newborn babies feel safest when they're close to their mothers. Holding your baby close to you right after the birth, skin-to-skin against your chest, helps your baby relax and prepares her to nurse within an hour or so. The majority of newborns soon become quite sleepy and not very hungry at all for another 2 or 3 days after the initial "golden hour" of alertness has passed (see page 73). Don't fret if you weren't able to do this, though; you can make up for lost cuddling time, and initiate breastfeeding, as soon as you're able to.

Proponents of on-demand feeding believe that your baby's initial days of sleepiness and low appetite are natural to give you both a chance to recuperate from delivery. They argue that during this period mothers have little milk (drops of colostrum only); if babies were meant to feed often and receive large amounts of milk, then mothers would have a full milk supply already at the time of delivery. Professionals who advocate on-demand feeding recommend allowing your baby to sleep as long as she would like to during this period and feed only when she seems alert and interested. They do not think it is a coincidence that a mother's supply of milk comes in on about the third day, which is exactly the time newborns start to become more alert and more interested in nursing.

Many breastfeeding advocates reject this approach. Instead, they recommend that feedings in the first days be vigorously encouraged. If you share this philosophy, help your baby become more interested in breastfeeding by holding her close as often as you can and spending time skin-to-skin. Soft slings and wraps (see pages 45–46) simplify baby-carrying, or you could put your baby inside a low-cut stretchy top to hold her against your chest.

When you bathe, skip the soap and use plain water to wash the top half of your body so that your natural odor—which your baby recognizes—won't be changed. Your breasts produce a scent to attract your baby, and she'll start looking for the source of your delicious milk.

If your baby seems fretful, keep her with you and your partner as long as possible until she settles

REASONS FOR PAINFUL FEEDING

- **Swollen breasts** Engorgement or fluid retention can make attachment difficult. Soften the breast with reverse pressure (see box, opposite page) or express a little milk. Nurse often and apply cold compresses between feedings. Too much pumping can exacerbate the problem.
- **Enlarged or inverted nipples** Nipple shape is genetic, but temporary swelling can affect it. Talk to a lactation consultant.
- **Blocked duct** If you feel a lump, massage it and apply a warm compress.
- **Mastitis** Blockages can put you at risk for mastitis, a breast infection. If you get a fever and body aches, call your doctor.
- **Thrush** Sore or burning nipples during or after nursing may indicate a yeast infection in your nipples or breasts. Call your doctor.
- **Raynaud's syndrome** When you nurse, small arteries in the nipples can constrict and blanch the skin, causing severe nipple pain. Talk to your doctor.

LATCH PROBLEMS

If your baby doesn't latch correctly, break the suction with your little finger and try again. If the problem persists, talk to a lactation consultant. Common problems include:

- **Baby not opening wide** Your baby may not open his mouth enough to fully attach.
- **Your baby's position** Make sure your baby is close enough to your breast, or his feeding reflexes might be compromised. He may squeeze or pull on your nipple, causing it to rub against the hard part of his mouth.
- **Tongue-tie** If there's a restriction under your baby's tongue, he may not be able to extend it far enough to attach well. A minor procedure can snip the tie.

down. Your family and friends will understand that it may be better for your baby to wait a bit before they give her a cuddle.

If your baby wants to feed but has a hard time latching on—perhaps because your breast is swollen with milk (see box, opposite page)—she may get frustrated and not want to try next time. Stay calm. Try expressing some milk to relieve engorgement and continue your efforts to nurse. Express milk frequently to help get your supply going until she's able to better attach herself. Talk to a lactation consultant for tips.

If she can't breastfeed, be very patient and gentle—and avoid pushing her head. If you give her expressed milk in a bottle, hold her close to your breast (with some skin contact, if possible) while you feed her.

Painful breastfeeding

Mothers and babies should enjoy breastfeeding for many months. It should *never* hurt: Any pain is a warning sign that something's not quite right. If it isn't comfortable for you, it won't be right for your baby, so it's worth getting help quickly. With good support, the pain will disappear, and you will soon be able to enjoy breastfeeding.

5 ways to heal or prevent soreness

1 **Make sure your breast is soft enough for your baby to grasp.** If your breast is very firm, press your fingers against your breast, about 2 inches behind your nipple, and push into your chest wall, working all around the darker areola until your breast gets softer. This is called "reverse pressure softening." Expressing a little milk out first with your fingers may also help.

2 **Hold your baby really close.** Lean back comfortably and let him lie facedown on you; his feeding reflexes may improve so he can open his mouth wider. If you need to hold him, support his shoulders and bottom but don't hold his head; his chin should press into your breast so his nose is free. One layer of clothes, or none at all, is all he needs—your body will warm him.

3 **Encourage frequent, short feedings.** Hold your baby or carry him in a sling. Offer your breast as soon as he looks interested rather than waiting for him to cry—he won't attach as well when he's upset.

4 **If your nipple starts to hurt a lot during a feeding,** carefully break the suction and try latching on again, or offer the other side. If you can't get him on comfortably, get help as soon

as you can. If your nipples are injured, pure lanolin may help them heal—other creams could irritate and change the taste of your skin.

5 **Keep your breasts well drained.** Offer alternate breasts at each feeding. Check your breasts for any lumps after a feeding and gently massage them to prevent blockages. If you need to express milk, make sure your nipple fits the pump flange well—some mothers need a larger flange—and soften your breast first, if necessary.

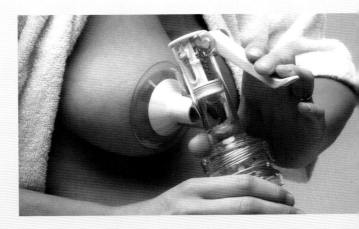

BREAST PUMPING TIPS

If you're breastfeeding when you go back to work, or you want to share feeding duties with your partner, you will need to use a breast pump to express milk. Here are some tips for pumping successfully:

◆ Buy the best pump you can afford, and a pumping bustier or hands-free model.

◆ Keep a pump at home and another at work. Also double up on the pump parts that need to be washed.

◆ In case of leaks, keep an extra bra, blouse, and breast pads in your office and your car.

◆ Arrange for a private space with electrical outlets where you can pump at work. If you're breastfeeding a child under the age of 1 and work for a company with more than 50 employees, U.S. law requires your employer to provide a private lactation room, and it can't be the ladies' room.

◆ Protect time for pumping by blocking it off on your schedule.

◆ Pump as soon as you get to work. In the morning you'll have more milk and you'll be less likely to put it off once you're involved in a project.

◆ No matter how busy your day gets, don't let yourself become engorged. This puts you at high risk for mastitis.

◆ Keep photos of your baby in your pumping bag to help stimulate milk production, or watch a video of your baby on your phone.

◆ If you express more milk than your baby immediately needs, you can freeze it: Date and double-bag the milk before freezing.

◆ Don't worry if you supplement with formula. Any breast milk is good. Your body will also adjust to a less-frequent feeding schedule, such as mornings and evenings only.

Well-meaning people may tell you that breastfeeding always hurts at first and that your nipples need to toughen up. While initial nipple pain may be a common experience, there is no evidence for this advice. Your nipples are meant to be sensitive so that your brain can release the hormones triggering your let-down reflex, and they shouldn't get damaged in the process.

You need to be comfortable, and your breasts should be soft enough for your baby to attach well and get the milk to flow easily. If they are hard and swollen, you can manually express a little milk so your baby can latch on more easily. When your baby is hungry and lying close to you, she should be able to move around and find your breast. She might need a little help getting there, but be gentle and don't use force.

If your nipples are sore during feeding, your baby most likely isn't latched on well, but there may be other causes for the problem (see page 78). Check your nipples after your baby has finished feeding—they should be the same shape as before. If they're squashed, pulled out, grazed, or blistered, your baby needs to latch on more fully, or your nipples will soon crack and bleed.

Another frequent cause of nipple pain is improper positioning. A common mistake is made in holding your baby in your crossed arms, beginning nursing with his head looking up at your nipple. Sucking at the breast in this position places extra pressure on the nipple, resulting in pain. To avoid this, place your baby so that his face is turned fully into your breast, with his chest parallel to your chest (see picture on page 75).

If you are struggling with breastfeeding because of pain, it's important to get help quickly; see page 81 for more information.

Support with feeding

You can easily find information on feeding your baby from books, websites, professionals, friends, relatives, and even strangers on the street—but how can you sort out the good advice from the bad?

Babies are the same the world over, and have the same needs for safety and good food, but their parents may have very different views on what babies need. Upbringing, personal experiences, and cultural beliefs can influence opinions and advice. The most helpful advice is based on facts and research on babies' biological and emotional needs—not on customs and beliefs. Even so, there are various philosophies, and experienced experts may have differing advice for you.

Considering advice

When evaluating advice, consider who it's coming from and what it's based on. Grandmothers, for example, are wonderfully experienced at caring for babies, but their suggestions might be out of date and no longer recommended.

If you're getting advice from professionals, take the time to understand their qualifications. Midwives and baby nurses have a basic grounding in infant feeding, but their advice may also be outdated. Primary-care physicians don't always receive good training on infant feeding— sometimes their only training is by a formula-company representative. But most pediatricians are quite knowledgeable on the ins and outs of breastfeeding and can be a helpful resource. All health professionals need regular training to stay up to date on the latest research. To ensure you get trustworthy information, look into the qualifications of the person providing it.

There's a wealth of resources to help parents make informed choices about breastfeeding. Several organizations provide online information, books, and other resources, and run support networks. Their publications on child care and feeding issues are based on the latest evidence.

Lactation specialists

International board-certified lactation consultants (IBCLCs) are professionally accredited breastfeeding specialists. Many have midwifery, nursing, or other healthcare qualifications. Some specialize as infant-feeding advisors in hospital maternity units; others are breastfeeding counselors with voluntary organizations or are in private practice. Make sure you're comfortable with a lactation consultant. Don't be afraid to switch right away if you're not. Time is of the essence in solving breastfeeding problems.

Accredited volunteer breastfeeding counselors (BFCs) have personal breastfeeding experience and are trained to listen to and support women as they learn to breastfeed. They can offer advice and help with establishing feeding routines and overcoming any difficulties.

La Leche League is an international network that supports breastfeeding women through mother-to-mother support, encouragement, information, and education.

Check your local community listings for support services in your area. Your hospital may be able to help you find the help you need. La Leche chapters, support chapters, and local volunteers can offer help in home visits, over the telephone, or in support groups.

Most important, see what works for your baby and your family. If the first person's advice doesn't solve a problem or you're uncomfortable for any reason, consult other professionals without delay. Your pediatrician often will be able to advise you, but if further help is needed, she can refer you to local resources for help solving feeding problems.

Bottle-feeding

Whether you're feeding your baby formula or breast milk in a bottle, wash bottles and equipment carefully. Soap and water, or cleaning in a dishwasher, have been shown to be just as safe as sterilization. Wash your hands thoroughly before feedings, too. If you're using formula, carefully follow the manufacturer's instructions to ensure your baby is well nourished.

Your baby should drink breast milk or formula until he is at least 1 year old. Don't give your baby ordinary cow's milk until he is about a year old: It contains high levels of protein and minerals, which can strain a young baby's immature kidneys and may be low in some nutrients. For example, cow's milk doesn't provide enough iron for young babies. Goat's milk and condensed milk are also unsuitable for young babies.

Types of bottles

When selecting bottles, you might have to try different designs and brands to find one with a shape and flow rate that your infant will accept. Because newborns consume only a few ounces at a time, start with small bottles (4 to 5 ounces) and low-flow nipples.

To avoid the chemical bisphenol A, opt for BPA-free plastic bottles or bottle systems with soft, disposable plastic liners.

For cleaning bottles, get a bottle brush, a drying rack, and a dishwasher basket for nipples and rings. If you'll be away from home, you'll also need a cold pack and insulated bag for transporting expressed milk or formula.

No studies have shown that one brand or design of bottle or nipple is better than any other one (despite advertising claims).

Breast milk versus formula

All baby formulas are carefully manufactured under strict government guidelines to ensure that they replicate human milk as closely as possible and provide the proper amounts of fat, protein, carbohydrates, calories, minerals, and vitamins that your baby needs.

Do not feel guilty if, for whatever reason, your child is formula fed. While breast milk is always going to be a little better, formulas are excellent at meeting your baby's nutritional needs.

Much has been said about the ability of breast milk to help prevent infections in newborns and young infants. Human milk contains maternal antibodies, immune system cells (lymphocytes), and a number of molecules that have antibacterial effects. Formula has none of these. But how important are these anti-infective ingredients of breast milk? In developing countries, where poverty, poor hygiene, and inadequate sanitation are common, breastfeeding is very important in preventing life-threatening infections. However, in the clean, modern environment in which we live, the risk of getting a serious infection is lower.

Studies show that in the first year of life, a breast-fed infant in the United States gets on average one

FORMULA

- Feed your baby freshly made formula whenever possible. Once a can of ready-to-feed formula is opened, or formula is mixed from powder or concentrate, it can safely remain in the refrigerator up to 48 hours. If formula not finished at a feeding is quickly placed back in the refrigerator at the feeding's end, it can be given at the next feeding with a clean nipple.

- You can give your baby a bottle cold, at room temperature, or warm—but not hot. Drop a little milk on the inside of your wrist; it should feel warm, not hot. If it is too hot, hold the bottle, with the cap covering the nipple, under cold running water. Don't warm a bottle in the microwave, because it can create hot spots that can possibly cause a burn in your baby's mouth.

- Measure correctly. Too much powder can cause constipation and dehydration; too little powder may not provide sufficient nourishment.

CHECKING A NIPPLE

Fill a bottle with formula or milk, attach the nipple, and hold the bottle upside down.
Formula should drip out at a steady flow of 1 drop per second. A small hole can be enlarged with a sterile needle.

less head cold or one less diarrhea illness than a formula-fed child. Breast-fed babies also get roughly half the ear infections. These numbers are averages, so some children get more and some fewer of these illnesses. Breastfeeding is still best, but when it comes to preventing infections, its advantage over formula in our society is relatively small.

Types of formula

If you're unsure which formula is best for your baby, your pediatrician can provide guidance. You can buy formula in powder, liquid concentrate, and ready-made forms at most supermarkets and drugstores. Powdered formulas are usually the least expensive. Ready-made formula is the most expensive, but the convenience may be worth it for the first few weeks as you get used to feeding. If your local tap water contains fluoride, you are helping your baby develop strong teeth that are less prone to cavities. (See pages 198–199 for more about fluoride.)

There are three basic types: modified cow's milk, soy, and hypoallergenic formulas.

Modified cow's milk

Most bottle-fed babies drink formula that is made starting with cow's milk, which is then modified to be closer to breast milk. If your baby was fed this type of formula in the hospital without any problems, there's no reason to change when you get home. Barring a medical problem, it is very unusual for a formula-fed baby not to gain weight properly, if he is allowed to take as much (or as little) as he wishes at feeding time. If your child is colicky or you think he may be having a reaction to the formula (see pages 171–172 and 177–182), ask your pediatrician's advice before you switch—the problem may not lie with the formula, but may have to do with feeding techniques, intolerance to a particular ingredient, or possibly a medical condition that needs treatment.

There are specialized formulas for bottle-fed babies who are allergic to or intolerant of cow's milk, or who have other feeding or medical problems.

How to prepare formula

Make sure your work surface is very clean and wash your hands thoroughly. Have clean bottles and supplies nearby.

If you're using powdered formula, use the scoop provided with the container to measure the amount of formula you need. Make sure each scoop is leveled off before pouring the powder into the bottle. Following the instructions on the formula container, measure and add the right amount of clean water, either bottled or from the tap. (If you use well water or aren't sure your tap water is safe, you can bring the water to a boil and then cool it before adding it to the formula.) Put the nipple and cap on the bottle and stir or very gently shake to mix the formula. Avoid forming bubbles.

With liquid concentrate, measure the amount of formula you need and pour it into the bottle; then add water and mix as described above.

Formula can be offered warm, cold, or at room temperature. To warm formula, hold the bottle under hot water running from the tap or set it for a few minutes in a pan of hot water. Squeeze a drop of formula on the inside of your wrist to make sure it isn't too hot. Don't use the microwave, as it can heat formula unevenly and result in very hot spots.

OUT AND ABOUT

If you need to prepare a bottle away from home, bring a bottle of water and measured formula in a clean container. (The one pictured here holds enough for three feedings.) You also could buy ready-made formula cartons.

Soy formula

Soy-based formulas contain no cow's milk proteins (the main source of formula intolerance and allergy) and no lactose (milk sugar). Many babies who cannot tolerate cow's milk formula will do well when switched to a soy formula. But beware that about 25 percent of infants who are allergic to cow's milk proteins are also allergic to soy products.

Hypoallergenic formula

Hypoallergenic formulas begin with cow's milk, the same first step as in cow's milk–based formulas. However, to make the formula hypoallergenic, the cow's milk proteins in the formulas are extensively hydrolyzed—broken down into very small pieces no longer recognized as cow's milk protein by the body. Hypoallergenic formulas tend to be harder to find, more expensive, and some have an unpleasant smell.

But if your baby can't do well on a cow's milk– or soy-based formula, they are worth it.

Feeding your baby

For the first few weeks, you might want to have some prepared, ready-to-use formula so you can feed your baby as soon as he's hungry. Waiting to eat can upset a baby so much that he'll refuse to feed. Avoid letting too many people give him a bottle at first; you or your partner should handle most of the feeding initially. Feeding time should soon become a relaxing, enjoyable occasion. You can encourage this by holding your baby close to you and maintaining eye contact with him. Soon, you'll see him grow excited when he knows his bottle is on its way.

If you have twins, it's easiest to feed both babies at the same time; see page 76 for tips on establishing a good schedule.

BOTTLE-FEEDING CAUTIONS

- ◆ Never leave your baby alone to drink from a propped-up bottle, even when he's older—there's a risk that he could choke.
- ◆ You should inspect nipples each time you wash them to ensure that they aren't worn or damaged (see page 83).
- ◆ Do not let your baby sleep with a milk-filled bottle in her mouth. If done repeatedly, the hours during which milk bathes the teeth can promote tooth decay, resulting in multiple cavities.

Bottle-feeding routine

Make yourself and your baby comfortable. Hold him securely in your lap with his head in the crook of your elbow and his back supported along your forearm. To help your baby relax, cuddle him close, talk, or sing. Watch him all the time and respond to his demands. Some babies like to pause for air or to burp; others prefer to keep feeding steadily until all the formula is gone.

If you warmed the bottle, check the temperature before giving it to your baby: Shake a few drops onto the inside of your wrist. If it feels too hot, you can cool it by holding the capped bottle under cold running water.

Offering the bottle

Show your baby the bottle

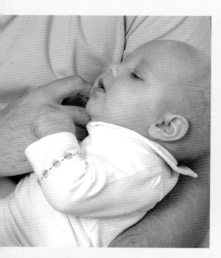

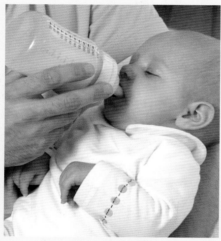

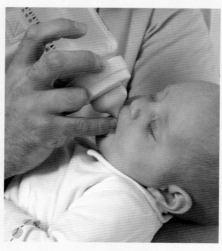

and then stroke his cheek to prompt his rooting reflex. He will automatically turn to you with his mouth open, ready to suck.

Hold the bottle at an angle of about 45 degrees so that the nipple tip is full of milk and there are no air bubbles. Offer the nipple to your baby and allow him to take it deep into his mouth and begin sucking. Keep the bottle steady so that he can latch on properly. Adjust the angle so that the tip is always full of milk.

Drinking his fill

Remove the bottle when your baby has finished feeding or you need to burp him: Slip your little finger into the corner of his mouth to break the suction. It is best to end the feeding with some formula still left in the bottle. If the bottle is empty, put a little more milk in it— he may still be hungry. Only when he stops feeding with formula left over will you know that he could have taken more but chose not to.

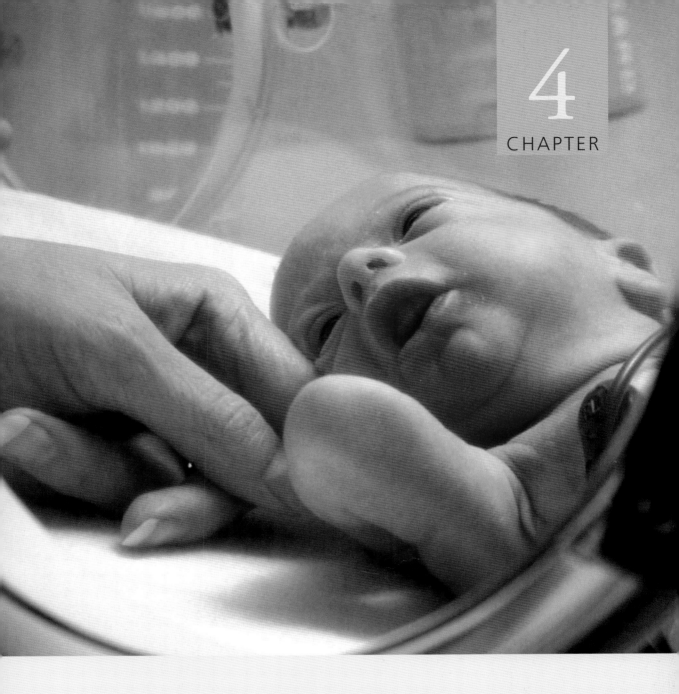

CARING FOR YOUR PREMATURE INFANT

In the hospital

If your baby was born well before her due date, you probably didn't have the pregnancy and delivery you expected. Instead of savoring a happy postpartum period at home with your baby, you may be preoccupied with worries about her health. If she was whisked away to the neonatal intensive care unit (NICU) or a special babycare unit after delivery, you may not have even had a chance to hold her. Watching specialists and nurses caring for her might leave you feeling helpless. Going home without your baby is especially difficult. Even if she has no serious medical issues and will be just fine after a short stay in the NICU, it's troubling to see her in the hospital— she looks so small and fragile.

You may feel isolated and alone, but you have company: Premature birth occurs in about 11 to 13 percent of pregnancies in the United States.

Spending time with your newborn will be a priority, but it's important to remember that you need to pay attention to your own well-being. You need to rest and recuperate after giving birth. Even if you had a relatively easy vaginal delivery, it may be weeks before you feel like your old self. And if you had a cesarean delivery, you'll need even more time to heal fully. You may be tempted to neglect your own needs so you can devote your full attention to your newborn, but it will be better for everyone if you take care of yourself, too.

Twins and more

Characteristically, pregnancies with twins (or more) result in earlier deliveries than singleton pregnancies. Although there can be other reasons for an early delivery, it seems as if the enlarging uterus runs out of room for the multiple growing babies and has no choice but to deliver them. The chance of preterm delivery increases with the number of fetuses a woman is carrying, and the typical length of gestation decreases.

The greatest challenge with twins and multiples is a practical one: There are more of them! In the NICU, this may lead to logistical difficulties, such as feeding multiple babies at once or producing enough breast milk. And of course, now you have two (or more) children to worry about.

If one of your twins is ready to come home before the other, you'll face unique issues. If your second child is expected to be discharged within a few days, the hospital might allow her sibling to stay in the hospital until both can come home. But you might find

---

MORE **ABOUT** | multiple births

Although twins make up most multiple births, triplets, quadruplets, quintuplets, and even sextuplets are becoming more common due to in vitro fertilization. Multiple siblings may result when the ovary releases multiple eggs, or when several embryos are transferred during fertility treatment. In these cases, each egg is fertilized separately, and nonidentical siblings, who can be of either sex, are conceived. Alternatively, a single fertilized egg can split and produce two, three, or even more identical embryos, always of the same gender.

Multiple births are always high risk: The uterus is capable of carrying, feeding, and providing oxygen for only a certain number of fetuses. With twins or more multiples, there's a greater likelihood the babies will be born prematurely and could develop health problems associated with being born early.

yourself dividing your time and energy between home and the hospital. Visiting one baby in the NICU requires that another adult be home watching her sibling. The baby at home will require much of your attention and care, and you may feel badly that your hospitalized baby isn't getting the same attention from you. If your hospitalized baby remains ill, you might worry that you're thinking of her too much. There are no easy answers, but you can reassure yourself that your hospitalized baby is in good hands, and you can lean on family and friends for emotional and practical support. In the best cases, it's a short-term problem, and you'll soon have both babies home with you.

Visiting your baby in the NICU

You'll probably want to spend as much time as possible with your preemie newborn. Being with her in the NICU will allow you to get to know each other. Your baby will certainly enjoy and be comforted by your voice and your touch, and you will be able to learn how to care for her under the helpful tutelage of the nurses.

It's important to strike a balance between visiting your baby and taking care of yourself, resting enough to restore your health after delivery. When you're released from the hospital, ask your doctor how often and for how long you should visit your baby. Depending on your condition, one visit a day at first

is likely plenty. Your visit might last a few hours if you can sit by her incubator, or less if you need to stand.

As you regain strength, you might want to try visiting in the morning to feed your baby, and then stay long enough to provide a second feeding before going home to rest in the afternoon. Then you could return for a brief evening visit. Full-term babies generally sleep 16 to 20 hours a day, and preemies usually sleep even more—your baby will probably be asleep for much of the time during your visits.

Your partner will also want to spend time with your newborn but will be under other strains. In addition to shuttling back and forth between home and the hospital, your partner will be trying to help you rest and recover, while managing household chores. Working partners may also need to return to work, though if your baby is seriously ill, it's worth looking into options for family leave during this trying time. In some families, parents alternate trips to the NICU, with one parent arriving in the evening after work. Partners can also wear themselves out by trying to do too much, so be careful. Your baby will need two healthy, well-rested parents when she comes home, because there will be much to do!

It's a great disappointment to have to leave your baby in the hospital when you go home, but there is a small silver lining to this dark cloud. Unlike mothers of full-term newborns, who have only a day or two

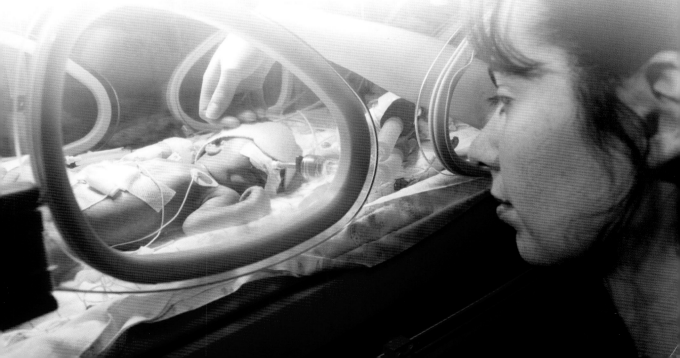

What is prematurity?

In humans, the time from fertilization of a mother's egg to delivery is normally 38 weeks. But we say pregnancy lasts 40 weeks, since historically it is timed from the beginning of a woman's last menstrual period (LMP), which generally occurs two weeks before ovulation and fertilization.

This method of counting is illogical, because it says your pregnancy begins before you're technically pregnant, but it's used by medical specialists around the world. So when doctors speak of the 36th week of pregnancy or say the fetus has a gestational age of 36 weeks, they are counting from the LMP.

Pregnancies don't all last exactly 40 weeks—there's a fairly wide range of what's considered a normal pregnancy. A newborn is said to be full term if she is born at 37 weeks of gestation or later, up to 42 weeks. Preterm labor occurs when the pregnancy ends before the 37th week of gestation.

Low birth weight and prematurity are not the same. While the two often go hand in hand, sometimes full-term babies weigh far less than expected. (They're described as being small for their gestational age.)

Prematurity is really meant to describe the inability of a baby's body to function the same way a full-term baby's body does. Using gestational age or birth weight to indicate the immaturity of a baby's bodily functions usually works, but not perfectly. Two children may be born at 35 weeks' gestation, but one's lungs or other body systems may perform much better than the other's. In other words, even though both were "in the oven" for the same length of time, one came out more fully baked than the other.

The age of a prematurely born infant may be described in one of two ways. The baby's chronological age is described in weeks or months since birth. The baby's corrected age, however, is her chronological age minus the number of weeks she was born prematurely. If your 9-week-old infant, for example, was born 8 weeks prematurely, at 32 weeks of gestation, her corrected age is 1 week. But this is only an approximation. It assumes that your infant now functions like a 1-week-old, full-term newborn.

Why do doctors use corrected ages? By using the corrected age, they can reasonably (but not exactly) compare infants born at different degrees of prematurity to each other and to corresponding full-term infants.

GLOSSARY FOR TALKING ABOUT PREMATURE BABIES

Full-term or term pregnancy	Pregnancy lasting 37–42 weeks
Premature infant	An infant, usually preterm, whose body does not function the same way a full-term baby's body does
Gestation or gestational age	Number of weeks or months of pregnancy counted from the LMP
Preterm infant	An infant born before 37 weeks of gestation
Late preterm infant	An infant born between 34 and 37 weeks of gestation
Low birth weight	Birth weight is less than 5 pounds, 8 ounces
Chronological age	Age since the time of birth
Corrected age	Chronological age minus the number of weeks a child was born prematurely. For instance: An 8-week-old baby who was born 5 weeks prematurely has a chronological age of 8 weeks and a corrected age of 3 weeks. It's the number of weeks since the LMP minus 40 weeks (i.e., if the baby had been full term).

in the hospital to get used to their infants and learn how to care for them, you will have much more time to become an expert in your baby's care. As you spend time in the NICU, the nurses will show you how to perform routine, daily tasks. You'll probably feel competent and confident in your skills by the time you bring your baby home. You'll know how to clean and change her, how to measure and administer her vitamins, how to pick her up and hold her, and perhaps even what her cries mean.

Very premature infants are frequently quite ill at first—their lungs, intestines, circulatory systems, and other bodily functions are immature. It's a good idea to be proactive while your infant is in the NICU and learn as much as you can about her medical conditions and how to manage them. Practicing care routines under the eye of a good neonatal nurse will prepare you for what you will need to do once your baby is home.

Life in an incubator

When babies go to the NICU, they are often treated first on open warming beds beneath radiant heaters. Once they're medically stable, most preterm and premature infants stay in an incubator.

An incubator consists of a flat infant mattress enclosed in a clear box with plastic-like walls and top, measuring roughly 2½ feet long, 1½ feet high, and 1½ feet wide. The incubator rests on a cabinet so that your newborn is waist-high off the ground. Most models allow access into the "living quarters" via a rectangular door that makes up the lower half of one of the long sidewalls. On one wall are two round, porthole-like openings that let your hands and forearms fit through.

An incubator protects your newborn and keeps her warm, while making it easy to keep a close eye on her. Feeding and common procedures, such as bathing, taking blood, and starting intravenous therapy, can be managed without removing her from her heated home. Through the porthole openings, you can touch and comfort her until she is well enough to be taken out and held. Incubators are not soundproof, so you can talk or sing to her from outside her safe haven.

Keeping warm

Incubators are heated because premature infants are not yet capable of maintaining their own body temperature. When your premature or preterm baby is allowed outside the incubator, she will be well bundled and will wear a hat.

Once a preemie in an incubator is the equivalent of 35 to 36 weeks' gestation, the temperature inside her incubator may be gradually lowered to see if she can maintain a normal body temperature while dressed in clothes. If she's able to do so, she can move to an open crib.

Physical contact

Even if you can't hold your premature or preterm baby in your arms yet, you can touch her and talk to her to show your love. This not only helps you feel better, but it benefits your baby: Studies have shown that, compared to other premature babies, those who are regularly touched and talked to grow faster and get home sooner.

Feeding

Very small premature babies usually aren't able to suck strongly, so they're initially fed with a small feeding tube inserted through the nose (a nasogastric, or NG, tube) or mouth (an orogastric, or OG, tube) to reach the stomach. Expressed breast milk or formula made for premature babies is measured in a syringe and dripped or pumped into your baby's stomach via the tube.

When your baby is older, she can receive bottle feedings while remaining in her incubator. To do this, sit next to the incubator with each hand and forearm through a porthole. Using both hands, sit her up almost upright, supporting the back of her neck and head with one hand. Hold the bottle in your other hand and place it in her mouth. Let her rest every minute or so until she drinks the prescribed volume.

The NICU nurses can show you some of the tricks of the trade for helping slow or reluctant feeders. For example, gently stroking your baby's cheek near the mouth often induces a sucking reflex and can get her to start feeding.

Breastfeeding in the NICU

Breastfeeding your preterm infant is a lot of work for you but valuable for your baby. Of the many advantages of breastfeeding (see Chapter 3), two are especially important for premature infants. First, babies who drink breast milk have fewer complications related to prematurity, most notably a lower incidence of a serious intestinal disease called necrotizing enterocolitis, or NEC. In addition, the antibodies and immune system cells in breast milk help prevent infections.

Most premature babies are not ready for breastfeeding right after birth. They are too sick to be fed or are not yet able to produce a strong enough suck (or both). If you want to breastfeed, you'll probably need to start by expressing milk for your baby using a pump.

For breastfeeding to be successful, you'll need to start pumping milk soon after your delivery and continue pumping often during the day, aiming to pump as often as your baby would feed. It requires a substantial time commitment: Even with the strongest pumps, a session often lasts 15 to 20 minutes. If you don't pump regularly, your milk supply will decrease. Rent a hospital-grade pump or invest in a good pump—either will be gentle but strong, which will save you time.

Stress and exhaustion can impair your ability to produce a good supply of milk. This is particularly troublesome for mothers of premature or preterm babies, who are often stressed and anxious. Mothers may spend all the time they can at their infants'

bedsides, neglecting their own need for rest and recuperation. It's important to take care of yourself. Your infant will benefit from having a calmer, rested mother in many ways, not the least of which is her mom's greater milk production.

Despite these obstacles, there's a very good chance that you'll succeed at breastfeeding. It's helpful to have a partner who shares your desire to provide breast milk to your baby, and neonatal nurses typically will encourage and support your efforts. The work required—the time spent pumping and the extra effort to breastfeed—is another way you can express your love for your baby. And you'll be supporting the medical staff in helping your baby reach maturity and good health.

Providing milk

Premature babies sometimes receive tiny feedings through an NG tube within a few days of birth. These are called trophic feeds, because they really aren't enough to be a significant source of nutrition. Instead, these small amounts of milk are given to stimulate the intestinal tract, in the hope that in the future feedings will go more smoothly. If your newborn's doctor recommends trophic feedings, you can supply expressed breast milk. Later, when more nutritious feedings are started, your milk (often enhanced by the addition of a breast-milk fortifier) can be given to your baby via a feeding tube. Even though her sucking efforts are weak at this stage and she won't get much milk, some doctors and nurses suggest teaching your infant to associate breastfeeding with the positive feeling of satiety. To do this, place her on your breast and encourage her to suck while the milk is delivered via the feeding tube. Subsequently, when she does develop a more mature suck and swallow mechanism, feedings can be at the breast.

MORE **ABOUT** | kangaroo care

Skin-to-skin contact with your premature baby when she is in only a diaper, with a soft cloth or blanket covering her skin, is helpful for parents and baby. With such kangaroo care, both parents can bond with their baby (see picture, page 94). Breastfeeding done this way is often more successful and has been shown to result in greater weight gain and earlier hospital discharge than conventional breastfeeding.

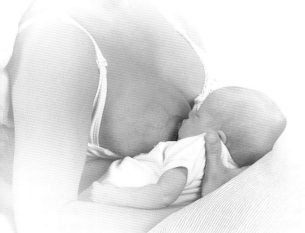

Producing and storing breast milk

If you choose to feed your baby breast milk, begin expressing milk within a day of your delivery to stimulate milk production. You won't be able to express much at first, because your milk supply isn't fully in for a few days. But express every 3 to 4 hours, if possible, because that will encourage a better supply of milk. You can pump milk in the hospital or at home; most NICUs have a quiet room reserved for mothers to express milk. Express your milk in sterile containers provided by the hospital. Label each bottle with your infant's name and the date the milk was collected. You may produce much more than your infant needs at first. Talk with the NICU staff about how much to bring to the hospital; the rest can be stored in your freezer at home for months.

Feeding at the breast

Getting milk from your breast is hard work for your preemie: It requires strong, sustained sucking, which takes up a lot of her energy. Let the staff guide you in how often to breastfeed your baby.

Communication with the NICU staff is important when breastfeeding. For example, if you're on the way to the hospital to breastfeed your baby, it's a good idea to call ahead and let the nurses know so they won't give your baby a bottle of expressed milk before you arrive. They'll also let you know if your supply of stored milk is running low.

Two breastfeeding positions that seem to work well are the "football hold" (see above) and the "cross-cradle hold" (see right). Both holds allow you to easily control your baby's head with one hand and hold your breast in the other. Many lactation specialists encourage "kangaroo care" or skin-to-skin contact (see box, opposite page). You may also be advised to use a nipple shield, which helps your baby get milk from the breast without having to generate as much negative pressure in sucking.

Monitoring success

The best indicator of the success of breastfeeding is whether your newborn's weight continues to increase. But when you first start breastfeeding, you can estimate how much milk she's taking in by comparing her weight before and after a feeding. Because 1 ml of milk weighs about 1 gram, a 25-gram weight increase after feeding suggests she took in about 25 ml of milk. Infant scales aren't always 100 percent accurate (see page 99), making this an imprecise approach. To be as accurate as possible, do not move the scale between taking the two measurements, and make sure your baby is weighed both times with the same clothing, the same diaper, and the same amount of added materials, such as monitor leads.

At home

Bringing your premature or preterm infant home will be exciting and perhaps a bit scary—you may feel overwhelmed at first by the responsibilities that go along with caring for her. However, the skills you learned from the nurses in the NICU will serve you well. Almost all the information covered in Chapters 1 and 2 applies to premature and preterm infants as well as to full-term babies, but a premature baby needs some extra attention.

In addition to the routine preparations for the arrival of a full-term baby, you'll need to consider some issues that are specific to preemies.

Practically speaking, you will need to have on hand smaller diapers, undershirts, and outfits (easily found on the Internet if not in baby shops), but you also may need to adjust your "nursing skills" when dispensing medications and vitamins (see also pages 339–340) and be able to follow very specific instructions about feeding schedules or caring for ongoing medical conditions. While discharge instructions will be relatively short for a late preterm infant whose only issue is slow feeding, there may be a great deal for you to do at home if your baby was much more premature or experienced complications.

Extra nursing care

Very premature infants often have continuing medical issues (see Chapter 13), so you'll need the NICU staff to teach you how to provide the special care your baby will need. In addition to vitamins and perhaps other medications, your baby may need oxygen or other special equipment or monitors. If your baby had major respiratory problems or apnea (occasional long pauses between breaths), you may be taught special techniques for cardiopulmonary resuscitation, or CPR, in the unlikely case that you will need to use them (see also pages 42–43).

Maintaining body temperature

Nearly all premature infants are unable to regulate their body temperature adequately at first. Full-term newborns can usually manage fine after a few hours, provided they're dressed appropriately, but preemies have a much harder time. Because of their limited energy reserves and lack of insulating body fat, their temperature can fall quickly if they aren't in a heated environment or wrapped in enough clothes or blankets.

Your baby won't be discharged from the NICU until he's able to keep himself warm if dressed properly. But generating heat uses up energy: The calories your baby uses to keep himself warm won't be used for growing and gaining weight. So you should minimize the time he's undressed or exposed to cooler temperatures. For a premature baby, always add two more layers of clothing than you need for yourself. Babies commonly wear hats in the NICU to prevent heat loss from their heads, but these aren't needed at home as long as the room temperature is above 68°F.

Germ control

A full-term newborn's immune system is weaker than that of an older child or adult. Premature infants have even less resistance to infection—the earlier they were born, the more immature their immune mechanisms. Babies born before 34 weeks of gestation also lack another component of immunity: maternal antibodies (see box, right). It's especially important for you to follow the precautions recommended in Chapter 2: Limit holding, touching, and close contact with your baby to only a few close relatives or friends, and only after they have washed their hands; don't allow anyone with a contagious illness to visit; and avoid public places where people are in close proximity.

Breastfeeding will help protect your baby from infection, since breast milk contains antibodies and immune cells to defend against many microbes.

Preventing infections

By making an effort to minimize your baby's exposure to germs, you'll hopefully be able to reduce the number of infections. But don't assume that your baby won't get any colds or infections just because you're careful. Infections such as head colds are inevitable. Here are some other ways you can help protect your child.

MORE ABOUT | maternal antibodies

Beginning in the third trimester of pregnancy, antibodies present in the mother's circulation can cross the placenta and enter the fetus's bloodstream. So at birth, a full-term baby is armed with a large stock of antibodies (provided by Mom) against bacteria, viruses, and pathogens he hasn't even encountered yet. Babies who are born prematurely, however, may not have been in the womb long enough to gather these antibodies.

Maternal antibodies have a limited life span: Over time, they're removed from a baby's circulation and cleaved to small molecules for later use by the body. By the time a baby is 6 months old, the level of antibodies has fallen low enough that the baby is more vulnerable than he was at birth. However, some of these antibodies can be detected as long as a year after birth.

Maternal antibodies also may play a role in some cases of newborn jaundice, the yellow skin coloring that occurs in some newborns (see page 363).

The yellow coloring is due to high levels of bilirubin, a molecular breakdown product of the hemoglobin in our red blood cells. Maternal antibodies may affect this process if the mother and baby have different blood types. Like everyone else, pregnant women have antibodies circulating in their blood that protect against foreign blood cells. If any maternal antibodies that cross the placenta are directed against the baby's red blood cells, an unusually high number of the baby's red blood cells are destroyed, creating more bilirubin and causing jaundice.

Immunizations

Vaccines are safe and valuable tools to prevent serious infectious diseases in full-term infants (see also page 336), and they also are effective in premature infants. The schedule for giving immunizations to preemies is the same as for full-term infants and is based on chronological age, not age-corrected for prematurity. If your baby remains in the NICU for 2 months or more, he'll receive his first immunizations there.

It's a good idea for parents, other adults in your household, siblings, and frequent visitors (including babysitters or nannies) to get immunized against pertussis (whooping cough) and influenza (the "flu").

Synagis

Respiratory infections usually consist of only a stuffy nose and a cough. However, in premature infants—especially those who required treatment for premature lungs and are still healing—head colds are more likely to progress to wheezing, bronchiolitis (see page 346), or pneumonia (see *Lung infections,* page 347). Many viruses can cause respiratory illness, but two of them—influenza and respiratory syncytial virus (RSV)—are notable for commonly infecting newborns and sometimes causing severe infections. Infants can receive the flu vaccine once they're at least 6 months old. All adults in your home, siblings, and frequent visitors should be vaccinated against the flu each year for their own protection and to lower the risk that your baby will be exposed to the disease.

There is no vaccine yet for RSV, but you can try to minimize its effect on your baby. The drug Synagis can prevent or reduce many RSV infections in high-risk infants. Synagis consists of antibodies against RSV made in cell cultures and test tubes. During RSV season, usually November through March, qualifying infants can receive monthly injections of the antibodies. Only high-risk children under the age of 2 may get the medicine, which is very expensive.

If you believe Synagis might help your child, discuss it with your pediatrician. Most insurance companies cover Synagis only if your baby meets one of the many very specific criteria listed in the box below, but such decisions can be appealed. A call to your insurance company and a letter from your baby's pediatrician explaining why Synagis should be given can sometimes be convincing.

6 reasons to try Synagis

1   Your baby is younger than 2 years old (chronological age) and required treatment such as oxygen or medications for chronic lung disease within 6 months of the start of RSV season.

2   She was born at or before 28 weeks of gestation and is 12 months (chronological age) or younger at the start of RSV season.

3   She was born between 29 and 32 weeks of gestation and is younger than 6 months (chronological age) at the start of RSV season.

4   She was born between 32 and 35 weeks of gestation and is younger than 3 months old at the start of RSV season or is born during the RSV season with one or both of the following risk factors: attends child care or another child younger than 5 years old lives in the same household.

5   She was born with congenital abnormalities of the airway, or with severe neuromuscular disease.

6   She has significant congenital heart disease and is younger than 2 years old.

Handling your baby

Although preemies are smaller than full-term babies, you can pick them up and hold them the same way (see pages 32–33). With experience, you'll learn how sturdy your child is and how much head support he needs until he's strong enough to keep his head from flopping down, back, or to the side.

Using a sling (see pages 45–46) to carry a preemie is controversial. A premature or low-weight baby is at a higher risk of suffocating in a baby sling. The Consumer Product Safety Commission urges extra caution if using a sling with any baby younger than 4 months old. A sling could restrict a baby's breathing if the fabric presses against his nose and mouth, or if the sling pushes his head to his chest.

However, carrying preemies in a sling offers health benefits. Holding your baby so he can hear your heartbeat and feel you breathing and moving can help him thrive and strengthen his emotional bond with you. In fact, preemies grow faster when frequently carried in a sling, which mimics the womb. A sling can also ease the transition from womb and incubator to the outside world.

If you're considering using a sling for your premature infant, talk to your pediatrician, research current safety guidelines, and vigilantly monitor your baby when he's in a sling. Opt for a ring sling that holds your baby in an upright position snug against your chest. Avoid bag or duffle slings, which hold your baby at hip level and can cause his chin to rest on his chest, a dangerous position.

Car seats

You'll need a car seat for your baby—you won't be able to drive her home from the hospital without one. But most infant car seats are designed for full-term babies and larger infants. When settled into one of these car seats, a premature baby's head may slump forward, which could block the upper airway in her throat and neck, restricting the flow of oxygen into her lungs. This can result in apnea (cessation of breathing for many seconds), bradycardia (slowing of the heartbeat), or desaturation (low oxygen level in the tissues).

Car seat challenge

To be sure your baby can travel home safely without suffering any of these complications, NICU staff may conduct a "car seat challenge" before discharge. Your baby will be attached to monitors tracking her heart rate, respiratory rate, and tissue oxygen level. She'll be placed into the car seat you plan to use regularly and observed for any signs of trouble; the American Academy of Pediatrics recommends preterm babies should be observed for 90 to 120 minutes.

If she shows no indication of apnea, bradycardia, or desaturation, she'll pass the challenge and be cleared to go home in the car seat. If she fails the challenge, the hospital might postpone her discharge or help you find a safer way to bring her home. Blanket rolls and supportive inserts might resolve the issues, or you may be advised to use a horizontal car bed.

Using a car seat

The general car seat guidelines, as described in Chapters 9 and 13, also apply to premature babies; however, there are additional recommendations just for them.

Use only first-stage infant car seats. A few models are designed to accommodate babies as small as 4½ to 5 pounds. For up-to-date advice on choosing the right model, go to the American Academy of Pediatrics' website (www.healthychildren.org) and review the car seat guide in the Safety & Prevention section. Some seats are designed for children who weigh more than 20 pounds; these are not safe for your baby.

The distance between the crotch strap and the back of the seat should be 5½ inches or less, and there should be no more than 10 inches between the lower harness strap and the seat bottom. Always use the car seat in the backseat of the car, with your baby facing the rear. When possible, an adult should sit next to her to make sure that your baby remains seated in the proper position.

To avoid slumping, your infant's back and buttocks should be squarely positioned against the back of the car seat. You can support her with special padded inserts when available, or rolled-

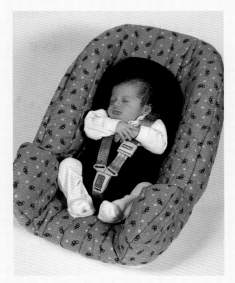

up blankets or towels placed on each side, cushioning her between the sidewalls and her head, shoulders, and legs. If the crotch strap can't be pulled tight enough to hold her securely, place another rolled towel under the buckle. The retainer clip should lie over your baby's chest.

Avoid seats with shields, abdominal pads, or arm rests—your baby could hit her head on these if the car stops suddenly.

The car seat should be reclined slightly backward so the baby's head and trunk are at an angle of 45 degrees above horizontal. Since the seat is facing the rear, the top of the seat tilts downward, toward the front of the car. You can put a rolled-up blanket or foam swim noodle under the seat to position it at the right angle.

Feeding and nutrition

Premature infants usually aren't discharged from the NICU until they can be fed successfully and are gaining weight steadily. But even those who are allowed home may not yet have perfected the skills needed to feed easily. Premature babies often feed slowly and suck less strongly and efficiently than full-term babies. Weak oral muscles, poor coordination of the tongue and pharynx, and the need to breathe frequently can also hinder them. For such small babies, the effort of sucking continuously at the breast or on a bottle can be exhausting. You'll probably be very good at feeding your baby after getting some practice in the NICU, but feedings will continue to be slow, and your baby may have to take several breaks to rest.

Preemies need proportionally more calories, protein, and fat than do typical newborns. They also need large amounts of calcium, phosphorus, and vitamin D to build strong bones, and iron to produce hemoglobin and new red blood cells. But the human body can work in amazing ways: The breast milk of mothers who deliver premature babies contains more of these nutrients than the breast milk of mothers of full-term babies. While this is a big help, a powdered breast milk fortifier is often added to expressed breast milk to ensure that a preemie gets plenty of calories, calcium, phosphorus, vitamins, and everything else she needs.

When premature babies are bottle-fed, at first they're usually given a high-calorie formula, with 24 calories per ounce and extra nutrients. They're later given transitional formula, with 22 calories per ounce and nutrients, and once they reach a target age and/or weight, they're switched to formula for full-term infants, providing 20 calories per ounce.

Some doctors may take a different approach and, for example, send late-preterm infants home with regular formula. But when your baby comes home, he'll most likely be getting premature infant or transitional formula. His doctor probably will recommend additional vitamins and iron drops.

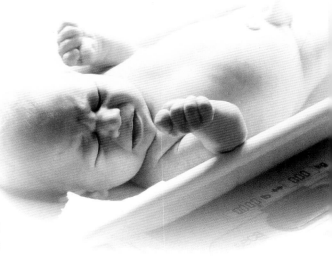

If you're breastfeeding, your baby also will need vitamin and iron supplements. If he gains sufficient weight while breastfeeding exclusively, he may not need any other supplements. Many breastfed preemies, however, need extra bottle feedings of fortified expressed milk or high-calorie preemie or transitional formula.

Timing feedings

Premature babies usually aren't very good at realizing they're hungry. Your baby won't be able to sense hunger and let you know by crying until he approaches the equivalent of full term (using corrected age). He also may not have developed the mechanism by which his hunger is proportional to the amount of calories he needs for healthy growth.

You'll need to initiate feeding at regular intervals, as directed by the NICU staff. They'll also tell you how much milk or formula your baby should be given during feedings, if you use bottles. While on-demand feeding is ideal for full-term newborns, preemies initially aren't capable of managing their hunger and feedings, so it's best to stick to the schedule recommended by his doctor.

Weight gain

Most babies leaving the NICU weigh less than comparable full-term infants of similar corrected age. This is due to several reasons. Oral feedings, for example, may have been delayed due to respiratory or gastrointestinal problems. The best place for an infant to grow to term is in the womb. Even with the many advances in neonatal care and nutrition, including intravenous feedings (hyperalimentation) and high-calorie premature infant formulas, medical science has yet to match the natural method in which nutrients from the mother pass through the placenta and nourish the fetus.

Once feeding is well established and your baby is getting full nutrition, he'll undergo what's called "catch-up growth." His rate of growth will exceed that of full-term infants of comparable corrected age. It's as if your baby understands that his weight is too low for his age and he's trying to match the weight of his full-term peers.

As your baby begins to take in enough calories, he'll grow remarkably quickly: Typically, he'll gain 20 to 30 grams—or more—per day. (An ounce is about 30 grams.) Like many parents, you probably will want to monitor your baby's weight gain frequently. Most experts advise against keeping a baby scale at home, however, out of concern that parents may become overly focused on a baby's weight.

MORE **ABOUT** | baby scales

When your baby was in the NICU, you may have noticed she gained weight erratically—one day she gained a tremendous amount, and the next day she gained almost nothing. Your baby might have ingested more calories on the days she gained a lot, but that usually isn't the explanation for such variations.

Usually weight-gain variations are due to inaccurate measuring. The NICU scales are calibrated and accurate, but no measuring device is 100 percent accurate. A good scale will provide a weight measurement that is accurate to within 1 to 2 percent of the true weight. So if the scale says your baby weighs 4 pounds, 6 ounces, her true weight may actually be as much as 2 percent higher or lower—or plus or minus up to 1.4 ounces. So if your NICU newborn weighed 4 pounds, 6 ounces yesterday and fed very well, yet weighs the same today, it's quite possible she actually did gain weight. In fact, due to measurement errors, she might even have weighed 4 pounds, 4.6 ounces yesterday and 4 pounds, 7.4 ounces today—for an undetected gain of nearly 3 ounces!

There are many variables that are relatively meaningless when weighing an older child or adult but that become quite significant when weighing a small infant. For example, if your baby has a large bowel movement or urinates shortly before being weighed, she could be as much as 1.5 ounces lighter than she was a few minutes earlier.

With all these small inaccuracies, it's best to focus on the general trend in weight gain. Follow your baby's progress over several days rather than focusing on the change from one weighing to the next.

Health concerns

Premature and preterm babies are subject to the same illnesses and medical issues as babies born at term (see Chapter 13), though some of these problems need special attention when they affect premature infants.

Reflux

Reflux, or regurgitation of stomach contents into the mouth or nose and esophagus, is common among full-term babies and even more prevalent in premature infants (see page 171). Simple measures can help—for example, keeping your baby in an upright position for 20 minutes after each feeding and providing smaller but more frequent feedings.

Keep in mind that the amount of spit-up is usually far less than you might guess by the size of the spill. It's usually no more than a nuisance and a mess, provided babies are gaining weight and aren't uncomfortable during feedings. However, if your baby seems to be in distress during feedings, consult your pediatrician.

Hearing loss

Inability to hear softer sounds is more common in premature infants. Diminished hearing ability may be the result of an infection, a side effect of certain drugs used to treat medical problems in premature babies, or simply due to prematurity. A hearing test is usually performed before babies are discharged from the NICU, but many physicians recommend a follow-up test several months later, especially for very premature infants. Early detection and intervention—hearing aids, speech and language therapy, programs designed for hearing-challenged children, and perhaps cochlear implants—have greatly improved the speech and language outcomes for infants with hearing loss (see page 374).

Retinopathy of prematurity (ROP)

Excessive growth of blood vessels in the retina (the back wall of the eyeball, where sensors of the visual system are located) can impair vision and in the worst cases cause blindness. It's most often found in preemies born at 31 weeks or earlier and weighing 2 pounds, 12 ounces or less, but it can occur in larger preterm infants too. Mild forms of ROP often heal on their own, but more serious cases need treatment to prevent significant vision loss.

Periodic eye examinations, often begun while babies are in the NICU, can monitor for ROP and, if it has developed, can indicate whether it's healing or progressing. At-risk infants will require follow-up visits with an ophthalmologist until the retina matures, and those with ROP will need to be monitored for progression of the disease and possible lasting effects on their eyesight, such as impaired vision, nearsightedness, amblyopia, retinal detachment, and glaucoma.

Dental problems

Infants who needed to have an endotracheal tube put down their throats to help them breathe, usually because their lungs were premature, are at increased

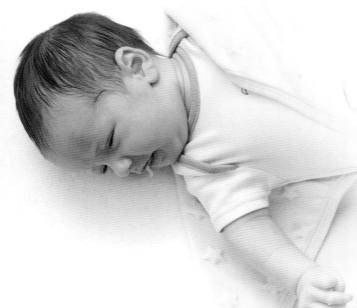

risk for dental problems—it's believed the tube can damage oral tissues. These dental problems include a high arched palate, deformities or defects in the enamel in the baby teeth that will later erupt, or even missing teeth. In rare instances, bilirubin—a normal waste product that is elevated in jaundiced newborns—or medications may stain the developing teeth. No specific treatment is needed, but your baby should have routine preventive care and visits to the dentist beginning when she's 12 months old.

Inguinal (groin) hernia

Early in fetal life, before the internal organs that distinguish males from females have developed, the testes or ovaries form in the abdominal cavity. In boys, each testis gradually travels to the scrotum, leaving the abdomen through a small round opening called the inguinal ring, beneath the skin and muscle, and passing between layers of muscles in the groin through a passage called the inguinal canal. Girls also have an inguinal ring and canal, even through the ovaries remain where they are formed.

As the fetus develops, and after the testes have arrived in the scrotal sack in males, the inguinal ring and canal are completely sealed. But if this passageway remains open, a piece of intestine can leave the abdomen and travel through it. If this happens, you might spot a bulge in the groin. It's usually about the size of a ping-pong ball. The protruding intestine may appear outside the abdominal cavity briefly before withdrawing back into its normal location.

Babies born prematurely are at higher risk of hernias in general, and boys and babies who require a ventilator are at greatest risk. If a hernia is discovered while your baby is in the NICU, it will usually be repaired surgically before his discharge.

If you're at home and notice a bulge in the groin, scrotum, or labia, try to photograph it quickly; it may disappear within minutes. Notify your pediatrician, who will schedule surgery in the near future to close the inguinal canal. If left untreated, there's a small chance of intestinal strangulation, a serious complication that occurs when part of the intestine enters the canal, gets caught, and becomes damaged when its blood supply is compromised.

Chronic lung disease

If your infant suffers from chronic lung disease, it will be diagnosed while she's in the NICU. Formally known as bronchopulmonary dysplasia (BPD), chronic lung disease most often develops in very premature infants who needed mechanical ventilation. It's caused by a combination of premature lungs, the higher concentrations of oxygen needed, and trauma from the pressure at which the air is delivered to the lungs.

Chronic lung disease is diagnosed by characteristic clinical and radiographic findings, including: persistent rapid, labored breathing; evidence of inadequate oxygen transfer in the lungs; and many tiny round areas of hyperaeration, which appear black on an X-ray and are surrounded by densities that appear white. Practically speaking, however, your baby has chronic lung disease if she continues to need oxygen 30 days after birth. She may need oxygen, oral medication, or both once she returns home until her lungs have healed.

Babies with chronic lung disease are more susceptible to complications when they get respiratory infections. To prevent infection with respiratory syncytial virus, or RSV, babies with chronic lung disease should be prescribed Synagis (see page 96).

Rehospitalization

Hopefully, your baby will thrive after her discharge from the NICU. Some babies who spent time in the NICU end up briefly hospitalized later for treatment of respiratory infections. Very premature infants and babies with chronic lung disease are the most likely to require a return visit to the hospital, but any premature infant can become very sick from a common head cold. The infection can spread to the lower respiratory tract, causing wheezing or pneumonia. It's a good idea to take careful measures (see pages 94–95) to minimize the spread of infections.

Growth and development

After discharge from the NICU, your baby will see his pediatrician frequently. At first, the visits will focus on your baby's adjustment to being at home, as well as how you're doing; feeding and nutrition; the status of any remaining medical problems; and his growth.

His growth probably will be measured against a standard growth chart. (Growth charts specific to small premature infants are used primarily for babies who are still hospitalized.) These charts plot your baby's age against his weight, height, and head circumference. (See pages 272–275 for a discussion of growth and development and of growth charts.) You'll use your baby's corrected age, rather than his chronological age, to chart his growth. Even so, your baby probably will start off in the lowest percentiles for height and weight. Some babies may stay there, but as your baby catches up he'll approach a level of growth more typical for full-term infants around the same corrected age, and eventually the same chronological age.

Pediatricians monitor development milestones in all babies, but they track premature infants particularly closely. Again, your baby's expected development will be based on his corrected age. For example, if your baby was born 2 months prematurely, he'd be expected to start smiling at a chronological age of 3½ to 4 months, or a corrected age of 6 to 8 weeks, since babies born at term usually start to smile when they're 6 to 8 weeks old.

Some babies "catch up" to full-term babies developmentally earlier or later than others. A healthy premature infant usually reaches the normal range without correction for prematurity by a chronological age of 12 to 18 months.

Milestones are a helpful way to monitor your baby's development, but try not to obsess over them. It's reassuring, of course, to see your baby reach milestones at his corrected age for the first several months and later catch up to full-term babies, working on skills appropriate for his chronological age. But even among healthy, full-term babies, it's best not to put too much emphasis on the timing of achievements. What's most important is not when he reaches milestones, but that he does reach them.

---

catching up

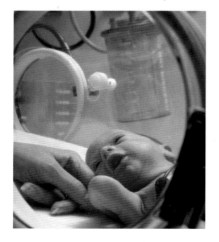

Catching up to full-term children is the result of two forces. Accelerated growth and development leads to true compensation for prematurity. And then, as children get older, the range of what's considered "normal" grows wider: A baby may progress at a steady pace a few months behind average but eventually will naturally fall within the normal range. For example, the typical full-term infant smiles between 6 and 8 weeks of age, a range of 2 weeks, but it is normal to begin walking anywhere from 10 to 18 months, a range of 8 months. If your child was born 2 months prematurely and is developing normally (according to corrected age), she will be "behind" when she smiles at 4 months of chronological age, but "normal" when she walks at 15 months of (chronological) age.

Parenting issues

Caring for a premature baby will profoundly affect you, as a person and as a parent. You're not the same mother or father you would have been had your delivery been full term. Your plans, hopes, and expectations will change dramatically. Instead of focusing on such mundane problems as learning to change a diaper or becoming comfortable with feedings, you'll be forced to deal with more difficult issues. Concerns about your newborn's health and safety can no doubt overwhelm you at first. You may wonder: "Will she survive? Will she be normal? Was this premature birth somehow my fault? What will I tell friends and relatives? How can I go home without her?"

At some level, you'll mourn the loss of the pregnancy, delivery, and postpartum time you didn't get to experience. You lost much of the third trimester of your pregnancy and all the experiences, both pleasant and unpleasant, that go with it. And now, instead of holding your healthy, full-term baby in your arms, surrounded by gifts and flowers, you're off to the NICU to visit your at-risk baby, who's attached to all sorts of machines, getting fluids intravenously, and perhaps receiving oxygen or mechanical ventilation. You expected to be the focal point of your newborn's life, but you're relegated to the role of bystander, watching the nurses and doctors care for her.

Initially, you may not understand what's being done for her, and you may not know how you can participate or help. You have lots and lots of questions, but when you ask the most important ones, the answers are often, "We'll have to see," or, "We can't answer that right now." You may still fear that your baby won't do well, that she might not end up a perfect, whole child.

If you planned to breastfeed your baby, prematurity or medical problems could mean you'll have to express milk for weeks before she can try to nurse at your breast. With time, effort, and energy—for expressing milk is an everyday,

around-the-clock chore—you may keep up a healthy enough supply to support her and be successful at breastfeeding. But if breastfeeding isn't an option, you may feel guilty that you're not doing everything you can to help your baby.

In time, you'll feel more comfortable in the strange world of the NICU. You'll begin to know the nurses and doctors caring for your baby; you may befriend other parents visiting their infants. The more you learn about your baby's condition and treatment, the less shell-shocked you'll feel. Yet your mood will continue to rise and fall with her progress. When all is going well, you may feel elated; setbacks, however, draw a dark cloud over your world.

Stress and exhaustion can strongly affect you. Perhaps you're angry with your partner. You may become critical of the care your baby is receiving, especially when something goes wrong. When the phone rings at your home, you may feel a flash of fear: "Is it the hospital calling? Is something wrong?" And you may be constantly asking yourself: "Will she get better? Will she ever be ready to come home? Will she grow up to be a healthy, normal child?"

This can be a traumatizing experience. As focused as you are on your baby in the NICU, you need to take some steps to care for yourself. Seek out support programs in your community or through your hospital. Try to find parents of preemies who are now thriving. They can be empathetic sources of support for you and your partner.

If you have local friends and family, let them help you. You may need to be clear and specific: Ask for meals, for help keeping up with household tasks, or even for some time alone if they're crowding you. Call long-distance friends or family when you need to hear a supportive voice.

How this affects you

All parents, regardless of the size or health of their newborn, want only the best in life for their baby.

Parents of babies who've never had a medical problem are still prone to worrying whether their children will be healthy or developmentally normal; for parents of premature infants, especially those coping with medical problems, this fear is compounded. The trauma of your experience, the uncertainty of your baby's future, and your sometimes well-founded fear of a bad outcome all have a profound effect on you and the way you'll feel about your baby.

Compared to other parents, mothers of special-care babies are much more likely to have a high level of anxiety and to suffer from postpartum depression. Part of your heightened anxiety is quite realistic and expected. Your baby may have been very ill; she still may be recovering from some of the medical problems she experienced. If you've brought her home, you've probably been given very detailed instructions about how to take care of her and about what signs constitute danger, requiring an immediate call to the doctor. You may even have been taught how to begin resuscitation efforts—just in case. No matter how small the risk of such an emergency or how reassuringly it's discussed with you, it's almost impossible to set aside the concern that your baby could suffer a life-threatening event at home.

Your anxiety is also fed by fears of what might happen in the future. When your baby is sent home, doctors usually can't tell you for certain whether your baby will have neurological problems, developmental delays, or learning disabilities. The more premature and critically ill your baby is, the more realistic your fears. But some of these problems, if they do occur at all, won't be apparent for months or years. "Will she be okay? Which problems might she face? How severe will they be?" No wonder you worry!

It's very hard to be a calm, relaxed parent when your baby has ongoing medical problems and you know she's at risk for rehospitalization or other sudden medical emergencies. Worries about her future health and development don't make it any easier. It's very difficult to strike an appropriate balance between worrying too much and not enough. You may receive well-meant advice to "Treat her like a normal baby"—and if your baby had few difficulties in the NICU and has no lingering medical issues, you probably should try to follow that advice. But if your infant had a stormy stay in the NICU or isn't completely healthy, or if you're a worrier by nature, you'll have trouble silencing the doubts and anxiety. Regardless of your particular experience, you can't ignore what you and your infant have been through.

On the other hand, if you view your baby only as fragile or sickly, you may become an overprotective, unduly anxious parent. If she has a runny nose, you may hurry to the doctor's office, fearing she'll develop pneumonia. You may have trouble being away from her or letting her do anything remotely risky, such as playing with other babies.

There's no simple solution. You'll need to make an effort to find the middle road. Over time, especially if your baby does well, you may be able to quell some of your anxieties. Even if your baby has "weak lungs" or faces disability, you'll probably find that being overprotective may meet some of your own needs but isn't the best approach.

All children need to assert some control over their world and show some independence. When they're permitted to do so, they feel proud. Stifling your baby's efforts to be more independent doesn't encourage her personal growth and sense of worth. Your anxieties and worry for her well-being are understandable, but she'll benefit if you try to hold these tendencies in check. With time and experience, instead of fretting over what she *can't* do, you'll probably find yourself marveling at what she *can* do. But she needs support and space to find that out for herself.

Finally, never lose sight of the fact that your baby, no matter how bright or how disabled, is a unique and wonderful human being. You'll love her no matter what the future brings. She is your special, priceless, adorable, loving baby.

YOUR BABY
MONTH BY MONTH

It sometimes seems that your wonderful newborn can only feed, cry, poop, and sleep, but he's able to do so much more. Even in the first week of life, your baby can recognize his mother's face (and his father's) and may imitate facial gestures—try making funny faces and see what happens. He also can distinguish his mother by smell and, sometimes, by voice.

Your newborn's primary activity is sleep, and this can occupy up to 20 hours of his day. Babies usually wake up for a feeding and then drift off back to sleep, but some are almost too sleepy to want to eat in the early days. If you are on-demand feeding, let him sleep as long as he wishes and feed him when he wakes up. But if you are feeding on a schedule, your newborn should eat every 2 to 3 hours. If he doesn't wake up, gently rouse him—try tickling him, holding him upright, or changing his diaper (never shake him!). You can tell your baby is getting enough milk if he feeds vigorously, seems content afterward, and has many wet and dirty diapers. Your newborn's feces can be very soft and frequent, particularly if he's breastfed.

Feces can vary in color from dark brown to yellow.

Some babies cry a lot! This doesn't mean you're doing anything wrong. You'll soon recognize your baby's cries—and whether he's hungry or wants something else (a clean diaper, to be warmer, to have some quiet). Your newborn is sensitive to loud noises, bright lights, and strong smells, all of which could make him cry. Rocking, singing quietly, or holding him so he can hear your heartbeat may help calm him. If you're breastfeeding, putting your baby to your breast is soothing. Swaddling your baby (see page 34) can help him feel secure; after all, he was used to being tightly held in the womb before birth.

Your infant doesn't have much neck muscle power yet. His head tends to fall back if you pull him to a sitting position; this is known as head lag. Support his head if you are lifting him or holding him in a sitting position (see pages 32–33). Your baby's arms move without any apparent control on his part, and his hands are often closed. Your baby has several reflexes at birth, such as tightly grasping an object placed in his hand, that slowly disappear. He will naturally turn toward a source of food and "root" for it with his mouth. A touch on the cheek can stimulate this reflex—he may even suck on your finger to see if it's a food source. If he's startled or his head is abruptly moved backward, he will bring his arms around to the front, as if to grab hold of you. This is called the Moro, or startle, reflex.

Your baby will begin to fixate with his eyes during the first week or two, but he can't yet follow a face moving across his field of vision. He can hear but doesn't turn toward sound; he may be quiet when there's a soft noise nearby.

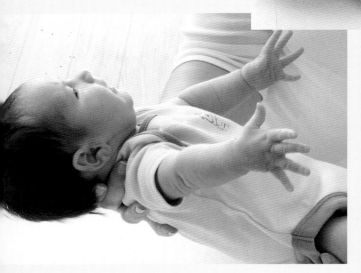

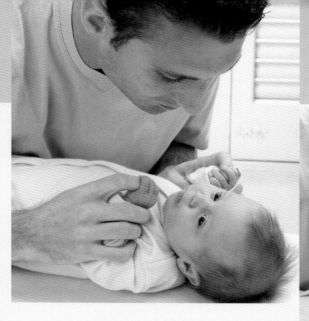

Now your baby seems much more alert. She's awake more of the time, is beginning to follow objects with her eyes and ears, recognizes you more clearly, and takes an interest in the world. She may stare at you intently while being fed. You may notice a smile, though this might be due to gas; the first real smile will be in response to a smile of your own, and it usually happens at around 6 weeks.

She might start to sleep for longer stretches at night, although this usually doesn't happen for another month or two. Your baby may be happy to go 3 to 4 hours between feedings during the day but still wants to eat more often at night.

She still cries frequently, usually because she's hungry or uncomfortable. Some babies cry a lot and lustily, particularly late in the day. This is often called colic (see page 177), but the cause is not really known and there is no cure. Try rocking and comforting her, and try to be patient—it gets better after a few months! Your baby also may make little noises when content, but she isn't cooing quite yet.

Her muscles are growing stronger, and she can hold her head up for longer, though it still lags when she's in a sitting position. She waves her arms and "bicycles" with her legs when excited. Her hands are usually closed, but she can open them and grasp a finger or other object placed in her palm. She's starting to learn the connection between what her hands do and what happens when they move, and

she will enjoy it if you move them for her.

To help her grow stronger, set her down, awake, on her stomach for a few minutes of "tummy time." Keep her engaged with toys or your face, and pick her up when she gets frustrated and has had enough.

Your baby probably needs lots of cuddling and holding. She may enjoy watching a mobile or other moving object placed in front of her, not too far away.

You can start playing games with her now. When she's on her changing table, with her face about 8 to 12 inches away from yours, lean toward her and talk happily. Pause and give her a chance to smile, gurgle, or move her mouth back at you. Try doing these things one at a time: Smile, stick out your tongue, or open and close your mouth exaggeratedly. She may start to imitate you! She'll also appreciate music, singing, and gentle splashing when you bathe her.

Your baby is growing rapidly, although how much varies greatly. Her size relative to other babies often has no bearing on her adult proportions.

TWO MONTHS OLD

Your baby is probably sleeping less during the day—and, if you're lucky, more at night! She may be aware of routines such as feeding and bathing, and get excited when she recognizes the signs. She's becoming more aware of the world and of the special people around her.

Your baby shows recognition by becoming excited—gurgling, smiling, and waving—when she sees people or toys that she likes. If you talk to her, she coos responsively. If she's crying, she may stop if you pick her up and speak softly to her. She probably enjoys being around people. If she's in the mood for company, she'll get upset if left alone.

Most babies this age like to be cuddled, but all babies are different. If you haven't already, now you'll start to see her temperament appear—how she reacts as an individual and a bit about what kind of a personality she'll have, whether outgoing and sociable or more reserved and thoughtful. You can help her by learning to respond in the way that suits her best.

Your baby watches objects more carefully when they're moved slowly across her line of vision, and she studies your face intently. She smiles more frequently and may laugh and gurgle. She also makes more varied noises.

She should be able to focus on her face in a mirror, if it's held close enough. Move the mirror slowly up, down, and around and watch as she tries to keep her reflection in sight. She loves it when you talk to her, and it's through the constant interaction of language that she'll learn her first words, though that is still a long way off.

Her hands are becoming interesting to her, and she may look at them and grasp an object for a very short time. She's starting to notice her fingers and may curl them around objects placed in them. Try putting your fingers in hers and gently rocking her from side to side. You can gently prop her up with cushions and put small, colorful objects within view.

Your baby is noticeably stronger. She can hold her head up for a few seconds if her chest is supported, and her back is straighter when she's held upright, though she is still some way off from sitting on her own. When she's on her stomach, she can lift her head up and arch her back; however, she may not be able to roll over, or to push up on her arms. Give her plenty of tummy time, which doesn't have to be on the floor. You can hold her on top of you securely while you're lying down or reclining.

Routines become more important as she gets older, particularly at night. Starting a regular bedtime routine should help avoid problems later and make it easier to one day settle her into her own bed. For example, after bathing and feeding, read the same book and play the same music at bedtime.

Her rapid weight gain will continue.

Now is the time for your baby's first immunizations (see pages 327 and 336). Though this may be an anxious time for you, most infants are only briefly upset by baby shots.

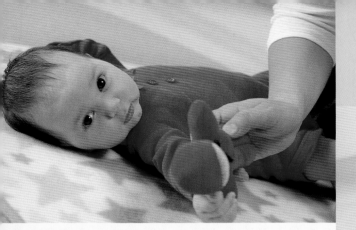

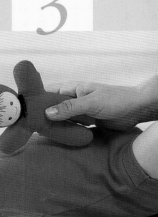

Your baby is becoming much more active and communicative. He responds more to routines and is more sociable. He smiles more frequently and at people other than his parents. He typically also makes more sounds, including cooing and squealing. Talk constantly to your baby—it engages his interest and helps familiarize him with the sounds and rhythms of words. You can have a two-way conversation without using proper words. He'll follow the expression in your voice and learn to recognize commonly used words; for example, talk about the parts of his body when bathing him.

His hearing and vision are becoming more accurate, and he is better at recognizing people both visually and by their voices. He can distinguish people who are farther away, and he can see several colors. He may show excitement when he hears music or a favorite song. At this age, he is most interested in interaction—the interplay of action and reaction, the response that he gets from an adult.

Movies and television may be colorful and interesting, but they cannot interact with him. He can learn much more from you, so digital entertainment should be used little, if at all. (The American Academy of Pediatrics recommends no TV for children under 2 years old.)

His neck and back muscles are strengthening, and he can support his head for a few minutes and sit, supported, for a longer period with his head and back straight. He prefers sitting to lying down, and takes a keen interest in his surroundings.

It's important to continue encouraging your baby to spend some time on his stomach, under supervision, each day. On his stomach, he will lift his head up. He may start to roll over—rolling from his stomach to his side then onto his stomach again. He'll keep trying this maneuver until he rolls all the way over onto his back.

He's likely using his hands much more and can put things in his mouth. Be careful to keep small objects out of his reach, so he won't try to eat them! In the bath, he is starting to splash and probably enjoys you trickling water down his body.

Your baby is more familiar with cycles of day and night, and, as a result, he may be getting better at sleeping through the night.

Crying is still common, and some babies still cry at night at this age. Stroking and massage can be very soothing. Colic usually stops by around 3 months, but there are still many other reasons for night crying—for feeding or company, for example—and for some babies it just becomes a habit. If crying is persistent, you may want to talk to your pediatrician to rule out any potentially treatable condition.

At 3 months, your baby may start to appreciate the feel of materials and the difference between hard and soft, warm and cool, furry and smooth. Give him toys and fabrics with different textures to grasp and feel.

Your baby now spends lots of time awake, although he still needs to nap during the day (and will for a long time to come). He may get excited when he sees the breast or bottle before a feeding.

He's more interested in the outside world and in a greater variety of toys—those that can be touched, watched, banged, and listened to. Encouragement helps him learn. Whenever he does something new or clever, react in a positive manner, for example, with a smile. Describe specifically what he did that you like and encourage him by telling him, in a very positive tone of voice, how much you appreciate his efforts.

Your baby is moving his body more actively and may begin rolling from his back to his front. If he spends time regularly on his stomach, he may roll from his front to his back—be careful where you place him! He likes kicking his feet and may play with his toes. He'll soon be able

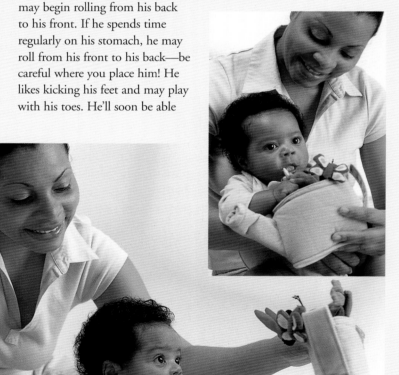

to hold his head up without support. When on his stomach, he can lift his head and shoulders while he rests on his hands and arms. He typically struggles to get objects that are out of reach. Try making it a fun game by placing an item just out of reach and cheering when he gets it. Given a toy, he might grasp it with two hands.

Communication is improving, partly through facial expressions—he's learning to recognize yours as you can recognize his, which are getting more varied. He makes a range of noises and babbles to himself.

He might know his name, though it might be a little longer before he does. He looks around to hear sounds, and waves and gurgles in anticipation of feeding and other favorite activities. It's getting easier to figure out what he doesn't like, too: He turns away from unwanted things.

Your baby's temperament is emerging more, and you'll see whether he readily accepts change or is slower to adapt. Pay attention to how he reacts to situations and do what you think best to build his confidence.

Your baby will get a second round of immunizations. He's more susceptible to infections because the immunity that passed across the placenta at birth is starting to wear off.

Recommendations on when to introduce solid foods vary greatly, but the majority of pediatricians advise starting between 4 and 6 months of age. See page 225 for more about when and how to introduce solid foods.

Physically, your baby is growing much bigger and stronger. She is nearly ready to sit up on her own and enjoys being propped up in a stroller, infant seat, or high chair, where she can turn her head from side to side.

If she hasn't started rolling before, she is likely starting to do so now; when lying on her front, she rolls onto her back and vice versa. She might be able to travel pretty far by rolling or thrusting herself forward, inches at a time, but she's a little young for crawling. She likely pushes up on her arms, stands supported with your arms under her shoulders, and enjoys bouncing. If supported, she jumps up and down and pushes off the floor or table with her feet; her legs bend and extend on landing and liftoff.

Your baby is much more adept with her hands. Hand her a rattle, and she'll shake it. She probably can grasp her toes and put them into her mouth—pay close attention to whatever else she might be trying to nibble on! She is enjoying more and more the pleasure of actively making noises and will be getting better at copying noises you make, as well as facial expressions. She babbles to express both happiness and unhappiness.

Games are growing more fun, and counting piggies leads to squeals of pleasure. If you ring a bell or squeeze a squeaky toy, she tries to find out where the noise is coming from.

She enjoys being taken around the house. You can point out familiar items, talk about them, and let her touch items, such as flowers and fabrics, rough and smooth surfaces, and other objects, to gain a sense of their differences.

Her vision and hearing are becoming more accurate. She likes studying faces and objects and looking at pictures in a book, so this is a good time to start reading more books with her. At this age, you'll mostly be pointing to pictures, but you can read short stories, too. She loves hearing your voice. You can give her sturdy board books or soft-covered

baby books to explore on her own.

Your baby becomes alert when someone enters the room, particularly if it's someone she knows. She probably tolerates strangers relatively well unless she is tired or hungry.

She is probably affectionate toward you: She may pat you or get excited when she sees you approach, and she may get upset when you walk away.

By this point, your baby is most likely settled into a daily routine with regular sleeping times, and she's probably sleeping a longer stretch during the night. It should be easier to leave her for short spells with someone you trust. She will more easily adapt to a new person if she's developed confidence that her needs will be met when she cries.

Before long, she'll be moving around your house. This is the time to check that you've removed things that could be dangerous (see page 311).

6 SIX MONTHS OLD

Halfway through the first year is a big milestone. Most babies double their birth weight by 5 to 6 months and triple it by a year. Not only is your baby bigger, but she's also more active and, if you have not already started them, she is ready to start eating solid foods (see Chapter 10, "Feeding your older baby").

Your baby's teeth may be starting to emerge (although in some families you may have to wait a few more months). Teething can on occasion be painful (see page 200), so she may be irritable and cry more than usual before a new tooth erupts.

She's moving around much more, rolling from side to side or creeping. She can support herself with straight arms and palms held flat on the floor.

If you put her into a sitting position, leaning with her arms in front of her, she probably can sit for a short period before tumbling to the side, forward, or backward. But your baby isn't safely stable yet, so be sure to keep soft cushions around her when she's propped up. She may raise her arms to be picked up.

Her neck muscles are strong now. When she's lying on her back, she can lift her head to look at her feet. She uses her hands more adeptly to find objects to play with and stretches out to reach them. Soon she'll start to transfer objects from one hand to another. She usually puts things in her mouth, so keep small items out of reach. Rule of thumb: Anything that fits through a toilet paper roll is a choking hazard.

Your baby will enjoy being held in a supported standing position and can use a jumper or bouncer. Jumping up and down can lead to endless joy, but don't leave her in a jumper for too long—make sure she gets plenty of time to practice moving around. Check that the bouncer is securely set up and always supervise her closely when she's using it.

Your baby babbles a lot and may make noises to seek attention. She's beginning to recognize words and listens when she hears her name.

Although she can't yet say meaningful words, she's starting to develop a conversational style—she'll enjoy getting a response from you. Play along with the conversation as best you can. When she seems to say something meaningful, answer her so she'll be eager to keep trying. Giving a running commentary on what she's doing, what you're doing, and even what the dog is doing is a great way to help her develop listening and language skills.

Her hearing is becoming more accurate, and she loves to play with things that make noise. She picks things up and shakes them, and enjoys hearing you making music and sounds. She also enjoys dancing—that is, dancing in your arms, with you moving her arms and legs to the rhythm.

A third set of immunizations is given at this age.

Your baby is more settled in his habits now. He probably has a daily routine for napping, feeding, bathing, and sleeping. He still takes two naps a day and most likely sleeps through the night.

Routine nighttime activities can help him relax and prepare to sleep—give him a bath, sing a lullaby, read a story, give him a massage, or rock him. If his afternoon nap extends too close to bedtime, you can try starting earlier or cutting it short.

Your baby probably weighs about a pound more than he did last month and is a little taller. He's becoming stronger and probably can sit unsupported with his back straight. If he hasn't started turning regularly from his back onto his stomach, he'll start doing it now. He might be able to get himself into position to crawl, though it probably will be a few months before he's on the move. Some babies, however, start crawling around now. If your baby is very active, he may pull himself to standing— though he may not be able to sit back down and will cry until you "rescue" him.

His motor skills are improving, too. He is probably trying to hold his spoon by himself and can drink from a two-handled cup, if offered (for more about introducing a cup, see page 227). He may appreciate a hard rubber teething ring to soothe his sore gums when he's teething. He's grabbing and picking up lots of toys, trying to transfer them from hand to hand. When he holds something, he examines it closely.

Your baby is trying new ways to communicate, such as babbling and stopping to listen when you talk. He might imitate some of the sounds that you make and may raise his arms to be picked up. He may look intently at strangers, unsure whether he likes them. You might want to start teaching him simple sign language (see page 176); he'll be able to use signs within a few months to communicate, typically well before he begins to master words.

Your baby's personality becomes more evident each day (for more about understanding your child's temperament, see pages 138–139). If he seems strong-willed and high-strung, you'll need plenty of patience (for tips, see page 291). Talk to him frequently, give him lots of cuddles, and distract him when he gets irritable. If he seems shy and sensitive, take it slow when introducing him to new people or places and stay nearby for support.

He'll enjoy playing with baby blocks and soft toys and being on the floor—keep encouraging supervised tummy time. He also may like being around other babies as long as you're nearby to boost his confidence. Continue to read, sing, and talk to him as much as possible.

Your baby is starting to go places, though he might manage it by rolling, rocking, scooting, or slithering commando style rather than crawling. He can now sit without support, and he might be able to pull himself up from a seated position. Once he starts moving around, it's very important to protect him from potential dangers. If you haven't already childproofed your home, you need to do it now (see Chapter 12, "Keeping your baby healthy").

Your baby is growing rapidly. To fuel his energy needs and make mealtime more interesting, you can start to feed him a wider variety of coarser foods—many of which you eat yourself. He may balk at being fed and prefer feeding himself. Offer food he can pick up with his fingers (see pages 231–232).

As your baby's pincer grasp gets more refined and he tries finger foods, he's also able to pick up very tiny objects. Continue to keep small items (anything that fits through a toilet paper roll) out of his reach.

Your baby may use simple gestures, such as shaking his head when he means "no" and pointing at things he wants you to give to him. He might repeat sounds such as "na na na" or "ba ba ba." He might even say his first word—probably "mama" or "dada" or maybe "uh-oh!"

Although he has a short attention span, your baby enjoys manipulating toys that squeak and playing games with you. He may start looking for toys that he has dropped. The development of object permanence—the understanding that things and people still exist even when they're out of his sight—is crucial to your baby's understanding of the way our social and physical worlds behave. When you leave the room, he's beginning to understand that you haven't disappeared forever. He realizes that when a ball rolls under a table, it sometimes reappears on the other side.

Your baby is also learning a bit more about himself. He enjoys looking in mirrors and seems to recognize himself. While watching himself in a mirror, he may touch his nose or pull his ear.

He might start to dislike or even fear strangers. Your baby might cry when you leave the room and may want more hugs and kisses. New faces represent new experiences, and he doesn't yet know if these will be enjoyable or unpleasant experiences. New activities, like being taken swimming, can trigger the same fear, so don't force new experiences on him.

He might choose a transitional object—a blanket or a soft toy (make sure there are no detachable parts)—to comfort him at these times and when he goes to bed. If he hasn't chosen something, you might want to choose a suitable object and make it part of his bedtime ritual.

This is the age of active motion: crawling, pulling up, and maybe cruising around the furniture, though the last is usually a bit later. It's important to remember that every baby is different; some crawl earlier, and some much later, so don't be anxious if she isn't on her hands and knees yet. Your baby might even be crawling backward if her arm muscles are stronger than her leg muscles. Encourage crawling by setting her on a soft carpet with lots of interesting toys within reach. Your baby likes toys with interesting shapes and patterns, and holes that can be searched safely.

She should be able to sit on the floor, amusing herself with nearby toys. She may be able to hold an object in each hand and bang them together.

Your baby's communication skills are improving steadily. She likely responds to her name and repeats one or more sounds. She tries to imitate what she hears, although her noises don't sound like real words yet. She's starting to make simple sounds such as "ba" and "da" that at first aren't used in context, but your responses will help her understand their meaning—she loves pleasing you. If you are using sign language with her, she may begin signing back!

She's showing emotions more readily: She gets upset if a toy is taken away or may cry if you look angry. She also may show sensitivity by crying when another baby cries. Your baby might be more clingy these days and afraid of things that didn't worry her before, such as loud noises or the bathtub.

As she better understands object permanence, she'll look for hidden objects. Games such as peekaboo are a lot of fun. Try hiding a toy under a soft blanket for her to "discover."

Her personality will shine more and more. She'll probably be determined and perhaps stubborn. Distraction is usually very effective; she's too young to understand angry words. She's able to let you know very clearly what she does and doesn't like.

Mealtime should be fun, particularly when she's able to participate. Eat meals together when possible and let her practice with finger foods.

Your baby is very curious about her world. Help her learn through her senses. Stimulate her vision with bright colors and hanging objects, her hearing with music or singing, her touch with different textures, and her taste and smell with food.

Your baby is starting to tease and test you. She learns quickly and is beginning to notice the things she can and can't do. She drops things from her stroller and waits for you to pick them up, and speeds off toward forbidden places. You need to watch her like a hawk—and have a lot of energy to keep up!

Your baby will soon be able to crawl up—but not yet down—stairs, putting her at risk of tumbling. You will need to teach her and practice with her repeatedly how to ease her way down backward rather than forward. She may be able to walk if you hold her hands and may cruise about the room using furniture for support. Some babies become expert at crawling and can get around very quickly.

Whether your baby is trying to stand up or is content to crawl, she loves pulling herself to standing and may be able to sit back down from a standing position, which is quite an achievement.

Her hands are into everything and she's more adept. You might be able to tell whether she's left- or right-handed. She can pick up tiny objects with her finger and thumb (her pincer grip); dirt and bits of dust and trash prove very attractive, so you need to be vigilant.

She can feed herself with her fingers and at least help hold a cup. She can start using a spoon, though the food usually falls off before she lifts it to her mouth. You can feed her with a second spoon at the same time to make sure she gets enough to eat.

Your baby is vocalizing more, though she's not expressing many understandable words. She likely communicates with gestures, such as holding out her arms to be picked up. She waves "bye-bye" and pats dolls and stuffed toys. She may shake her head and say "no," though it doesn't always mean what it seems; she loves to copy other people. She's happy when you encourage her and upset if you're angry; she may cry if another baby gets too much attention. She may react shyly to strangers, turning away and putting her head on your shoulder or leg.

Your baby now knows where things belong, and that they don't disappear when out of sight. She handles objects more appropriately, such as shaking a rattle. She's beginning to imitate gestures—you can have a lot of fun with clapping and copying games, such as pat-a-cake.

Settling her down at night isn't always easy. Try to repeat the same routine at the same time every night. When you put your baby into her crib, she may pull herself up and protest loudly, because life is full of exciting events, and she doesn't want to miss a thing.

climbing upstairs, give you a present while cruising, and wave while turning around. He can hold a crayon and may be able to use it, though he can't draw anything recognizable. He holds his arms and feet out when you dress him.

His language is more apparent; he probably can speak a meaningful word or two and vocalizes a lot. Encourage him as much as possible by responding to him as if it's a conversation. He'll copy the expression on your face, along with more of the words he hears. He enjoys both the stories and pictures in books and can link sounds to pictures—for example, pictures of animals and the sounds they make. He may even turn the pages of a book, though not in a logical way!

Your baby's personality is more evident. Now that he knows much more about what he wants, he can become very frustrated if he can't get it. This frustration can erupt in all sorts of situations—at home, at the supermarket, or on the bus. Try to remain calm and be patient; the best approach is distraction: Point to something that's even more interesting and go up close to have a look. Babies have very short memories, and he probably can't keep the original idea in his head for more than a minute or two, so he might forget all about it.

He's also more sensitive to your feelings. He knows when you aren't pleased and may hide his face or turn away. Some babies enter a clingy phase and don't want to be set down. Don't worry, and don't try to force him to let go—it will pass.

Your baby is able to enjoy more sophisticated games, including water games in the bath; games involving music, rhythm, and movement; stacking items and tossing and rolling balls; and games with mirrors. Keep it varied and interesting, and he'll repay you with laughter. He also enjoys new experiences—such as going grocery shopping, having a meal in a restaurant, or being introduced to new textures and tastes.

Your baby is probably underfoot most of the time and enjoys cruising around the furniture. If he stands, then he can sit down—usually by holding on to something for support. Some babies can walk on their own before they're a year old; others don't take their first steps until they're closer to 18 months old, so don't worry if your baby isn't inclined yet. If he isn't walking on his own, he's developing skills—he likely can walk a bit if you hold one of his hands.

Even if he's walking, he still spends much of his time crawling—especially if he wants to get somewhere quickly. But he prefers being upright to being on his back and may protest when you lay him down for a diaper change. He also can do more things at once: He typically can hold an object while

Your baby has reached a magical milestone: He's 1 year old and now a toddler. He may be standing on his own or even walking; don't worry if he isn't, as many children do so later. Given the opportunity, he may start to crawl up and down the stairs.

He can hold something in one hand while using the other (multitasking), and he can hold two objects in one hand. He loves banging items such as spoons together and clapping. Although bath toys are fun, he's probably just as happy playing with soap suds.

He understands much more of the world around him; he may know some parts of his body (and even

point to them when asked where they are), some animals and their noises (which he may repeat), and the names of familiar people. He says a lot of nonsense words he made up himself, but he may be able to say several meaningful words—though he often gets them wrong (such as mixing up dog and cat). Even without words, he can clearly indicate what he wants by pointing with his index finger. His memory is better, and he has favorite books he loves to have read to him again and again. Favorites may include books with funny actions or animal sounds, and he may point to named objects.

Your toddler might even demonstrate awareness of cause and effect. For example, if his toy is resting out of reach on a towel, he might pull the towel toward himself to reach the toy.

He probably loves giving and receiving hugs and kisses and can never have enough. He also appreciates humor. This is a good time to gently introduce rules—for example, no biting, no hitting—because he can start to understand them. Comment when he does the right thing. Avoid scolding; your job is to teach him positive behaviors, and he's far too young for punishments.

He's attracted to the TV and probably knows what the buttons are for, but you should limit screen time. (Experts recommend no TV at all until your child is 2.) Your toddler needs interactive experiences; reading a book and talking to him will do more to help his language development than watching TV will. Given the opportunity, he pounds on your computer keys. Your toddler especially likes toys that allow him to mimic what he sees you doing, such as playing with a toy telephone.

If your child still uses a pacifier, it's time to wean him from it, according to American Academy of Pediatrics guidelines. A pacifier can sometimes interfere with speech development as well as affect the teeth. And if you haven't already done so, it is also time to switch from bottles to a cup.

Your toddler's physical growth isn't as rapid as it was in the first 12 months, but each month still brings new skills, and your toddler's personality is shining through more clearly. She may be able to walk now, though this depends on confidence; some toddlers are better at crawling and don't yet want to work on mastering walking. Be patient, give her opportunities to test her skills, and don't push.

She's getting much better at using her hands, particularly using her finger and thumb (her pincer grip) to pick up small objects. She watches objects that are dropped or thrown as they fall to the ground and enjoys throwing things.

At mealtime, she's more adept at using a spoon and managing a cup, but because she rotates her hand frequently, she often spills whatever she's trying to eat. Give her plenty of time and practice, and she'll get better at it.

Your toddler is curious about everything and getting more experimental with toys. If she's walking, she enjoys pulling things behind her or pushing things in front. Toys that make noise are particularly entertaining. Messy play is very fun for her; you can introduce her to finger paints, shape sorters, and blocks. She might be able to place one block on top of another.

She expresses her desires more strongly and can be very determined about getting her own way. She does not understand about danger and staying safe, so be sure your home is well childproofed. Ideally, she should have a safe place to play freely with her toys, without being continually warned, "Don't touch that!"

Your toddler enjoys hiding games—either you hiding behind something and popping your head out, or hiding a favorite toy to see if she can find it. She can probably play on her own for a while, though she prefers to have you around. She's ready for games involving instructions—"Please show me the pony" or "Where is mommy's nose?" She

also likes activities during which she can anticipate actions—such as finger-play songs like "The Itsy Bitsy Spider." These kinds of activities help build her communication skills and sense of trust, and enhance social interaction between you.

She may give you a kiss if you ask her for one!

Your toddler is learning language quickly—though as with walking, there's a wide range for when children reach this milestone. She understands much more than she can say—she may have only 3 or 4 words but understands up to 50. When you ask, "Where's Daddy?" she looks in the right direction. She can point, if asked, to parts of her body, such as her nose. She tries hard to repeat words and sounds, and usually gets them right.

Your child is using gestures more, such as waving and clapping, and may wave "bye-bye" when asked. Like most toddlers, she loves repeating songs with accompanying gestures, such as raising her arms for "up," and giggles loudly when you join in. She doesn't quite understand stories, but greatly enjoys looking at pictures in a book. Describing and pointing to objects in the pictures will help develop her language skills. The best books for this age have big pictures and not many words.

Your toddler enjoys applying herself to a problem and perseveres in finding a solution by trial and error, such as playing with a sorting toy to put the right object into the right opening. She still needs help, but try to let her work things out herself. She loves putting small things into bigger things and taking them out, such as putting blocks in kitchen containers and removing them. She may start building—you can encourage this by joining in with blocks at her level, constructing a tower and then knocking it down, or making a bridge or a train. Now that your toddler can open and close doors, you'll want to double-check your childproofing. If you haven't already, secure cabinets and

drawers with childproof locks. Stock one unlocked cabinet with child-safe kitchen items—pots, plastic bowls, wooden spoons—for her to play with.

She's steadier on her feet and can stand for longer periods. She can bend over and stand up again without losing her balance. She doesn't like being restrained—once she starts to walk, she'll want to head off in all directions. When you're out and about, you may find it difficult to keep her within a safe distance without too much protest.

Your toddler now understands "no" and accepts rules, such as not tearing books, but might not be able to control her urges. Watch your response: If you laugh when she does something she shouldn't, she'll take that as approval and do it again. If she gets angry, react calmly, and she'll get over it.

At meals, offer a range of healthy foods and let her feed herself. The best way to avoid food refusal, which some toddlers show at this age, is to not worry or comment on how much she eats.

Your toddler has a real sense of humor and is starting to do funny things to get attention—including things that aren't allowed. She's probably very affectionate and loving toward you and wants your reassuring presence; however, she may be shy with babysitters and new people, and she may start to cry if someone she doesn't know picks her up or smiles at her. Don't worry; some toddlers need a little more time to warm up to people. She may carry a security item, such as a toy or blanket. She still doesn't understand the concept of danger, so it's helpful that she wants to stay close to you.

But now your toddler may be testing her limits. She may shout to show how powerful she is. She may demand, with persistent finger-pointing, objects that are out of reach. She may have a temper, but this still is best dealt with calmly and quietly. Distraction is usually very helpful to calm her.

Common household objects are very interesting to her and are cheap and fun toys. She likes stacking pots and pans, filling them with toys, and banging them together to make noise.

Your toddler can likely begin to participate in her own daily care. She can hold her feet out when it's time to put on socks and shoes. She knows that a washcloth is for cleaning her face and hands and can start to do that herself. She can hold a cup and drink from it, but she still knocks it over frequently—you may want to use a cup with handles and a spout to minimize mess.

She stares at objects for a long time to try to understand what they are, particularly if they move in an unusual way, such as a mobile in the wind. She likes using building blocks and can pick up small objects with great accuracy using either hand. She may carry her toys around, though not very carefully, and regularly throws them to the floor.

Although she can get around pretty quickly now, she's not completely steady on her feet and may bump into things; she probably walks with her feet kept wide apart. She may enjoy pushing a wagon or doll stroller and is starting to play chasing games, such as hide-and-seek.

Your toddler is endlessly curious, so make his environment safe to explore. If your home is danger-free, you won't have to keep warning and redirecting him. You also can let him play independently out of sight for a few seconds without worrying. But silence is always alarming where a toddler is concerned—trouble is almost sure to be brewing!

This is a wonderful age for learning how the world works. Your toddler enjoys playing with different materials—sand, dirt, and water—and with different textures, such as plastic, wood, cloth, and metal. He enjoys throwing a soft ball and may be able to retrieve a rolling ball, but make sure he learns that throwing hard or heavy objects isn't a good idea and may hurt.

He's probably starting to run. Falls are inevitable,

but as long as he's on a soft surface he's unlikely to injure himself. He loves to push things; if you provide him with a little cart, he can put his toys in it and learn about wheels. He's getting better at climbing, going upstairs on his hands and knees. He may climb out of anything you put him in, including his crib. Your toddler likes to carry things and turn the pages of a book. Above all, he wants to be independent. Don't be surprised if he pushes your hand away when you try to help.

Switches are fascinating to toddlers. Once he learns how to turn something on and off, he'll want to do it over and over. It's good to avoid watching TV or playing video games when he's around. (TV is not recommended for children under age 2.) Instead, talk to him, play with him, or show him lots of colored pictures in books and magazines.

His understanding is growing by leaps and bounds, and he is learning more about routines—holding out his hands to be cleaned when they're dirty, for example. He likes to mimic household activities, such as sweeping and cooking, and may be able to identify and fetch objects. If you say, "Please bring me the book," he might carry it to you.

At meals, he should be able to drink from a cup with less mess and feed himself most of the time. He still isn't very adept at using a spoon, but he wants to practice—he doesn't want you feeding him.

He's using more and more words every day, and he's starting to enjoy funny noise words, such as "splat" and "boing," particularly if you accompany them with actions.

Your child is learning more about how you expect him to behave. Explain what you want him to do with simple words and keep it short. Children get lost in long explanations.

Your toddler enjoys simple jokes—talking in a funny voice, making animal noises, using silly made-up words, and mimicking funny expressions.

She thinks she is the most important person in the world and expects to get everything she wants, and she will be greatly disappointed when she doesn't. When your toddler gets frustrated, distracting her appropriately can stop the flow of tears and help restore her good humor.

This is a good time to establish and follow clear routines; toddlers thrive when things happen at the same time every day. Establishing routines doesn't mean you have to work by the clock, but if you do things in the same order, life will run more smoothly—particularly at bedtime.

Rules are important, too, provided you don't have to keep saying "no." You also want to limit them to important issues, such as no hitting or biting. The best way to enforce rules is by making them easy to follow: If you don't want your child to play with something, keep it out of her reach.

Safety is a big issue at this age. Your toddler is blissfully unaware of everyday dangers, such as standing up on a chair or stroller, climbing down stairs, putting small objects in her mouth, missing a step going out the front door, and, of course, walking onto a busy road. It's important to teach her what's age appropriate about common potential hazards (see page 306), but your constant vigilance is still always required.

Your toddler loves playing with a range of toys now. Good choices include simple puzzles and an activity board with lots of different parts she can manipulate. She can likely throw a soft ball, build a small tower of bricks, and copy a bridge or other simple types of structures.

If you haven't introduced crayons yet, this is a good time to give your toddler some chubby nontoxic crayons and paper. She also can try finger painting; if you're worried about her putting paint-

covered fingers in her mouth, try edible finger paint or make your own by using pudding or mixing a bit of food coloring into plain yogurt.

Eating at mealtimes is still erratic. Healthy snacks, such as bananas, applesauce, or yogurt, throughout the day are good for her body and her mood. See Chapter 10, "Feeding your older baby," for ideas.

Now your toddler is always on the go. Although her gait continues to be uncertain, she is getting better at running without falling; she is steadier while walking, too. Her climbing skills continue to improve; she can climb into and sit on chairs. She should be able to crawl downstairs backward safely, though you still need to watch her in case she rushes and tumbles. If she isn't walking at all yet, it's a good idea to consult her pediatrician.

As she grows more independent, she can entertain herself for long stretches of time. But her attention span is still short, and she rarely sticks to one activity for more than a few minutes.

She is starting to have strong feelings. You can help by giving her names for her feelings so she can understand and cope with them. For example, you might say, "It's a little scary visiting a house where there are lots of people you don't know, but you will feel better soon, and I am always here for you." She's angry if she doesn't get her way; when she does get upset, try to stay calm and either distract her or remove her from the situation.

Consistent rules are important. Help your toddler understand that some places are out of bounds and that some possessions must be treated carefully.

Your toddler's expanding vocabulary makes it easier for her to tell you what she wants. She still uses sounds and gestures, pointing to desired objects and repeating what you say. She may vocalize to herself when playing and may start singing, too. She understands many more words than she can say and may carry out simple tasks, such as, "Please put the teddy bear down." Each child is unique and reaches these milestones in her own time. However, if your toddler isn't saying more than five words by now, you should check in with your pediatrician.

She's much more accurate when stacking and sorting toys, fitting shapes through holes and puzzle pieces into their slots, and using blocks for building, although she frequently fumbles and drops whatever she handles. She should be able to build a tower of three blocks and use a pencil to scribble back and forth and make dots. She also is beginning to enjoy pretend games and imaginative play. She likes to push toys, sometimes using one toy to push another. You'll notice that your toddler is developing a hand preference. She demonstrates her improved dexterity in taking off gloves and socks and unzipping things.

Your toddler seems to learn something new every day—the pace of language development is particularly rapid. He can name common objects pictured in books and probably shows sustained interest when you read to him. He has a good idea of what belongs to him and where common household objects "live"—this is a good time to encourage him to help with simple chores. He likes to help and will appreciate being recognized for doing a job well. Let him sort laundry with you, dust shelves with a sock on his hand, put away groceries, pick up toys, or feed the family pet.

He enjoys taking a toy, usually a cuddly animal, on expeditions and has a firm favorite. He may start to take a security blanket, too.

Outdoor play is more complex, thanks to his strengthening manipulative and locomotive skills. Get him outside every day if you can, even in the rain, so he stays fit and healthy. Not only will it help keep his boundless energy in check, but he'll also develop balance and coordination and understanding of distance, height, and space by running, jumping, climbing, and swinging.

He also enjoys pretend play, though not with other children quite yet. He mostly plays on his own, though sometimes he'll grab toys from other children. When he does, gently return the swiped object or help the children to share. This is a good time to start talking about sharing, which isn't an easily learned concept.

He can use a stick to reach other toys and is developing an understanding of tools. He probably can stand on one foot while holding on to something for support, kick a ball, throw a ball overhand, and run without falling (sometimes).

He can help dress and undress himself, and makes a good effort to wash his face and hands. He can feed himself with a little less mess and is learning to brush his own teeth, with help. He might let you know if he has a soiled diaper, or he might become uncooperative during diaper changes. Some toddlers get interested in potty training about this age. If he is ready and interested (see page 219), give it a try; if he resists or shows no interest, don't press it.

You might be dealing with more testy behavior, particularly in a more determined child. There may be tantrums, screaming, shouts of "No, I won't," and sometimes running away. This may test your patience, but remember that a positive approach is most effective (see page 294).

Settling to sleep at night might be more difficult. A consistent bedtime routine helps, with a period of winding-down time each night.

Most toddlers have at least 20 words by this point, although the exact number can vary greatly from child to child. She may be starting to put words together into short sentences. She loves to name things and may ask for toys and food. She can follow more complicated instructions when she's in the mood and can name the parts of her body. She enjoys being asked questions and is starting to learn about being polite. You're her role model, so be sure to set a good example. Her sense of humor is becoming more apparent.

Your toddler probably enjoys music, and you can expose her to all different kinds. If you play a musical instrument, let her look at it and investigate how it works, and play her a simple tune. She might sing along! She can certainly dance, and you can teach her about rhythm using two spoons, a drum, a keyboard, or your voice and hands.

She's developing a much better understanding of what things are for, from dishwashers to cell phones, and may want to get involved if she sees you at the computer. She is also better at problem solving and

may be able to fit puzzle pieces more accurately or attempt more difficult puzzles.

Reading books is a great pleasure for both of you; she can turn the pages and join in with retelling a familiar story. She has favorites and may want to read the same one every night. She may pull you along to show you something interesting. When she encounters something new, help her understand it with a simple explanation.

She may enjoy dressing up, which is a fun way to spend an afternoon. She can start to use clay, face paints, and generally anything that makes a mess. She's more sociable, although she still plays alongside but not with other children—this is called parallel play.

Your toddler is getting more helpful at getting herself dressed each day. It takes a little longer to have her help, but it's good practice for her. Everything she learns to do herself is a step toward greater independence—and it will make your job easier in the long run. She'll feel very proud when she's done it herself.

She might have some awareness of concepts such as time—she may be able to wait quietly for something for a few minutes, for example. She also might be starting to understand concepts such as up, down, big, and small.

She may have a good grasp on what belongs to her and other people, though she is chiefly concerned with what belongs to her. She might put this knowledge to use by being helpful sometimes, and can put away her toys when asked.

At meals, she may be fussy and balk at new foods. Avoid battling over food—she's sure to win. Your job is to provide healthy food; her job is to decide what and how much to eat. Relax and don't worry. Keep introducing new foods, along with some familiar ones, and praise her for trying even one bite. She'll start eating other things soon enough, particularly if she attends child care or participates in a playgroup where she might want to copy other children.

Your toddler is turning into a big kid! She's reaching big milestones in language, social development, physical strength, and personality. Her language should be easier to understand, and she enjoys using it. Get ready for some chattering! She refers to herself by name and is beginning to say "please" and "thank you," although she still needs your good example and may need reminders. She understands some complex sentences and requests, and she likes to answer questions. Her vocabulary is extensive, and she probably uses many two-word and even perhaps three-word sentences. She can point to and name familiar objects.

Your toddler has mastered some new skills, such as climbing on and off furniture, running, and throwing a ball (though she can't yet catch one), and she keeps very busy trying out these new feats. She can climb up and down the stairs with two feet on each step. She may be able to walk backward and can jump with both feet off the ground. She may dance to familiar music.

By this point, you may notice certain characteristics emerging, such as a dislike of loud noises, or new fears. These usually don't last long. Offer reassurance and understanding, and try not to pressure her.

She can sit in a chair on her own and look at picture books for a short period—she still loves to have you read to her, too. She likes to open boxes to discover what's inside and recognizes her own image in a photograph.

Your toddler does not want to share yet. Keep explaining cooperation to her and setting a good example. It's very important for toddlers to learn that they're not the only ones with needs and that others have needs too, but this lesson requires time, patience, and repetition.

Your toddler may hit or bite other children. When she does, remove her from the situation with a calm but firm "no" and tell her it is not okay to hit or bite. If she does it again, then this would justify going home or the use of a time-out (see page 300).

She can likely build a tower at least four blocks high and construct other shapes, such as a bridge or steps, and enjoys scribbling and drawing circles. Provide plenty of paper and nontoxic crayons for her masterpieces.

When she grows frustrated, try to respond with understanding and compassion. Help her do things on her own whenever it's appropriate.

She is most likely aware when her bladder is full and she needs to urinate; she also may know when she needs to pass a bowel movement. If so, she may be ready for toilet training (see page 219). Again, this isn't something to push; she needs to go at her own pace. Girls are likely to reach this milestone sooner than boys.

Physically, your toddler is getting stronger and is proud of what he can do by himself. Some children now can jump with both feet off the ground, balance on one foot (although not for very long), walk backward, and run fast. Most toddlers can stop to pick things up as they walk, push a cart, pull a toy, or maneuver a ride-on toy.

Your toddler's language is becoming exciting and more vivid. He's using more complex words (such as "under" and "on top") to describe where things are and their properties ("round" or "hard"), and he uses sentences more effectively. He can sing some words of songs and enjoys participating in group musical events. He may talk to himself a lot!

Your toddler is getting better at drawing and may be able to draw straight lines and more complex shapes, such as circles. He probably enjoys painting and making pictures with finger paint, which help develop both his tactile awareness and motor skills.

He has figured out how to screw and unscrew lids and turn handles and knobs, which means you need to be careful about safety risks. But he also knows how to unwrap presents, which provides opportunities for fun. Wrap up pretend presents for him to rip open. Familiar toys feel like new discoveries when they're packaged in crinkly paper.

Your toddler wants to investigate more and more: "What's in here? What's that? What is this button for?" The more he can understand, the more he wants to learn. You can never explain too much; just be sure to use simple terms. Soon he'll be able to tell the difference between 1 and 2, but he probably can't count any higher yet.

At this age, both boys and girls often like to play house with dolls, particularly feeding and getting the dolls ready for bed, and they may engage in other caregiving activities.

Socially, he's probably more ready to be separated from you. This depends, however, on his confidence and feeling of security, which are related partly to his temperament and partly to the opportunities he has been given in the past. Don't push him to separate—this will upset him. Gently and gradually build up his confidence. When you correct his behavior, don't put him down or criticize him. Keep your explanations simple and concrete. Be sure to comment when he's being well behaved.

Many children this age still suck their thumbs. Babies around the world turn to their thumbs for comfort and security. It usually isn't a problem at this age, though later on it could affect his developing teeth. There are ways to gently discourage thumb-sucking, such as offering a favorite toy, stuffed animal, or blanket as a substitute, or making him sock puppets to wear, but it isn't a big issue at this age.

Learning about emotions is as important as learning about numbers, and it's good for your toddler to recognize when she feels angry or anxious. Help her put this into words. When she gets angry, point this out and help her cope with the emotion. Your getting angry too will only increase the tension.

Her language continues to expand. She enjoys reading games: Ask her to finish a word or sentence, or change it to something else as a joke. You can also mix up song lyrics for a laugh. Her memory is very good—she's learning numbers and may begin to count. She's also getting better at sorting objects by shape, size, and perhaps color. Ask her to name the colors of things you see: balls, cats, cars, or flowers, for example. She knows the difference between big and little, and probably between high and low.

Physically, she's stronger and enjoys active games; this is a good time to start working on ball skills such as throwing, catching, and kicking. Learning about coordination takes time and considerable practice. She might be ready to ride a small bike with training wheels.

Battles are inevitable, but try to avoid having them over food. Remember, it's your job to provide the food and her job to choose what and how much to eat. Candy and sweets become a temptation at this age, however. Making them a forbidden food will increase her fascination with them, so offer them as occasional treats and serve up healthier options, such as frozen juice or yogurt.

Your toddler enjoys outings, but probably wants to bring along some favorite toys. Before bringing her into a new situation, prepare her by explaining what will happen and who she will meet; some children are more wary than others, and this will help to make her comfortable. She may begin to play with some children rather than alongside them.

At 2½ years old, your child is well into toddlerhood, and potentially the tantrums, rages, and defiance that can go with it. Your child wants to test limits— and needs to as he learns about the world and strives to become more independent. Clear, consistent rules will help teach your child how to behave and help him feel more secure.

Daily routines will make life easier and can help avoid emotional traumas. Aim to serve meals at the same time each day. Eat together as a family whenever possible. Your child appreciates this social time and learns how to behave at meals by watching you. He can be a real helper, lending a hand with simple household chores, such as putting dirty clothes into the laundry basket. If you have a young baby at home, he might be able to help with his younger sibling.

More and more, your child enjoys using words and language, and he has prolonged conversations

using more complex words. He probably knows some nursery rhymes.

He likes to learn the different meanings of words and frequently asks, "Why?"—so you need to be prepared to give simple explanations for all sorts of complex questions, from the difference between dogs and cats to why cars don't go on the sidewalk. It's important to give a good explanation, even if it needs to be repeated the next day. This requires patience, which can be in short supply in a busy household, but you'll be rewarded when your toddler uses the information months later.

Your toddler is increasingly adept with his hands. He can hold a pencil in his preferred hand and use it to copy a circle as well as horizontal and vertical lines. He probably draws more neatly, and you can make a game out of tracing around familiar objects and shapes, such as jigsaw puzzle pieces, hands and feet, and stars and circles. He likes to operate switches and press buttons, and he has a lot of fun with flashlights and battery-operated toys. At the beach or in the sandbox, he has an easier time filling a bucket with sand.

Your child's coordination is also improving. He probably can climb on simple play equipment with confidence, walk on tiptoe, and jump with both feet. He has a better understanding of time, though he might not wait patiently when told, "It will be only 10 more minutes."

If your toddler is starting preschool soon, you'll need to help him get ready for it. For example, he will need to gain confidence in being apart from you for short periods. Before he starts school, visit the facility together. Try to get to know the teachers and begin learning about routines at school.

Your child is likely developing richer and more secure relationships with people outside her immediate family, such as grandparents, uncles, aunts, and close family friends. Their children or her cousins may be her first close playmates.

She's increasingly interested in other children and can interact more with them, addressing them with requests and orders, particularly concerning her toys. Even if she tends to be bossy, she may be starting to share; be sure to nurture this valuable trait. If she attends day care or preschool, she's getting a lot of practice with socially helpful skills, such as taking turns and sharing. She can tell the difference between boys and girls.

Physically, your child is getting more coordinated when climbing and running. She walks upstairs taking turns with her feet, climbs well on play structures, balances on one foot for a significant time, and kicks a ball with reasonable accuracy.

Your child is learning up to 50 new words a month now! She can talk in longer sentences and still enjoys the sounds of words, particularly those that sound funny or rhyme. She can describe things she's done and is beginning to use the word "I" in reference to herself. She's more specific when answering questions and can be clear, but sometimes the words come out wrong.

She's getting better at dressing herself and may be starting to undo buttons and snaps. Encourage this new independence; self-care is an important developmental skill. If she has favorite clothes, she may have a tantrum if she isn't allowed to wear them. Unless inappropriate for the weather or activity, as much as possible, let her choose her clothes or give her limited choices: "The red or the blue shirt?"

She may enjoy constructional play using blocks and should be able to play meaningfully with toy

cars and dollhouse furnishings. Trial and error is an important way for her to learn. Let her try playing with toys belonging to an older child (provided they're safe). She likes to "read" books that relate to familiar activities, such as going to the store, eating meals, and playing with toys.

Your toddler is starting to distinguish colors; she can match colors but may not be able to name them. She's interested in drawing and painting, and loves crayons and paint. She may be able to draw more accurately and may draw part of a figure.

She may be able to control her bowels and bladder during the day and perhaps at night, but don't push this too fast! The more you pressure her, the more determined she might become to do the opposite.

Your child may be watching some TV shows or movies. Don't let her spend too much time sitting in front of a screen (the AAP recommends no more than 1 to 2 hours of television per day for children over age 2), and make sure what she's watching is appropriate for her age and of good quality.

Now that your child is almost three, she is really becoming a little person who can have a conversation, understand an explanation, and help you out. She still can be difficult, oppositional, and resentful of being told what to do. Remember this is all part of her learning to be more independent, on the one hand, and more compliant with rules and expectations, on the other. Left on her own, she still is very likely to do something unsafe. But much of her development depends on the example you set for her, and the discussions you have will help her become a more polite, helpful, and considerate child and playmate.

She enjoys playing with friends, and this is the chance to help her with sharing. Talk with her about taking turns; when you supervise playtime, make sure turns are handled fairly. Explain about saying "please" and "thank you"—and make sure you do the same.

Point out why some things are necessary (putting toys away after playing with them, for example) and why some things mustn't be done (such as hitting other children). But explain it simply and briefly. Using an angry voice or lecturing makes it less likely she'll listen.

Children of this age prefer consistency in their activities and schedules—dressing the same way each day and reading books without any changes—though this will ease up over the next few months. Some girls and boys this age can be aggressive; many are easily frustrated, and they use the word "no" constantly. Your child isn't able to modulate her behavior easily, but you can help her understand what she's feeling. Note when she plays nicely and be consistent when you correct her for undesirable behavior, and ask other adults who care for her to do the same. She'll learn. At this age, children have

varying abilities to control their emotions; some are calmer, but others still struggle. Some children are extremely confident; others are insecure.

Your child now refines her motion by adjusting her speed, dodging obstacles, turning corners, and making sudden stops. She's more effective at using her hands to put puzzle pieces together correctly.

Your child takes great pride in being independent and wants to do more and more by herself. You can encourage her by offering her simple and easy jobs. She can help you around the house—for example, putting dirty clothes in the laundry basket. In the kitchen, you can have her stir ingredients, bring the cereal box to the table, or put clean spoons away.

She always wants to know, "Why?" This can be wearing, but it's important always to give a reason—this is how children learn. She likely talks in full sentences. Most adults probably can understand what she says and what she means. Some children stammer or mix up words; if she does this, try not to draw attention to her mistake but use the correct words yourself. For example, if she mixes up pronouns and refers to another girl as "he," answer her by rephrasing what she said but substituting "she."

Your child loves playing games, and there are plenty that can revolve around familiar things in your home. A simple box of dress-up clothes offers endless opportunities for pretend play.

This is a good time to introduce books with more complex stories—let her choose books that you can read together. Reading together regularly will boost her language skills, and if you can, make up stories to feed her imagination.

She's getting better at eating neatly and is still likely to have strong food preferences, not eating what she doesn't like. Eating together as a family is good for bonding, as well as developing her language and social skills.

From this point on, your child will spend more and more of his time away from you. As parents you will still be the most important people in his life, but he'll take enormous pleasure in new experiences and spending time with other people.

As he spends more time away from you, he needs to learn about potential dangers and staying safe. He's beginning to understand and recognize danger but isn't safe on his own yet; even if he knows something is potentially dangerous, he may forget or be unable to control his curiosity. He's old enough that you can start helping him understand whom to trust and whom to be wary of. Remember that he'll learn best if you compliment his behavior when he does what you expect and want him to do; when he doesn't, explain to him why it was wrong and what he can do instead.

It's a good time to think about how you expect him to behave socially. Rules that are laid down now and enforced consistently should be readily accepted. Help your child learn to talk about his feelings by teaching him words he can use to describe them.

He enjoys playing in a group and pretending, which can lead to endless fun with friends. Mechanical and building toys are popular at this age. Plenty of time playing outside and climbing on play structures will help your child be physically agile.

He can participate in family activities much more now; he may be able to play simple, age-appropriate board games and can share in hobbies, such as gardening. He enjoys joining you for a bike ride and swimming, and may be ready to go see a movie.

He now boasts improved self-help skills; he should be adept with his fork and able to dress and undress himself (except tying his shoes, and perhaps successfully handling buttons), wash and dry his hands, eat neatly (most of the time), and possibly use the toilet and wipe his bottom. (Toilet training happens at a range of ages. See page 219 for more information about readiness.) He can be helpful at home by putting away his toys and clothes and helping to set the table. He may be able to pour out his cereal. Make chores fun and acknowledge him when he does well. If helping becomes routine now, he'll be less resistant about pitching in when he's older.

His understanding and speech are now very good; he uses longer sentences and complex prepositions such as "inside," "on top of," and "inside out." You can have a conversation. He knows his name and can repeat it; you may want to teach him his address or your telephone number. He has some understanding of time concepts, such as yesterday and times of day, and he can learn some numbers. He knows the difference between large and small and singular and plural, and he can identify colors and match shapes.

APPROACHES TO PARENTHOOD

On being a parent

New parents learn quickly that each baby is a unique individual and that what's considered "best" for some children might not suit their baby—or them. Trends in parenting come and go. When you were young, for example, you may have been encouraged to listen attentively, to follow strict guidelines, and to value school achievements above all else. Today, children in the United States are often encouraged to be independent thinkers, to make decisions for themselves, and to develop their potential in nonacademic areas, such as music, art, and drama.

You'll make parenting choices every single day. You'll need to decide how to manage your baby's daily care, your toddler's tantrums, your preschooler's progress, and your growing child's friendships. You can't sit on the fence: A child needs a positive, confident parent who sets clear limits.

Many factors influence your parenting. What you read in books and magazines, what you watch on television, and what you see among your friends and family all affect your approach. More important, your personality, your baby's personality, and the way the two of you interact will guide your parenting. Once you're a parent, it's good to reassess

THE CHILD-ORIENTED PARENT

Philosophy You believe the best way to raise your baby is by responding to her emotional and physical needs as they emerge. When she cries, you immediately comfort her. If she's hungry, you immediately feed her. If she's bored, you quickly try to entertain her. With this approach, your baby drives your actions. By the time your child is 3 or 4 years old, life will have evened out, and she'll have learned to fit in with family routines and to recognize that other people have needs, too.

Impact On the positive side, your baby might never have to wait; her needs are satisfied instantly. She might never feel alone, isolated, or ignored. On the negative side, she may miss out on opportunities to develop resilience and coping skills of her own.

THE SCHEDULE-BASED PARENT

Philosophy You believe that routines are very important for children and that it's vital to stick to a set schedule as much as possible. You encourage activities, such as feeding and sleeping, at predetermined times.

Impact Most older babies thrive on a schedule, especially when it comes to naps and bedtimes (see pages 161–163 for more about sleep routines). However, newborns need to eat when they're hungry, and babies don't tend to organize their sleep patterns until around 3 months. On the positive side, with multiple children a schedule can help you slot time to meet each child's needs. However, you'll have to adapt your routine as your baby's physical needs evolve—when he needs more food and sleep during growing phases, for instance. On the negative side, your baby may resist the imposition of a fixed schedule if it doesn't meet his physical and emotional needs.

your beliefs. You may want to replicate your own happy upbringing, or you may reject your parents' approach and decide to go in a new direction. As you get to know your baby better, you'll intuitively make changes to match your baby's needs. Your parenting skills will develop and improve over time, matching your baby's development.

Parenting styles

There are as many styles and approaches to parenting as there are parents! Parenting is an ongoing, evolving process, but it's good to be thoughtful about what kind of parent you want to be. One system for classifying parenting styles looks at how parents respond to their children's needs and desires, and the extent to which they encourage their children to adapt to family schedules. Looked at this way, parenting styles may be described as child-oriented, schedule-based, or flexible (see boxes).

Most professionals encourage a flexible parenting style (see sidebar on page 143 for details on how to put this into practice). But there is no one-size-fits-all approach, and you may find that another style better suits your family. A flexible approach, of course, allows you to use what appeals to you in child-oriented and schedule-based approaches and to adapt it so it works for your family.

Regardless of which style suits you best, remember that children thrive best in loving environments with clear guidelines for behavior. Your love and the structure you build for your child's behavior are the basic ingredients that will lead you to succeed as parents and will allow your child to become the best person he can be.

Working as a team

In a two-parent family, it's important that both parents agree on one approach. You and your partner don't need to be carbon copies of one another; on the contrary, your child benefits from your individual natures and personalities. But broad consensus on primary parenting concerns—such as behavior, relationships, and routine—is essential.

For example, in families considering attachment parenting, an intensive, child-centered approach (see page 141), it's essential that both parents are fully committed to the philosophy and practice. It requires a great commitment, involving nearly constant physical contact with your baby, and cannot succeed if one parent is skeptical or reluctant.

This is true of all approaches to parenting: Parenting requires a major commitment from both partners. When both parents work together and compromise, your child will benefit from the consistency, and your relationship with your partner will strengthen. Unfortunately, when there is no agreement on what rules to follow and how to enforce them, your child will become confused and will not know how to behave, and you and your partner may face more tension in your relationship.

THE FLEXIBLE PARENT

Philosophy You believe each child is an individual with her own particular blend of characteristics. You observe your child's needs, such as general sleeping patterns and playful periods, and establish routines around them, yet you're willing to adapt them as your baby's needs evolve. Your parenting style has a consistent theme, but you adapt your techniques as circumstances and your child change. You take the strengths of the other two styles and blend them.

Impact On the positive side, you allow yourself flexibility depending on your child's age and stage of development; the needs of both child and parents are deemed important. However, on the negative side, a growing baby can get confused if you're inconsistent in similar circumstances.

The effect of temperament

Your baby began showing his temperament the moment he was born. He may have sucked well and enthusiastically during his first feeding or sucked slowly and seemed passive. Perhaps he wriggled about when you first held him or snuggled close to you. At birth, his responses to different situations reflected his temperament: This innate temperament is the foundation for his life-long personality.

Temperament profiles

Numerous individual traits go into making a child's temperament. With such a wide range of ways each trait can vary, no two children have exactly the same temperament. Yet psychologists have been able to identify clusters of characteristics that allow them to classify children into three basic temperament profiles. You may find, however, that your baby can't be neatly categorized because he shares features from more than one type—about 1 in 4 babies are hard to classify before they're a year old.

The main temperament profiles are:
- *Easy* The easygoing baby is a pleasure to be with because he's very even-tempered and typically responds positively to anything that happens around him. He welcomes and readily adapts to new experiences. His mood and behavior are regular and predictable.
- *Difficult* The hard-to-manage infant is very active most of the time but is easily irritated and unsettled, his moods vary dramatically, and his behavior doesn't follow a predictable pattern. He doesn't like change and takes a long time to adapt to new situations or unfamiliar faces.
- *Slow to warm up* The slow-to-warm-up child reacts mildly to most things. He approaches life cautiously. He is unenthusiastic about new experiences but doesn't have strong negative reactions—if he doesn't like a new toy, he'll turn his head away rather than push the toy away.

Personal characteristics can emerge and develop throughout childhood, but your child's personality was roughly formed at the time of birth and will be largely settled by the time the preschool years are over. A significant challenge for you as a parent is to help your child use his temperament in positive ways, even when some aspects of his personality appear to be undesirable. Take, for example, his strong determination to get what he wants. This trait can cause problems when your child challenges you, but it can be an asset when he has a goal he wishes to reach or a skill he would like to master.

A child who has an easy profile is certainly less work, and there will likely be fewer daily struggles; but there is no temperament that is better or worse than the rest. The profiles are just different.

What if your child has a difficult profile? You will still love your child, and you will still want to guide him to be happy and well behaved. But the techniques you will use to accomplish this may not be the same as those used by the parents of a child with a different temperamental profile.

Let's say your son has a difficult profile. One day in the park, you see another mom effortlessly get her child to do whatever is asked; meanwhile, you are struggling with yours at every turn. You may be tempted to view the other mother as a skilled parent and judge yourself poorly. But before you think less of yourself and worry about what you're doing wrong, realize that if the other mother's child had your child's temperament, and your child was the easy one, most likely the other mother would be the one questioning her parenting skills.

Sources of temperament

Exactly what goes into creating a child's individual temperament is a mystery. Studies comparing the temperaments of identical twins with those of nonidentical, fraternal twins have found that there is more similarity in temperament among identical than nonidentical twins, especially during the first year of life. This strongly suggests a genetic component is at play—that your baby inherits part of his temperament profile from his parents.

Environment also plays an important part. The more parents smile and show affection to their baby, the more likely he is to be socially responsive and happy. Home environment clearly matters and can shape a baby's behavior, steering him in a particular direction but not changing his basic nature.

Even if your baby fits one of these temperament profiles, his personality is unique. It doesn't matter whether his traits are inherited or environmental— what matters is that you respond to him positively, in a way you're comfortable with. So if you're a loving, affectionate person with a relaxed manner, then stick to that approach even if your baby is fretful and hard to manage.

A lot depends on the way you manage your baby's temperament profile. If your baby dislikes change, for example, you may be tempted to be very cautious and avoid new experiences. While placing him in uncomfortable situations should generally be avoided, you will still want to improve his adaptability by rewarding behavior that is more desirable, when it occurs, and supporting him when he is challenged with change. You may find that with time he gradually becomes less moody and more accustomed to change.

As a parent, you can't change your child's basic temperament; you can, however, do your best to bring out his strengths and try to improve on areas of weakness.

Matching style to temperament

Before your child was born, you already had ideas about parenting. Maybe you were certain that the best way to bring up a baby is to have firm limits so that he quickly learns what he can and cannot do, or maybe you thought that if you were reasonable your child would do whatever you requested. Whatever you expected before your baby was born, the challenge now is to see how your ideas fit with the very real hands-on job you're facing.

Evidence suggests that no matter what parenting approach you take, it will be most effective if it takes into account the individual emotional needs of the child. You and your child, in effect, work together.

If your child has a quiet and withdrawn temperament, insisting that he try to be the life of the party is setting him up for failure. But gently introducing him to a range of social experiences will help build his social confidence. You cannot squash the determination of a curious toddler—nor should you—but you can channel his curiosity in a positive direction, for example, by encouraging him to complete a difficult task that he's already started.

It's important to adjust your expectations for your child's behavior with his temperament in mind. If he is easygoing, be firm and expect him to follow the rules you propose. On the other hand, if he is stubborn and strong-willed, be prepared to give in more to his desires and allow him greater latitudes in his actions. (See Chapter 11 for more on matching your expectations to your child's temperament.) Adapting your parenting strategies to take into account your child's temperament encourages him, in turn, to adapt his personality to meet your expectations—and that is usually a recipe for a successful, happy family life.

MAIN COMPONENTS OF TEMPERAMENT

Activity level Some babies are quick, energetic, and vigorously active; others are more relaxed and content to move at a slow, steady pace.

Irritability Some babies are easily upset, while others aren't rattled by everyday experiences.

Soothability When babies are upset, some are easier to calm down and soothe.

Fearfulness Stimulation can excite one baby and scare another. Some babies are more easily frightened than others.

Sociability Some babies smile and coo when someone approaches; others may become anxious and cry.

Parenting as partners

You and your partner inevitably will disagree at times on what parenting style to employ. When this happens, try to resolve the disagreement privately, when your child isn't listening. Presenting a united front lets your child see that you both support each other. This boosts her confidence in you as parents, and her sense of emotional security. Raising a child is not an exact science! Every parent has an opinion about the best way to manage bedtime routines, discipline, feeding, tantrums, and so on. And that's fine. After all, there's usually more than one way to do anything, and it's perfectly normal for parents to have minor disagreements about parenting.

But major problems can arise when you have a serious difference of opinion about how to raise your child. A sustained disagreement between you and your partner can have significant consequences for the entire family. These problems include:

- *Inconsistency* Your growing child needs a consistent structure at home, a predictable set of rules that she is expected to follow. If you tell her one thing and your partner tells her another, there is no consistency. At first, this will confuse your child; as time goes on, it will make her feel anxious and insecure.
- *Tension* Serious disagreements—whatever their nature—affect the atmosphere at home. You feel tense, your partner feels tense, and before you know it, your baby feels tense, too. In a strained environment like this, tempers become frayed. Soon everyone in the house is irritable and bickering.
- *Manipulation* Over time, children learn to exploit differences of opinion. When your child doesn't get what she wants from you, she'll go to your partner, hoping for a different answer. Your child is naturally only interested in achieving her goal, and she'll approach the parent most likely to give in to her.
- *Resentment* No one likes to feel as if her views are being ignored. If either partner isn't feeling

valued, resentment will soon set in, and your self-confidence as a parent will drop rapidly. If the situation persists, these negative emotions will intensify and can have negative consequences for your relationship with your partner.

Working together

For the sake of everyone's happiness, talk frequently about your individual approaches to parenting. Try not to fight about differing child-rearing beliefs in front of your child. She doesn't want to see you squabble and will be upset by it.

You may dislike what your partner has to say, but you're each entitled to have an opportunity to share your opinions. Your partner holds views just as strongly as you do and may be just as resistant to alternative suggestions. That's why you need to

express your ideas to each other. When each of you has your say, it helps reduce tension and avoid a confrontation. Set aside some time specifically to discuss matters on which you may disagree. Once you've each had a turn to say what you think, and you've considered each other's comments, talk about why each of you might feel the way you do. Reflecting on your childhoods and the ways you each were brought up will often help you understand each other's perspective.

Together, consider the strengths and weaknesses of your alternatives. Be honest with each other; don't reject your partner's ideas just because you didn't think of them first yourself. Be prepared to accept that your way might not be the only way or the right way. Talk through the pros and cons of each approach and try to resolve the conflict without unnecessary confrontation.

Once you've agreed on a strategy, make a commitment to carry it out, consistently, for a certain period of time—perhaps 2 weeks. Then evaluate how successful it is. If the strategy is working, you can both be pleased with yourselves. If it isn't working, then make a commitment to try the alternative you discussed. It's okay to work some things out through trial and error.

Single parenthood

As a single parent, you're running the show: On a day-to-day basis, you won't have routine disagreements to sort out. Of course, you may have friends and relatives who offer different opinions, but by and large it's you who calls the shots. But as the sole decisionmaker, you need to be confident in your judgment as a parent—and that isn't always easy. You're bound to doubt yourself at times. Try to go easy on yourself—read the Dos and Don'ts in the boxes on page 145 and keep them in mind.

When you have a hard time deciding which strategy to follow, consider the pros and cons of your alternatives, seek advice from people whose opinions you value, and try one strategy for a period of time. It's okay if it doesn't work—revisit your alternatives, choose another strategy, and give it a try. There's rarely only one right answer.

ATTACHMENT PARENTING

Attachment parenting is an intensive child-centered approach. In it, parents focus on forging a very close bond with their child by being as physically—one parent is constantly with him to promptly meet his every need—and emotionally connected as possible. The idea is that you're building a harmonious, mutually responsive relationship and helping to instill trust and confidence.

Babies raised this way aren't expected to remain dependent on their parents forever. On the contrary, proponents say that these babies develop healthy independence because they trust their parents will keep them safe, and they feel confident exploring their world.

William Sears, MD, who developed the term, lays out seven principles: bonding at birth, breastfeeding, baby-wearing (or having your baby in your arms as much as possible), co-sleeping in a family bed (the American Academy of Pediatrics believes co-sleeping may be dangerous and advises against it), responding to a baby's cries, avoiding attempts to "train" your baby, and striving for balance.

Whether attachment parenting is the best way for a baby to become attached to a caregiver is open for discussion.

There are a number of child psychologists and child-care experts who disagree with this method. Constantly holding a baby, responding immediately to all his cries, and doing nothing to displease him, they argue, can lead to a child who is demanding and needy.

If you're interested in attachment parenting, consider the points made by both its advocates and critics, and be aware that it requires a considerable commitment from both parents. Attachment parenting can be tremendously satisfying for parents who have patience and interest in making such a commitment.

Practicing your approach

Most parents agree that the three biggest challenges in raising a baby are managing his feeding, sleeping, and crying. (See Chapters 3, 7, 8, and 10 for more detailed information on these topics.) A baby who cries all the time, refuses to sleep even when exhausted, and constantly demands food can quickly fatigue even the most energetic parent.

Bear in mind, however, that no matter what style of parenting you adopt, your baby's feeding and sleeping patterns will change rapidly, especially during the first few months. For the first 6 to 8 weeks, your baby must be fed every few hours; by the time he's 6 months old, his feeding needs begin to resemble those of an older child. A newborn needs to sleep as much as 80 percent of the day and probably has seven or eight naps in a 24-hour cycle; by the time he's a year old, his total sleeping time probably will drop to about 13 hours a day.

Adjusting your responses

How you respond to your baby depends on your personal preference and natural style. Most parents tend to use a mixture of schedule-based and flexible approaches. It's a question of balance.

Take crying as an example. Unless your baby is a newborn, there's usually no need to rush to him the moment he cries, nor is it a good idea to ignore him altogether. A reasonable approach is to judge the situation (you'll learn what different cries mean) and avoid setting hard-and-fast rules about picking him up or leaving him. Sometimes your baby needs a clean diaper or cuddles, and other times he may be just fussing and can manage without you by his side the moment he whimpers. Consider varying your response, depending on the circumstances. The same approach applies to feeding and sleeping.

Possible problems

Whatever your parenting approach, things won't always run smoothly. Here are some common problems and some strategies for dealing with them.

You are feeding your baby on demand but are becoming worn out by frequent feedings.
One of the challenges of on-demand feeding—especially if you are breastfeeding—is determining when one feeding is actually over and the next one begins. This is particularly important when a baby is a slow feeder. If it seems you are feeding constantly, you will soon become exhausted. To avoid this, try doing the following:

- *Introduce some structure.* You don't have to switch to a rigid schedule, but you can aim for approximate feeding times. Even if you start within a half hour of your planned start time, you'll most likely notice a difference.
- *When the feeding is over, stop.* Decide how you'll judge when a feeding is over—for example, when your baby stops sucking for more than a minute. When you see that sign, it's time to end the feeding. If you're breastfeeding, break the seal by inserting your little finger gently at the corner of your baby's mouth.
- *Get some rest.* If possible, ask your partner (or a good friend) to give your baby a feeding—use expressed breast milk if you're breastfeeding. You might even want to designate one particular time—for example, at night—and do this regularly. Once you feel a bit less tired, you'll be able to think more clearly.

You are attempting to follow advice to let your baby "cry it out" and not liking how you feel.
The decision to let your baby "cry it out" for any reason—for example, with certain sleep-training methods—is a personal one. Advocates for and against such methods abound. (For more on crying, see Chapter 8, "Crying and responding.") How you respond to your baby's crying is a personal choice—do not follow parenting advice that makes you feel uncomfortable. Simply put, if you feel the best response at the moment is to pick him up, do so. Yet you don't always need to pick up your baby to

quiet him. You could leave him in his crib and pat his back, stroke his face, sing softly to him, talk in a calming tone, or offer a pacifier.

Your baby has an erratic sleep schedule.
Your baby's need for sleep changes as he grows (see page 155). You might be trying to maintain a schedule that no longer works for him. Another possibility is that you're giving up too quickly and not sticking with one schedule for long enough. Try the following:

◆ *Keep a sleep diary.* Try to note the times your baby sleeps during a 7-day period to give you an idea of his natural sleep rhythms. Then try to impose some structure around this basic pattern.

◆ *Be adaptable.* If you see that he's outgrown the schedule that used to suit him, then change it. Remember that your baby needs less sleep as he grows older, and the gaps between each period of sleep become longer.

◆ *Don't give up too quickly.* With every schedule-led approach, there will be times when a baby doesn't seem to fit in. But that doesn't mean you should give up. If you stick with it for a few more days, he'll probably sleep more predictably.

Early constant cuddling results in a child who cries unless he is held all the time.
You cannot spoil a newborn by holding him too much. As your baby gets older, though, he's alert enough to learn the connection between his tears and physical comfort. You've taught him inadvertently that crying is an effective way to get your attention. He enjoys cuddles and is determined they will continue. Try the following:

◆ *Recognize the source of the problem.* Admit to yourself that it's really you who has to change your behavior, not your baby—he's just doing what comes naturally to him. Make up your mind to change the way you respond to him when he cries.

◆ *Soothe without holding.* If you feel unable to leave your baby alone when he cries, soothe him without taking him in your arms; close, loving,

FLEXIBLE APPROACH

Feed your baby on demand. You have a rough idea of how far apart feedings should be, but you're prepared to be flexible depending on your baby's evolving needs. If she cries between feedings, is unable to settle down, and indicates with mouth movements that she's searching for food, you set aside the schedule and feed her rather than allow her to continue being upset.

Try to fit sleep times to your baby's natural sleep rhythm. You have an idea of how much sleep your baby needs and when she gets tired and is most likely to sleep. You aim to settle her down at these times and have devised good naptime and bedtime routines to support this effort. But you're also willing to adapt the sleep schedule to suit your baby's changing needs.

Pick your baby up when she cries. You think that a baby who cries is unhappy or distressed and needs attention. You go to her and try to figure out what the problem is and solve it, whether it be with a dry diaper or hugs. Whatever the cause of her discomfort, you believe it may intensify if ignored. Your responsiveness helps your baby feel secure.

How this affects your baby She probably feels generally happy and comfortable. Any distress when you set limits is most likely transient and soon resolved; she knows her needs will be met and is learning self-control.

How this affects you Your days (and nights) have some structure and rhythm, but you may still feel you have little control over your baby's schedule. Changes in your baby's natural patterns require adjustment on your part.

physical contact can include stroking his face, patting his back, and holding his hand. Resist the temptation to lift him up.

- *Pick him up when he isn't crying.* Not only do you want to teach him that crying won't always result in a cuddle, you should also teach him that he can get a hug from you without crying. Pick him up for a cuddle when tears aren't flowing down his face.

When success is elusive

Despite your best efforts, there will be times when it seems nothing you are doing succeeds in resolving a difficulty you are having with your baby—and this can be very dispiriting. Before he came along, you probably viewed yourself as competent, caring, and effective, and you may even have had responsibility for managing others. But now you sometimes find yourself stunned by your baby's ability to thwart your every strategy!

And then there is the exhaustion. In his first weeks, your baby's constantly changing sleeping and feeding needs turn night into day and day into night, as you search for the solution that will keep him content and predictable. You may feel you're on an endless chase to find the "right" schedule for him:

Just when you've achieved your goal, he changes yet again. There's no need to panic: This is an inevitable consequence of normal development. Virtually every parent endures the same frustrating experience.

Try not to take it as a failure on your part—instead, try to see it as a learning experience. It isn't all about you. Your baby often cries for reasons that are totally unknown to you (or to anyone else). This doesn't mean that you're doing something wrong or failing as a parent. Part of the solution usually involves adjusting your parenting philosophy and management strategies as your child grows and develops over time.

You will have an easier time getting on the right path if you establish clear, realistic targets. If your baby doesn't feed well, for example, there's no point in trying to limit feedings to 10 minutes—that's simply unrealistic, and you'll be setting yourself up for failure. A more appropriate goal in that situation might be to have a minimum break of 2 hours between each feeding.

If you don't achieve your goals right away, don't give up. It isn't reasonable to expect your baby to change his behavior quickly. Stick with one strategy for at least a couple of weeks before deciding whether to try something else instead.

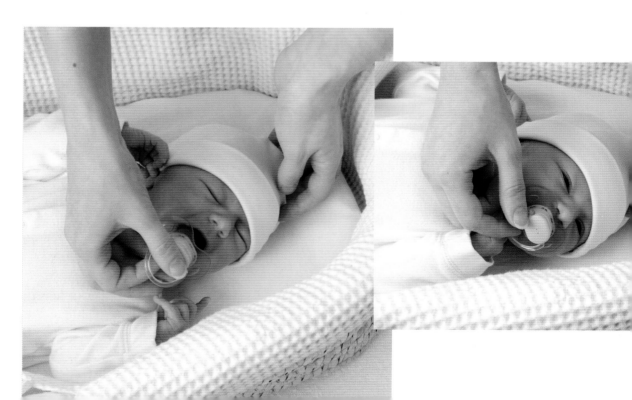

You'll have the most success if you aim for gradual improvement. Your young child won't change overnight, but he makes improvements in small, graduated stages. If you feel your baby cries constantly, for example, set small, attainable goals, such as keeping him calm and settled for 5 minutes without tears, but steadily try to lengthen the amount of time he's able to go without crying.

Staying confident and positive

If you're dealing with a challenging baby, a few setbacks as you try to achieve your goals with him can chip away at your confidence. Many factors can contribute to a feeling that you aren't enjoying being a parent: a demanding, hard-to-console baby; your exhaustion; or the feeling that all the work of parenting is falling on your shoulders. Here are some warning signs that your confidence is crumbling and you are finding little happiness in being a parent:

◆ You have more than passing doubts about the way you manage your baby, and you constantly wonder if there's a better way to handle him.

◆ One day runs into the next, with no perceptible

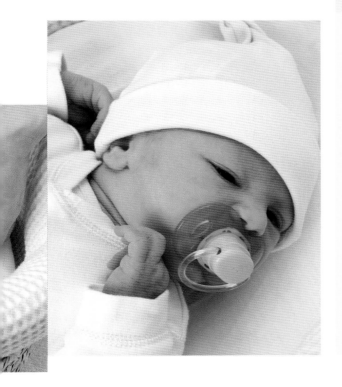

DO

Do carefully consider alternatives. There is no need to rush into things. Consider the implications before choosing a particular strategy to use with your infant.

Do follow through. Once you've made up your mind what to do, stick with it consistently for a few weeks before evaluating whether it's been successful. Your child may be resistant to change, but it could get easier over time.

Do be prepared to admit you've made a mistake. Recognizing that you need to do something differently is a sign of your emotional strength, not emotional weakness. If something isn't working, reevaluate your approach and try a new plan.

DON'T

Don't assume you're wrong. The way you're raising your child may very well be just what she needs. Just because your friends have a different approach doesn't mean they're right and that you're mistaken. Believe in yourself.

Don't always go for the easy option. Raising a child sometimes involves hard decisions, especially when it comes to discipline. Resist the temptation to go for the soft option just because you think it will be easier.

Don't give up and change too quickly. You won't always get the results you hope for right away. Your child takes time to adapt as she grows. Once you've decided on a course of action, don't let yourself give up on it too quickly.

7 tips to restore yourself

1 **Get help, if possible.** Get your partner involved or seek support from family or friends. With recharged emotional batteries, the challenges you face won't seem so formidable.

2 **Be willing to change.** Every so often, step back and have a good look at the way you manage your child. Are these methods appropriate, and have you adapted them as she's grown and developed? Self-questioning can help keep your ideas fresh.

3 **Recognize that others are like you.** No one is perfect. Acknowledging that you're not alone in having self-doubts will help your confidence.

4 **Tell yourself you're doing a good job.** Even if managing your baby is sometimes a struggle, you're probably achieving more than you realize. Don't lose sight of things that are going well.

5 **Look for change, don't place blame.** Search for ways to change your behavior so that your baby changes hers. Don't blame yourself or your baby.

6 **Get back in charge.** A challenging infant can take over your life, leaving you feeling passive. Make clear decisions about how you want to manage your baby and follow through with confidence.

7 **Give your baby lots of cuddles.** No matter your parenting style, give your baby lots of hugs and cuddles. Loving, physical contact helps form an emotional attachment and makes you and your baby feel better about each other.

interval between them. You feel as if each day is the same—dominated by your baby's routine.

- ◆ Time is at a premium, and you never seem to have a moment to yourself. The daily demands of caring for your baby occupy every second that you have available.

- ◆ You constantly ask other people for advice before making a decision about your baby, because you're sure they know better than you.

- ◆ At night, you lie awake worrying about your relationship with your baby. You're especially worried that he may not love you.

If any of this sounds like you, it's time to shift your perspective. Every parent has moments of self-doubt—not only is that normal, it's healthy. But when self-doubt gets the upper hand, you need to turn things around so that you feel you're back in the driver's seat. It's hard to take time to refocus and reenergize when you're burned out and frustrated, but it's worth the effort. For help, check out the tips at left, the flexible parenting practices on page 143, and the Dos and Don'ts on page 145.

Many of the signs that suggest you need to refocus and reenergize can also signal postpartum depression. Try the suggestions at left, but if you don't see significant improvement soon, speak to your doctor and get help right away.

MORE ON PARENTING

There is much more on parenting and shaping your child's behavior in Chapter 11, "Interacting with your growing baby." Feel free to skip there now to learn more on this important subject. The section on Discipline (see pages 289–300) will help you understand why your child behaves as he does. There you will find helpful discussions on topics such as when to be strict, when to give in, and strategies to avoid struggles.

Parenting twins

If you thought one baby would be challenging, you've probably discovered that twins can be twice the usual expense and work—but also twice the fun! And that makes family life very special for you.

Parents of twins face particular challenges simply because of the twins' closeness in age, their special relationship to each other, and their underlying need to develop as distinct individuals despite being part of a twosome.

Identical twins usually look the same to people who don't see them daily and don't get to know them as well as you do, but you'll probably notice subtle physical differences. Even identical twins, but certainly fraternal twins, have different personalities, and they develop at different rates.

Twins sometimes develop a secret language, one that adults may not understand. Make a point of having plenty of language-based activities, particularly when your twins are toddlers. Talking to them is especially important: Research shows that twins are often slower than singletons at developing language skills.

Similarities vs. differences

Perhaps the biggest issue you face when raising twins—apart from the physical task of caring for two babies of the exact same age at the exact same time—is to balance their similarities with their differences, ensuring that each child is allowed to become a unique individual.

People love to see a matching set. They think it's cute for twins to wear coordinated outfits, particularly when they're identical twins, and to be regarded as one unit rather than as separate individuals. That's okay early on, but eventually each child's distinctive skills and personality start to show through. Your twins will feel stifled if they aren't allowed to develop in their own unique ways.

Similarities between twins are easy to deal with. You can provide the same household, toys, and food. Their differences, however, are harder to manage. It's much more demanding if, say, one twin likes to play indoors while the other prefers to play outdoors, or if one is easygoing while the other becomes upset over the slightest change in the

- The most common complaint of parents of twins during the first year is the physical strain of managing two sleeping and feeding schedules simultaneously.
- Identical twins have greater similarity in heartbeat, pulse, and breathing rate than nonidentical twins, suggesting these physical dimensions are inherited.

family routine. Yet managing such differences is part of the job when parenting twins.

Do your best to encourage each twin's individual interests and talents. One twin might enjoy stories while the other might prefer jigsaw puzzles: Provide opportunities to meet these different interests whenever you can, despite the practical difficulties. Don't worry about how supporting their differences might affect their relationship with each other—rest assured they will remain close, even as they grow more distinct. And they will quickly accept each other's particular strengths and weaknesses. You can help this process along the way by:

- *Taking an interest in what each of your twins does*, regardless of whether both babies' interests coincide.
- *Giving individual time to each.* Try to spend a few minutes alone with each twin every day; don't only spend time with them together.
- *Encouraging each twin to delight in her sibling's achievements.* This helps nurture their respect for each other.

Nurturing individuals

It would be nice if you could use the same approach with both twins when it comes to setting expectations and managing behavior. But the reality is that you need to match your parenting style to each twin's developmental needs and temperament. One might be outgoing and the other one shy. One might be easygoing and the other more of a handful.

Put simply, what works with one might not work with the other.

Each twin has to develop her independence and learn to stand on her own two feet. At some point, she'll be separated from her sibling, at least temporarily. Your twins will form friendships with different children, and their distinct personalities and abilities will lead them through different paths in life. Many parents of twins put their children in different classes at school to help nurture their individual identities.

Bear in mind, however, that your twins may resist such a move. After all, they're used to each other's company day and night, and they may not have felt the need to develop the range of social skills necessary to socialize well with their peers. With your support, they will learn to mix confidently with other children their own age, even when their twin isn't alongside.

Getting advice

Life with a baby is often hectic. You have to make so many decisions—some major, some minor. You have to make parenting choices from the moment your baby is born, and you'll be needed indefinitely. Like every parent, you'll sometimes question your skills and abilities. You want the best for your baby, and you don't want to make any mistakes in raising him.

It's hardly surprising, then, that you may want advice from people you consider more experienced than you. Advice from parents, grandparents, close friends, healthcare providers, and anyone else whose opinion you value can be very helpful, enabling you to make an informed choice about what to do. Of course, there may be people who give an opinion without being asked!

Being open to advice is better than isolating yourself. If you feel uncertain about your parenting abilities, you might find yourself avoiding other moms and dads. Such a buffer might feel more comfortable, but it won't help you improve your parenting skills in the long run.

3 reasons why it's good to listen

1   **You learn from others' mistakes.** There's no point in making a mistake someone else has made already.

2   **You learn from others' successes.** Listening to the way someone else resolved a problem means that you can try a similar strategy with your baby.

3   **You learn from others' uncertainty.** It's always good to have confirmation that you're not the only parent who sometimes feels unsure.

When there's too much advice

When too many people give you advice at once, it's hard to know whom to listen to—particularly when you get conflicting opinions and each person offering advice acts like an expert! Keep in mind that people's views are generally based on their own limited experience and influenced by their own and their children's personalities—although that generally won't stop them from sharing their firm opinions with you.

If you're confronted by a barrage of unsolicited—and often conflicting—advice about how to raise your baby, remember there is no right way to raise a child. True, there are universal rules about parenting, such as the need to love your baby, the need to help him fulfill his potential, and the need to stimulate him through play. But there are plenty of ways to meet these needs—not just one.

Remember that what suits one baby might not suit another. The fact that your sister's baby liked a particular musical toy doesn't mean that your baby will necessarily enjoy it, too. Each child is different, even when they're in the same family or they come from similar backgrounds.

Trust your instincts and don't disregard your core beliefs. There's no point in trying to heed advice that runs counter to your fundamental beliefs, because you won't be able to follow it.

Sometimes you may completely disagree with another person's approach to parenting. Even so, it can be beneficial to consider that person's point of view and try to understand it. You don't have to do the same thing, of course. It's prudent to avoid saying anything critical or disapproving (no matter how tempted you might be) to other parents. You're unlikely to change their minds, and they probably won't change yours.

6 things to consider when you receive advice

1 The giver Resist the temptation to reject advice simply because you find the person giving the opinion irritating. You might be surprised to find a differing opinion has some merit and can help solve your problem. It's wise to be respectful even if you disagree with someone's advice. It was probably offered with good intentions, and there's no point in snapping a rebuke. And you may discover that the advice is helpful the next time.

2 The giver's experience Keep in mind that everyone's experience is limited. Even a parent who's raised five children might not have faced the same parenting challenges that you're dealing with. A grandparent doesn't necessarily have all the answers, either, despite having been a parent for far longer than you.

3 Appropriateness You should never follow advice that makes you uncomfortable. If you believe your baby is too young to digest solid foods, don't listen to the relative urging you to give her rice cereal. Have confidence in yourself. If you feel conflicted, seek another opinion from someone you trust.

4 The final word What should you do if you can't decide between different points of view, or if you and your spouse disagree on an important issue? It is often helpful to have someone whom you respect give a careful, considered opinion that takes into account your and your partner's parenting styles, and your child's temperament. One person who has wide experience in dealing with all types of children and all types of parents may be able to fill this role for you: your pediatrician.

5 Parenting trends Some parenting habits follow trends. Believe it or not, decades ago child-care experts warned mothers not to let their husbands play with the baby after coming home from work, because the change in routine would upset the baby. Assess whether you might be following the latest parenting craze—good or bad—instead of something with years of research-driven data to back it up, and then let that knowledge inform your decision to follow the pointers, or not. Regardless, if a piece of advice doesn't seem logical, it probably isn't; trust your intuition.

6 Ownership Never lose sight of the fact that you are the parent. You have the right to tactfully ask people to give you breathing space. It's often hard to say no, especially to someone you love and respect, but it's your right as a parent. You may need to be assertive with those giving you advice.

Second-time parents

Just when you're finally feeling confident about managing one child, along comes the second! Of course, you will become adept at parenting two kids in time, but your stamina, patience, and self-confidence may be taxed in the early weeks and months. Caring for two young children is obviously much more demanding than caring for just one.

Luckily, you now have plenty of experience to draw on. You long ago took off your parenting training wheels, and you're no longer a novice. Many of the things you used to worry about with your first baby—how to hold her, how often to bathe her, how to help her fall asleep—don't even give you pause this time around. You're more practiced, more knowledgeable, and more comfortable about taking care of a young child than you were with your first baby. This helps you be a more effective parent from the start. Despite your considerable experience, however, you'll face new tests and challenges now that you have two. Here are some of the common challenges you might encounter, and some advice on how to handle them.

Your toddler insists you feed her lunch just as you start to breastfeed your new baby.

- She probably makes this demand just for the sake of attention, and it's perfectly okay to give her some. Let your toddler sit with you and play a game or look at a book while you breastfeed her younger sibling. As long as she feels she's getting some interest from you, she'll be happy.

    But when both children want your attention at the same time, which child should get preference? A good guiding principle to use is this: Go to the one who needs you most at that moment.

    Many parents of two children feel guilty that they spend more than half their time with their older child. But older children have many more needs and are very effective at refocusing your attention on them. Your new baby, on the other hand, requires much less of your time.

Your baby has fallen asleep, and it's time to take your 2-year-old to a parent-and-toddler playgroup.

- You could take your baby with you, and hopefully she'll continue to sleep. Second children get used to being dragged around. On occasion, you could ask another parent in the group to take your toddler while you stay with the baby. You need to be prepared to be flexible, especially when things don't go according to plan.

When shopping with your children at the supermarket, your toddler keeps running away.

- If you can, avoid the problem by leaving your older child with a relative or friend while you shop. Alternatively, you can keep her close by securing her into a stroller or the grocery cart while carrying your infant in a sling or baby carrier. One way or another, you need to control your toddler's movements and keep her safe.

Once you've dressed the children and everyone's ready to leave the house, your toddler wets herself as you close the front door.

- Stay calm: Accept that you will arrive later than you intended—people expect young families to be late anyway. Change her wet clothes for dry ones and go on with your plans. These accidents happen frequently with young children.

Your baby is fussy and won't sleep, your older child is moody and whining, and you're expected to visit someone that afternoon.

- As much as you want to go out as planned, consider canceling your outing. Otherwise, you're probably setting yourself and your children up for failure. You can reschedule the visit for another day when everyone is in better spirits.

The techniques that worked with your first child don't work with your second.

- Your second child has a different temperament

(harder to soothe, more strong-willed). You may have to tailor your approach to meet her individual nature for things to work better.

Managing with more than one

Keep in mind that many people know what it's like to have two young children—they've faced the same challenges you're coping with right now. So if you have to change your plans at the last minute, change them—nobody will be surprised. If you need extra help in order to get through the day with two young children, ask for it. Rest assured that you're not alone in struggling to meet the practical demands of parenting more than one young child at the same time. Here are some tips to help you cope.

Be adaptable. When it comes to household chores, for example, eliminate as many as you can. You'll find that the world continues to turn even though your house or apartment is less tidy. If possible, hand off some domestic chores to your partner, postpone them until you have more time to tackle them, or hire someone to do them. By limiting your domestic routine to include only necessary chores, you're able to concentrate on the more important business of raising your kids.

Do your best to plan your days, especially during the week, so that there's some structure to your time.

Children and babies are unpredictable, developing their own schedules independently of any hopes you have, but some attempt at planning is usually better than none. For instance, plan a trip to your friend's house, even if you need 2 days of organizing to manage it. This helps you have a feeling of control, a sense that you're in charge of your family—rather than your family being in charge of you.

Acknowledge your limitations. Confidence and self-esteem as a parent are vital, and it's only natural that you want to know you can be an effective parent. But it's healthy to recognize your imperfections. Nobody has an unlimited supply of energy. Take help when it is offered, and ask for help when it is needed. You'll be amazed at how refreshed you feel after someone else has taken care of a task or your children for an hour or so.

Pay attention to the good stuff. When you're caring for young children, the routine of feeding, bathing, and diapering can quickly dominate, making every day seem the same. Don't lose sight of the terrific developmental changes taking place as your children steadily improve their skills. They're easily overlooked in the haze of exhaustion, chores, and basic family pressures, so try to keep them in focus. Concentrate on your achievements and your children's progress to see the joys of being a parent!

SLEEP MATTERS

Getting enough sleep

Every adult needs sleep in order to function. Without enough, we lack energy, become irritable, and have problems concentrating. The same can be said of infants, so it's especially important that your baby gets enough sleep. Newborns sleep an average of 16 hours a day, with about half of this time at night. Your baby will wake up hungry every few hours and need to be fed. But be patient, it will get better over time!

The phases of sleep

There are two main types of sleep: light and deep. These are divided into several sequential phases. First we enter a state of drowsiness, which is followed by light sleep. We then pass into dream sleep (also known as REM, or rapid eye movement, sleep), and eventually into deep sleep. Then we return to dream sleep, light sleep, and back to drowsiness before we wake fully.

When your baby is in dream, or REM, sleep, you'll be able to see her eyes moving under her eyelids; her body will sometimes twitch, and her breathing will be irregular. During periods of quiet sleep, she'll take deep, regular breaths. Occasionally, her whole body will jerk before becoming still again.

Everyone repeats the sleep cycle several times a night, waking occasionally. Unless we're disturbed when we're awake, we simply go back to sleep—come morning, we've had a good night's rest and usually don't remember waking up.

Learning to settle themselves back to sleep is a skill that babies develop over time. Settling your baby down when she's awake instead of waiting until she's asleep is one way to encourage your baby to do this. While a newborn needs to be fed when she wakes up, with an older baby, you can also try gently patting her and speaking softly to lull her back to sleep instead of first picking her up or feeding her.

Baby sleep patterns

Some babies need more sleep than others, and some may start sleeping longer stretches at night earlier than others. Try not to let the question, "Is your baby sleeping through the night?" bother you. (Realize, too, that "sleeping through the night" has meanings ranging from 6 to 8 hours in a row, to just

waking once for a feeding, to letting you sleep your usual night's sleep without interruption.) With time, usually around 3 months, the duration and timing of your baby's sleep periods will become more predictable, with longer stretches at night.

For the first few weeks, your baby will sleep a lot, but unfortunately seldom longer than 2 to 3 hours in a row. If there is a stretch of 4 to 5 consecutive hours, it will usually be in the afternoon (not during the night). As she gets older, her sleep patterns will change, and she'll need less sleep. When she's between 3 and 6 months old, she'll probably sleep for about 15 hours in total, mostly at night and with two or three naps during the day. By about 6 months, your baby may have only two daytime naps—and she may sleep up to 8 hours in one stretch at night.

By the time she's 12 months old, she'll probably sleep about 14 hours total. Her nighttime sleep could stretch to 10 hours, and during the day she might take two naps lasting up to 2 hours each. After 1 year, she may need only one nap a day.

Parents' sleep needs

It's true that nearly all parents are tired. Starting shortly after your baby's birth, you will begin regularly suffering from sleep deprivation, and though it does get better, it is an ongoing issue for a long time. Lack of sleep can profoundly affect your energy level, mood, and ability to concentrate. When you're exhausted, it's easy to become irritable and even resentful of your precious new baby.

The common advice is to sleep when your baby sleeps—with good reason. Seize opportunities to nap, even if you rest for only 15 minutes. It's tempting to "get some things done" while she sleeps. But try not to worry about a messy house, since prioritizing napping or going to bed early will help you cope better with babycare duties, particularly at night in the early weeks.

You and your partner will develop a system that works best for your family. If you're bottle-feeding, you can take turns

handling nighttime feedings. If you're breastfeeding, your partner may be able to handle changing and burping, help you find other times to rest, or give your baby a bottle of expressed milk.

To keep nighttime disruptions as brief as possible for you and your baby, make things as easy as you can. Having your baby sleep in the same room as you, but not in your bed, makes it easier to feed her right away and prevents her from getting too upset, which might make it harder for her to settle down afterward. If you're bottle-feeding, use prepared formula. Keep everything you need for feeding and diaper changes close by.

Safe sleeping

Your baby will spend a lot of his time asleep, so it's important to make sure he's safe and comfortable by ensuring his crib is a danger-free, secure place in which to sleep. You should also follow the recommendations for minimizing the risk of sudden infant death syndrome (SIDS) (see page 63).

Where your baby sleeps

Experts recommend that you have your baby sleep in your bedroom, but not in your bed, for up to 6 months to reduce the risk of SIDS. Whether you breast- or bottle-feed, this also makes it easier to settle your baby back to sleep after nighttime feedings. While your baby can sleep in his crib from the get-go, in the early weeks you might prefer something small and cozy, such as a bassinet, instead of a crib. Keep in mind, however, that he'll quickly outgrow a small bassinet or cradle and be ready to move on to a crib.

The crib and mattress

It's best to purchase a new crib if you can. With a secondhand crib, you may not know its history or if it meets current safety standards. If you do use a secondhand crib, make sure it meets the latest safety regulations, and be sure to check that it hasn't been recalled by the U.S. Consumer Product Safety

Commission (www.cpsc.gov).

Whether you opt for a new crib or a used one, check it over carefully. It should be stable with no sharp edges. To ensure your baby's head can't become trapped, make sure the slats are no more than 2⅜ inches apart and that there are no cutouts in the headboard and footboard. Check for missing hardware, splinters, and chipped or peeling paint.

Drop-side cribs are now prohibited from being sold in the United States. These cribs were popular for many years: One side could be lowered, making it easy for parents to pick up their babies and set them down gently without back strain. These cribs have been blamed for scores of injuries and some deaths, and millions of them have been recalled. The CPSC urges parents not to use these models.

Look for a movable mattress base that can be lowered as your baby grows and becomes more active. Once your baby can kneel—and later stand—make sure the sides of his crib reach his chest so there's no risk that he can fall out. Once the top of the crib side is under his chest, lower the mattress. Most children can stay in their cribs until they're at least 2 years old. When the mattress is in the lowest position and a child learns to climb out, some parents choose to put him in a bed. Some cribs convert into beds, but this can be expensive.

Buy a new crib mattress to reduce the risk of SIDS. Make sure that the mattress is firm and fits snugly into the crib so that there's no risk that your baby could become trapped between the mattress and the crib frame. In a full-size crib, the mattress must be at least 27¼ inches by 51⅝ inches and no more than 6 inches thick. You shouldn't be able to fit more than two fingers between the mattress and the crib sides.

You have a lot of options for a mattress: foam, natural fiber, coiled springs, hypoallergenic, etc. Foam mattresses usually are less expensive, while natural fiber ones generally last longer. A waterproof cover will make it easy to wipe up any messes.

Never leave toys or bottles in your baby's crib; they're choking and suffocation hazards. If your child goes to bed with a favorite plush animal or blanket, remove it after he falls asleep until he's a year old. The American Academy of Pediatrics discourages the use of bumper pads, which pose a suffocation risk. If you use bumpers, they should be thin, firm, well secured, and not "pillow-like." Knot ties, which pose a strangulation risk, tightly and cut off extra fabric. Once your baby can push up on hands and knees, remove bumpers and any mobiles over the crib.

Sleep position

Always lay your baby down on his back. Research has shown that this is the most effective way to reduce the risk of SIDS. Once your baby begins to roll over, you should still put him down to sleep on his back, but you don't need to return him to his back every time he rolls over onto his tummy. By this stage, he's at a lower risk of SIDS, and moving him probably will disrupt his sleep.

The CPSC advises against using sleep positioners, citing the risk of suffocation. For tips on reducing the chance of your baby developing flattening of the skull in the back (plagiocephaly), see page 29.

Bedding and nightclothes

Don't use blankets or pillows. They put your baby at risk of suffocating and can cause him to overheat, another SIDS risk. Use a fitted cotton sheet that won't bunch up when your baby moves around, and make sure the sheet is well secured. Your baby can use a small, light blanket after 6 months, when he'll be able to remove it or crawl out from under it. If you use a blanket, position your baby so his feet touch the end of the crib and tuck the edges of the blanket securely under the mattress. Make sure the blanket doesn't go higher than your baby's chest.

Ideally, your baby's room will be warm enough that he can sleep in lightweight clothing. Make sure there are no drawstrings or anything else on his clothing that could catch on something. He should sleep in snug clothing made of flame-resistant fabric. All he really needs is a diaper and a snug, footed outfit.

If you're concerned your baby won't be warm

SWITCHING TO A TODDLER BED

Toddlers typically are able to climb out of their crib at 18–24 months. Luckily, the way they do it—first putting one leg over the top edge and then the other, turning themselves around so they face the crib—makes them land on the floor feet first. Injuries occurring when a child climbs out of his crib are very unusual but can result when other furniture is too close to the crib. If you fear your child will hurt himself when he learns to climb out, place some pillows on the floor next to the crib.

While many parents choose to begin using a bed for their child as soon as he can climb out of the crib, there is another point of view. A number of pediatricians recommend keeping him in his crib even after he can climb out. The vast majority of crib "escapees," if promptly returned to the crib, will soon tire of climbing out after doing it a few times and will not do it again. Once this point is reached, you can continue using the crib for naps and bedtime until he doesn't fit in it anymore, often around age 5. Each time, put him back and say, "Stay in your bed," without much ado. After he has "forgotten" how to climb out, you can rest assured that when you are asleep or just out of the nursery, he is safely in his crib.

If you opt to switch to a bed when your child learns to climb out of his crib, be prepared for him to leave the bed frequently. Switching your toddler to a bed is often giving him a license to come and visit you during the night, which may disrupt your sleep. When he sleeps in a bed instead of a crib, it is much harder to stop his escape. If your child climbs in bed with you during the night, it's important to decide whether it's okay. Being inconsistent will confuse your child and make it harder if you later decide he should always stay in his own bed.

enough, try swaddling him, or using a wearable blanket or sleep sack. These have sleeves and snaps or a zipper down the front; the bottom may have a gathered opening or be closed, like a bag. As he grows older, he may find a sleep sack restrictive. To avoid having him overheat, leave his head uncovered.

Monitoring your baby

If you cannot hear your baby cry from your present location in your home, a monitor can help you listen while your baby sleeps in another room. Be aware, however, that babies are noisy sleepers. As long as you are where you can hear your baby crying, you will hear him loud and clear if he needs you. Routine use of monitors has not been shown to be helpful in preventing SIDS.

The right temperature

You want your baby's room to be comfortable while he sleeps, but not so warm that he overheats. Ideally, keep the temperature in your baby's room between 68°F and 72°F. Air conditioning is fine as long as your baby doesn't get too cold. Preventing overheating reduces the risk of SIDS.

Babies' hands and feet tend to feel colder than the rest of their bodies. To get a good sense of how warm he is, feel his tummy. You can remove a layer of clothing if your baby feels too warm, or add one if he feels too cold. Check on him a few minutes later to make sure he's comfortable. On hot summer nights, your baby may be fine in just a diaper. Don't position the crib too close to a heater—it could cause your baby to overheat.

Pacifier

The American Academy of Pediatrics (AAP) recommends offering your baby a pacifier when putting him to bed during the first year. However, the AAP guidelines also state that if your baby refuses a pacifier, don't force the issue. Do not reinsert a pacifier after your baby falls asleep.

Research indicates that use of a pacifier reduces the risk of SIDS, perhaps because a pacifier keeps a baby's tongue from falling backward and blocking the upper airway. If you're breastfeeding, however, wait until your baby is at least a month old before offering a pacifier so he can get used to feeding.

Pacifiers have some drawbacks. The pacifier can fall out of your baby's mouth, causing your baby to become distressed when he can't find it. If he uses it for naps and at bedtime, he may also want it more often during the day. Frequent pacifier use can limit his vocalizing. And down the road, you may have a hard time persuading him to give it up.

CO-SLEEPING SAFETY

The American Academy of Pediatrics recommends having your baby sleep next to your bed, but not in it. Its guidelines advise returning your baby to her crib after nighttime feedings, even if you're breastfeeding, for at least the first 3 months.

Do not co-sleep if you or your partner is a smoker—this increases the risk of SIDS.

If you want to co-sleep, you should bear the following in mind.

- Your mattress should be flat and firm.
- Bedding and clothing should be light, and the room shouldn't be too warm.
- Your baby must not be able to fall out of bed or get trapped between the mattress and the bed frame or wall. Make sure that she can't be covered by a pillow or bed covers.
- Both parents must be aware that the baby is in bed with them.
- Once you've fed your baby, place her on her back for sleep.
- Babies shouldn't sleep next to other children or be left in a bed on their own.
- You shouldn't sleep with your baby if you're very tired or if you've drunk alcohol or taken drugs or medication that may make you sleep heavily.
- Beware that falling asleep on the sofa or in a chair while holding your baby is associated with an increased risk of SIDS.

Managing sleep

Whether your baby likes to snooze at every opportunity or gets by on fewer hours, whether she is a night owl or an early riser, you can set the scene for her to sleep well—and get the sleep you need, too. In the early weeks with your newborn, your job is to make your baby's environment safe and conducive to sleep. Between 2 and 3 months, your baby will be able to start organizing her sleep patterns. Most families find that babies respond well to consistent sleep routines, although these will change as your baby's needs change. Establishing consistent routines early on can provide a foundation for good sleep habits.

An individual approach

Like every aspect of raising a child, there's no single perfect way to handle bedtime. You may be flexible or prefer a structured approach—and your baby may gravitate toward one approach or the other. Your approach will also evolve as you learn more about your baby's individual needs. However, it is clear that her development relies on getting enough sleep when she needs it. The habits that you establish early on are essential to setting a sleeping pattern that meets her needs. Friends and family often will offer lots of advice on how and when to get your baby to sleep. This can be a big struggle if your baby is fussy, has colic, or is a light sleeper, but remember that as parents, your wishes should trump all others.

Co-sleeping

Some parents sleep with their baby in one bed, a practice the AAP discourages because co-sleeping can put a baby at risk of overheating, injury, and even death. If you opt to share a bed with your baby, it's crucial that you understand the risks and take every precaution to keep your baby safe (see box, opposite page).

Despite these risks, co-sleeping does have benefits: the closeness of being together and the convenience of having your baby close by for nighttime feedings. Breastfeeding mothers who sleep with their babies can get more sleep during the night, and their babies tend to breastfeed longer. Many babies who co-sleep with their parents seem to sleep better, too.

You may find it hard to sleep when your baby is in bed with you. Your baby may find it difficult to sleep when you aren't with him, which limits your activities and later can make it harder for him to transition to sleeping in his own bed. Co-sleeping also can affect lovemaking. If you're interested in sharing your bed with your baby, consider the pros and cons, and make sure your partner is supportive.

The early weeks

Your newborn baby will probably sleep much of the time—an average of 16 hours. She'll likely nap frequently and wake every couple hours or so for feedings. In the first few weeks, you're starting to get to know each other. While it's too early to establish a formal routine, you can take the first steps toward helping your baby learn to sleep well.

Anticipate sleepiness

Putting your baby to bed at the right time will give her the best chance of falling asleep peacefully. With babies, a natural bedtime often falls between 7 p.m. and 8 p.m. This can be hard on working parents because they have less time with their baby awake in the evening. But if your baby misses her preferred sleep time, she may become alert and active again even though she's really overtired.

In the first few weeks, she'll grow tired quickly and easily. Think of offering sleep every couple of hours. If your newborn has been awake for 2 hours, try to settle her down for a nap. The goal is to anticipate the need for sleep before your baby starts to yawn or rub her eyes. If you notice these signs of sleepiness or others, such as pulling on an ear or fussiness, act immediately. This will help her get the sleep she needs for her development.

5 ways to help your baby unwind

1 **Talking** Tell your baby it's time for bed and talk to her soothingly as you get her ready. Although she doesn't understand your words yet, they'll become familiar and pleasurable as part of her routine.

2 **Bath** Many babies find a bath enjoyable and relaxing, but some are more excitable. If your baby gets active or cries at bath time, you might want to save the bath for another part of the day and try another calming activity. After a bath, put a clean diaper and her pajamas on her.

3 **Stories** It's never too early to start reading stories to your baby. Even before she can understand the words or pictures, she'll love cuddling with you and listening to your voice. She'll respond to the rhythm of nursery rhymes and enjoy their familiarity.

4 **Singing songs** Most babies love music and lullabies. You can choose a particular song that means it is bedtime. Your baby will come to recognize it and associate it with sleep. Some babies like to go to sleep to the sound of music playing softly. Other babies like a white-noise machine.

5 **Cuddles** This is a lovely way to help your baby feel reassured and loved before she goes to sleep.

Let your baby settle herself

Your newborn baby will wake frequently during the night, usually because she's hungry. When she's older, she'll still wake up periodically, but she won't need to be fed, although she may be in the habit of taking a feeding then. That's when you can help her learn how to settle herself back to sleep without her getting upset or needing attention. For example,

give your baby a little more time to settle down, or stroke her back, rather than picking her up.

Your drowsy newborn will easily drift off to sleep in your arms, often during feedings. But after the first few weeks, give her opportunities to settle herself to sleep. Put her in her crib in the evening when she's sleepy but still awake, rather than waiting until she's asleep. Try to do the same at naptimes. She'll sometimes need comforting, but after 3 months or so, she'll probably be able to drift off to sleep happily on her own. By this age, she probably can manage without feedings for longer stretches at night, and she'll be more likely to sleep for longer stretches if she's able to settle herself down.

Make night and day different

Newborns don't care much whether it's daytime or nighttime. After about 2 weeks, though, it's good to start helping your baby understand the difference so she'll associate nighttime with peacefulness and sleep, and daytime with activity and wakefulness.

Try to keep nighttime feedings as quiet and peaceful as possible. Keep the lights low, and talk as little as possible. Avoid turning on the television or music. If you want to leave a night-light on, make sure the room is only dimly lit. Daylight can sometimes cause your baby to wake up very early, ready to start her day. If this is a problem, you can hang blackout curtains to block the sunlight.

During the day, it's fine to feed your baby in a lively and noisy environment.

Create a good environment for sleep

Your baby needs to feel safe and secure before she goes to sleep. Some babies feel cozier in a small space in the first few weeks, so you may want to put her to sleep in a bassinet. Some babies like to be swaddled (see page 34).

Your baby's room should be quiet, but don't worry about keeping the rest of the house silent. Babies are very solid sleepers and can seemingly sleep though loud noises. The normal background noise of a family home in some cases can soothe her. She also may like to hear music quietly playing as she settles down for sleep.

Make sure your baby isn't too hot or too cold: Dress her appropriately and try to keep her room at a comfortable temperature (see page 158).

Comfort items

You may want to give your baby a comfort object, something familiar—perhaps a favorite blanket or a toy (make sure there are no removable parts and that it is age-rated for babies)—to help her soothe herself at night. If you do, remove it from her crib after she's asleep for the first year to ensure her safety.

A bedtime routine

A few weeks after your baby is born, you can begin familiarizing your baby with the concept of bedtime and start to develop a nighttime routine. You can't legislate how much sleep your baby needs, but you can influence when she sleeps and help her get settled down.

By this point, you'll most likely have figured out the times your baby gets sleepy. Let this guide you as you set a bedtime and times for her daytime naps. You don't need to be very strict about keeping to these times, but it's helpful to stick to them as much as you can as long as they're working for you and meeting your baby's needs. Keep in mind that some babies are more flexible about schedules—and more easy-going about sleep in general—than others.

Getting ready

There are no rules for establishing a bedtime routine—create one that suits your baby and your family's lifestyle. Keep your routine simple so that it becomes familiar to your baby and also so that babysitters and other people caring for your child can easily replicate it.

Near the end of your baby's day, encourage activity and interaction to help your baby use up plenty of energy before sleep. After this playful session, though, try to keep the atmosphere quiet and calm. Set the scene for bed by winding down playtime and having a quiet and relaxing period (see box, opposite page).

Once you've decided on a routine, stick to it as much as you can. Your baby will enjoy this special time you spend together and will come to anticipate

it with pleasure. Once established, your baby will become sleepy as the routine progresses, even if she initially is not tired.

Some ways you can get your baby ready for bedtime include:

- *A walk in the stroller* This can be a calming and soothing way to prepare for bedtime. But if possible, avoid using this as a default way to get your baby to sleep before putting her in her crib. This could make it harder for her to learn how to settle herself later.
- *Massage* A gentle massage before bed can relax and calm your baby. You can start doing this after she's about 2 weeks old.
- *Swaddling* Swaddling your baby is a successful strategy to soothe her and keep her from jerking herself awake (see page 34).

In the crib

As you put your baby in her crib, talk gently to calm her. Show her that you'll be close by. Some parents leave the room right away; others linger. If you want to stay in her room as she falls asleep, gradually reduce the time you spend in her room, so she doesn't need you to be there in order to fall asleep.

If your baby cries out, give her a few minutes to try to settle herself before you return. But don't leave her too long—you don't want her to become distressed and to associate bedtime with being upset. Talk to her and pat her on the back, but unless she's a newborn, try to leave her in her crib. You can try waiting a little longer each time to respond to her, to give her a chance to soothe herself. Do respond right away if she has a need, for example, if she's crying because she needs her diaper changed. This will tell her that someone will come if she needs it.

If all else fails

As you will quickly discover, the first weeks with a newborn are exhausting, and you will soon become quite sleep deprived. Do try to follow the advice above for getting your baby to sleep during the first weeks—it will result in good sleep habits that will make sleeping through the night easier to accomplish later. But if you find these suggestions

aren't helping you, do whatever it takes to get her (and a minute later, you!) to sleep. Remember that even if your methods don't encourage the most desirable sleep habits, getting some sleep—and your survival—depends on your finding enough rest. You can always undo bad sleep habits later.

From 3 months

You'll probably have introduced a bedtime routine by now. Hopefully this includes putting your baby to bed at the same time each night, when she's drowsy but not yet asleep. Try to stick with it, even when you're sleeping away from home.

Around this time your baby's sleep patterns should become more predictable, and you'll have a better sense of when your baby is ready for bed and can set a more fixed bedtime. Her internal clock recognizes day and night, and she can go longer stretches at night without a feeding. If you have a routine in place, stick to it. If you don't, it's never too late to start one. Your baby may still be wide awake at bedtime, but you'll probably find she's ready for sleep once you start getting ready for bed.

If your baby stays up past her bedtime, she could get overtired and become alert again, and it will be much harder for her to settle down. Keeping as close as possible to set times for naps and bedtime will help ensure that she gets the sleep she needs when she needs it.

Babies typically find predictable routines comforting. By now, your baby will know what happens at bedtime and what these activities mean—that it's time for bed. Your baby will have more predictable patterns of eating and playing, too.

Sleeping during the day

Most babies continue to need two naps until at least the age of 1 or so, and then can drop down to one. Sleeping during the day helps your baby to make the most of her activities and, if timed right, will help her sleep well at night. You may be tempted to keep her awake during the day in hopes that she'll sleep better at night, but this won't work. An overtired baby sleeps less soundly than a well-rested one—sleep begets sleep, you may hear wise parents say. The timing of the last nap is also important—it shouldn't be too close to bedtime.

A daytime nap routine works well for many babies. Start each nap with a brief sleep routine. You can borrow from your bedtime ritual: talking to her quietly, singing a lullaby, and dimming the lights. You'll come to understand what times of day she tends to get tired, and you can schedule naps accordingly—before she gets overtired. It's helpful to have a quiet, calming time before naps. If your baby doesn't settle down as easily during the day, experiment with different times and strategies until you find a routine that works for you. For example, some babies take long morning naps; others prefer a longer afternoon nap.

If possible, keep at least 3 hours between the end of the last nap of the day and bedtime. Similarly, avoid letting her nap shortly after waking up in the morning. An interval of at least 2 hours is preferred between wake-up and naptime.

If you're struggling with sleep problems, see pages 164–168 for possible solutions, and talk to your pediatrician for additional advice.

Multiples

It's tricky enough to get any baby settled down for sleep. It's even harder with multiples, who can have very different personalities and metabolisms—which consequently can lead to very different eating and sleeping habits. You may find it easier for everyone if you put your babies down to sleep at the same time from the start, so they establish a routine together. A sleeping schedule can help your babies' body clocks get set to the same rhythm. Be sure to lay your babies down on their backs (see page 157).

If your babies are waking up hungry at different times during the night, feel free to go ahead and wake up the second one when one wakes up for a feeding. This will ensure a minimal number of nighttime feedings and more sleep for you. Then they can settle back down together afterward and give you more time to sleep. It may take a while to establish a routine in which both babies wake up at the same time for feedings, but if it saves you time in the long run, the effort may be well worth it.

When you're juggling babies, it's difficult to get through the day without a rest period for yourself, especially if you're breastfeeding. If your babies regularly have a long afternoon nap, try to get some sleep at the same time. Your health and well-being are much more important than catching up on chores. If at all possible, try to get household help, so you can focus your energy on your babies.

Sleep problems

Most babies—even the soundest sleepers—have sleep-related trouble at some time or another. Lack of sleep interferes with your baby's development and enjoyment of life. And problems such as nighttime disruptions and early-morning waking will prevent you from getting a good night's sleep. It's in everyone's best interest to deal with sleep problems promptly and effectively.

Difficulty getting to sleep

Some babies have a harder time than others settling down at night, but there are ways to help things along. If your baby isn't settling down easily, first revisit your bedtime routine to make sure you're setting the scene for a good night's sleep. Put your baby in the crib at the same time each night.

One approach is to try leaving your baby for a few minutes to settle himself—be prepared to let him cry a bit. After you put him in his crib, say goodnight and leave the room. If you return to him, avoid taking him out of the crib. Talk to him for a minute or so, pat his back, and leave again, disturbing him as little as possible. Gradually increase the amount of time you wait before responding to his cries, and make the intervals between visits to him longer.

If your baby has become used to having you around as he goes to sleep, teach him to be able to settle down on his own once he reaches 3 months of age. Try a gradual approach. Move a little farther from his crib each night until you're outside the room when he goes to sleep. If he cries, return after a few minutes to comfort him, but gradually increase the interval between leaving him and returning. He'll get used to going to sleep on his own without feeling that he's been abandoned.

Also observe how your baby responds to different sounds. Many babies don't mind hearing background noise, so normal household sounds aren't usually a problem—although some babies

are exquisitely sensitive to sound. In his first weeks, playing quiet music or using a white-noise machine can help soothe some babies to sleep. Audiobooks may also be helpful—your baby won't understand the story, but the quiet voice may lull him to sleep. You can even record your own voice reading a story. Some parents have luck with the sound of a clothes dryer, a vacuum, or running water. But once he is 3 months old or so, the best habit is falling asleep without music or auditory aids.

Night waking

Your baby will wake up to eat frequently at night in the early months. This is normal and—though exhausting for you—necessary. Once he's a little older and is physically able to sleep longer without eating, he may continue to wake up more out of habit than necessity. It is at such times, when you have ruled out the other reasons for waking, that you can take steps to encourage him to go back to sleep on his own.

When your baby wakes during the night, it is important to run through the checklist (see box, above) to rule out any problems. As your baby gets older, you'll learn his different cries and will frequently have a good idea of what's wrong.

6 reasons for waking

1 Your baby is hungry.

2 He has a dirty diaper.

3 He's too hot or too cold.

4 He's teething (from about the age of 6 months; see pages 200–201 for more information on teething).

5 Your baby doesn't feel well.

6 He simply misses you and wants your company.

To help your baby to sleep longer stretches at night, stick to a consistent bedtime routine and remember to emphasize the difference between night and day. One caution: It can be tempting to take your baby out of bed and lull him back to sleep while you watch television. However, this can backfire in the long run because it contradicts the message that nighttime is a quiet, calm time to sleep.

A familiar object, such as a favorite blanket or a soft toy (safety rated for babies, with no removable parts), can comfort your baby and help him fall asleep when you aren't nearby. Babies have a keen sense of smell; an item that you've held, which smells like you, can be very comforting. If your baby goes to bed with a comfort object, remove it after he falls asleep until he's a year old. Toys or blankets are suffocation risks and should not be left in a crib.

3–6 months

Once your baby can go longer without eating, he'll be able to sleep longer at night. But first he must

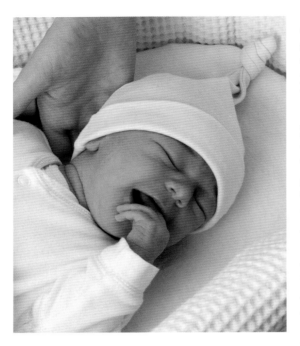

and mobile. That's a lot of fun during the day, but at night they can have a hard time sleeping—they wake up to move around. Stick to your approach for handling night waking. Being consistent is likely to be rewarded sooner or later.

Teething can be uncomfortable enough that your baby may wake up during the night. He is in discomfort, but it's still worth leaving him for a little while to try to settle himself down so that he might get through teething without developing a habit of waking at night. Talk to your pediatrician before using over-the-counter pain remedies (see pages 200–201 for more about teething).

By now, you usually know when your baby is hungry. If he wakes up, but it isn't his normal time to eat, avoid offering a feeding and allow him to settle himself; otherwise he could develop a pattern of waking for feedings that he doesn't really need.

Controlled crying and "no-cry" methods

Once your baby is 3 months old, if you choose to, you can try using a controlled-crying approach to help him learn to soothe himself at night. With this method, you go to your baby's side when he cries at night, but you don't pick him up, cuddle him, or turn on a light. Your goal is to disturb his environment as little as possible. Just talk to him soothingly to reassure him that you're still around, and to assure yourself that your baby is well. But keep your visit brief (a minute or so). Gradually increase the length of time you wait before responding to him. Wait 5 minutes the first night and 10 minutes the next night. Continue increasing your response time. This can be very difficult for parents, but there's a good chance it will work if you stick to it. If you're consistent, he probably will stop crying within a week or two and begin going back to sleep on his own.

Some parents prefer "no-cry" methods, out of concern that it's too upsetting to babies to be made to wait before being comforted. If you want to try this approach, first establish a consistent bedtime routine and make sure your baby is able to get himself to sleep when he's put to bed. If he cries during the night, take him out of his crib and rock

learn to settle himself to sleep without your help. He may cry for a while when he wakes, but eventually he should go back to sleep. The technique of letting him cry for increasingly long periods of time has a high rate of success. But many parents find it distressing to leave a baby to cry for any period of time. For these parents, there are other, less-extreme ways of dealing with nighttime waking, and you will find an approach that suits you.

6 months and older

Sometimes babies who have generally slept well begin waking up at night. Separation anxiety is normal at this stage of development, and it may be reflected in night waking—your baby may wake as part of his normal sleep cycle, and then become anxious because you're not there, or bad habits can develop quickly during an illness, when waking at night is expected. It's still a good idea to give him the chance to go back to sleep on his own, but don't wait too long to return to him. Left alone for too long, he may become distressed and have an even harder time settling down.

From this age, babies start to become more active

him to settle him down. The goal is for him to go to sleep during the night just as he does at bedtime. However, there is a chance that your baby will come to rely on you to be there when he wakes at night.

Remember that even without any sleep-training methods, 50 percent of 6-month-olds and 75 percent of 1-year-olds will be sleeping through the night on their own.

Toddlers

Older children may start waking up at night for several reasons. These include:

- *Disruption to the normal routine* Any change in your child's usual circumstances, such as going on a trip, an illness, or moving to a new bedroom, can disrupt sleeping patterns. Your child may wake up early or have trouble falling asleep.
- *Teething* Your baby might be uncomfortable, but still give him a chance to try to settle down on his own.

- *Fear of the dark* This is very common and usually can be eased with reassurance and subdued lighting or a night-light in the room.
- *Nightmares and night terrors* For toddlers, unpleasant dreams are particularly distressing because they feel more real than the nightmares adults experience. Toddlers continue to remember bad dreams and remain upset and afraid. Nightmares are usually brief and followed by a period of wakefulness when your toddler will need comforting. If he wakes up, reassure him that he's safe by hugging him, and reassure him that you will protect him. To help minimize bad dreams, limit stimulation, such as television, loud music, or noisy games, before bedtime. Night terrors, on the other hand, can disrupt his sleep without actually waking him and need to be handled differently. Night terrors occur less often than nightmares, typically when your child is sick or overtired. Your child may sweat, scream, and

7 ways to encourage sleep

1 Make sure your baby's last nap of the day isn't too close to bedtime, and that his daytime naps aren't too long.

2 Have a period of active play before beginning the calm-down time of your bedtime routine.

3 Start your bedtime routine every night at the same time.

4 Set bedtime for when your baby starts to become sleepy. (Or, for babies older than 3 months, pick a bedtime that suits your family's schedule and teach him to become tired at this time.)

5 Give your baby a chance to settle down to sleep on his own—don't feed him or play with him until he sleeps.

6 Make your baby's room a peaceful haven with dim lighting—try using a night-light or leaving a light on outside the room.

7 If your baby is upset and fretful, rock and soothe him.

thrash about. His eyes may be open and he may sit up and even talk, although he's still asleep. The scary part for your toddler is that he doesn't quite know where he is, who you are, or what's happening. If your toddler is having a night terror, sit beside him until he returns to peaceful sleep, but don't hug or soothe him—he may not realize who you are. He will probably fall back asleep, peacefully, within a half hour.

◆ *Feeling worried and anxious* Many things may make a toddler feel anxious: a new sibling, a parent away from home, starting preschool, or sleeping in a strange room. Try to find out what's worrying him. Stick to your routines, but understand that he'll need extra reassurance when he goes to bed. If he's sleeping in a strange bed, such as on vacation or when visiting relatives, bring some favorite toys or blankets to comfort him at night. (Remove them after he goes to sleep until he's 1 year old.)

In all these instances (except night terrors, when it is best not to go to your child), hug and reassure him. But do insist that he stays in his crib or bed. (Do not take him into your bed unless you want him with you regularly. Be aware that sleeping with Mom and Dad is highly desirable to a child, and after a few nights of this, he may soon insist upon it.) Tell him you will check on him in a few minutes and leave the room. Return every 5 minutes or so until he is asleep.

Early waking

Some babies simply need less sleep than others and always wake up early, no matter what. But you can take some steps that may help you and your baby get more sleep. Gradually moving bedtime later usually offers no help. Most babies will wake up just as early as they did before, but instead of being refreshed, they may be grumpy and tired. It's counterintuitive, but an early bedtime could help your baby sleep longer (sleep begets sleep), so you can try that, too. Your growing baby may need less sleep during the day. You can try shortening his naps or even eliminating one. However, it's important that he gets enough sleep during the day so that he

doesn't get overtired. Although many activities come to interfere with it, a nap is of great benefit to most prekindergarten children.

When your baby wakes up in the morning, give him a few minutes; each day increase the time you let him cry before you go in (controlled-crying method). He might settle himself back to sleep or amuse himself happily in his crib for a while, giving you the opportunity for a little more much-needed rest. If early-morning sunlight is waking up your baby, hang blackout curtains in his room. Leave some books or toys (that don't make noise) in the crib for him to play with if he is over a year old.

Getting your child to sleep later is ideal, but more realistically, the goal for an early-morning waker is to get him to remain quiet and occupied until a more reasonable time. If you try these tactics but nothing seems to work, you might have to accept that your baby is an early riser. If you go to bed earlier yourself, you'll be better able to cope with the early mornings and even enjoy them as a special time with your baby.

Be consistent

However you handle bedtime and night waking, consistency is essential to help your child settle into a pattern. Think twice before allowing your child to climb into bed with you. Aside from the risks of co-sleeping (see box, page 158), he'll see being allowed to climb into bed with you as a reward for waking—and after a few nights, you may find he's developed a habit of waking at night so that he can join you. This interrupts your sleep, and you won't sleep as soundly with a toddler in your bed. Even if you need to repeatedly return to his room to reassure him, you'll avoid a subsequent sleep problem.

Sometimes sleep problems are related to medical conditions. If you have any concerns, seek advice from your pediatrician.

Finally, do your best to keep bedtime a positive experience. Try not to send your child to bed feeling unhappy. And there's no need to insist that he fall asleep right away. Toddlers often will talk or sing in their bed until they fall asleep.

CRYING AND RESPONDING

Purposeful crying

Because babies can't talk and explain what they want or what's upsetting them, they communicate by crying. Your baby was born already knowing how to cry loudly, and in a way that will get your attention. Whether by design or evolution, crying serves the human species well because it alerts parents that their baby has a need. Responding promptly to your baby when she cries makes her feel loved and builds her trust in you, a key element in bonding.

Unfortunately, crying is a general alarm that signals only that your baby needs attention. Her crying doesn't reveal exactly what she wants, needs, or is feeling. As you get to know her better, you'll get a lot of practice deciphering her cries—newborns and young infants cry, on average, 2 to 3 hours a day (although usually not all at once!). Soon, you will be able to make a pretty good guess as to why she's crying. Do not hesitate to pick her up to comfort her; you cannot spoil a baby by holding her too much.

Likely reasons for crying

If your baby starts crying and it's been more than 2 hours since she last ate, she's probably hungry again. Go ahead and feed her. If she calms down, then she was crying because she was hungry. But if your baby continues to cry after you feed her, you need to look for another reason for her tears.

Crying that begins less than 2 hours after your baby's last feeding is less likely to be due to hunger. First look for another reason for her cries: Does she have a dirty or wet diaper? Does she just want to be held? Is she overstimulated? Is she bored? Is she hot or otherwise uncomfortable? Perhaps she needs to be burped or needs to satisfy her urge to suck. Go through the checklist: Check her diaper, pick her up, burp her, eliminate any unnecessary activity, initiate some play, remove or loosen some of her clothes, and let her suck on your finger or a pacifier. If one of these solutions stops her crying, then you've found the reason for her distress. If you

3 recognizable cries

Babies cry whenever they want something or when something bothers them. They have different types of cries for different situations. You will learn to recognize them over time.

1 **Hunger cries** are both braying and rhythmic. They're often accompanied by kicking or other rhythmic movements.

2 **Pain cries** are louder and more intense than other cries.

3 **Boredom cries** are irregular and uncoordinated. Your baby will pause between cries to see if you respond.

try everything but she continues to cry, try feeding her. It might be earlier than you expected her to eat, but hunger, as you know, doesn't follow an exact schedule.

Less common causes of crying

Usually, feeding your baby or offering one of the comforts previously detailed will calm her crying. But when nothing seems to work, there's a chance your baby has a feeding problem, such as gastroesophageal reflux disease (or GERD; see box, above), a milk allergy or intolerance, an illness, colic, or chronic hunger.

A feeding problem

When babies cry because they're hungry, they usually become content the moment they receive breast milk or formula. But what if your baby begins to cry while you're feeding her?

If she starts crying a few moments after she begins to suck, she might be having difficulty latching on to the breast (see pages 74–75)—despite her efforts to suck, she's not getting much milk. Similarly, in the first days of breastfeeding, your baby might not be able to get much milk from your engorged breast just after your milk comes in.

If your baby sucks strongly at the breast or bottle for a minute or so and then stops sucking and begins to cry, she may be impatient. After a month or two, many breastfed babies get frustrated when milk comes slowly and steadily from the breast, instead of in larger amounts all at once. Your baby may be saying to you, "I want all my milk right away—not a little at a time!"

Bottle-fed babies may act the same way if the hole in the nipple is too small or is clogged, so that the milk flows more slowly than they want. If you suspect this problem, buy a nipple with a larger hole or poke holes in the head of the nipple with a sterile pin (see page 83).

It may sound difficult to figure out the problem if your baby cries during feeding. But it isn't too hard

Babies with gastroesophageal reflux disease (GERD) regurgitate stomach contents—stomach juices and partially digested milk—up to the esophagus and mouth. Most babies with reflux suffer no discomfort, but a few babies with reflux feel burning pain in the esophagus when stomach contents arrive there. Reflux and crying occur during feeding or shortly after.

to pinpoint what's going on. The first two reasons for crying—poor latching on and breast engorgement—happen in the first days of breastfeeding. Impatience usually doesn't show up until several weeks of age and is readily diagnosed. If it occurs in a breastfed baby, she'll feed well and happily after you pause the feeding to calm her down. In a bottle-fed baby, the cause becomes obvious if a faster-flowing nipple cures her crying.

Pain caused by GERD is dramatic. In this condition, crying also begins shortly after a feeding begins. Efforts to calm your baby as you would if she were just impatient won't be very successful. If your baby spits up often, GERD might be the cause; if she doesn't, you probably can rule it out. Your pediatrician can help you decide if your baby has GERD, and if she does, he'll tell you what you can do to improve her symptoms.

Discomfort due to milk allergy

Only a small minority of infants who react to cow's milk have a true allergy, according to the medical definition of the word. An allergic reaction to cow's milk occurs soon after exposure to the allergen, usually between a few minutes after starting the feeding and up to an hour afterward. Crying might be the only symptom, but usually there are other reactions: vomiting, paleness, and, less often, wheezing or signs of severe allergy such as hives, shortness of breath, or shock. People who are allergic to cow's milk produce antibodies against cow's milk proteins of the IgE class.

Most children who react to cow's milk are intolerant of cow's milk protein—they aren't actually allergic because they don't produce antibodies. An allergic reaction usually appears soon after feeding, but crying related to milk intolerance could start anywhere from 1 to 24 hours after feeding. A dairy intolerance shows itself primarily by excessive crying and sometimes even by blood in the stool. With such a lag before your baby shows symptoms, it's easy to miss. Keep in mind that the exposure could be from formula (which is made with cow's milk) or through breast milk, since partially broken-down molecules of milk protein absorbed by a mother's intestines when she ingests milk can appear in her breast milk. So you may need to experiment with your dairy intake to help figure out if your child has a milk allergy or intolerance. Also keep in mind that removing dairy from your diet if you're a breastfeeding mother does not just mean avoiding cheese, milk, and ice cream. Casein and whey, two components of cow's milk, are present in many prepared foods. If your baby has a true allergy or intolerance to dairy, you may need to read every food label carefully to make sure you don't ingest any casein or whey while breastfeeding your child.

Fussy spells and colic

Babies with fussy spells and colic (see also pages 177–182) usually feed very well—they don't cry during feeding. Fits of nighttime crying are long and loud but don't center on feeding time.

Rare causes of chronic fussiness in babies who otherwise seem fine include infant glaucoma (elevated pressure within the eyeball) and hair-tourniquet syndrome (a strand of hair or a fabric thread somehow ends up tightly encircling a toe or finger, constricting blood flow and causing pain).

Illness

If your baby has a sore throat, stomachache, or other aches and pains associated with illness, she'll be cranky and may cry excessively. Usually there will be other signs that she's sick: fever, cough, runny nose, or diarrhea. Your sick baby probably won't feed as well as she usually does, but she won't cry only during feedings. If she is relatively young (under 3 months old), your pediatrician will likely want to hear from you. In older infants, your doctor may recommend giving her acetaminophen (such as infant Tylenol), which can relieve her pain and ease her crying.

Chronic hunger

A breastfed baby may cry excessively when she isn't satisfied with the amount of milk she's getting, but crying usually doesn't signal that your baby isn't getting enough milk on a daily basis. Babies who are chronically hungry are inactive, perhaps to conserve energy, and seem accustomed to their low-calorie diets. They may actually cry very little. This probably won't be diagnosed until a checkup, when it is discovered that she's not gaining enough weight. But if you suspect she is not getting enough milk, discuss this with her doctor.

Responding to crying

You'll want to soothe your distressed baby, no matter why he's wailing. Responding to him when he's crying shows him that you love him and strengthens the bond between you. Comforting him also makes you feel good. But are you spoiling him if you always pick him up as soon as he cries?

The short answer: No, you can't spoil a baby.

People who believe babies can be spoiled think it's a mistake to quickly respond to all your baby's cries. By doing so, they think your baby will become dependent on you and won't learn to calm himself. He'll demand to have you with him constantly.

However, it's more likely that the opposite is true: If your baby needs frequent tending, he probably is the type of child who needs more soothing. It's just his temperament. Each baby is born with a unique temperament. Your baby may be outgoing, fearful, upbeat, anxious, stubborn, or sensitive (see page 139). Not every aspect of his personality is evident at birth, but you'll see signs of some traits. He might be content to lie quietly in his crib for long periods, for example, or he may need you to soothe him.

It's absolutely fine to give your crying baby a few minutes on his own and give him a chance to try to calm himself. In the long run, you do want him to learn this valuable skill. But once it's clear that it isn't working, go ahead and pick him up. You're not spoiling him; you're giving more comfort to a baby who needs comforting.

When to respond

With time, you'll become skilled at knowing how best to respond to your crying child. Avoid extremes: Rushing to soothe him every time he cries will keep him from learning how to self-soothe, but if you ignore his cries, he could be suffering from pain, illness, hunger, or injury unnecessarily. Your response is critically important to his emotional development. The comfort you provide when he needs you confirms your love for him and lays the foundation for him to learn to love others. The art of parenting involves finding the happy middle ground. If you're unsure about how quickly to go to your crying child, here's a guide:

Respond promptly when your baby:
- Is hungry. (This doesn't apply to toddlers who are stalling at bedtime by asking for food.)
- Is ill.
- Has an injury or is in pain.
- Is afraid or having difficulty in a social situation.

Respond after a few minutes when:
- The cries don't signal anything urgent.
- You're teaching your baby to soothe himself.
- You're in the middle of doing something and can't leave it immediately.
- You need a few minutes to yourself (going to the toilet, showering, etc.) and he's in a safe place where he can't get hurt.
- You're teaching him good sleep habits (such as falling asleep by himself or not being fed during the night).

Try not to respond at all when:
- Your toddler is having a temper tantrum. Responding to it reinforces the behavior; in time, he'll calm down if you ignore his behavior. If you're in public, you can pick him up and remove him from the room, but try not to say too much.
- Your baby (or toddler) is demanding your attention for a nonurgent matter, and you need to finish what you're doing. Situations involving separation anxiety often fit into this category. For example, if you're dropping your child off at day care, have a good-bye routine, such as a special hug, and then go. If he starts crying, picking him up delays the inevitable, since you still need to leave, and it will prolong the crying. Typically, once you're gone, he will be fine after a surprisingly short time.

How to respond

By far the best way to calm your upset baby is to pick him up and hold him. Singing; talking in a soft, soothing voice; and, for some newborns and young infants, swaddling can help. Try bringing your baby into a dimly lit, quiet room or go outside. Pay attention to what sounds your baby likes. Sometimes listening to wind chimes, running a vacuum cleaner, or hearing music will soothe a baby (see opposite page for more tips). As you get to know each other, you'll discover the most successful ways to comfort your baby.

Sucking

Babies have a natural urge to suck. Pacifiers soothe some babies, especially those with a strong desire to suck. Guidelines from the American Academy of Pediatrics recommend offering a pacifier at naptime and bedtime for the first year (after the first month if you're nursing). Using a pacifier has been found to decrease the risk of sudden infant death syndrome (see page 63). However, do not try to force your baby to take one or reinsert a pacifier once your baby is asleep.

If you're breastfeeding, you can often calm your baby by letting him breastfeed longer. He won't get much nutrition from the extra minutes of sucking, but he may find it comforting. This solution is time-consuming, though, and can result in sore, cracked nipples—which, in turn, leave you at risk of an infection. (Pure lanolin ointment can help protect your nipples and aid healing.) To prevent this, you can gently break the seal of your baby's mouth with your little finger once he is no longer actually swallowing milk.

Another option is to let your baby suck on your finger. Hold your pinky palm side up, bent in the shape of a letter "C," and insert it into your baby's mouth until the tip of your finger rests against his hard palate. (Be sure to keep your pinky nail short!) Substituting your finger for the pacifier can require you to hold your infant for long periods of time.

MORE **ABOUT**   pacifiers and breastfeeding

Some people believe that by sucking on a pacifier, a baby may suck less at the breast—diminishing a mother's milk supply. Additionally, some people warn that infants may suffer from "nipple confusion" and not suck properly at the breast because of their experience with sucking on a pacifier. However, these conclusions may not be warranted. The argument against pacifiers is based on studies that have a large flaw: In these observational studies, investigators did not randomly assign babies to one group or the other. Instead, the parents decided on their own whether to use pacifiers with their babies. This is problematic because babies vary in the intensity of their need to suck—it's quite possible that the infants whose parents gave them pacifiers were the ones with the most intense sucking urges. In *other words, a baby who cries often because she needs to suck on something is more likely to be given a pacifier. So these trials may show only that babies with a strong urge to suck don't breastfeed for as long as those who have a weaker urge. It may be these babies' personal characteristics, not pacifier use, that determine when weaning occurs. Moreover, a baby who's always eager to suck will breastfeed long and often. Perhaps his mother stops nursing sooner than other mothers because she finds it too time consuming. There's no reliable evidence that nipple confusion actually occurs in newborns. They are typically smart enough to learn to suck successfully on pacifiers and also at the breast. Recent well-designed randomized studies have shown that pacifiers do not cause shortening of the duration of breastfeeding.*

Soothing techniques

Holding

Pick up your baby and hold her close to your body, so she can hear your heartbeat or your voice as you sing to her, or carry her in a sling or carrier. Many babies find this reassuring.

Swaddling

Snugly wrapping your baby replicates her experience in the womb and can help settle a crying baby to sleep. See page 34 for step-by-step guidance.

Bathing

Some babies love to be placed in a bath and have warm water gently splashed over their bodies. Alternatively, take your baby into the bathtub with you and hold her close in the warm water. (Have someone nearby to help you get out.)

Stimulation

Some babies are easily bored! Try showing your baby a toy or mobile with bright colors, or put on some upbeat music and play with her.

Rocking

Gentle motion can help her calm down. Rock her in a bouncy chair, or hold her while you rock in a chair or glider. Sway with her against your shoulder or in your lap, or dance slowly with her in your arms.

Going out

A walk in the open air seems to work with some babies. Sometimes just the change of scenery going from inside to outside helps.

Baby sign language

When your baby is about 6 to 7 months old, you can begin teaching her sign language—and by the time she's 8 or 9 months old, she may be able to sign back to you!

While you can develop your own gestures, most parents use standard hand signs developed for the deaf, known as American Sign Language (ASL). There are signs for "milk," "hungry," "tired/go to sleep," "diaper," "more," and just about everything you might need. The baby in this photograph is signing "please." With sign language, your baby can communicate clearly with you well before she's able to speak.

When the idea of teaching babies with no hearing impairment how to sign first began to catch on, some people worried that using signs would delay speech development. Research has shown this is not the case. In fact, some studies show that babies who learn early on how to communicate with sign language develop spoken language sooner.

Scientists believe that the nonverbal communication between parents and their baby gives the baby's brain a major head start in learning to talk. Previous studies have indicated that this effect is related to how the parents talk to the child. Now it's apparent that how parents gesture to their children also affects their children's vocabulary.

Recent research has revealed that pointing and gesturing at a toddler around the age of 14 months has a significant effect on her ability to make conversation when she reaches school age.

How to teach signs

If you don't know sign language, you can learn enough to share with your baby with the help of books or an ASL dictionary— several websites offer free video and image dictionaries.

To teach useful signs to your baby, sign the word when it's relevant. Use the sign for "milk" when you are about to breast- or bottle-feed; sign "time to sleep" when it's time for a nap or to go to bed. You can choose whether to say the word at the same time you sign it or just sign it. In fact,

some experts on signing advise against saying the words while signing—they say your baby probably will learn the concept sooner if you use only sign language and no spoken words.

By using sign language, you and your baby can avoid some of the frustration that comes when she's unable to explain to you what she wants. With less frustration, your baby will most likely cry less.

Most children don't have a handful of spoken words until they are 15 to 18 months old, and for some it takes even longer. But at 8 or 9 months of age, a baby can learn enough words through sign language that the two of you may be able to "talk" together by signing.

Colic

Colic refers to long episodes of crying by healthy babies, for no apparent reason. It's been estimated that as many as 20 percent of infants suffer from this condition, but that figure includes many babies with milder forms.

During a bout of colic, a baby who has been acting fine all day typically brings her knees up to her abdomen suddenly, clenches her fists, and begins screaming. And she screams for hours, despite your best efforts to respond to whatever she might need and to comfort her.

These crying spells usually start at 2 to 4 weeks of age, gradually increase in duration and intensity, and peak at about 6 to 8 weeks of age. After that peak, symptoms generally decrease dramatically. Episodes become milder until they disappear, usually at about 3 months of age but occasionally not until 6 months. Colic usually occurs in the evening, ending between 11 p.m. and midnight for many babies. In the most severe cases, babies may cry all day or all night long.

Colic occurs equally in girls and boys, in bottle-fed and breastfed infants, in rich and poor families, in first-born children and subsequent babies, and in babies born vaginally and by cesarean section.

Most pediatricians view colic as an essentially benign condition, with no lasting effect on a child. But colic can have a pronounced effect on parents.

After many long nights of listening to their baby cry, often without being able to calm her down, parents might find their feelings toward their baby changing. They may begin to find parenting less rewarding and fail to develop as close a bond with their baby as they might under normal circumstances. It's natural, of course, to even feel angry at times toward a baby for being so difficult. But when parents feel only aggravated and annoyed, negative emotions and sometimes behavior can usurp their expressions of love. When a baby's colic has finally eased, the way her parents view her and respond to her may have changed. Moments of intense parental frustration and anger during episodes of colic can even lead to child abuse. If you ever feel as if you're going to lose your temper or harm your baby, put her in a safe place, like her crib, and leave the room until you've calmed down.

Colic also might affect a baby. Some studies suggest that babies who suffered from colic are more prone to feeding and sleeping problems, have more-difficult personalities, and may have behavior problems in preschool. It seems logical that repeatedly enduring such intense crying without relief can affect a child's emotional development. But is the cause colic, or is some other factor at work? For example, a baby with colic may simply be born with a more-difficult temperament that would have led to the same behavioral outcome even if she didn't go through weeks of colic. Or perhaps the weeks of aggravating colic have affected her parents'

RULE OF 3s

The long-standing definition of colic goes back to Dr. M. Wessel. In 1954, he defined colic as crying by an otherwise healthy and well-fed baby that lasts for at least
- 3 hours a day,
- 3 days a week,
- 3 weeks in a row.

You really don't need this definition to tell you if your baby has colic—the wailing will certainly happen almost every evening. And of course you don't have to wait 3 weeks to be sure it is colic. But having a widely accepted meaning for colic is useful for classifying patients in research studies.

For parents, a more practical definition of colic is: daily episodes of loud, continuous crying with no apparent cause that are difficult to relieve and very distressing to you.

7 common theories about what causes colic

1 Intestinal immaturity and gas. During attacks of colic, infants look as if they're suffering from abdominal pain and often pass gas. This theory doesn't explain, however, why colic occurs mostly in the evening and isn't immediately present at birth, and why colicky babies generally have the same posture and facial expressions as they do when they cry for other reasons.

2 A reaction to cow's milk proteins. These proteins can be ingested through formula or transmitted via breast milk after a mother drinks cow's milk or eats foods that contain cow's milk proteins. A small percentage of colicky infants dramatically improve when they're given a hypoallergenic formula or their mothers omit dairy (or another suspicious food) from their diets. However, this doesn't work for most infants with colic, and it doesn't account for the fact that colic occurs mostly in the evening.

3 Inexperienced parents are missing their baby's signals and are unresponsive to her needs. A published study demonstrated that in one group of mothers and their babies, colic could be reduced by teaching mothers to better recognize cues from their babies and to react more immediately and effectively. However, most mothers and fathers of colicky babies have no problem recognizing and answering their baby's wants and needs.

4 Being overtired. It's well known that tired infants and children are fussy and cranky. The timing of colic could be related to the fact that tiredness is greatest at the end of the day. Colic resolves around the same age that babies who don't have colic develop a greater sense of night-day cycles and longer nighttime sleeping intervals. This seems logical, but there is no evidence that colic is a sleep problem.

5 A very fussy temperament. As with all personality traits, there is a continuum of colicky infants: Some don't have fussy spells at all, many have mild cases of colic, and others have terrible colic. Many times, too, at least one of a colicky infant's parents was also colicky as a baby. It could be inherited, like some other personality traits.

Several experts suspect that some babies with colic have a heightened sensitivity to sensory input. They're greatly bothered by noises, bright lights, and skin sensations. In these babies, colic may be caused by what they perceive as an environment full of such stimuli. However, there's no solid evidence to confirm or deny this hypothesis.

6 A result of "bad" bacteria outnumbering "good" bacteria in the intestines. Infants with colic have been found to have significantly fewer non-pathogenic bacteria, such as lactobacilli, in their stools than other infants. When lactobacilli were fed to colicky infants in one small study, most found some relief from their symptoms; infants not given the probiotics did not improve. However, this doesn't explain why the symptoms are worse at night.

7 A result of pressure on the back of an infant's head during delivery. Such pressure may disrupt the normal function of the back of the skull and upper vertebrae, the bones surrounding the spinal cord in the neck. This explanation is proposed by advocates of cranial osteopathy, but there's no widely accepted supporting evidence.

parenting style and damaged the bond between them, leading to future behavioral issues.

If you're struggling with colic, it's important to focus on the experience of most pediatricians, who find that nearly all babies and parents who have endured colic go on to have loving and caring relationships.

Traditionally, colic has been thought to be caused by abdominal pain attributed to gas or intestinal immaturity. In fact, the word "colic" comes from the Greek "kolikos," meaning "of the colon." This hasn't been satisfactorily proven, nor have other theories about what causes colic (see opposite page).

Many scientists regard colic as a set of symptoms resulting from not one, but several, possible causes. Several of the theories proposed as causes of colic may be correct. All we know for sure is that there's still much to learn about colic.

Treatment

There are three categories of popular treatments for colic: nonspecific, specific, and ineffective. Nothing has been shown to be completely effective, but if anything seems to soothe your baby for even a few moments, it's worth continuing. You'll find out what—if anything—works for your baby through trial and error. Sometimes, you simply won't be able to soothe her. When nothing seems to work, swaddle your baby (see page 34), lay her down in her crib, and turn the light off. Sometimes just letting her cry for several minutes can help a great deal. Don't ever feel that her persistent crying means you're failing as a parent. Sometimes no one can calm a colicky baby.

Nonspecific measures

None of these remedies addresses the underlying cause of colic, but some occasionally give temporary relief—with an emphasis on "occasionally." Motion, massage, vibration, and certain holding positions may help (see page 181), though none has been scientifically proven to work.

Another option is chamomile or fennel tea. In studies, giving chamomile or fennel tea, at room temperature and in a bottle, to a crying baby was more effective than a placebo. Some herbal teas can be unsafe for babies, so check with your pediatrician before trying this, and make sure any tea you provide is purely chamomile or fennel.

Specific treatments

Some treatments are specific to particular

theories about what's causing colic. These include eliminating milk or foods that may cause gas from the mother's diet for breastfed infants and switching to a hypoallergenic formula for formula-fed children (gas and allergy theories); teaching parents to pick up on clues to their baby's needs (parent-infant interaction theory); letting your crying baby scream until she tires of it and falls asleep (sleep problem theory); placing her, swaddled, in a quiet environment with minimal sensory stimulation (temperament theory); or giving probiotics (bacterial imbalance theory).

Specific treatments work dramatically for very few colicky infants, perhaps because a combination of factors causes colic or because none of the theories is correct. Probiotic treatment, which is relatively new, is intriguing and shows much promise, but further studies are needed to determine its effectiveness.

Ineffective treatments

Generations of parents have tried over-the-counter remedies, such as gripe water or Mylicon, and most will swear that they work. However, there's no evidence that simethicone, the main ingredient in Mylicon and other colic remedies, is helpful in treating colic; in fact, studies have found it only as effective as a placebo in relieving colic symptoms. Gripe water also lacks any proof of therapeutic value. Most likely, symptoms improve because of the natural course of colic (see box, below) rather than manufacturers' claims.

Coping with colic

When the hours of crying first begin, you'll probably worry that something is seriously wrong with your infant. It's a good idea to visit your pediatrician to rule out any medical issues.

Colic unfortunately begins when you're emotionally vulnerable: You're new to parenting, and you may feel insecure in your new role. You're also exhausted from providing around-the-clock care for your infant. You may feel, at some level, that your baby is crying because you aren't a good enough parent. Every parent experiences self-doubt at times, but it's important that you don't blame yourself. Do your best to help relieve your baby's distress, but if nothing works, try to let it go. Blaming yourself only compounds the problem—your frustration and anxiety may become apparent to your baby, making her more uneasy. In particular, mothers coping with post-delivery hormonal changes may have a hard time with mood swings and sadness. (See page 182 for some coping strategies.)

MORE **ABOUT** | the natural course of colic

Colic gradually increases in severity and peaks at 6 to 8 weeks of age when, abruptly, symptoms usually quickly improve. This may explain why simethicone, gripe water, and other so-called remedies, which have no proven effects, are regarded by many parents as "miracle cures." If you start using one of these supposed remedies out of desperation as colic nears its peak, the dramatic improvement that follows may be credited to the remedy when, in fact, the baby's crying was about to get better all by itself.

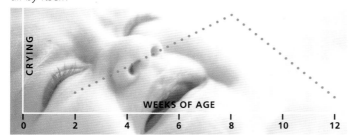

Ways to try to ease colic

Motion

Hold your baby in your arms and rhythmically rock her back and forth, place her in an infant swing or use a bouncing seat, or settle her in a stroller and rhythmically push it forward and backward. One of the most effective techniques is taking a colicky baby for a ride in the car. Of course, your baby must be in her car seat while you drive.

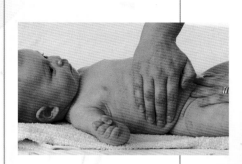

Massage

Using a cupped hand, gently knead your baby's belly, working from side to side and then clockwise. Only do this when your baby is not distressed.

Vibration

Some people think vibration and noise help because they mimic the baby's uterine environment. To try this method, place your baby in her infant seat and hold the seat on top of an operating dishwasher, washing machine, or dryer.

Alternatively, put her in her crib and then turn on the vacuum cleaner and lean it against the side of the crib.

You also can try a soothing noise machine.

Tiger in the tree

You can try this holding position when your baby is relaxed or crying and when she's naked or dressed. Hold her so that she lies supported over both your hands. With your fingers spread, try to gently knead both sides of her tummy. You can walk around with her or lay her over your knee in this position.

6 ways to survive the weeks of colic

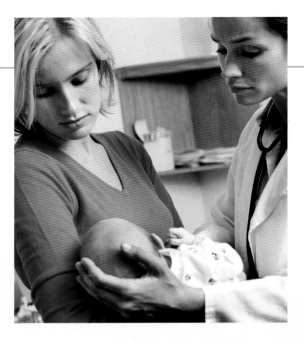

1. **Bring your baby to your pediatrician's office.** As soon as you become concerned about the long bouts of crying, have the diagnosis of colic confirmed. This should reassure you that there's nothing seriously wrong with your baby.

2. **Get support.** Besides commiseration and empathy, let others in your inner circle help you by donating their time. Sharing the difficult evenings with another understanding person is helpful. Just walking away from the screaming for a short period allows you to compose yourself. If someone can give you time to take a nap, exercise, or get out of the house, you'll be much better prepared for another evening of screaming.

3. **Use the power of positive thinking.** Although you know intellectually that you're not to blame for the colic and that it eventually will go away, emotionally you're very likely to sometimes ignore these facts, feeling hopelessly unable to deal with this seemingly never-ending torture. Tell yourself repeatedly— even leave messages around your home—that you didn't cause the colic and the episodes will end soon. The power of positive thinking can help you get through this unpleasant phase.

4. **Realize your role.** Once you've convinced yourself that you're not to blame for the colic, you can focus on how you can help your baby. Use the nonspecific techniques on page 181. Discuss specific remedies with your doctor and partner to see whether any might be appropriate. Remind yourself often that, as the parent, your job is to help your baby through this difficult period. The best way to help is to try to remain as calm as you can and continue to be a source of love and comfort.

5. **Be wary of postpartum depression.** Bear in mind that depression is more likely to be an issue if your baby is demanding. At the very least, stressful evenings listening to relentless crying, exhaustion, and the sense that the crying will never go away can contribute to feelings of depression. If you're very sad, lacking energy, tearful, or feeling hopeless, call your doctor.

6. **Recognize angry feelings.** It's the rare parent who never gets frustrated with a crying child. You might even feel angry at your baby sometimes. This is normal and understandable. However, if these feelings occur repeatedly, or if you're tempted to strike your baby, or pick her up and shake her, stop and get help immediately. You need a break from your baby, a chance to get some rest and relaxation. You must enlist your partner, family members, or friends to help you. Of course you don't want to hurt your baby, but if you're very tired, isolated, frustrated, and angry, you may lose control and lash out at him. Get help before you get to this point!

CARING FOR YOUR OLDER BABY AND TODDLER

Nurturing independence

Now that the early months are over, you might be surprised at how steadily your baby gains weight. She's getting bigger, and hopefully her sleep is becoming more regular, which means that you too may be getting more sleep and enjoying being a parent a little more.

Each month brings new abilities—and challenges—but you're likely more confident in being able to interpret your baby's needs and look after her properly. Some babycare tasks seem like ancient history, such as tending to the umbilical cord stump or a circumcision, and ongoing tasks, such as changing diapers and feeding, have become almost second nature to you.

The 6-month mark can be an exciting one for parents, as this is typically when your baby shows the beginnings of physical independence: She can probably sit up without support, eat solids, and make conversation—even if it is just babble. These new developments will likely shift the way you care for her, such as mealtimes in a high chair, baths in a standard tub, and more engaging playtimes. And they will offer you glimpses of her personality and budding emotional independence.

The months leading up to a year hold even more milestones, namely mobility for your child.

3 ways to help bring out your child's best

1 **Help your child feel confident.** Expect your toddler to achieve. You're an important influence on the way she views herself; if she believes you think she can learn to crawl and later to walk, then she'll try a little harder because she'll believe in herself, too. Keep a positive view of your child even when progress is slow. Remind yourself that change and advancement are always possible; low expectations may lead to underachievement.

2 **Treat your child as special and unique.** While your child may inherit characteristics similar to yours, she remains an individual. You can help her develop her full potential by recognizing her unique strengths and weaknesses, and by supporting her according to her individual needs.

3 **Be a good role model.** Your child watches you, copies you, and is heavily affected by you at all times, so it's hardly surprising that she may start to behave like you. Make sure you act as you'd like your child to act. Be aware of any behavior that doesn't promote her well-being and, if necessary, work to change it.

A crawling baby will signal that it's time for you to take inventory of potential hazards in your home—and everywhere else. You may be surprised at how fast she can move, as well as how far she can reach, once she begins to pull to standing. Her voluntary actions (including moving her hands and fingers to point) will show you what interests her. When safe, allow her to explore the objects of her fascination.

Once your baby reaches 12 to 15 months—at which point she is considered to be a "toddler"—she'll begin to have her own, often strong, opinions about what she will and won't do, where she will and won't go. Bathing your toddler and getting her dressed may prove to be more difficult than it was a few months ago. Your relationship will start to deepen—and once she begins to communicate with words, she'll have more to say about what's happening to her. In addition to the practical work of parenting (cutting nails, brushing hair, etc.), you'll also need to contend with your toddler's willingness (or unwillingness) to cooperate with your efforts.

Your toddler's drive to assert herself has its roots in early infancy: It's what enables her to gradually progress from reflex-driven behavior (such as the startle reflex, see page 28) to increasingly controlled, voluntary actions.

Long before 24 months, your toddler will seek out more independence. You may sometimes find her behavior difficult, but remember that her attempts to be assertive are a positive expression of her growing independence and abilities—not defiance and naughtiness. As much as possible, when she tries to do things on her own, give her a chance. When you step in to help, approach it as a teaching opportunity—for example, by talking through what you're doing as you do it. Let her explore and experiment, and let her help you with simple tasks, even if the chore takes twice as long. The goal is to promote your toddler's resilience and self-esteem, and the best way to do this is to ensure that you have a loving, nurturing relationship.

Building your relationship

As your baby grows and develops, you'll find that you're no longer simply a caregiver for a helpless infant, attempting to understand and meet his needs. Your baby quickly will become a toddler—an eager participant in your relationship who is better able to communicate his wants and desires, and get you to respond the way he wants.

Two-way communication

Within just a few weeks of birth, your baby began to communicate by using a wider range of responses than crying. For example, he may have indicated he disliked something by beginning to fuss, turning his head away, arching or stiffening his back, sucking his thumb or fingers, or refusing to establish eye contact. This last gesture was particularly important, because eye contact is one of the primary ways that babies communicate before they can speak. (Other means include crying, of course, and combining gestures with sounds, facial expressions, and gazing.) It's good to continue to look into your baby's eyes when you feed, change, and comfort him. If you talk to your baby at the same time (see box, opposite page), he will learn the basics of language. He'll soon develop a repertoire of imitative vocal sounds.

Your 6-month-old doesn't understand what you're saying, but he's following your intonation patterns, the rhythm of your speech, and any accompanying hand gestures and eye contact. In time, the sounds of specific, frequently occurring words will become familiar, and they may very well be his first words.

With each month that passes, your child plays a more active role in your relationship. He probably already stretches his arms toward your face as you approach his crib, showing that he wants to be picked up and cuddled. When you hold him, he likely intentionally snuggles his face against your neck, embraces you with his arms, or strokes your face. He'll even begin to figure out what makes you smile and what encourages you to pay attention to him—such as smiling at you and uttering sounds

such as "ma"or "da."

All of these actions and more are the start of lifelong communication. He will soon be running to you with arms outstretched, and running away from you hoping you'll give chase. Actively interacting with him will strengthen your bond and give him confidence.

Smiling and laughter

Your baby began to smile at you practically from the moment he was born, but you didn't recognize the slight changes at the corners of his mouth as a smile. Over the first few weeks, he "practiced" smiling and learned to produce a recognizable smile at about 6 weeks in response to a favorite toy, a funny noise, or something you did. At about 2 months, he probably smiled in response to your smiles—true "social" smiling. Now, when he sees you smiling, he smiles back to tell you that he feels the same way.

Soon, your baby will learn to use different types of smiles—with closed lips or open mouth—to influence the way you communicate with him. He'll laugh if you tickle him or make an entertaining sound. Laughter, like smiling, promotes the ongoing exchanges between you and your baby. It also ensures that whatever made him laugh in the first place is repeated, as you'll be encouraged to make your baby laugh again.

Pointing

At around 6 months of age, your baby may begin pointing to objects out of his reach, and you'll respond by picking up the toys and giving them to him. By the time he's about a year old, he'll point not just to indicate a need but also to share an experience with you. He may point to another baby or toddler in a stroller to tell you that he finds the other child interesting. Your toddler also will use pointing to demonstrate that he knows a word for something. If you ask him, "Where are your feet?" he'll point to them. Even when he begins to speak,

Talking to your baby

When parents talk to babies or young toddlers, they instinctively adjust their speech to what's known as "baby talk" or "motherese." Using a high-pitched voice and a wide range of intonation patterns, often with a rising tone at the end of each sentence, captivates babies and gives baby talk its singsong quality. It's more than just sound and pattern: Parents frequently use their child's name, pose questions, prompt their child to respond, use explanatory hand gestures, and include regular physical contact. They refer to what can be seen, heard, or felt at that moment using short, simple sentences, and their speech is relatively slow and rhythmic, with lots of repetition. When a baby or toddler "says" something, her parents expand on this to make it a two-way exchange, as much like a conversation as possible. When your toddler points at what you're wearing and says, "Mommy's dress," for example, you may reply, "Yes, that's Mommy's dress. It's Mommy's party dress. It is red with pretty white flowers. Do you think Mommy's dress looks nice on her?"

Experiments have demonstrated that only hours after birth, newborns show a preference for baby talk over normal talk. It's very important to your baby's acquisition of language. But baby talk's real value is not in teaching vocabulary and grammar—it's in improving comprehension and promoting sustained interaction between parent and child so that a child is encouraged to pay attention to, understand, and experiment with speaking. As your baby gets older, you'll naturally adjust your speech in relation to her responses, comprehension, and, ultimately, her own language production. You'll begin to use longer sentences with new structures.

Early preverbal communication between adults and infants shares many qualities with later language behavior and, in fact, lays the foundation for what will become real, spoken dialogues. It also gives infants a sense of their own capacity to communicate and to be in rhythmic interaction with their parents, particularly if their parents respond sensitively to their attempts at turn-taking.

Just as in adult conversations, in these early exchanges with your baby, one of you will be active while the other is quiet, and then you'll reverse roles. You'll pay close attention to each other's response and react appropriately; parents respond in ways designed to keep the "conversation" going. Your baby may slowly build up her responses, crescendo, and then go quiet and wait to see what you do next. You may react with more enthusiasm, mimicking your baby's facial expressions and starting a new cycle of excited dialogue.

Age 1 to puberty

1 Place one hand on your child's forehead, gently tilt his head back, and lift his chin. Remove any visible obstructions from his mouth and nose with your finger.

2 Pinch his nose closed. Take a breath and place your mouth over his mouth. Blow gently into his lungs, for about 1 second, pause, and give another breath, looking along his chest as you breathe. Take shallow breaths and do not empty your lungs completely. As his chest rises, stop blowing and allow it to fall.

3 Holding your arm straight, place your hand on the center of his chest. Using the heel of your palm, press down one-third the depth of his chest 30 times at a rate of 100 compressions per minute. Depending on his size, you might need two hands. After every 30 chest compressions give 2 breaths (as in step 2).

4 Continue with cycles of 30 chest compressions and 2 breaths until emergency help arrives.

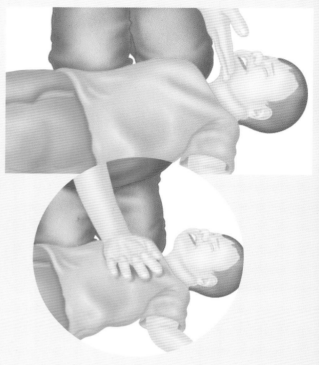

Recovery position for toddlers

This position will safeguard your toddler's breathing if she is unconscious, if she's had a serious injury, or if she's in shock.

Place her on her side with her lower arm at a right angle. Move her other arm so that the back of her hand is underneath and against her cheek. Pull up her top knee until her foot is flat on the floor and her leg is positioned at a right angle to her body. Make sure that her airway remains open by lifting her chin. Keep checking that she's breathing until help arrives. If she stops breathing, treat as for unconsciousness (see above).

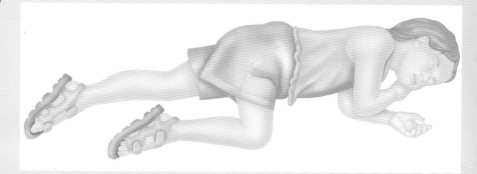

he'll regularly use pointing to complete an idea. For example, your toddler may point to his head and say "hat" to ask that you put his hat on.

Recognizing Mom and Dad

During the first weeks of life, your baby became increasingly sensitive to the differences in the ways you and your partner speak, smell, move, and handle him, and the special ways each of you responds when he smiles, coos, or kicks his legs. By 3 months, he formed a very detailed impression of his parents. This influences the way he'll interact with each of you and how you, in turn, react to him. When he sees his mother approach, he may anticipate being fed and make appropriate gestures. If he hears his father's voice, he may become excited and kick his legs because he thinks he's about to enjoy some playtime with him.

Playing games

From the age of about 3 months, your baby began to recognize the difference between an angry tone of voice and a pleased tone, and during the next few months, he'll learn what actions will elicit each response. By around 8 or 9 months of age, he'll be able to remember a whole repertoire of behaviors that get the kind of attention he likes best—extra cuddles, praise, smiles, and laughter. He even may try to mimic the little games you play with him—teasing by holding out a toy and snatching it away just as you're about to take it, or playing his own version of peekaboo. Teasing games are an important part of learning about giving and sharing. Although these games can begin as early as 6 months of age, it will be some time before your baby will actually give you his toy happily—as far as he's concerned, teasing you does not entail having to give up his possessions. In fact, the toy is largely incidental in this act. And he isn't trying to fool you by making you believe you will get the toy and then pulling it out of your reach. At this early stage, he's simply imitating behavior that he knows results in laughter.

Gender-related play

Studies show that, however unintentionally, parents often encourage different activities and behaviors for girls and boys. For example, dads tend to initiate rough-housing with sons but engage in quiet, nonintrusive play with their daughters. Why this happens is another nature vs. nurture debate. Is it because of innate gender differences, cultural expectation, or—most likely—both? On one hand, neuroscientists continue to discover ways that boys and girls develop differently, starting from infancy. (One gender's ways are not better or worse; they're just different from the other's.) However, parents, too, obviously influence their children's attitudes and behaviors. While it's natural for children to imitate the same-sex parent, it's also important for parents to be aware of gender stereotypes and avoid reenforcing them. A good strategy is to provide a wide variety of play opportunities and experiences that support the development of many different skills (see Chapter 11, "Interacting with your growing baby"), see what interests your child, and go from there.

Keeping your child clean

Your child doesn't need daily baths to stay clean, although this has become a tradition in many cultures. But to maintain cleanliness she will need a lot of help from you. In addition to bathing her and washing her hair, you'll need to teach her to wash her hands regularly, particularly before eating and, later on, after using the toilet.

Hygiene

Some people maintain that homes and children should be kept scrupulously clean to protect against infections; others believe that a little bit of dirt never hurt anyone. Standards for hygiene vary for every family, but there are some basic practices you should follow to help your child stay healthy.

Not only is it impossible to protect your baby from every illness and infection, but she'll need to build up her immunity against common diseases.

It's important to try to balance between under- and overprotection while imparting personal hygiene rules to last her through life.

Children are particularly vulnerable to stomach ailments involving diarrhea and vomiting, as well as diseases picked up outdoors. You can help to combat this by teaching your child good hygiene habits.

When your child begins feeding herself, get her into the habit of washing her hands before eating or touching food, and teach her not to eat any fruit or raw vegetables before they've been washed. Wash her hands (or use a hand sanitizer) after being out in public, such as going to the grocery store, playing outside, or touching pets. Supervise her handwashing until you're satisfied she's done it properly. Make sure your toddler knows which washcloth and towel are hers—it's better for hygiene, and it may encourage her to use them.

Many toddlers rely on blankets for comfort; if your child has one, try to keep it clean. Wash it frequently—if she's reluctant to give it up for any length of time, wash it when she's asleep and less likely to miss it. (To avoid this problem, buy three or four identical blankets and regularly rotate and wash

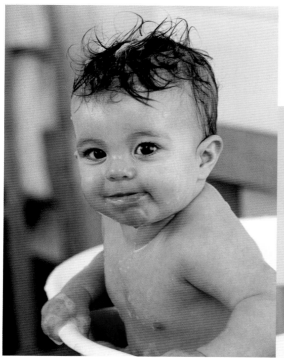

them, so they "age" about the same degree.)

Toddlers who crawl or play on the ground or in sandboxes and then put dirty fingers in their mouths, or those who eat dirt, are at risk of toxocariasis (see box, right), a disease caused by roundworm infection.

Try to keep your child from eating dirt, sand, or grass, and discourage her from sucking on dirty fingers. Trim her nails short to minimize getting dirt stuck under them. If you have a sandbox, keep it covered when not in use. If you're out with your toddler, carry moist wipes to clean her hands.

Baths

Even if your baby screamed through baths as a newborn, she'll probably enjoy bath time as she gets older. In fact, it may be harder to get her out of the bathtub than into it! Bath time is a wonderful opportunity for your baby to relax and have fun. She

The tiny eggs of Toxocara—a species of roundworm—are found in the feces of infected dogs and cats, and can remain viable in the ground for years. Disease resulting from ingestion of eggs is rare, but can cause asthma, upset stomach, listlessness, and even blindness. It's treated with antiparasitic drugs and sometimes with steroids to relieve symptoms. If you own pets, you can reduce the risk of roundworm by having kittens and puppies treated for worm prevention, and keeping cats inside.

can play with water toys, learn her body parts and how to wash them, or sit and listen to you tell her a story. When she's more verbal, it also can be a time to sing songs, talk about all the events of her day, or play word games. Bath time is a chance for you to have your baby all to yourself when she's at her best. And you can have it every day! If you wish, you can build this into her evening routine before bedtime.

Daily baths can be fun, but they aren't necessary. It's okay to give your baby a bath every 2, 3, or even 5 days as long as you clean her face and neck after eating, carefully clean her bottom at diaper changes, and bathe her when she gets especially dirty. Another option is to give her a quick sponge bath outside the tub between baths.

Once your baby can sit up well—at about 6 to 7 months of age—you can bathe her in a bathtub. Safety at bath time is paramount. Don't fill the tub too high: 2 to 3 inches of water is enough. Test the water temperature with your elbow to make sure it isn't too hot before you put your baby in the water. Keep her away from the faucets so she won't touch them and get scalded. It's also a good idea to turn down your water heater to 120°F. To prevent slipping, put a rubber nonslip mat on the floor of the tub or use a plastic infant bath inside the tub. Either lift her out of the bathtub or hold her hand when she climbs out. Never leave your baby alone in the tub, not even for a moment.

Bubble baths can be tremendous fun for many children but can infrequently cause minor problems. Bubble bath is nontoxic and washes away easily, but

Soaps and shampoos marketed for babies are supposedly gentler on the skin and sting less when they get into your baby's eyes, but they don't have any advantage over adult products. The main advantage of baby products is that they're more enticing to your child—they may have a cartoon figure on the label, for example. One type of soap or shampoo is much like another, and there's no clear best choice to use with your baby. Of course, manufacturers would like you to think that their product is the *best, but their claims are unsubstantiated—no inter-product comparison studies have been published. If your child has sensitive skin—and even if she doesn't—you may prefer to use a nonsoap cleanser. Some parents are concerned about parabens and phthalates in their babycare products, and until more is learned about their long-term effects, the American Academy of Pediatrics recommends limiting your baby's exposure to these elements unless indicated for a medical reason. Check ingredient lists.*

occasionally, sitting in bubble baths can irritate the area just outside the vagina in girls or the urethra in boys, sometimes leading to a bladder infection. If

your child develops any rash, redness, or irritation, discontinue bubble baths.

There's no compelling reason to use specially formulated baby soap products (see box, above). Many pediatricians recommend a nonsoap cleanser, which is less likely to dry out or irritate your child's skin, or a moisturizing soap, such as Dove. But you can also use soap formulated for adults.

Bath-time battles

Sometimes bath time isn't all splashes and giggles. Bath time can turn into a struggle, especially when your child is grumpy or you're out of patience after a long day at home or at work. The solution might be as simple as ensuring that your child gets to bed on time and doesn't miss her naps, so she doesn't get overtired. For more help on avoiding these battles, and teaching yourself how to be more patient, see Chapter 11, "Interacting with your growing baby."

Some young children are frightened of being in the water. As silly as it may seem, some toddlers are afraid of baths because they wrongly believe that when the bath is over, they will go down the drain with the used water. To overcome this fear, let your child play with toys in a sink full of water. Let the water out, and she will see that the toys remain in the sink once the water is gone. By repeating this many times, you will help her get over her fear. If your child develops a fear of bath time, try making it more fun by adding a mild bubble bath, soap crayons, or water toys, or by singing appropriate nursery rhymes, such as "Rub a dub dub, three men in a tub." If your toddler is scared of getting her face wet, show her how to blow bubbles in the water. Taking her swimming or letting her play with the garden hose also may help her.

Your child may feel more comfortable in the water if you join her in the tub. Let her splash you or pour water over your head and then do the same to her. Or let her bathe with friends—they can have a lot of fun together. (Never leave the children unattended.) Perhaps she'd prefer taking a shower with you. But if she still resists getting into the tub, don't force the issue. If nothing else works, have her stand in a basin of water while you wash her, or stick with sponge baths until she's ready to give the tub a try again.

Shampooing

Even when baths are a blast, shampoos often aren't. Your baby probably will come to enjoy lying back in the tub and wetting her hair, but at first she may be afraid to let her head go underwater. She's unlikely to protest having her scalp scrubbed, but she may be terrified to have water poured over her head to rinse away the shampoo. She's probably afraid of the discomfort from getting soap or shampoo in her eyes. You can help ease her fears with a special shampoo hat, a dry washcloth held gently over her eyes, or other simple tricks (see box, below).

Products for babies really are no better than those designed for adults (see box, opposite page), but baby shampoo can help. Baby shampoos sting less than adult shampoos when they accidentally get in the eyes, but they still cause some discomfort.

4 ways to make shampooing easier

1. **Sit your baby in the tub, tilting his head backward.** When you rinse, most of the water and suds will wash backward, away from his eyes, without causing any discomfort.

2. **Fold a dry washcloth in half and hold it against your baby's eyes and forehead** to shield his eyes from soap and water.

3. **Have your baby wear a shampoo hat or visor.** Basically, a shampoo hat or visor consists of only the rim of a hat. It goes across your baby's forehead, just over his ears, and around the back of his head. When you pour water over your baby's head, the hat will keep the water from getting in his eyes.

4. **Shampoo as infrequently as possible. Your baby doesn't need a daily shampoo**—in fact, you can go several days between shampoos if you need to.

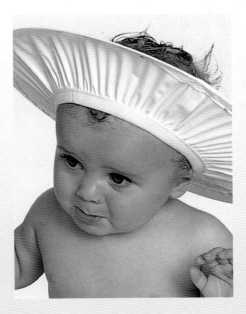

Skin, hair, and nail care

Newborns often have dry, coarse skin for the first few weeks of life, and peeling is common. But after this initial stage, babies usually have soft, moist skin—the kind of skin that makes most adults jealous! If your older baby has a skin problem, it will most likely be dry or irritated skin.

If your baby was born with a full head of hair, much of his hair, especially on the top of his head, may have fallen out. If he spends a lot of time on his back, he may also have a bald spot where he rests his head. If your baby has lost his hair or was born with very little hair to start with, don't worry—it will grow in. It's not uncommon for even 1-year-olds to have nominal hair growth.

Your baby's nails will be growing, too! Fingernails grow quickly, but toenails grow much more slowly and require cutting much less often.

Dry skin

If your baby has dry skin, you'll be able to feel it: When you gently rub your hand over his skin, it will feel rough to your touch. If you look closely, usually you can see fine, white flakes or small bumps on the surface of dry skin. You may also notice dry patches—areas of dry, rough, slightly raised skin that in light-skinned children look pinker than surrounding skin.

Some children inherit a tendency for dry skin from their parents; in others, dry skin results from a lack of moisture in the air at home (common when the heat is on in the winter) or from being in the water (bath or swimming pool) too long. If your baby's skin is chronically dry and itchy, he may have eczema (see page 357).

Dry skin can be very uncomfortable and itchy for your baby, and treating his skin will make him more comfortable. To help heal your baby's dry skin, bathe him less frequently. When you do give him a bath, use moisturizing soap (or a nonsoap product) and apply a moisturizing lotion to his skin immediately after you gently pat him dry with a towel. A humidifier in his room to add moisture to the air may help.

Irritated skin

Rubbing and wetness can irritate your baby's skin, particularly in the diaper area and on his face.

Diaper rashes are most likely to develop on skin where a wet or dirty diaper comes into direct contact with the skin. Urine and feces can break down the protective surface barrier on your baby's skin and allow irritation. The rash is unlikely to spread to nearby areas that get wet but don't rub against the diaper, such as thigh creases.

Cheek and chin rashes also are common. The culprit is usually saliva, but milk, food, and material regurgitated from the stomach also can injure the skin's surface. Spitting up, if it occurs, is likely to begin soon after birth and can go on for months.

USING MOISTURIZER

Which moisturizer is best for dry skin? As with soaps, many moisturizers are marketed for infants. They're generally mild, but as a result, they usually don't moisturize as well as adult lotions. Any adult lotion will do. There's little difference between brands of lotion when it comes to effectiveness, but there's a huge difference when it comes to price. If your baby has sensitive skin, you may want to use lotion that is free of dyes and perfumes. Tip: If you have been rubbing on the lotion just after baths or once a day without success, try applying the lotion two or even three times a day.

Saliva is the most likely cause of cheek and chin rashes for your older baby. Drooling begins at an early age, but your baby likely started drooling much more after the first 3 months. This is often attributed to teething, but it has little to do with that—it's because his salivary glands are maturing.

When your baby's skin is wet from saliva or spit-up and is rubbed against his favorite blanket or your clothing when you hold him close to you, a pinkish-red patch of irritated skin can result. Sometimes wind or cold weather can cause similar skin irritation.

Young children also can develop yeast rashes. Many diaper rashes become secondarily infected with yeast after a few days. The recesses within neck skin folds are also prone to yeast infection. At about 2 to 3 months of age, your baby probably developed a "double chin"—or even "triple chins." Drool and excess milk often find their way deep in the creases of these folds, where the warm, moist environment is very favorable for the growth of yeast. Be sure to keep those areas clean.

It isn't realistic to expect your baby to stop spitting up or drooling. But you can help him by providing a protective barrier to keep those liquids from getting onto his skin. A thick ointment, such as A+D or Aquaphor, will also decrease friction between the sheets, blankets, or clothing and your baby's skin. If wind is bothering your child's skin, apply ointment before going outside in cold weather. To prevent wetness in his neck folds, use a bib. When he does have a rash in his neck folds, gently stretch open the fold during diaper changes and clean that area with a wipe.

For more on diaper rashes, including how to avoid them and ways to treat them, see Chapter 2, "Caring for your newborn."

Hair care

Hair on your baby's head is intended to keep him warm, although it doesn't perform that function very well. Beyond acting as a visual characteristic that helps distinguish your baby from others, hair is mostly a nuisance for parents. It needs to be washed,

dried, combed, brushed, and periodically cut. Most babies don't like putting up with any of this.

In addition to the hair on his scalp, your newborn might have had fine, dark hairs all over his body, especially on his back, forearms, and temples. These newborn hairs often disappear gradually during the first few months. But in some babies, this newborn body hair may persist or continue to grow except on the face, neck, hands, and feet. Body hairs are normal and are most noticeable on children with dark hair. This is usually an inherited trait, often occurring when a baby's father has a lot of body hair. It's best to ignore body hair, unless you find hair in your baby's pubic area. Small, fine hairs in your son or daughter's genital area also are of no concern, but if the hairs are long, curly, or thick, talk to your pediatrician. It may be a sign of premature puberty, a rare condition.

Haircuts

It isn't easy to cut a baby's hair. Many babies are very uncomfortable and fearful when scissors or clippers are near their heads. Even under the best conditions, it may seem impossible to get your toddler to sit still for more than a few moments. Your best bet is to find a barber or hairstylist who has a lot of patience and preferably has experience cutting children's hair. There are even salons that specialize in children's haircuts, providing child-size chairs and plenty of toys to help children feel at ease.

Nail care

You won't need to trim your toddler's nails as often as you did when he was a newborn—he'll need a trim every 5 or 6 days now. There are several ways to manage the task, but none is very easy and none is likely to make your child happy.

Even small nail clippers designed for babies can

tips to make hair care easier

1 **Keep hair short.** Short hair is much easier to care for than long hair. When brushing becomes a battle, it may be time for a haircut.

2 **Distract your baby.** Brush her hair while she enjoys a more pleasant activity.

3 **It's easier to comb hair when it's moist or wet,** so comb your baby's hair right after towel-drying it at bath time or lightly spritz it with water from a spray bottle before combing.

4 **Use a detangler.** If your baby has long hair, strands may become entwined and stuck together. Untangling hair is uncomfortable while brushing. Spray-on detanglers will save the day.

3 tips for cutting nails

1 **Cut straight across the top of the nail.** Sculpting a curved nail at the growing end isn't necessary and requires a great deal more time and skill.

2 **Cut your baby's nails when she's sleeping** or effectively distracted during a quiet activity.

3 **Have two people share the job.** One person is responsible for holding the finger straight and still, while the other cuts the nail.

be hard to use because it's easy to accidentally snip off a little skin from a fingertip. But by the time your baby is 6 to 9 months old, her fingers are bigger, and it's easier to position the clippers so they can be used more safely. Trimming nails with your teeth risks introducing infection—germs from your mouth can get into tiny breaks in your baby's skin around his nail. A soft emery board is a safe and gentle way to file down his nails, but it can be time-consuming to shape each nail.

A good option is to use baby scissors, which have one sharp cutting blade and one dull, rounded blade. To use baby scissors, position the dull blade facing downward with the sharper blade on top. The dull lower blade will not cut the skin on the finger, and the upper blade can still cut the nail.

Your baby's toenails grow much more slowly and don't need to be kept quite as short as his fingernails, so they don't need to be trimmed so frequently. Check for sharp edges; it can be painful if these catch on clothing.

Any redness, inflammation, or hardness around a nail may indicate an ingrown toenail. If you notice these signs, talk to your doctor.

Tooth care

Begin taking care of your child's teeth when the first one appears, typically at about 6 to 7 months. At this stage, you can simply wipe her teeth with a clean washcloth after each meal. The main goal of oral hygiene now is to prevent caries, or cavities, in her baby teeth. Newly erupted baby teeth don't yet have a fully developed, toughened outer enamel surface to protect them, so they're more prone to decay and erosion. Your doctor may prescribe fluoride to help in the development of healthy teeth.

Dental checkups

Your pediatrician will check your baby's gums at her early checkups. Pediatric dentists recommend that you schedule your baby's first visit with them when her first tooth comes in. However, a number of pediatricians advise waiting until your child is no longer afraid at medical checkups and will open her mouth when requested. Using these criteria, her first visit may not be until she is about 2½ years old, but then the visit will likely be an enjoyable one.

At her annual dental checkups, your dentist will check that her teeth have erupted normally and have no problems. Some dentists apply a protective fluoride solution to the teeth for extra protection against cavities.

Contact your dentist if you notice any problems with your child's teeth, such as a chipped or injured tooth, a discolored tooth, or teeth that are painful or sensitive when she eats hot or cold foods. If you suspect an issue, don't wait to see the dentist until your child is in pain; you don't want her to associate dental checkups with pain.

Fluoride

While there is a large genetic aspect to why some children get more cavities than others, regular brushing, dental care, and fluoride can lessen the number. Sodium fluoride has been proven to help children grow stronger teeth and suffer fewer cavities. Research shows that children in communities that have fluoride added to their water supply have a 20 to 40 percent reduction in cavities. Fluoride also contributes to stronger bones. Many, but not all, municipal water systems add tiny amounts of fluoride to drinking water to improve the oral health of everyone in the community. If you're not sure whether your tap water contains fluoride, check with your local water authority or ask your pediatrician or dentist. But if your

---

MORE **ABOUT**   cavities

Cavities are not isolated problems: They're an infectious disease caused by bacteria living on gums. Under certain circumstances, such as when a tooth often has small pieces of sugary foods sticking to it, cavity-causing bacteria can grow to large numbers and begin to digest the tooth's surface enamel. Your baby's first teeth are temporary, but it's important to be vigilant about tooth care. Some babies are particularly prone to cavities: In these cases, parents will need to be extra careful about oral hygiene. Cavities cause painful toothaches, and filling cavities can be uncomfortable. Poor dental hygiene allows the "bad" bacteria that cause cavities to populate the gums and oral cavity, and "good" bacteria become much less numerous. You might think that cavities in baby teeth are insignificant, since an affected tooth will fall out in a few years and be replaced by a new, adult tooth. But if there are already cavity-causing bacteria in your child's mouth from dental decay, a grown-up tooth erupting in the same spot will be surrounded by the bad bacteria, and your child will be at much higher risk of developing cavities.

water comes from a well, however, you can assume that there is no fluoride in your water.

Both pediatric dentists and pediatricians recommend that babies get fluoride regularly. Ingested fluoride even aids teeth as they develop in the gums, before they erupt, so it's more effective in preventing cavities the earlier it's started. Your child can get fluoride through several means (see below), including fluoridated toothpaste—though pediatric dentists and the American Academy of Pediatrics recommend not using fluoridated toothpaste until your child is at least 2 years old. She probably won't start spitting out toothpaste until she's 3 or 4 years old, so she'll ingest some toothpaste when she brushes her teeth. (Be sure to use only a tiny smear of toothpaste.)

Fluoride is tremendously helpful if used properly, but excessive amounts of fluoride can cause problems for your child's teeth. This means you need to make sure your baby gets enough fluoride—but not too much. A baby can have too

PACIFIERS AND TEETH

While the American Academy of Pediatrics recommends offering your baby a pacifier at sleep time during the first year, overuse can lead to problems as your baby's teeth grow and develop. The longer your baby uses a pacifier, the more likely it is that it will reshape the inside of his mouth, which can affect how his baby teeth—and later his permanent teeth—meet when biting. It's a good idea to try to wean him off the pacifier early. Some experts recommend taking away the pacifier as soon as your baby can reliably bring his hand to his mouth (about 3 months of age); others advise removing it when he's about 1 year old. If he's still using a pacifier regularly when he's 2 or 3, he could develop a cross bite, with his upper teeth going behind his lower teeth instead of in front of them.

5 ways your child may receive fluoride

1 **Breast milk** Fluoride is passed from a mother to her child through breast milk. Many mothers produce milk with enough fluoride to satisfy a baby's requirement, but some mothers don't.

2 **Formula mixed with fluoridated water** Parents can mix formula with low-fluoride bottled "baby water." Mixing powdered or concentrated formula with tap water that has been fluoridated, though, is safe.

3 **Drinking fluoridated tap water** Many communities add fluoride to their tap water. Most commercially available water filter systems don't remove the fluoride.

4 **Toothpastes that contain fluoride** Parents can use toothpaste with fluoride for children once they are over 2 years old.

5 **Fluoride supplements** Your doctor may prescribe fluoride, available alone or with vitamins A, C, and D.

Teething

Teething refers to the discomfort your baby feels immediately before the eruption of a new tooth. People tend to blame all sorts of problems on teething, making it a catchall diagnosis, but symptoms must be linked directly to the appearance of a new tooth to be considered teething.

Symptoms

Historically, teething has been said to last for 2 to 3 weeks before the arrival of a tooth, and quite a few symptoms have been attributed to it. However, teething doesn't cause the heavy drooling and desire to chomp on hard objects that is typical of babies beginning

at about 3 months of age. Nor is it responsible when your baby is fussy or sleeps poorly for a few nights in a row, but is fine during the day; this is usually simply the result of bad sleep habits. Other symptoms often attributed incorrectly to teething include high fever, diarrhea, poor appetite, vomiting, coughing, and runny noses.

Why is there so much confusion about teething? Because 20 baby teeth erupt in the first 2 to 3 years of life, and many, many illnesses also occur during these same years. By chance alone, sometimes a tooth will appear at the same time as a cough or an episode of diarrhea. It's human nature to try to find causes for effects, and it's easy to assume that the new tooth is causing the illness. But it's just as logical (and equally incorrect) to conclude that the illness caused the tooth to erupt!

It's true that teething sometimes can cause minor discomfort, but studies of large groups of children have shown that symptoms such as fever and diarrhea occur just as often in weeks when no tooth appears as in weeks when a tooth does erupt.

Easing discomfort

Most teeth erupt without any detectable pain or discomfort. An erupting tooth occasionally can cause some fussiness, drooling, and a desire to chomp on a hard object. But if these symptoms

appear at all, it's only in the day or two before the tooth erupts.

When your child seems uncomfortable due to teething, give him a hard, safe object to chomp on. A cold object is especially soothing to many infants and toddlers. A liquid-filled teething ring that can be frozen is often comforting. Some parents simply offer their baby a frozen bagel—if you try this with your baby, be sure to take it away before it grows soft and pieces can break off.

If teething pain seems more severe, you can try medication. Acetaminophen (such as infant Tylenol and others) is an excellent and safe pain reliever. Another option is a topical anesthetic such

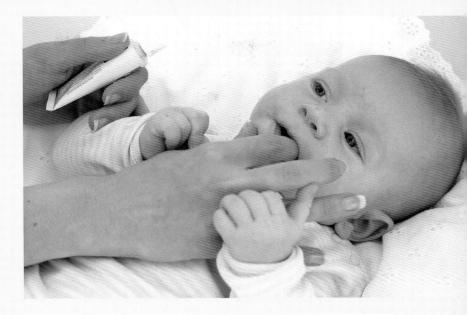

as Orajel or Anbesol, which both contain benzocaine. Rubbing the anesthetic onto your child's gum numbs local nerve endings. To use, apply a small amount of the liquid or gel to the sore area of gum with a clean fingertip and rub in gently.

Never use benzocaine-containing teething products with infants under the age of 4 months. Be sure to use only a small amount and follow the manufacturer's instructions to avoid the risk of methemoglobinemia—a rare complication that occurs when too much topical benzocaine is absorbed through the gums into the bloodstream.

On rare occasions, the eruption of a tooth is preceded by the appearance of a purple blood-filled cyst about ¼ inch in diameter on the surface of the gum, overlying the spot where the tooth will soon erupt. The cyst invariably ruptures as the tooth emerges, and a few drops of blood may appear in your baby's mouth. Both an eruption cyst and the small amount of bleeding are normal and harmless.

ORDER AND TIME OF ERUPTION OF TEETH

Exactly when each tooth erupts will vary, but a baby typically has all her primary teeth by the time she's 3 years old.

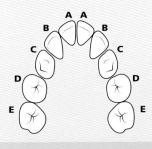
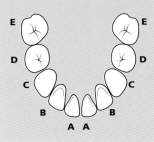

UPPER

A Central incisors 8–12 months

B Lateral incisors 8–12 months

C Canines ("eye teeth") 16–22 months

D First molars 13–19 months

E Second molars 25–33 months

LOWER

A Central incisors 6–10 months

B Lateral incisors 10–16 months

C Canines ("eye teeth") 17–23 months

D First molars 13–19 months

E Second molars 23–31 months

much fluoride if she gets it from more than one source or if she swallows large amounts of toothpaste containing fluoride. Make sure your baby gets fluoride from only one source—fluoridated water, toothpaste, or a supplement, not a combination. If you use fluoridated toothpaste, use only a smear for children under 2 and a pea-size dab for children ages 2 to 5 to ensure they reap the benefits of fluoride without the undesirable effects. To lower the risk of too much fluoride, the American Academy of Pediatrics and pediatric dentists recommend no fluoride supplements be given until 6 months of age. However, if you mix powdered or concentrated formula with water, it is safe to use fluoridated tap water for children of all ages.

Brushing teeth

Start the lifelong habit of cleaning your baby's teeth as soon as her first tooth erupts. Use a wet washcloth at first to wipe her teeth and then switch to a small, baby-size toothbrush with soft bristles. Ask your pediatrician or dentist if you should use toothpaste or only water. If she recommends toothpaste, find out whether it should be fluoridated or nonfluoridated. When your toddler is 3 years old, you can use an electric toothbrush, which may be more effective at cleaning teeth.

Most experts recommend brushing your child's teeth twice a day, once after breakfast or in the

BABY-BOTTLE CAVITIES

Terrible cavities may develop simultaneously in several teeth if your baby is allowed to sleep with a bottle of milk or formula. Saliva will wash away any milk from the last feeding given before she's placed in her crib, but a bottle left in her mouth for hours overnight continuously bathes her teeth with milk. If this is repeated week after week, she may develop multiple cavities. This also can be a problem for breastfed babies who spend each night sleeping at your breast. Continuous exposure to breast milk over weeks and months can lead to significant tooth decay as well.

morning and once in the evening. If you can, add flossing to the routine.

Most parents prefer to brush their child's teeth before the bedtime feeding. Brushing her teeth after the last feeding could disrupt the quiet, calm mood you're encouraging as she gets ready for bed. Your baby's saliva will wash away any milk on her teeth, so don't worry—feeding her milk after brushing her teeth won't cause cavities. However, don't let her take a bottle to bed (see box, above).

It's very important, however, to brush well to remove any bits of solid food clinging to her teeth. Saliva won't wash away such small bits, and the food can remain in contact with the tooth for hours. This allows cariogenic bacteria to do what they do best: start creating cavities.

If you permit your toddler to have candy and other sweets, brushing her teeth is especially important because sugary foods are most likely to stick to her teeth and promote cavities. Although this is not widely appreciated, it is not the sugar content of candies but their ability to stick to teeth that is the greater factor in increasing the risk of cavities. If you can't eliminate sweet foods completely, try to limit them to occasional treats.

Some parents enforce a family rule that if their child eats a sticky, gooey candy, she must brush her teeth immediately afterward. If you decide to impose such a rule for your child, you may see three positive results. 1) Your child will learn quickly that the stickier candies are the ones most likely to cause cavities (that's why she has to brush right away); 2) she won't be able to eat sticky candies outside the house if her toothbrush is at home; and 3) sticky, gooey candies become much less of a treat when an

extra brushing of the teeth must follow promptly.

In contrast to sweets, cheese is a great acid neutralizer—you may want to encourage your child to eat some after meals.

Brushing your child's teeth may be more challenging than you expected. Many children don't like the sensation of the toothbrush rubbing against their teeth and gums. However, they usually enjoy the taste of toothpaste! And many toddlers with strong opinions—that is, most of them—want to do it all by themselves. Of course, they usually just suck on the toothbrush to enjoy the toothpaste and rarely brush very effectively. You will need to do some brushing too in order to make sure her teeth are clean.

Have your child sit on your lap and let her "do it herself." Then, take the toothbrush (or use a second one) and quickly get in the real brushing. Try to use circular motions, but do what you need to do to clean each tooth thoroughly, front and back. Children's teeth have very deep fissures, so take extra care to ensure you clean properly and get into those grooves. Ninety percent of all tooth decay in young children happens in the back molars.

There aren't many teeth to brush at first, but new teeth will soon emerge and your job will get harder. Your child probably will need some help with brushing until she's about 7 years old.

If your baby resists or struggles, be firm and insist on brushing. Although her baby teeth eventually will be replaced with the permanent set (this begins at about the age of 6), it's important that you and your baby take good care of her first teeth. Dental decay can be painful and will require treatment, an unwelcome experience that can often be avoided. Also, a child may become self-conscious about a

7 ways to be kind to teeth

1 **Encourage your toddler to drink water** when he isn't having milk. You'll be helping him establish a good habit, and in most communities he will also be receiving fluoride in the water.

2 **Avoid giving your child sugary drinks,** including juice and fruit drinks.

3 **Don't leave your baby's bottle in his crib or allow him to use it as a pacifier.** If your baby needs a bottle to settle down, fill it with water. (Babies receiving breast milk or formula generally do not need supplemental water—they get the hydration they need from the milk.)

4 **Take your baby away from the breast between feedings;** avoid letting him use your nipple as a pacifier. Gently insert your little finger to break the seal once your baby is no longer swallowing. Breast milk, like formula, can cause damage if it's in constant contact with his teeth.

5 **Serve your child fruit, rather than sweets, to end meals.** Whole fruit is naturally sweet but doesn't contribute to dental decay like sugary foods and drinks.

6 **If you offer sweets, try to limit them to treats after meals** rather than as snacks between meals, and offer them before you brush your child's teeth.

7 **Remember that sticky, gooey candies are most likely to contribute to cavities.** Avoid these or else institute a rule that your child must brush his teeth immediately after eating them (see page 203).

tooth that's discolored or has a filling. If your child resists brushing, try to encourage her cooperation by brushing your teeth together, so she can copy you and have fun, too. Let her hold the toothbrush, and put your hand over hers to guide her efforts. Give her some control—let her choose the toothbrush and maybe give her a special toothbrush holder. Take turns cleaning her teeth.

But if a struggle is inevitable, given your child's temperament, settle for as much as you can accomplish without engaging in a full-out battle. You may have to let her try to brush her teeth on her own, even though you know she isn't very effective at it, or you may need to take a few days off from brushing. Sometimes a trip to the dentist or pediatrician is helpful because having an "expert" tell her she must brush may change her behavior. Keep trying.

Thumb-sucking and pacifiers

Many babies enjoy the sensation of sucking their thumbs or pacifiers. But both can lead to problems if they continue for too long (see box, page 199). Most children spontaneously stop sucking thumbs or pacifiers between the ages of 2 and 4, so give your child the opportunity to do so unless you or your child's dentist notice that her habit is already affecting her teeth. Abruptly weaning her off the pacifier can lead to other poor habits, such as sucking on her fingers, so gently but firmly encourage separation from the thumb or pacifier with positive, loving support. It may take several attempts before she completely breaks the habit.

Your toddler might respond well to a reward system, perhaps using a chart with star stickers to mark successful days. Or your toddler may find it easier if you substitute another comfort item. Avoid bartering and bribery, but be sure to compliment your toddler and tell her how proud you are when she forsakes her thumb or pacifier.

Feeding

At 4 to 6 months, your baby will start to eat solids. Detailed information on how to approach this and recipes to try are found in Chapter 10, "Feeding your older baby."

Eating with the rest of the family is an important part of your child's social development. If you have your evening meal late, and your child has already eaten, you can still have him sit with you and nibble on finger foods. If you can, try to have breakfast with your child and share weekend meals.

At mealtimes, much more than food is going into your child—he's learning skills, such as how to use eating utensils, how to communicate, and how to share and enjoy food. If you make these relaxed and happy occasions, your child will enjoy and learn. Otherwise, sitting down and eating at a table can bore your child or turn into a battle of wills. Remember that children copy adults: If you eat your food with enjoyment, your child is more likely to do so as well. If he becomes bored at the table, let him get down from his chair and play on the floor.

Be realistic about what you expect from your child. A mess is inevitable when he's learning to feed himself. Cover him with a large bib and put some newspaper or plastic covering on the floor where he's seated. Most toddlers learn to spoon food into their mouths without too many spills by the time they're 15 to 18 months old, although finger foods may be quicker and easier. Your child also may want you to feed him sometimes, but once he can feed himself this is best avoided. (Letting him handle the feeding and determine how much he wants to eat will make food struggles unlikely.)

Don't worry too much about table manners at this age, but do teach him some limits. At this age, for example, it's reasonable to teach him that it's unacceptable to throw food on the floor or at someone. If he's stopped eating and is just playing with his food, you can remove him from his chair before he gets too restless.

By the age of 3, most toddlers and preschoolers can handle a fork and spoon with some dexterity but

will need help with a dull knife, particularly when cutting large pieces of soft food. It's smart to allow more time than you think you need for mealtimes as your child learns to feed himself—and applaud his efforts. Offer small servings; give seconds if he asks. Keep in mind your job is to offer a range of healthy, tasty foods; your child's job is to decide how much and what to eat. Don't offer bribes for finishing his meal or reward him if he eats everything.

High chairs

Make sure your child's high chair is sturdy and has straps at both the waist and crotch. It should be secure enough to keep your child from standing up. Padding should be easily removable and washable. Look for a tray that's large enough to support your child's arms, has raised edges to catch spills, and can be easily removed for washing. If space is limited, look for a chair that folds up or can be moved with lockable wheels. If your baby can sit up without support, another option is a chair that hooks onto the dining table.

Eating out

If you go out for the day, bring along plenty of kid-friendly snack foods, such as fruit, sandwiches, crackers, pieces of cheese, and water or juice—toddlers get irritable if they don't eat for a long time. Carry wipes or cloths to clean your child's hands before eating and his mouth afterward.

While the idea of eating in a restaurant can be intimidating to many new parents, it's a good idea to take your baby out to eat so he'll learn to dine in company and be sociable. It's also an opportunity to experiment with new foods.

Choose a family-friendly restaurant that provides high chairs, order food that is quick to prepare, and bring familiar snacks in case your baby rejects what you order or grows restless while waiting for his food. Eat a little early or late to avoid mealtime crowds. You also can bring a portable chair or booster seat if your baby can sit without support.

5 ways to minimize mess

Many children prefer to do everything with food but eat it. Don't worry—this is a just a phase. Stay patient, and avoid making a fuss.

1 **Set the high chair on a plastic tablecloth or newspaper** to make cleaning the floor easier.

2 **Draw a circle on the high chair tray to show your baby where to put her cup.** Until she learns to stop tipping her cup upside down, use a lidded spill-proof cup.

3 **Make a game out of taking her to the sink to wash her hands** when she gets very messy.

4 **Use a plate with deep sides and compartments** so she can pick up food easily. A bowl with a suction-cup base may help.

5 **Use a plastic bib** with a compartment to catch food. A useful alternative is a plastic feeding apron. The apron covers the front of the torso and the arms, fastening behind your child's neck.

Clothes and dressing

Buying clothes and dressing your child can be fun, but remember the point is to keep your child appropriately warm or cool and protect her from the environment. There's no need to dress her in stylish, expensive garments. Keep in mind that her clothing will get dirty and will need frequent washing, and that she'll soon outgrow her outfits—including the ones you bought big "for her to grow into"!

Practicality is a top priority when choosing clothing. Many children don't like to have clothing pulled over their heads, so look for tops with wide openings. If your child keeps putting her hand into her diaper, you might want to continue to use undershirts that snap at the crotch. But if you're working on toilet training, dress her in outfits that allow her to undress quickly to sit on the potty— dresses, skirts, or pants or shorts with elastic waists.

Once your baby is 9 or 10 months old, she may be very uncooperative when it's time to get dressed. And it gets worse! It's normal for 1-year-olds to squirm and resist; by the time they're 2 or 3, they often shout "no!" and refuse to get dressed.

You can try to make dressing easier (see page 208), but if distracting her, giving her choices, or being firm doesn't succeed, you have a decision to make: Is it more important for you to get your way or avoid a tantrum? Your answer will help you decide what to do. If your toddler wants to go outside in cold weather without a coat, you'll probably feel strongly enough about it that you won't give in, and you'll accept that she'll have a tantrum. If she'll put on a coat but refuses to wear mittens, however, you may be comfortable letting her go without mittens. Bring them along, and when her hands grow cold, you can ask if she'd like to put them on now.

Give yourself more time than you think you need to get your child dressed in the morning. You may have to get up earlier to avoid having to hurry, which makes everything worse. Children tend to slow down and resist more when rushed. If all else fails and you have to get out the door at a certain time (for instance, to drop your child off at daycare so you can get to work), the night before, have your child take a bath; put on clean daytime clothes, like a knit tunic and leggings; and wear them to bed.

Self-dressing

Around the age of 15 months, your toddler likely will be taking the first steps toward dressing independently. You may find it difficult to get her to stay still long enough for you to dress her! If your toddler is reluctant to get dressed, try making a game of it. When you pull a sweater over her head, play hide-and-seek: "Where's your head gone? Oh, there it is!" If she refuses to put on her coat before going

5 techniques to make dressing easier

1 Distract your child. It might be easier to dress your toddler while he's busy with an interesting toy or book.

2 Be firm. If your child has an easygoing temperament, you'll probably be able to overcome his resistance simply by being firm.

3 Give choices. If your toddler thinks he's getting his way and you're getting your way too, you both win. Offer him a choice of two or three shirts, for example. If you let him make the decision, he will feel in control and will be more cooperative. And you accomplish your goal of getting him dressed without a struggle.

4 Allow plenty of time. If you aren't in a rush, then you can say to your toddler, "Would you like to get dressed now or in 2 minutes?" After picking the 2-minute option a few times, he may be ready to get dressed without a fight. Or you may be able to get one sock or another piece of clothing on him each time you broach the subject. Eventually he'll be fully dressed.

5 Humor your toddler. It's always a good idea to pick your battles. If your son wants to wear the same green T-shirt every day and has a tantrum if he can't, then wash it, if necessary, and let him wear it. Or buy several identical ones and rotate them so they wear out at the same rate. This is certainly preferable to battling every day. If your daughter wants to wear only dresses, have plenty of easy-to-wash ones on hand. If your son wants to wear only rain boots, let him. It can be easier to let your child have his way, and there's no harm done.

it is!" If she refuses to put on her coat before going out, take it with you and offer it to her after a few minutes outside. She's more likely to accept it if she's feeling cold.

Singing can also help a reluctant toddler to get dressed. Learn and share a song about getting dressed, or make one up yourself. Encourage her to sing along with you. Get a picture book about getting dressed and read it together. If your child is cranky in the morning, feed her breakfast before getting her dressed.

At 18 months, your toddler may have discovered how to remove her clothes, and she'll have a lot of fun taking off her diaper, shoes, and socks. But she'll also be learning how to cooperate, such as raising her arms for you to pull off a shirt.

Dressing your toddler is a good opportunity to teach her about the parts of her body, types of clothing, how they're worn, why you're putting them on, and what they do. This will help her learn to dress independently. Talk about what you're doing: Explain that her snowsuit keeps her warm and dry, the zipper keeps her snowsuit fastened, the hat goes on her head, the scarf keeps her neck warm, boots keep her feet dry, and so on.

Very young children don't usually care what they wear. But by the age of 3, your child may have very definite likes and dislikes and can be fussy about certain clothes. Let her choose what to wear as long as it's practical, and don't criticize her choices. She won't be the first toddler out and about in a mismatched outfit or favorite Halloween costume!

Helping her dress herself

You can do the job more quickly by yourself, but learning to dress herself is an important step for your toddler toward becoming independent and self-reliant, and you'll appreciate it in later years.

Don't expect too much at first, but offer a hand if she wants it. Try not to interfere or laugh if she gets it wrong, or she may become angry or discouraged. Allow her some independence in choosing what to wear, even if you don't like the colors she selects. To minimize arguments, put only clothing that you want her to wear in accessible drawers. Avoid

fighting with her about clothes. When she's old enough, let her choose what she wants to wear from a suitable range of summer or winter clothing.

Set out clothing items so your toddler can put them on easily. For example, lay out shirts with pictures on the front facing down, so that they're facing away from her when she puts them on. Lay out pants with the waist closest and the front facing up. Set out a shirt or pullover facedown with the neck opening farthest away, and teach her how to burrow into these from the bottom.

A "learning to dress" doll can help your toddler practice working with snaps, laces, and zippers.

Fastenings

When your toddler is learning how to use a zipper, teach her to pull it away from skin and clothes to prevent catching. When she's learning to use the toilet, dress her in pants with elastic waists that are easy to pull up and down. Later, when she learns to use buttons, teach her to button from the bottom up—this will help avoid getting the buttons in the wrong holes. Keep in mind that buttons and other small fastenings that could become separated from your child's clothing are choking hazards. Avoid clothing with these types of fastenings until your child is over the age of 3: Instead, opt for outfits fastened with zippers, Velcro, snaps, or elastic.

Shoes

Kids don't need to wear shoes unless their feet need protection from injury—for example, from sharp objects on the ground, cold, heat, snow, or water. At home, let your baby go barefoot or walk around in nonslip socks. Soft-soled shoes that slip on over your baby's feet are fine for crawlers and prewalkers. Children don't need shoes until they are walking, and then they need firm but flexible shoes.

Most special-occasion shoes, such as sandals or boots, don't meet recommended criteria for children's footwear (see box on page 210), especially in the area of flexibility. Do your best to find satisfactory shoes in these cases—don't let style overcome comfort and safety. Boots, of course, can't be low-cut, because they need go above the ankles to

5 features to look for in footwear

1 **Bendable** You should be able to bend the shoe or sneaker, with the toe end and heel end both going upward and downward.

2 **Sturdy** The shoe or sneaker should be sturdy but bendable. Stiff soles are not recommended.

3 **Low-cut** Shoes should be low-cut; they shouldn't rise to the level of the ankle.

4 **Contain an arch** You should be able to feel an arch inside the shoe with your fingers.

5 **Fit well** The shoes must fit well. You should be able to place just your index finger between the tip of your child's big toe and the end of the shoe while he's standing. In the store, put the shoes on your child and wait about 10 minutes or so; then check for red marks on her skin, indicating a pressure point. If you spot a problem area, try another pair.

To avoid the hassle of tying shoelaces over and over again, look for sneakers and shoes that use Velcro fasteners.

Socks

Be careful choosing socks for your child—it's important that they fit correctly. If they're too big, they can cause pressure and ruin a correctly fitted shoe; if they're too small, they'll scrunch your child's toes and will be uncomfortable. Check regularly to make sure your child's socks still fit her. You also don't want socks that are so tight that they leave a red mark or ones that are so loose your child constantly pulls them off—although taking her socks off gives her a chance to develop hand-eye coordination and dexterity.

Look for cotton socks rather than acrylic or wool. Cotton lets feet "breathe," allowing moisture to escape, and minimizes the possibility of fungal infections, such as athlete's foot.

Laundry

Children generate a lot of dirty clothes. Fortunately, there's no need to separate your child's laundry from your own or to use a special laundry detergent. If your baby has sensitive skin, opt for a detergent that's hypoallergenic and is free of dyes or fragrances. You'll need a good stain remover, and a bucket for soaking soiled items is a good idea, too.

Sleeping

When your child is between 12 and 18 months old, he'll most likely begin to need less sleep. (See chapter 7, "Sleep Matters," for more details on sleep.) He will probably drop one daytime nap as he starts to find more exciting activities to do around the house. This transition is not always smooth: Nighttime sleep problems can occur as he starts asserting his independence (see pages 167–168).

The amount of sleep a toddler needs varies from child to child; some toddlers need more and others less. A bad temper and fussiness can be signs of insufficient sleep. Be realistic about how much sleep your child needs. If your 2-year-old sleeps only 11 hours at night and you put him to bed at 7 p.m., then don't expect him to sleep through until 8 the next morning. Generally, you can count on about 12 to 14 hours of sleep, including naps, for a 1-year-old; 12 to 13 hours, including naps, for a 2-year-old; and 12 hours for a 3-year-old.

Naps

Nearly all toddlers nap each day until they're at least 2 years old, and most still need some daytime sleep up to the age of 4 or 5. Try not to let preschool, toddler classes, or playdates interfere with this important rest time. Your child will nap as long as he needs to, usually at the same time each day. If your child's naptime isn't convenient to your schedule or is so late in the afternoon that it's making his bedtime too late, try a gradual approach instead of trying to introduce a different naptime suddenly: Shift his naptime earlier by just 10 to 15 minutes each day until he's falling asleep at a better time.

Some toddlers refuse to nap, but even these children still need to rest during the day. If your child needs some downtime but won't go to sleep, try regular quiet time. Let him play quietly with some toys or books in his bed, or put on an audio book or soft music. You also could use this time to read to him.

You can encourage your child to continue taking naps. Ease him away from energetic activity some time before you want him to nap; offer him a snack that encourages sleep, such as milk and a complex carbohydrate (like a banana or whole-grain crackers); make sure his room is darkened; and settle him down much as you do at bedtime. If he's resisting a nap because he doesn't want to lose your company, try spending a little time with him reading or just relaxing together.

Moving from a crib to a bed

When you put your toddler into a bed is a personal preference. Typically, parents make the change once their children can climb over the top of their cribs. However, many pediatricians recommend keeping children in their cribs until kindergarten, when they are approaching the point of being too big to fit in them anymore. Once a child climbs out of his crib, promptly return him; in a few days, he will most likely tire of exiting and will remain in his crib.

When a young toddler who sleeps in a bed wakes up at night, he frequently heads straight for his parents' bed. Decide if this is okay with you or not, then respond to your child consistently, either welcoming him or returning him to his own bed at

1 **Set a time for your child to go to bed** and stick to it. Give her plenty of notice as bedtime approaches.

2 **Bathe your toddler shortly before bedtime** each night; allow her to play a little but don't let her get too excited.

3 **Put her in her pajamas**; give her milk or an unsweetened snack before brushing her teeth.

4 **Don't leave the room right away** once she's in her bed. Spend some quiet time with her— chat about the day's events or read her a story.

5 **Tuck her in** and give her a cuddle and a good-night kiss. Leave the room before she's asleep.

night. But unlike returning him to his crib, repeated efforts to get him to stay in his bed are often unsuccessful. The frequent nighttime visitor can become a problem for your uninterrupted sleep.

When you do switch him to a bed, your toddler's bed should be low to the ground so that he won't hurt himself if he tumbles out. You may want to set up guard rails along the sides or position cushions next to the bed until he gets used to the new space.

Most toddlers won't object to moving to a bed, but some are reluctant to leave a familiar environment. If space isn't a problem, keep both the crib and the bed in the same room for a few weeks so he can sleep part of the time in each.

Make the switch at a time when your toddler is fairly settled—there are no new siblings, you aren't toilet training or weaning him, he is not recovering from an illness, and your family is not preparing to go on vacation. Any source of stress could make the transition more difficult.

Your child probably will enjoy helping to pick out new bed linens, but narrow down his choices in the shop, or he'll soon become frustrated or difficult. It's a good idea to cover the bed with a waterproof pad under the sheet, in case accidents occur.

To help your toddler get used to his new bed, he can bring along a favorite blanket and crib toys, although he might prefer a new stuffed animal as a companion for his big bed.

A bedtime routine

Just as you did when your child was younger, a simple and soothing bedtime routine (see box, above) for your toddler helps him feel secure and is the first step in preventing sleep problems. Set the scene for sleep well before bedtime by winding down energetic activities and spending some quiet time together before bed. Whether you include a bath, story time, or a quiet lullaby in your nightly ritual, try to keep to your routine as much as possible so your child understands that this particular sequence of events will lead to going to bed and sleeping.

Out and about

The old adage, "There's no place like home," may well have been coined by a parent just returning from an outing with her child! The idea of visiting loved ones and enjoying time with your child together sounds wonderful, but then you realize it involves toting along the diaper bag, playpen, stroller, portable crib, and all sorts of toys and paraphernalia for a child who may be fussy and upset away from home.

Small, local trips are relatively easy to manage, but longer trips and vacations can present a host of potential difficulties.

Close to home

A short trip is much easier than a longer one because there's less you need to manage. Your child's mobility will be limited only briefly, you need to bring only enough with you for her immediate needs, delays while you get everyone into the car or wait for a bus are minimal, and it's usually easier to plan your outing around your child's routines. And if the trip isn't going well, you can just turn around and go home.

Whether you're off to the park, the playground, the supermarket, or the museum, it pays to be prepared. It's a good idea to keep a small bag packed with a couple of diapers, a change of clothes, baby wipes, tissues, plastic bags for garbage, snacks, and a bottle of water. If she's old enough, let your toddler carry a lightweight backpack with a favorite toy or comfort item and her own drink and snack.

Don't go anywhere where your active toddler will be confined to her stroller for too long. If you take the stroller, try to avoid carrying too many things. A large shoulder bag or a backpack should hold everything you'll need.

Using a carrier

When your baby was younger and lighter, she could sit against your chest in a carrier. But as she gets heavier, especially if you intend to do a lot of

walking, you may want to invest in a backpack so she can sit up and look out, and her weight will be evenly distributed over your shoulders and across your hips. The best ones have sturdy metal frames and adjustable seat heights, and stand securely on the floor when you put your baby inside. Backpacks and back carriers are made for children about 6 months and older, when they can support themselves sitting up and their neck muscles are quite strong.

Shopping with a toddler

Many parents would rather not shop for food or other essentials with a lively or bored young child in tow, but it's hard to avoid. You may need to try several strategies to prevent these outings from

becoming a hassle.

- Decide on the rules that suit your family, such as never buying candy in supermarkets, and do your best to stick to them.
- Try to go to the supermarket when it's quiet and when neither of you is tired or hungry. Bring crackers, a banana, or another simple snack in case your child gets hungry.
- If you can, try to make it a learning experience. Let your child help choose what you're going to buy—ask her if she wants red or green apples. If she's old enough, let her look for items on the shopping list. Tell her what to look for, or draw pictures of a few items and ask her to remind you what's on the list.
- If possible, go to stores with well-maintained restrooms that have changing facilities—and make sure you know where they are!

- Take your child to small specialty shops occasionally, such as a bakery or deli. You can talk about how the food is made or see how food is cut up or weighed.
- If you have a lot of shopping to do, try to take a break outdoors so your child can run around and get some energy out.

Local excursions

With a little effort, everyday outings can be fun learning experiences for your child. Even before you get where you're going, you and your child can talk about the sights along the way. Point out the differently shaped clouds and ask her what animals she thinks they look like. Look for her reflection in puddles. Discuss dogs, buses, or items for sale in store windows. When outside, look out for things to collect and use to make collages or a nature display.

6 ways to ensure a pleasant trip

1 **Bring distractions.** Keep your child busy by taking along books, toys, games, and coloring books and crayons. Bring DVDs to play in the car, on the plane, or in your hotel room to help prevent boredom.

2 **Bring food.** If your child has strong opinions about food, make sure her favorites are available during your trip. Bring a snack or two on board the bus, plane, or train, and on daily outings as well. Don't assume your child will like food prepared in restaurants, even though it looks the same as when you make it; it's a good idea to bring a sandwich or small meal in case she objects to the food that's served.

3 **Follow routines.** As much as you can, keep your child on her usual daily schedule. The happiest children are those who get to bed on time, take their naps, and eat at their usual times throughout the day. Disruptions in routine often lead to cranky, uncooperative children.

4 **Always consider your child's nature.** She'll most likely be fascinated by a new environment but feel a bit disturbed and insecure away from familiar surroundings.

5 **Carry a first-aid kit.** (See box, page 216.)

6 **Childproof any new surroundings.** Whether you stay in a hotel or in someone's home, inspect it as soon as you arrive. Bring a roll of duct tape, which can be used to cover outlets, hold curtain cords out of reach, and keep cords from lamps and alarm clocks out of the way. See Chapter 12, "Keeping your baby healthy," to learn about potential hazards.

Seed pods, feathers, leaves, pinecones, and grasses are all collectible.

Regular visits to the park can be a good way to provide your child with plenty of exercise, and it's a good place for you to meet other parents with children of a similar age. Your child will enjoy playing on playground equipment, digging in the sand, playing with water, or just running around. (Safety note: Never go down a slide with your child; depending on her coordination, stand on the side and guide her all the way down or catch her at the bottom.)

Even if it's raining or snowing, you can dress your child in suitable clothes and take her outside to play or for a short walk. Go on a puddle hunt in the rain and let her splash in her boots. If you see a rainbow, ask her if she can name any colors. Encourage her to stick her tongue out to taste rain, snow, and icicles. Let her see what footprints she can make. Let her throw snowballs at a wall, have a pretend snowball fight, or teach her how to make a snow angel.

On everyday walks, try to vary your route so that your toddler sees new things. Add to her experiences by including interesting places to visit, taking into consideration her age and personality. If she seems fascinated by animals, she might welcome a visit to the zoo, pet store, or a farm. Talk to her about the animals, what they are, the sounds they make, and so on. Keep the visits short to avoid boredom. When you get home, look through an animal book and see if your child can spot the animals she saw. Your child may enjoy going to the airport to watch planes take off and land, going to the train station to see trains come and go, watching construction workers use a steam shovel or other equipment, or, if you live near the water, going on a boat trip.

Long-distance travel

Traveling long distances away from home with your child requires considerable time and effort—not just

PARENTING**TIP**	traveling by air

At the airport, don't check your stroller with your other baggage. Check it at the gate just before you step onto the plane; it should be waiting as you exit at your destination. You'll appreciate being able to use the stroller as you make your way through airport security and to the gate. If you travel by plane a lot, consider purchasing some gear designed specifically for traveling with young children, such as a combination car seat/stroller, a wheeled rack for a car seat, or a child's airplane safety harness.

to get there, but before you leave and while you're there. Time away is bound to be less restful than when you traveled without a baby, and your child's routines will strongly influence your daily plans.

If your child has a food allergy, diabetes, asthma, or other diseases where symptoms may appear suddenly, keep with you (do not put in checked luggage) the appropriate medication, such as epinephrine injections, insulin, or asthma medications, as well as a written prescription and contact information for your child's pediatrician. If your child frequently gets ear infections or swimmer's ear, you may want to discuss with your

pediatrician taking an oral antibiotic or ear drops along with you.

By car

Always make sure your car seat is properly adjusted for your child and correctly installed (see page 97). Stop every hour or two to change her diaper or to let her use the potty, and to move around and burn up some energy. If you can, try to do most of the driving during the hours she usually sleeps. Eat meals at her usual times and allow at least 2 to 3 hours for her to wind down before bedtime.

By train and bus

Train and bus travel can be more difficult than car travel. There may not be any diaper-changing areas, and there may not be anyone available to watch your child while you use the toilet. You'll have to place your child in a car seat on the seat next to you and hold it in place with one hand, or hold her on your lap the entire trip.

If you have the option of choosing among several

TRAVEL FIRST-AID KIT

- ◆ Sunblock
- ◆ Insect repellent, if needed on your trip
- ◆ Infant pain reliever
- ◆ Prescription medication and a written prescription
- ◆ Adhesive bandages in a range of sizes, along with antibiotic ointment (such as Bacitracin or Neosporin) for cuts and scrapes
- ◆ Antihistamine (such as Benadryl) for allergic reactions or car, motion, altitude, and sea sickness; check with your pediatrician about usage guidelines
- ◆ Vaccination record and health insurance card, as well as contact information for your child's pediatrician

---

departure times, pick the one that coincides with naptime or makes it easiest to follow your child's daily schedule. On a train, you may be able to alleviate boredom by walking with your toddler to another car. Many trains have dining cars, which offer more activity to watch and a place for a treat; some provide electrical outlets for electronic devices. If your child gets bored easily, you may want to bring along a portable DVD player or watch a movie on your laptop.

By boat

On a small boat, secure your baby on your lap. Both of you must wear a life jacket, and you need to supervise your toddler closely at all times. On large boats and cruise ships, be sure to childproof your cabin as soon as you arrive.

Sea sickness is another form of motion sickness. Dramamine and acupressure bands may help; scopolamine patches aren't recommended for young children. An antihistamine (see box, below) may help. Consult your pediatrician before your trip.

By air

Many airlines recommend that babies shouldn't fly until they're at least a month old, but you can safely take her earlier if you wish. Flights are the fastest way to reach your destination, but traveling by plane is challenging. (Tip: Bring on board a change of clothes for yourself and two for your child.)

You'll need to check with your airline to find out what kind of ticket and seat your baby requires. If she's very young, you may be able to hold her on your lap, but this may not be practical or comfortable on a long flight. Keep in mind that the safest place for your child at any age is in her own seat, secured in her car seat, which can be held tightly in place with the plane's seat belt. Check ahead of time to make sure your car seat or harness is approved by the Federal Aviation Administration. Before your travel, review your airline's policies regarding travel with children, and clarify any questions you have.

Getting through security

Going through security can be very stressful with

children. In addition to taking off your own shoes, coat, belt, and any metal items, you'll need to take your child out of her carrier, remove her shoes, and send all your gear—even your child's blanket or teddy bear—through the scanners. Your stroller will need to be folded and sent through the X-ray machine as well.

Allow yourself ample time to get through security. Be patient and calm, and do your best to avoid getting frazzled. If you get anxious and stressed, your child will, too. It's a good idea to prepare her for this process before your trip, particularly if she's attached to a blanket or favorite toy and may balk at sending it through the X-ray machine. Older children will need to walk by themselves through scanners.

Prepare as much as you can before you get to security: Gather up any items that will need to go through the X-ray machine, and remove extra layers of clothing. Locate any items, such as a laptop or liquids, you need to remove from your bags. When you get to security, look for specially marked family lanes; you'll feel less pressure to rush. Tell the security personnel if you have liquids—such as breast milk, formula, or medication—for your child.

Before your trip, be sure to review the latest guidelines from the Transportation Security Administration (www.tsa.gov). At the time of this writing, liquids are limited to 3.4-ounce containers packed in one sealed, quart-size plastic bag. You're allowed to bring breast milk, formula, juice, and medication exceeding this amount in "reasonable" quantities. Pack conservatively and carefully.

Exotic travel

Before travel to developing countries, talk to your pediatrician. Find out if vaccinations or malaria prophylaxis are needed, and learn what you can do to prevent (and treat) traveler's diarrhea and other potential health issues. Do this on the early side— you should get any vaccines at least a month before your departure.

Travel-related problems

Although most trips will prove to be trouble free, it's best to be prepared for problems. There are a

few conditions that are related to travel in which treatments suitable for adults may need to be adapted for children.

Car and sea sickness

Motion sickness with associated nausea and vomiting results when the eyes make rapid movements to follow and refocus on moving objects. A good way to avoid it in cars is to position your child in the middle of the backseat. Cut cardboard to form blinders and tape them onto the sides of her car seat to keep her from looking out the side windows. Looking straight ahead can help her avoid these rapid eye movements. Some doctors recommend giving an age-appropriate antihistamine, such as diphenhydramine (Benadryl), dimenhydrinate (Dramamine), or meclizine (Bonine), to prevent motion sickness. These probably will make your child sleepy.

Car sickness sometimes occurs because a child has developed a habit. Such children seem to throw up whenever they're put in their car seats and the car begins to move. They typically vomit shortly after the trip begins, but sometimes it starts even before they move. If your baby has developed this habit, for whatever reason, the best thing you can do is have a plastic bag on hand as you strap her in her seat and wait for her to throw up. Try not to show any emotion or disapproval: With many children, any reaction—

even though it's negative—reinforces their behavior. Usually, after one or two episodes of vomiting, the rest of the trip is uneventful. You may want to pack extra outfits, wipes, and plastic bags, and perhaps put a towel under your child if you think she's likely to throw up.

For young children suffering from sea sickness, try rest and an antihistamine.

Earache

When flying, changes in air pressure during takeoff and landing can lead to earaches. This isn't as common as believed: According to one study, only 6 percent of children suffered ear discomfort during takeoff and 10 percent felt discomfort during landing.

The Eustachian tube in the ear is responsible for equalizing air pressure in the middle ear with pressure outside the body. If the Eustachian tube becomes "stuck" in a closed position—for example, if your child has a head cold or allergies—it won't be able to equalize the pressure, and changes in cabin pressure as the plane ascends or descends can cause pain. Swallowing and chewing cause the Eustachian tube to briefly open and close, allowing it to equalize pressure, which eases discomfort. It's a good idea to nurse your infant or give her a bottle—or, if she's older, something to chew on—during takeoff and landing.

However, this might not work if your child has a head cold. If she has a cold when you fly, bring a child-safe painkiller with you on board in case she does get an earache. If she has an existing ear infection, it's okay for her to fly: Any pus or fluid in the middle ear will have a protective effect on predictable pressure changes.

Altitude sickness

Altitude sickness isn't a concern on airplanes, thanks to pressurized cabins. But if you're visiting someplace several thousand feet higher than you're accustomed to, the oxygen level in the air is lower, and you may develop altitude sickness. Symptoms include crankiness, decreased appetite, headache, and sometimes vomiting or rapid breathing. Jet lag and changes in routine can cause the same

symptoms in your child, so you need to be alert to how she's feeling.

Your child's body will adjust to the change in a day or two, but until then her symptoms may be troubling. Older children and adults can benefit from medications to prevent and treat altitude sickness, but these usually aren't given to infants and toddlers. You can help your young child, however, by giving her extra fluids and ensuring she gets adequate sleep before you travel and after you arrive—dehydration and tiredness seem to exacerbate the symptoms of altitude sickness. Some experts recommend giving an antihistamine to help children with symptoms of altitude sickness, but it's unclear whether the medication treats the symptoms or just puts a cranky child to sleep.

Jet lag

Rapidly changing from one time zone to another disrupts a person's 24-hour internal biological clock (circadian rhythm). If you travel across several time zones, your child may become cranky and experience tiredness and headaches. Fortunately, jet lag seldom occurs in trips with a time zone shift of fewer than 3 or 4 hours, and it's much less likely to be a problem when you travel from east to west than when going west to east.

To combat jet lag, arrange flights to suit your child's normal sleep patterns, if possible. An overnight stop along the way can help. Keep your child hydrated, and when you reach your destination expose her to sunlight to help reset her internal clock. Some experts recommend giving your child melatonin—half an hour before bedtime the first two nights after you arrive—to help realign her body's rhythms. If you're only going to spend a few days in a different time zone, you may want to keep her routines based on the time back home. For longer stays—more than 3 days—consider shifting your routines to match the local time.

Toilet training

At birth, bowel movements occur automatically. Newborns have what's called a gastrocolic reflex, which essentially means that when milk enters their stomachs, their lower intestine is stimulated to push out a bowel movement. By the time your baby is a month or two old, this reflex is weaker, and he needs to help push out his stool. He'll begin to urinate or defecate almost immediately after feeling the urge.

The earliest sign of physiological readiness for toilet training usually appears between 18 and 30 months of age: You'll notice that your toddler seems to sense a bowel movement coming and will go to his room, into a closet, or to another "private place" to squat and have the bowel movement.

When to start
For toilet training to succeed, your toddler needs to

be physically and behaviorally ready for the process. First, he must sense that he needs to urinate or defecate and be able to hold in his excretions until he can get to the potty. Second, your toddler also must want to use the potty. Most toddlers, especially girls, are physically ready by the time they're 2½; it's far more difficult to actually get your toddler's consent to be trained.

Doctors and child-care experts may have different views on when and how to approach toilet training, but they agree that parents should never battle with their children over using the toilet. You cannot win a struggle over toilet training, unless, of course, your toddler lets you. Toddlers can be very determined to get their way: If your child is resolute that he won't go on the potty, there is little you can do to make him urinate or defecate outside his diapers. A few toddlers who are upset or anxious about toilet training may show their unhappiness by holding in feces for several days, becoming quite constipated.

Many parents buy a potty when their baby reaches 18 months and set it next to the adult toilet; others wait for signs of interest. You can start taking early steps toward toilet training once your child begins to show interest, such as sitting on the potty with his clothes on, or when he is able to keep from having a bowel movement until he gets to his private place. You may want to start reading a book about using the potty, or get a potty-training doll, as a low-pressure way to encourage your toddler's interest in using the potty.

Choosing a potty
There are dozens of potties available. How do you choose? And which one is best? Any one will do. Colors, decorations, music, and other enticements to encourage your toddler to sit on the potty probably will lose their novelty very quickly. The most significant choice is between a potty chair, which sits on the floor, or a potty seat, which fits over the adult toilet seat.

Potty chairs set on the floor allow your toddler to sit comfortably and securely with his feet on the floor—he might feel safer here than on the large toilet. Potty chairs usually have a removable, bowl-like receptacle for waste products; urine and feces can easily be dumped into the toilet, and then the bowl can be cleaned. You can put the potty chair wherever your toddler is—you can keep it in the bathroom or bring it outside when he's playing in the yard, so he won't have to go far to use it. The biggest disadvantage with using a potty chair is needing to clean it every time it's used.

Potty seats adapt a full-size toilet to the smaller dimensions required to seat a child. The central opening is smaller so that your toddler won't fall into the toilet. He'll need a step stool to climb onto the seat, or he'll need your help—though some seats have attached steps. Potty seats don't need to be cleaned after every use, and they're usually portable—you can even bring them on trips. But you can use

WHY DOESN'T SHE WANT TO GO ON THE POTTY?

There are numerous explanations for why your child might not want to be toilet trained. Whether you agree with the psychoanalytical or behavioral view on this subject, one thing is clear: Your child likes her diapers and is very content to continue to use them. She doesn't seem the least bothered by the discomfort of a wet diaper, nor is she "disgusted" by having stool against her skin. The thing that truly motivates your child to be toilet trained is her desire to gain your approval. A kind and gentle approach to toilet training your child is more likely to succeed than a sterner, more demanding style.

them only with full-size toilets, so your child will need to be able to get to the bathroom. It's a minor inconvenience to move the seat out of the way so adults can use the toilet, and then the seat needs to be put back in place so it's ready for your toddler.

Getting started

Once you have your potty, the next step is to lure your toddler into using it. Don't try this during a stressful time, such as before a move, when you're about to have another baby, or during major holidays—your child will need a lot of your attention while you're potty training him.

Some children may be curious or want to imitate the adults and will sit on the potty on their own, or they may try it while you use the toilet at the same time. Others may need to be asked. If you sense, by your toddler's facial expression and behavior, that he's about to poop, ask if he'd like to sit on the potty. Praise him when he sits on it, even if nothing comes out or he keeps his clothes on. When he finally pees or poops while sitting, tell him what a big boy he is. Some parenting experts recommend giving a small reward—a tiny candy or a sticker—

for success using the potty, but others recommend against it. If you do want to use rewards, offer one right away. Don't expect your child to stay dry for a day or a week before receiving a reward, as toddlers have no sense of time. If you want to build up to a bigger treat, such as a new toy, you can use a chart and stars to reward positive potty action. Once your toddler has earned enough stars, he can get his toy—but don't take it back if he has an accident. For some children, the stars alone are reward enough.

It's common for a child who has shown interest in sitting on the potty to suddenly decide that he no longer wants to sit there. If this happens, drop the subject of toilet training for a short while. Wait a week or two before asking him again if he'd like to sit on the potty. As long as his answer is no—whether expressed verbally or by his actions—back off and try again later. Eventually, he'll say yes.

Training boys

Boys are generally slower than girls when it comes to toilet training. Boys usually start to pee by sitting on a potty, so your son will have to be shown how to point his penis downward to direct the pee into the potty. Once he stands, you'll need to show him where to stand and how to aim into the bowl. Some parents put a square of toilet paper into the bowl for "target practice."

How long will training take?

If you're consistent about having your child sit on the potty, he has an easygoing temperament, and he is motivated, he could be toilet-trained by the time he's 2½ years old.

toilet-training tips

1 **Don't use underwear** until your toddler has gone several days without an accident. She'll be more likely to succeed at staying dry when she finally is in underwear.

2 **Use underwear as a reward** for her progress in learning to use the potty. If she asks you to put underwear over her diaper, don't—you'll lessen the value of underwear as a reward.

3 **Be prepared for frequent stops to use the potty for** the first few weeks after your toddler is able to stay dry all day. She'll want to go to the potty whenever she feels a small urge to pee or poop, since she wants to avoid accidents. It can be hard to find a suitable toilet quickly when you're out shopping or at the park, so have a plan for getting her to a toilet when she feels she needs one.

4 **Dress for success.** Make sure your toddler wears easily manageable clothing—pants that can be pulled down or a skirt that can be lifted up readily.

NIGHTTIME TRAINING MYTHS

Parents sometimes try these strategies to help their children stay dry at night, but none of them addresses the neurological reason for bed-wetting.

Myth: Restrict liquids after dinner. The theory here is that if your toddler is given less to drink, she'll produce less urine, and her bladder will fill less during the night. Restricting your toddler's fluid may delay the time until her bladder fills—but wetting at night is seldom due to a bladder with too small a capacity. It isn't the volume of urine that causes a child to wet, but the fact that when her bladder is distended, her brain is unaware of the fullness signal. If this myth were true, an adult who has a lot to drink before bed should also have nighttime accidents. But this doesn't occur, because his brain recognizes the signal from the bladder and he will either wake up to go to the bathroom or will just "hold it in."

Myth: Wake your child before you go to bed and put her on the potty. This technique may avoid bed-wetting, but it doesn't mean your child is able to stay dry at night. Getting your child to empty her bladder after she's slept a few hours will delay the refilling of her bladder until she wakes in the morning, but if her bladder is distended later in the night, she still won't sense it and she'll have an accident.

Myth: Don't use diapers or pull-ups at night—after your toddler wets herself a few times, she'll be discouraged from wetting again. This assumes that your child is wetting the bed at night on purpose or because she's too lazy to get up to go to the bathroom. But most children don't realize they're wet until they wake up in the morning. Going without a diaper or pull-up at night will only result in a lot more laundry to clean.

Do your best to avoid struggling with your child. Trying to force your child to use the potty only prolongs the process, and makes both of you unhappy. Furthermore, you'll lose the battle. If your child is determined not to use the potty—or simply not ready for whatever reason—he might not be trained until he's 3½ or older. This takes longer, but when he's ready to use the potty, toilet training will be more pleasant and will take just a few days.

The most important thing is to not get stressed about potty training. Your child will pick up on this tension and pressure, which can delay progress. Ignore any judgmental looks or comments you might get when you say your toddler isn't potty-trained yet. Trust that you know what's best for your child and trust that your child does, too. He will—when he is ready and willing—use the potty.

Nighttime training

Staying dry at night is a totally separate talent from staying dry during the day. If your child is dry during the day but soaking diapers—or his bed—at night, he isn't being lazy: He's sleeping deeply and his brain misses the signal from his full bladder. Not only is he oblivious that he's urinating, but the wetness doesn't even wake him.

To remain dry at night, your toddler must sense a full bladder during sleep and respond to the signal either by "holding in" urine or waking and going to the bathroom. A certain neurological maturity is required to detect the signal. Some children are sufficiently mature at the same time as they master daytime training; others might not achieve maturity until they're 5, 6, 7, or even older. Your child will stop nighttime wetting when he's able to sense the signal from his bladder during sleep, and this is genetically determined. If you or your partner took a while before staying dry at night when you were young, you may have passed this tendency on to your child.

FEEDING YOUR
OLDER BABY

Ready for solid food

Introducing solids to your baby's diet is an exciting time for both of you and a natural part of her development. Gradually introducing her to a wide range of tastes and textures will eventually lead to her enjoying the same meals as the rest of the family. Remember, it's a slow, gradual process, so take it easy and enjoy!

When to start solids

The American Academy of Pediatrics recommends waiting until your baby is 4–6 months old before introducing solid foods. Breast milk or formula alone will meet all your baby's nutritional needs for the first 6 months, when no other food is needed. Since there are numerous variations, however, speak with your pediatrician for a more personalized recommendation on how and when to start solids.

Experts continue to debate about the best time for infants to start solid foods. Forty years ago it was common to start solids at 2 months of age. For the last 30 years, however, waiting until the age of 6 months has been the usual recommendation. And now, experts are saying 4–6 months old is best. Don't be surprised if the advice parents receive about introducing solids changes yet again!

All babies are different and have different needs, and it's up to you to decide when your baby is ready (see box below for readiness signs). Don't feel pressured to start solid food earlier than you feel is right. If your baby was born prematurely, be sure to consult your pediatrician to determine when to introduce solid foods. Also, in families with a history of weight problems or allergies, your doctor may have special instructions about the introduction of solid foods.

Once started, solid foods can supplement breast milk or formula in providing for your baby's nutritional needs, particularly when it comes to iron. Requirements for protein, thiamine, niacin, vitamins B6 and B12, magnesium, zinc, and sodium also increase between 6 and 12 months.

It will take some practice and experience before your baby ingests much solid food. But in learning to bite and chew, your baby is also acquiring skills important for speech and language development.

When you offer solid food, also continue to breastfeed or provide formula to your baby until he's 1 year old. The American Academy of Pediatrics recommends that breastfeeding be continued for at least the first year of life and beyond for as long as mutually desired by mother and child. For those using formula, at 1 year of age you can stop offering formula and introduce cow's milk.

7 signs your baby is ready

1 She seems unsatisfied after a breast- or bottle-feeding and hungrier than usual.

2 She's interested in your food.

3 She makes chewing motions.

4 She can close her mouth around a spoon.

5 She holds her head up well.

6 She can sit up with support.

7 She can move her tongue back and forth.

Solids: start to 12 months

Many foods are suitable for babies 4–6 months and older (see page 236 for important exceptions), provided they're puréed and very soft. It's best to start slowly by introducing your baby to one variety of infant cereal or one type of fruit, vegetable, or meat at a time, especially if there is a family history of allergies. Most pediatricians recommend beginning with foods that are unlikely to cause allergic reactions or stomach upset, including single-grain cereals; low-acid fruits, such as apples or pears; and starchy vegetables.

Choose a time of day when you aren't rushed and your baby is well rested and in a good mood; midday usually works well. Eating is a new skill for your baby, so don't expect her to get it right from the start. Don't be upset if she seems to spit food out at first. This is perfectly normal. It doesn't matter how much she eats early on: Your first goal is to get her used to taking food from a spoon. Keep in mind that it will be some time before she's able to feed herself with a spoon (see page 233).

Talk to your baby throughout the meal, and be positive and encouraging. Smile, and try not to be

DID YOU KNOW...

Babies are born with an extrusion (spitting out) reflex that causes them to push their tongue forward when food touches it. This disappears by about 6 months of age. Some experts have theorized that since infants push all foods out of their mouth, they aren't intended to start solids until this reflex is outgrown.

bothered by the inevitable mess.

Start gradually. Her first meal should be smooth, almost liquid in consistency. Most families begin with rice cereal, mixed with breast milk or formula for a familiar taste. (Starting with rice cereal is a tradition, but you could just as well start off with oatmeal or barley cereal.) Begin by offering some puréed food (see page 226) on the tip of a soft baby spoon or a clean finger. You might want to give your baby a little breast milk or formula to ease her hunger, but as she gets used to solid foods wait until after her meal to give her milk. Your baby probably won't eat more than a teaspoon or two of the purée at first. Don't worry about how much she's getting. These first solid foods supplement the nutrition she's getting from breast milk or formula, and her appetite will vary from one meal to the next. Once she's eaten a bit of food or is no longer interested in the spoon, offer her breast milk or formula.

Putting cereal in your baby's bottle as a way to deliver solids is not recommended. Experts feel that children should be allowed to choose how much cereal they want, and then decide how thirsty they are for breast milk or formula. Combining the two ingredients in one bottle allows no choice—if she wants cereal she must also drink; if she wants to drink, she must also eat.

Introduce new foods slowly for the first few weeks. Give her the same food for 3 to 5 days in a row so she can get used to new tastes and so you can monitor her for any adverse reactions. You may want to keep a food diary to note what she seems to like and dislike, and to gauge whether there's any sign of an allergic reaction. A rash, diarrhea, a bloated tummy, or increased gas could indicate an allergy. If your baby refuses to eat a particular food, don't give up on it entirely. Wait a week or two and offer it again—her tastes may change, and she may decide she likes it after being offered it several times.

Don't be surprised when your baby's stools look and smell different after she starts solids. This is perfectly normal. She may become constipated, perhaps because her digestive system is getting used to food. If your baby becomes constipated, introduce more fruits and vegetables, which are richer in fiber, and consider offering prune juice.

You can eventually share many family meals with your baby (watch out for ingredients your baby hasn't been exposed to yet). For more ideas, see the recipes at the end of this chapter.

GETTING EQUIPPED

There's no need to invest in a lot of gear, but a few things are especially useful:

- Bibs—you'll want plenty! Plastic-backed bibs prevent food and drinks from soaking through to clothes, and some have sleeves for better coverage. Molded plastic bibs with a trough to catch dropped food are helpful with older babies who have started feeding themselves.
- 2–3 shallow, soft feeding spoons
- 2 nonslip plastic bowls
- Strainer
- Steamer—this isn't essential, but steaming helps retain water-soluble nutrients in fruits and vegetables
- Mini food processor, blender, and/or food mill—these make light work of puréeing and finely chopping meals
- Cup with two handles

Very first foods

It makes sense to introduce infant cereals first and to give them often. Infant cereals (rice, oatmeal, and barley) are fortified with extra iron (see box, opposite). Aside from breast milk or formula (also fortified with iron), cereal is the other major source of iron in the first year of life.

Most babies triple their birth weight by 1 year of age. This rapid growth requires not only an increase in bone and muscle size, but also an increase in blood volume. As a result, between birth and your baby's first birthday, she will also have to have about triple the number of red blood cells to fill her now larger arteries and veins. And each red cell requires much iron—one iron molecule is needed to build each molecule of hemoglobin. Muscle cells also require iron. So, your child's iron requirement in her first year is huge. This is why pediatricians recommend giving iron-fortified infant cereals early (in the sequence of new foods) and often.

But after cereals, which foods to give next? Some parents introduce vegetables before fruits, assuming that if their child begins to like vegetables before trying sweet fruits, she'll continue to like vegetables later. In truth, though, it doesn't work this way. Nearly all babies like fruits and vegetables quite a bit until they reach about 15 months old. Then, no matter what foods you gave first, many start to turn away from vegetables (and from some fruits as well!).

Consider starting with foods that you eat. Research suggests that babies prefer food that they were exposed to in the womb or through breast milk. Mild-tasting, single-ingredient purées are a good starting point (see recipes on pages 250–251). You can buy jarred purées or make your own. To prepare your own, wash fruit and scrub vegetables thoroughly, and then peel them, removing pits, cores, or seeds. Roughly chop them and add to a saucepan with a small amount of water. Cook until tender, then purée in a blender until smooth.

Try:

- Vegetables such as yams, squash, and carrots
- Fruits such as bananas, pears, and apples
- Dry infant cereal prepared with breast milk or formula

Milk matters

For the first year, breast milk or formula remains a vital source of nutrients for your baby. As she eats more solid foods, she naturally will drink less. Let your baby decide for herself how much of each she would like. At this age, eating more and drinking less (or vice versa) is perfectly fine.

Do not give your child cow's milk before 12 months. Some babies can't yet tolerate the proteins in cow's milk. It also contains too much salt and protein and not enough iron or other nutrients.

Water

Your bottle- or breastfed baby does not need to drink water, unless advised by her pediatrician. The main component of all milk is water. So your baby will get all the fluid she needs by just taking the amount of formula or breast milk needed to satisfy her hunger. You can give your bottle-fed baby cool water during hot weather, but this isn't necessary and should be in addition to and never instead of formula or breast milk. Like water, fruit juices are of little nutritional value and should be avoided or at least limited.

Introducing a cup

Like so many other aspects of beginning new foods,

opinions on when to introduce a cup and what kind to use also vary. Most pediatricians suggest starting to use a cup somewhere between 6 and 12 months of age. All agree that the longer a child keeps her bottle, the more difficult it will be to wean her from it. For those who advise introducing a cup at the earlier end of this age range, the idea is to gradually familiarize your child with the cup over the next months. Those who recommend switching to cups

at a year mean to abandon bottles at the same time that formula stops. By switching to whole cow's milk and giving it only in a cup, it is likely that your child will drink far less than before, with the bottle. This is generally helpful, because children need much less milk going forward, and too much milk may interfere with hunger for solids. Children who drink the most milk, or fluid of any kind, at this age often are the slowest to gain weight.

As for what type of cup to use, again pediatricians are divided—this time among those who prefer open-top cups and those who recommend lidded or sippy cups. The rationale for open-top cups is that lidded or sippy cups can affect your child's teeth, gradually pushing the front teeth forward. But this seldom happens unless the cup is constantly in her mouth. The advantage of lidded or sippy cups is obvious—much less mess!

Vitamins and supplements

Formula-fed babies usually don't need any vitamins or nutritional supplements, provided they're drinking at least 8 ounces of formula a day. All the vitamins and minerals required are in the formula.

The American Academy of Pediatrics recommends giving breastfed babies a vitamin D supplement beginning at 2 months until they begin to drink vitamin D–fortified milk at 12 months. Your baby might need additional supplements if she's a vegetarian or if you're vegetarian and breastfeeding. Ask your pediatrician for advice.

Fluoride is not contained in formula but may be contained in the water used to mix powdered or concentrated formula. Bottled waters (except for a few marketed only for babies) do not contain fluoride, while most, but not all, municipal water systems add fluoride to tap water. The breast milk of mothers who receive adequate fluoride often has fluoride in it; but in some cases, the mother's milk is low in fluoride. Many pediatricians recommend supplemental fluoride starting at age 6 months for breastfed babies without another source of fluoride and for formula-fed babies not getting fluoridated tap water. (See "Tooth care," pages 198–204.)

Baby-led eating

Your baby's first experiences with solid food may be both exciting and challenging. By being flexible about when and what your baby eats, and following your baby's cues and her physical reactions to new foods, you can avoid struggles over meals and enjoy the process of eating together.

The best time to feed your baby is when she's well rested and not fussy. Learning to read her cues can help you gauge when she's ready to eat, but before she gets too hungry (and can't focus on the task at hand). While crying is sometimes a sign of hunger, your baby may also open her mouth wide when she sees food, kick her legs and swing her arms, and bob her head forward.

Providing a variety of different tastes, colors, and textures is the ideal way to start your baby on her journey to healthy eating. Gradually introduce her to a wider variety of foods, paying attention to her responses. When giving your baby a new food, offer a small amount, and realize that this will be a completely new taste and texture experience for her. Even if she takes only one bite, that's fine. Over time, your baby's tastes will change. Don't be surprised if foods she originally had no interest in someday become her favorites. Between 6 and 9 months tends to be a time when babies are more open to trying new foods.

When you first begin feeding your baby solid foods, it can be difficult to recognize whether your baby is full or still hungry. Babies' and toddlers' appetites vary from day to day and even from meal to meal. It's completely normal for them to eat little at one sitting and more at another. When they are allowed to rely on their own internal fullness cues, they are usually quite adept at deciding how much or how little food they need.

Your baby should be the one to tell you when she's had enough. Recognizing the following signs of fullness can prevent power struggles and battles at the table:
- Turning her head away
- Leaning backward
- Refusing to open her mouth
- Playing with her food

After the sign for "I don't want any more" is given, offer your baby an appropriate drink (see pages 227 and 228)—she may be thirsty or may want to further satisfy her hunger with a drink instead of solids.

EATING TOGETHER

Mealtimes with your baby aren't just about good nutrition. They are special family times that allow you to interact, bond, and watch her experience the joys of discovering new flavors and textures. Learning to read baby's signals will make feeding a happy time for both of you.

Adding foods: 6–12 months

Once your baby is happily eating one "meal" (which is probably just a few tablespoons) a day, then you can add a second meal and eventually, over the next few months, a third. If you add new foods to familiarize your baby with different tastes and flavor combinations, you'll reap the benefits: Studies have found that children who have been exposed to a variety of foods from an early age are less likely to be fussy eaters later on in life. Researchers have found that between the ages of 6 and 9 months, children are especially receptive to new tastes and textures. Their experiences during this period may define their palate.

All babies are different. Some take to eating solids readily, happily accepting new foods, while others take longer. Don't panic or rush things. The most important thing is that mealtimes are as happy and relaxed as possible. Your job is to provide healthy food; your baby's job is to decide what to eat.

Preparing your baby's meals

To help your baby establish good eating habits, it's important at this stage to introduce a wider range of fresh foods, including a greater choice of fruit and vegetables along with carbohydrate- and protein-rich foods (see page 234–235). You'll probably find that many of your own meals—such as broiled fish or chicken, thick soups, soft pasta in tomato sauce, or vegetables in cheese sauce—are suitable for your baby. Make sure that all meat or fish is free of bones. Be careful to read ingredient lists on processed foods so you can avoid preservatives, sugar, salt, and cow's milk in various forms, such as whey powder.

Your baby should eat anywhere from a teaspoon to a whole bowlful of food at each meal. Try to respond to your baby's appetite: Continue to give him more if he's still hungry, but don't force him to eat if he seems full but has eaten only a small amount.

Your baby can now move on from runny purées to chunkier purées and even mashed or finely minced foods. If your baby spits out lumps at first, which is very common, slow down and increase the texture of his food gradually, making it lumpier and slightly more challenging to eat. Try to keep individual ingredients separate at first so your baby can get used to each unique taste and texture. Many babies will soon welcome mixed ingredients, but some prefer to continue trying one type of food at a time.

Until your baby is eating the same food as the rest of the family, you might want to prepare baby

meals in bulk and freeze them in single portions for future use. To store food for later, cool food as quickly as possible and refrigerate for up to 2 days. To freeze food, wrap single servings in freezer paper or divide and freeze in ice-cube trays. Once the cubes of food are frozen, transfer them to a freezer-safe container. Be sure to label all containers with the contents and date. To use frozen food, thaw single servings in the refrigerator overnight.

Thoroughly heat thawed foods and stir to break up any hot spots. Let cool until the food is at the right temperature for your baby. Discard leftovers; don't reheat or refreeze.

Organic food

As your baby graduates to solids, serving organic food can reduce her intake of the pesticides, hormones, and antibiotics often used in agriculture today. While you may have to pay more for organic food, some experts believe it is worth it; however, others disagree, and organic food has not been proven to be nutritionally superior to conventional.

Whether or not to buy organic food for your baby is a personal choice, which availability as well as price may influence. It does not need to be an all-or-nothing proposition. If possible, buy organic milk and meat, because pesticide residues are stored

KEEP IT CLEAN AND SAFE

- Wash your hands thoroughly with soap before preparing meals, and make sure the rest of the family does the same.
- Be meticulous with hygiene and cleanliness. Make sure all bowls and spoons are clean.
- Give your baby her own utensils; always be near her to avoid any risk of choking.
- If serving food from a jar, check that the jar isn't cracked or leaking, that the expiration date hasn't passed, and that the safety button on the lid is down. Wipe the lid to remove dirt. Listen for a popping sound when you open the jar. If the seal has been broken, throw away the food.
- Don't serve your baby straight from the jar. Scoop out a serving and place it in a bowl. Don't let a spoon that's been in your baby's mouth contaminate leftovers in the jar.
- Refrigerate leftover fruit and vegetable purées for 2 to 3 days.
- See pages 309–310 for more on food safety.

in fat, and organic thin-skinned fruits and vegetables that absorb pesticides more readily, such as peaches, apples, nectarines, strawberries, pears, carrots, and potatoes. To remove pesticides, germs, and wax, scrub produce (organic or not) in warm water, with a vegetable brush, and dry it with a paper towel.

Finger foods

By 9 months, introduce your baby to finger foods—foods she can pick up with her fingers. You'll probably find your baby loves finger foods; not only do they help to soothe sore gums and make great snacks, but they also encourage independence with

The texture of your baby's food should keep pace with his progress. Start by puréeing food to an almost liquid consistency, then gradually serve thicker and lumpier food. Then you can mash, mince, or finely chop his food.

self-feeding. Finger foods allow your baby to practice chewing. Make sure finger foods are big enough to pick up but not big enough to be a choking hazard. O-shaped cereal, such as Cheerios, has all the qualities of the ideal finger food: It's easy to grasp and hold, it's the right size, it is easily mushed by the gums, and it is not hard or difficult to chew and swallow. Remember to remove any cores, skin, seeds, or pits from fruit, and never leave your baby alone while he's eating. Avoid giving him sweets such as cookies or cake so you don't encourage a sweet tooth.

When your child first learns to eat finger foods, she will probably, on a number of occasions, allow a piece of food to go to the back of her throat, where it will trigger a gag reflex. To many observers, the cough and gagging that results is interpreted as a choking emergency. On the contrary, the gagging prevents food from "going down the wrong pipe" by forcing it forward. Choking almost never occurs when finger foods with the characteristics described above are given.

Choking occurs when an object enters the wind pipe (trachea) and obstructs air flow. If your child has an episode of gagging, very little is required: Count to 10 or gently pat him on the back (which is more for you than to help your child!).

Good options include small pieces of:

- Steamed vegetables such as diced carrots, peas, sweet potato chunks, or broccoli florets
- Fruit such as pieces of banana, mango, melon, or peach
- Cooked pasta shapes
- O-shaped cereal or rice cakes

Commercial baby foods

You might like the idea of making all of your baby's food, but mixing in occasional jars of prepared food is typically more realistic, manageable, and practical for most parents. When you buy commercial baby foods, check labels for unwanted additives, sugars (dextrose, sucrose, glucose), artificial sweeteners (aspartame, saccharine), salt, and thickeners such as modified starch. You may prefer organic jarred baby food, but foods from the major makers of jarred baby food are all of high quality and come very close to home-prepared foods.

Milk and drinks

Breast milk or formula will continue to be your baby's main source of fluids. He will probably drink about 16 to 20 ounces daily. Breast milk or formula feedings ensure that your baby gets nourishment designed for his needs. At meals, breastfeed or offer formula after he eats so that he doesn't fill up on liquids before trying his meal.

If your baby becomes ill and loses his appetite, he will typically still want to drink and should continue to have formula or breast milk.

Don't give your baby cow's milk until he's 1 year old. Sheep's or goat's milk is not recommended. Make sure all milk your child drinks is pasteurized. Avoid giving your child more than a small amount of water or juice.

Vegetarian diets

With a little planning and attention, a vegetarian diet can provide all the nutrients your baby needs for growth and development. As with any diet, variety is key. Make sure you provide protein from

a variety of sources including nuts (if there is no sign of an allergy within the family), seeds, eggs, yogurt, cheese, and beans (including lentils and tofu), and combine them with fruits and vegetables rich in vitamin C to boost iron absorption.

A meat-free diet is naturally high in fiber, and too much could lead to an upset stomach, low energy intake, and inadequate amounts of iron, zinc, and copper. Because of this, avoid giving your young baby large quantities of brown rice, whole-grain bread, or whole-grain pasta. Try to make lentils and beans a significant part of your baby's diet; they're an important source of iron and make a great base for many savory dishes such as soups, stews, and dips. Make sure your baby is getting enough B vitamins, iron, and zinc, in particular.

- *B12* is found in eggs, cheese, textured vegetable protein, and fortified foods such as breakfast cereals and yeast extract.
- *Iron* is in beans, lentils, leafy green vegetables, eggs, tofu, dried fruit, brown rice, and whole-grain bread. As iron from these sources isn't always well absorbed, it's important to also offer iron-fortified cereal or iron-fortified infant formula. Depending on your baby's diet, you may want to speak to your pediatrician about using an iron supplement.
- *Zinc* is in tofu, dairy products, beans, lentils, whole grains, and yeast extract.

Consult your pediatrician about whether your vegetarian child should have a multivitamin or an omega-3 supplement.

Self-feeding

Many babies love to feed themselves from an early age—your baby might even grab his feeding spoon from you! It can make mealtime more challenging for you, but this growing sense of independence is very good for him (and it encourages good hand-eye

Artificial colors, flavorings, stabilizers, and emulsifiers are added to food—even baby food—to make it more attractive and tastier, and to help it last longer. It's important to read labels carefully to find ingredients under less familiar names, including sugar (glucose, fructose, high-fructose corn syrup, and dextrose), salt (sodium chloride), and preservatives such as sodium benzoate, sodium nitrate, and sodium nitrite. If you want to raise a vegetarian child, check for additives made from animal sources (such as gelatin, cochineal, and carmine).

coordination). Let him have his own spoon while you continue feeding with another one—things may get messy, but that's half the fun!

Your baby probably won't be very good at using a spoon for a few months, and most of his meals may end up on the floor or smeared on his high chair rather than in his mouth. Put a plastic sheet or newspaper under his chair to make cleanup easier, and try to handle any mishaps calmly. Remember that throwing or playing with food signals that the meal is over. You can make it easier for both of you by offering foods that are easy to scoop onto a spoon such as mashed potato, cooked rice, and cereal. Finger foods and meals cut into manageable chunks rather than mashed are easier to pick up and may ease any frustration; the more he's allowed to use his hands, the sooner he's likely to become more accomplished with a spoon. He'll enjoy becoming more involved in mealtimes.

Three meals a day

If your baby is happily eating the meals you give him, you can start to increase feedings with solid food from two to three meals a day by the time he's about 8 to 9 months old. His daily diet should include a variety of fruit, vegetables, dairy products (cheese, yogurt, but not cow's milk), and protein-rich foods (see page 234). Introduce new foods gradually. If your baby rejects a new food, wait at least several days and offer it again, or serve it in a different form or prepared differently. He probably can eat most family meals.

The number of children with allergies and food intolerances is on the rise. A true allergy involves an immediate immune system response, resulting in symptoms such as hives. The most severe response is anaphylaxis, which can be fatal (see page 377). With a food intolerance, the mechanism causing the symptoms, such as upset stomach or diarrhea, is different, and there is no risk of anaphylaxis.

Many food allergies start in early childhood. Eight foods account for 90 percent of all food-allergic reactions: cow's milk, egg, peanuts, tree nuts, fish, shellfish, wheat, and soy. Foods such as berries, citrus fruit, and tomatoes can also cause allergic reactions. Food allergies can manifest as colic, upset stomach, rash or hives, asthma, eczema, breathing difficulties, swelling of the throat, and anaphylactic shock.

To monitor for adverse reactions, introduce allergenic foods one at a time and wait several days before introducing other new foods. This will detect children innately allergic to the food in question. However, an allergy may still appear later on, after several exposures.

If someone in your baby's immediate family has a peanut allergy or other allergic conditions such as asthma, eczema, or hay fever, your baby is at a higher risk of developing a peanut allergy. Children with one allergic parent carry a 30 percent risk of becoming an allergic person themselves; having two such parents pushes the risk up to 70 percent. Allergy experts until recently had advised that children at high risk should not be exposed to peanuts until they are at least 3 years old. However, studies did not support this recommendation—delaying the introduction of nuts did not prevent nut allergy.

The American Academy of Pediatrics says if there are no allergies in your family, you can give eggs and ground or crushed peanuts to your baby after 6 months.

WHAT BABIES NEED

Babies grow quickly in the first year and require a lot of energy for their size. Aim for a balanced diet with an emphasis on fresh foods. Look at how your child eats over the course of a week rather than day to day—infants can have erratic eating patterns.

PROTEIN FOODS
(about 2–3 servings a day)
These foods provide a good source of protein, essential for growth and repair in the body. Offer a combination of protein foods to get a good mix of essential amino acids. For proteins, a serving is 1–4 tablespoons of jarred meat; 1 ounce cooked lean meat, poultry, or fish; 1 egg; or ¼–½ cup cooked beans.

- Low-mercury fish
- Tofu
- Meat and poultry
- Meat alternatives such as textured vegetable protein
- Well-cooked eggs
- Beans and lentils

FISH NOTE
(limit to 2 servings per week)
Hearing about the high levels of mercury found in some fish might tempt you to skip serving it to your child. However, fish is a great source of protein and important nutrients, including omega-3 fats such as DHA and EPA, which foster brain development. Opt for lower-mercury seafood such as chunk light tuna, catfish, domestic crab, mackerel, U.S.-farmed coho and silver salmon and wild salmon, sole, freshwater trout, and U.S.-farmed tilapia. To make fish shopping easier, go to www.montereybayaquarium.org for a pocket guide or smartphone app listing the safest choices.

CARBOHYDRATES/STARCHY FOODS
(about 3–4 servings a day)

Listed below are foods that are excellent sources of energy, vitamins, minerals, and fiber. Bear in mind, however, that while a diet rich in fiber is perfect for adults, babies find fiber difficult to digest. Avoid giving your baby too many high-fiber foods. For carbohydrates, a serving is 2–4 tablespoons of infant cereal; ½ ounce ready-to-eat cereal; 2 ounces cooked cereal, rice, or pasta; ¼ slice of bread; or 1–2 small crackers.

- Sugar-free breakfast cereals and oats
- Pasta and noodles
- Rice
- Bread
- Potatoes

FRUITS AND VEGETABLES
(3–4 or more servings a day)

Fresh, frozen, and canned fruit and vegetables are an essential part of a baby's diet. They make ideal first foods and provide rich amounts of vitamins, particularly vitamin C, minerals, and fiber. Offer plenty of foods containing vitamin C (also good for the immune system, hair, skin, and nails) because they aid in the absorption of iron. Try to provide your baby with a variety of fresh produce. For fruits and vegetables, a serving is 1–4 tablespoons of jarred fruits or vegetables; ¼ cup raw vegetables or 2 tablespoons cooked vegetables; ½ small piece of fruit; or 2 tablespoons diced fruit.

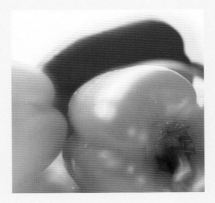

- Applesauce
- Banana
- Mango
- Melon
- Strawberries
- Carrot
- Broccoli
- Peas
- Snap peas

Whole nuts and peanuts Nuts and peanuts shouldn't be given to children under the age of 5 because of the risk of choking. Finely chopped nuts and peanuts are okay to introduce after 6 months.

Sugar Foods made from refined sugar are high in calories, have less nutritional value, may lead to obesity, contribute to tooth decay, and can spoil a child's appetite. Sugary foods—such as doughnuts, cakes, and cookies—often include a lot of fat.

Honey Don't give your child honey before she turns 1: Honey sometimes contains a bacterium that has been known to cause infant botulism. After the age of 1, a child's intestines are sufficiently mature to prevent the bacteria from growing.

Cow's, sheep's, or goat's milk Cow's milk shouldn't be given to children until they are 1. Milk doesn't supply adequate iron or other nutrients for infants, and some young babies aren't able to tolerate the proteins quite yet. Also, milk allergy is the most common allergy among children. Sheep's and goat's milk are generally not recommended for children, and only pasteurized milk should be used.

Raw or undercooked eggs Cook eggs completely so that the whites and yolks are both solid. Raw or partially cooked eggs may be a source of salmonella, a cause of food poisoning. Parents used to be advised to delay introducing eggs, but the American Academy of Pediatrics says it's fine to offer whites or yolks after 6 months if your baby isn't at high risk for allergies.

Salt Too much salt can overwhelm a baby's immature kidneys. Do not add salt to your baby's food, and limit naturally salty foods such as bacon, soup stock, and yeast extract. The American Heart Association recommends that children between the ages of 1 and 3 should consume no more than 1,500 milligrams of salt a day; babies should have even less.

Shellfish, such as shrimp and mussels Avoid shellfish due to the slight risk of food poisoning. When served, cook thoroughly.

Marlin, shark, swordfish, tilefish, and king mackerel These types of fish have been found to contain significant amounts of mercury. It's a good idea to limit or even totally avoid these types of fish because mercury can affect a child's developing nervous system.

Foods high in saturated fat Avoid giving too many fatty foods such as butter (small amounts for cooking are okay), fatty meat and meat products, cookies, pastries, and cakes.

MEAL IDEAS from 8 months old

Try mashed or finely chopped foods rather than puréed meals at this stage. An asterisk (*) indicates a recipe given at the end of this chapter.

BREAKFAST
- Oatmeal with Apricot Purée*
- Whole-grain baby cereal with chopped fruit
- Date and Vanilla Breakfast Yogurt*
- Fruit muffin and plain, unsweetened yogurt
- Hash browns with hard-boiled egg
- Roasted tomatoes with hard-boiled egg

LUNCH
- Well-cooked scrambled eggs with low-sodium baked beans and strips of toast
- Chicken soup with rice
- Baked potato with salmon
- Simple Hummus* with strips of pita bread and steamed vegetables
- Pea Soup*
- Pasta with pesto and broccoli
- Baby Vegetable Risotto*

DINNER
- Pasta and vegetables in cheese sauce
- Ground 95-percent lean beef and vegetable casserole
- Beet, Squash & Quinoa*
- Diced fish sticks with peas and carrots
- Grilled fish with rice and vegetables

DESSERT
- Rice pudding
- Plain, unsweetened yogurt with fruit (stewed or puréed)

Family meals: 9–12 months

As your baby approaches her first birthday, she's probably enjoying sitting at the dinner table to join family meals. She can enjoy most of the same foods as the rest of the family with a few important exceptions (see page 236), so you won't have to prepare special meals for her as often.

Benefits of eating together

Although your little one is just an infant, it's not too early to think about inviting her to join you at the dinner table. Even if it's only for a few meals a week, eating with your baby is an investment guaranteed to reap meaningful rewards later. Including her at the table makes her feel like an important part of the family. Perhaps that's why families who eat together are closer and have fewer struggles with picky eating than those who don't. What's more, children who eat with their families have healthier diets. They also get better grades and are less prone to depression

and behavior problems as they get older.

To keep your baby from fussing, consider feeding her before mealtime and then let her sit in her high chair and play with a special set of toys. You can also involve your baby by talking to her and telling her the names and colors of the foods she's eating.

Menu options

You'll find healthy recipes at the end of this chapter that both you and your baby will enjoy.

If you've been serving commercially prepared jars of food, try to start incorporating some homemade foods. You can prepare meals for your baby in bulk and freeze them in baby-size portions.

Your baby should be starting to eat chunkier foods, which you may want to serve in a nonslip bowl so she can more easily practice feeding herself with her fingers or a spoon. Eating coarsely mashed, finely chopped, grated, or minced foods

SNACKS

- Hard-boiled egg, cut into pieces
- Strips of bread or toast
- Rice cakes (small pieces; unsweetened)
- Pita bread with hummus
- Grated cheese
- Steamed vegetable sticks
- Slices or small cubes of soft fruit
- Dry, sugar-free cereal
- Yogurt, plain and unsweetened
- Tofu

helps her practice chewing skills and facilitates her speech development. She may balk at more coarsely textured foods at first, but don't give up. Take it slowly and try to be supportive and positive.

Finger foods are perfect for practicing self-feeding. You may find that she forgoes her spoon entirely in favor of using her fingers, and that's fine. Self-feeding is an important stage in a baby's development, as it helps hand-eye coordination and encourages independence.

Meal patterns

Aim to give your baby three meals a day, keeping the same schedule each day. Older babies tend to thrive on routine, and they need a lot of energy in relation to their small size. You may want to make lunch her main meal if she's alert and not too grouchy. If your baby has started to crawl or is going through a growth spurt, she may need healthy snacks between meals to keep her energy levels sufficiently high. One snack between regularly scheduled meals should suffice. Sugary, salty, high-fat, and highly processed snacks are not recommended, as they are low in nutrients and high in calories.

Never force your baby to eat, as this will only put her off food altogether. If you're worried she isn't eating enough, talk to your pediatrician. She can review your baby's growth chart and her progress,

and probably will assure you that your baby is fine. If she seems active and lively, then she's probably getting enough food for her energy needs.

Other drinks

If you haven't done so yet, try transitioning your baby from the bottle to a cup with two handles. If you're breastfeeding, you can introduce water in a cup after 6 months. The skills learned by drinking from a cup are believed to be better for speech development and for her developing teeth. You can offer whole cow's milk after 1 year. Avoid low- or nonfat milk until after she turns 2 years old, as the fat in the milk aids proper brain development. Avoid giving your child more than a small amount of juice.

Trouble-free mealtimes

Your baby is unlikely to love every meal she's offered, but don't get upset if she turns her nose up at something. Wait a few days and then offer the food again, perhaps in a different presentation. Keep in mind that your job is to serve a variety of healthy, age-appropriate food. Your baby's job is to decide what and how much to eat. Many babies want to be more independent at this stage and may become choosier about what they eat. If you stay calm when she asserts herself, she'll be less likely to use mealtime as an opportunity to test your patience.

1 year old

Just as you've gotten comfortable feeding table food to your older baby, who may happily wolf down almost everything you offer, don't be surprised if he suddenly becomes very fussy about what he eats. This is normal. It's good to remember that this is a stage your toddler is going through, and it typically won't cause long-term health problems. Continue to offer as varied a diet as possible, encompassing a wide range of colors, textures, and flavors.

Look at what your child eats over the course of a week rather than in a single day: You may find that overall your child is eating a good, varied diet, despite the occasional meal left uneaten. Most important, don't panic if your child goes through periods of eating less. He's likely growing less but still is eating what his body needs. Include in meals a healthy food you know your toddler will eat as well as a variety of other foods. Rest assured, if offered healthy options, no child will starve himself.

As he continues to grow and become more active, though, your child's energy requirements will increase from the ages of 1 to 3. Continue to serve him two to three servings of good-quality protein per day along with a variety of fruits, vegetables, and dairy products, such as plain yogurt.

If your child becomes picky about what he eats, avoid calling attention to it. You never want eating to turn into a power struggle! The upside is that a picky eater is likely to be highly in tune with his body's signals of hunger and fullness, which can prevent future overeating. Also, studies have found that you can be born with certain taste preferences, so your baby may be genetically inclined to genuinely dislike certain foods.

Experiment with different foods and how you prepare them. For example, your toddler may find the taste of certain vegetables overpowering. Try offering milder-tasting orange vegetables such as squash, sweet potatoes, or pumpkin. Your child may reject plain raw broccoli, but eat it up if it's steamed, roasted, or offered with a dip.

WHAT TODDLERS NEED

CARBOHYDRATES/STARCHES
4–5 servings a day

Breads, cereals, pasta, noodles, rice, and potatoes are excellent sources of energy, fiber, vitamins, and minerals. Potatoes provide useful amounts of vitamin C, which is found mainly just under the skin, so avoid peeling them if you can. Thin-skinned potatoes can simply be scrubbed. Add sweet potato, rutabaga, or parsnip to mashed potatoes to boost their nutritional value.

A serving is 3 ounces cooked cereal, rice, or pasta; 1 ounce ready-to-eat cereal; ½ slice of bread or ¼ English muffin; or 2 small crackers.

PROTEIN
2–3 servings a day

Low-fat meat, poultry, fish, eggs, and legumes are rich in vitamins and minerals. If your child is vegetarian, offer her a mix of protein foods including beans, lentils, tofu, nuts, and eggs.

Oily fish is the richest source of omega-3 essential fatty acids, which have been found to benefit the brain, eyes, and skin. You can give your child up to 2 servings of fish a week. Low-mercury options include salmon, mackerel, herring, sardines, chunk light tuna, and trout. Omega-3 is also found in nonfish sources such as walnuts, flaxseed, canola oil, pumpkin seeds, soybeans, and fortified eggs, drinks, and cereals.

Red meat and liver are rich in iron, but trim any excess fat. Lean, good-quality ground meat can be transformed into homemade burgers and meatballs, or served in pasta sauce or stir-fries.

A serving is 1½ ounces cooked lean meat, poultry, or fish; 1 egg; ½ cup cooked beans; or 2 tablespoons smooth peanut butter.

DAIRY PRODUCTS
2–3 servings a day

Whole milk, cheese, and yogurt provide protein for growth and development, and calcium for teeth. Together with vitamin D, which is added to cow's milk, they help make bones and teeth stronger. Childhood is a crucial time for tooth and bone development, and growth during this period continues to influence bone health in adulthood.

Unsweetened Greek-style natural yogurt is a useful alternative to cream in cooking because it's rich in calcium and protein; use it in sauces, soups, and pies—both sweet and savory. (See also page 243.)

A serving is ½ cup milk, 3 ounces of yogurt, 1 ounce natural cheese, or 1½ ounces processed cheese.

FRUITS AND VEGETABLES

5 servings a day

Whether fresh, frozen, canned, dried, or juiced, fruit and vegetables provide a host of vitamins and minerals, especially vitamin C, that are vital for good health. A minimum of 5 servings a day is recommended.

It probably isn't a surprise to learn that most children don't eat enough fresh produce—most parents struggle to get their children to eat their greens. Be careful not to present vegetables as less enjoyable than other foods. Model good habits by enjoying vegetables when you eat with your child, and avoid power struggles over eating them.

Try presenting fruit and vegetables in different ways. For example, many children turn their nose up at cooked vegetables but will happily eat them raw, including thinly sliced sticks of cucumber, carrot, and red pepper. Vegetable sticks are good for dunking into dips, so serve them with nutritious guacamole or hummus (see page 254) and you'll double the health benefits. Alternatively, incorporate vegetables into fritters or casseroles, or, if the going gets really tough, it's fine to toss puréed vegetables into sauces, stews, and soups. It may be easier to encourage a love of fruit, but again maintain interest by offering different types and presenting them in various ways.

A serving is ¼ cup raw or ⅛ cup cooked vegetables, ½ small piece of fruit or ⅛ cup cut fruit. This would be the rough equivalent of 1 tangerine, half an apple or banana, 5 grapes (cut grapes in half), a floret of broccoli, a dessert spoon of peas or carrots, or 1 tomato.

... and what they don't

SUGAR AND SWEETS

Most children naturally have a sweet tooth (breast milk and formula contain plenty of milk sugar, called lactose) but hold off on giving your child sugary foods as long as is feasible. Foods made from refined sugar are high in calories and can spoil a child's appetite for meals containing more nutritious food. Furthermore, they can lead to tooth decay. What's more, sugary foods often include a fair amount of fat—just think of doughnuts, cookies, and cakes.

Nevertheless, an outright ban can backfire, making candy even more desirable! It's fine to offer the occasional treat to teach your child about moderation and balance—just don't fall into the habit of providing sweets on a daily basis. Foods sweetened with artificial sweeteners are not recommended.

MEAL IDEAS from 1 year old

BREAKFAST

- Unsweetened breakfast cereal with milk
- Banana & Blueberry Smoothie*
- Cinnamon French Toast*
- Plain, unsweetened yogurt with mixed berries
- Hard-boiled egg with strips of toast

LUNCH

- Chicken and bean stew
- Baked potato with steamed broccoli florets and cheese
- Cheddar & Pita Salad*
- Pizza wedges with steamed vegetable sticks
- Thick vegetable and pasta soup
- Toasted tortilla wedges with dips
- Root Veggie Stew*
- Pasta with tomato sauce
- Marinated tofu with noodles
- Creamy Guacamole* with dippers
- Stir-fried tofu with peas
- Quesadilla wedges with cheese or mashed beans

DINNER

- Spaghetti Bolognese
- Lamb for Baby*
- Creamy Pumpkin Risotto*
- Shepherd's pie
- Pork and noodle stir-fry
- Veggie Quesadilla*
- Turkey Burgers with Pineapple Relish*
- Savory Brown Rice*

DESSERT

- Mixed Fruit Compote*
- Frozen yogurt
- Fruit Swirls*
- Cottage cheese with fruit purée
- Tropical Fruit Salad*
- Strawberry mousse

*in recipe section

SNACKS

- Hard-boiled egg with strips of toast
- Thin sticks of cheese with apple slivers
- Cheese or fruit muffin
- Small chunks of melon or other fresh fruit
- Hummus and bread sticks
- Rice cake with smooth nut butter
- Mashed banana sandwich
- Pita bread with hummus and steamed carrot sticks
- Meatballs with quartered cherry tomatoes
- Plain, unsweetened yogurt with mango
- Whole-grain muffin
- Small chunks of soft, fresh fruit
- Raisins or chopped, dried fruit
- Cottage cheese

Keep it healthy

When it comes to feeding toddlers, striving for a balanced diet can intimidate even the most nutritionally aware parent. Try not to worry. As long as your child eats a good mix of foods on a regular basis, he'll get all the nutrients he needs.

Take care that your child's diet doesn't have too much fiber or not enough of it. Avoid excessively fatty foods, but do not restrict fats. Children need a certain amount of fat for normal growth and development. Not all fat is bad, and it has important roles throughout the body. Unsaturated fat found in vegetable oils, oily fish (see page 234), and avocado is an important contributor to good health.

Try to provide a good mix of high-energy, nutrient-dense foods based on the recommended food groups (see pages 240–241) each day. Obviously, what your toddler eats must take into account if he's on a special diet, has a food sensitivity, or demonstrates strong eating preferences.

Snacks

Older babies have high energy requirements for their size, but they often won't consume three full meals a day. So they need small, frequent meals and two or three healthy snacks each day. Your baby probably will want a snack midmorning and another in the afternoon. Most toddlers would be happy to graze and nibble all day long, but to make sure snack time doesn't interfere with mealtime, offer your toddler healthy, fresh snacks at the same time, two or three times every day. Avoid giving snacks close to mealtimes. If your child is very hungry a little while before a meal, give him the upcoming meal early, rather than providing a snack. Avoid sugary, salty, or fatty processed foods.

Milk and water

Now that your baby is 1, he can drink cow's milk. Give your baby whole milk at first. Reduced-fat milk is fine after the age of 2. If your toddler is still drinking from a bottle, switching from formula to milk is a good point to transition to a cup. If you're breastfeeding, continue as long as you and your baby would like. Your body will adjust your milk supply

IRON NEEDS

Iron deficiency is a common problem for young children. Encourage iron-containing foods (see page 227), especially red meats, if your child likes these. To help him absorb this important mineral, serve iron-rich food with vitamin C–rich food; for example, squeeze fresh lemon juice over fish or serve marinara sauce with meatballs.

If your child is vegetarian, remember that iron from non-meat sources is more difficult to absorb, so more is needed in the diet. Every day, give your child iron-rich foods, such as beans, lentils, green leafy vegetables, dried fruit (particularly apricots and raisins), as well as fortified breakfast cereals.

to match your child's needs. He most likely will nurse less once he starts eating more solid food.

Water is also considered a good supplemental drink for children. Juice is recommended only in limited quantities.

A common reason for a toddler eating poorly and gaining weight slowly is excessive fluids. By drinking large amounts of water, juice, or even milk, your child may feel full and have no desire to eat more nutritious, higher-calorie foods at mealtime. If this sounds like your child, your pediatrician may recommend limiting the total daily amount of all liquids to 18–20 ounces. On the other hand, if he drinks a lot but he is gaining weight nicely, there is no need to restrict fluids.

Supplements

Most healthy children eating age-typical diets do not need a multivitamin. If you're concerned your child isn't getting all the nutrition he needs, talk to your pediatrician about your child's specific nutritional needs. Surprisingly, though, even children with very limited menus may not need to take vitamins.

2 years and older

As your toddler becomes more active, she'll need more calories to give her the energy she needs. Encourage your child to eat a variety of foods so she gets a wide range of nutrients (see pages 240–241 for guidelines).

Work on establishing a regular eating pattern based on three meals plus two or three snacks a day. Some toddlers continue to dislike lumps or chunks of food; finely chopping your toddler's food might make it more acceptable. Finger foods are a great way to encourage your toddler to chew foods and enjoy meals with a coarser texture.

If your toddler is in daycare or preschool, look for a facility that offers fresh, healthy lunches and snacks. Talk to your child's teachers and other parents to find out what foods are offered. If you or the staff are concerned about what your child is eating, you can always ask if you can supplement with a lunch or a snack from home.

Good eating habits

Your toddler is becoming increasingly aware of the world around her, and with this comes a new sense of independence and free will—with both its positive and not-so-positive side effects. But studies show that parents who encourage good eating habits from an early age are very likely to see the benefits in the long term. A few points to keep in mind:

- Don't get hung up on the mess your child makes; there's plenty of time to improve this in the future. Your toddler will continue to make a mess when she eats—crumbs become a way of life! While ideally you'd like her to eat with a fork or spoon, she'll use her fingers much of the time.

- It isn't always feasible for the whole family to eat together, but you'll reap the benefits when you do, even if you can manage only communal mealtimes on weekends. If family dinners are tough, try coming together for breakfast, or have your toddler enjoy a bedtime snack while you eat a late dinner. Eating together encourages chatter and discussion between parents and children, and gets everyone away from the television or other electronics. Children learn good eating habits from their parents, so make sure you eat your vegetables, too!

- Be patient and persevere. If your child decides to try even a small mouthful of food, you're making progress, and she may find she likes it after all. Some people say it takes an average of 10 "tastes" for a child to accept new foods. It can take even more. The theory is that if parents continually expose their child to a new food, eventually she'll learn to like it. Keep in mind you can prepare a simple food, such as carrots, in different ways, even with spices such as ginger or cinnamon, each time.

- Try to make food exciting. You don't need to spend hours arranging food to make faces, but try to provide different colors, textures, and shapes at each meal. Interesting or colorful plates, bibs, cutlery, and place mats can help, or try presenting food by theme—maybe a meal of all orange food,

or foods that are round. Steamed vegetables are more brightly colored than boiled vegetables. Try naming foods based on your child's interests— Pilot's Peas, Engineer's Oranges, Ballerina's Bok Choi, Star Wars Spinach. Imaginative and attractive presentation can make the difference between a child eating or refusing a meal.

- Many parents fall into the trap of believing children prefer bland or so-called kid's food like pasta in cheese sauce or simple sandwiches without condiments. In fact, children like stronger flavors and may happily try curries, stir-fries, chili, and the like.

- Even if you've managed to keep your child away from sugar so far, it becomes increasingly difficult to restrict sugary foods as she gets older, interacts with other children, and is more aware of child-oriented brands with brightly colored cartoon-character packaging. Everything in moderation seems to work for most parents, but opt for treats with the least amount of food coloring, additives, and preservatives.

- One of the best ways to get your child interested in food is to include her in preparing the meal, even if it's as simple as giving a sauce a quick stir or pouring some cereal into a bowl. To teach her to pour liquids, first pour them into a small measuring cup with a spout, then have her pour them into a cup.

- Invite your child to help with food shopping. Let her choose among healthy options, weigh fresh produce, or unpack the shopping cart.

Picky eaters

All children go through stages of picky eating. Their appetites can be unpredictable and are often influenced by how much they are growing at the time. If your child is going through a picky stage, the best strategy is to continue to serve a variety of healthy food and ignore your child's choices. Remember, your job is to decide which food to serve and when to serve it, and your child's job is to choose what and how much to eat. Keep in mind that no child will starve himself. Children are remarkably good at titrating what they eat to match their nutritional needs.

Most important, do not make eating into a power struggle. You will lose. Forcing your child to eat is a no-win situation for both of you. Conflict and tension only make the situation more difficult and may lead your child to use mealtimes as a way of seeking attention. It's very frustrating when your child rejects a meal you've lovingly prepared, but remember that children are remarkably clever at picking up on the anxieties of their parents and may well tune into your own frustrations about their not eating. To keep meals enjoyable and preempt battles:

- Always serve one healthy food you know your child likes.
- Encourage your toddler to try one mouthful, but always give her the option to say "no, thank you."
- Notice and comment positively when your child tries something new, but don't make a big deal out of it.
- Serve small portions; offer seconds if she gobbles up food.
- Peer pressure can work both ways: Ask a friend of your child's who you know to be a good eater to come for lunch. Children often learn by example, and if your child sees her peers eating all sorts of foods, it may well encourage her to do the same.
- Make eating fun: Picnics, even if you're only arranging a blanket on the floor, or a theme based on a favorite game or book can be real winners.
- Don't fall into the trap of bribing your child with dessert or candy. If you plan to serve dessert, offer a small portion alongside her meal and don't make a big deal about it.
- Offer previously rejected foods prepared in a different way. Often children are particular about texture and may love carmelized, broiled broccoli after rejecting soft, steamed broccoli. Cooked veggies a no-go? Try offering salads with ingredients your child picks out.
- If your child is going through a no-veggies phase, provide plenty of fruit options.
- Try not to spend too much time preparing meals; if you've put in a big effort and then your child doesn't eat anything, you are more likely to feel frustrated or angry.

Weight issues

Americans are becoming increasingly obese, and unfortunately children also are part of this epidemic.

In the United States, rates of childhood obesity have more than tripled in the past 30 years. As of 2008, nearly 32 percent of children between the ages of 2 and 19 were overweight (almost 17 percent were obese—about 12.5 million children)—and 10

percent of preschoolers between the ages of 2 and 5 were obese.

Obesity puts children at risk of ailments more common among adults, including diabetes and heart disease. They're also at greater risk of suffering sleep apnea and bone and joint problems.

Many experts link the rise in obesity to the growing presence of fast-food outlets, advertising, and the overwhelming array of cakes, cookies, candy, ice cream, potato chips, convenience foods, and soda in stores. Lifestyle also plays an important role. The popularity of video games, television, and computer activities means children are less active and aren't burning as many calories.

However, inactivity and poor nutrition aren't the entire story behind obesity. Family history and genetic influences also play a significant role.

The best way to prevent a child from becoming overweight is to breastfeed exclusively for 6 months and teach good eating habits early on. However, it's important to develop a healthy family approach to food and exercise for weight management. Try to stick to a routine of three meals a day plus two healthy snacks. Less screen time and more outdoor time is always a good idea. If you're concerned about your child's weight, talk with her pediatrician.

Milk and drinks

If your toddler eats well and has a varied, balanced diet, then you can switch her to reduced-fat milk once she's 2 years old. Your child can now drink whichever low-fat milk the rest of the family drinks (usually 1-percent or skim milk).

If you're breastfeeding, your child will also continue to receive fluids from breast milk.

Many children will happily go for hours without drinking anything. Offer fluids (milk or water) at meals and snacks. Roughly speaking, the average 2-year-old needs about 5 cups of liquid a day. About 2½ to 3 cups of that should come from milk and the rest from water. Avoid or limit juice.

DID YOU KNOW...

Exactly how diet influences behavior isn't known for certain, but a poor diet can definitely exacerbate destructive behavior, restlessness, poor concentration, learning difficulties, clumsiness, irritability, and poor social skills.

However, these links between diet and behavior can be more complicated than you might imagine. For example, parents commonly say that eating foods that contain sugar causes their child to misbehave and to become "hyper." Research, however, has shown that this is not true. For example, in one study, scientists selected a group consisting of parents who believed their children's behavior was negatively affected by sugar-containing foods. In random order, half of the children were given a food high in sugar and the others were given an identical food with no sugar. Parents then observed their child's play behavior and were asked if, based on the behavior witnessed, they thought their child had received sugar. Just as many parents whose children got sugar said that the food had made their child "hyper" as did parents whose children got no sugar.

While studies like this one don't totally eliminate the possibility that there are a few children who are affected by sugar, they do demonstrate that most parents wrongly blamed the sugar for their child's misbehavior.

MEAL IDEAS for toddlers

BREAKFAST
- Oatmeal with mashed banana
- Unsweetened breakfast cereal
- Poached egg with toast
- Plain, unsweetened yogurt with honey and granola
- Oatmeal with fruit purée
- Pancakes with fruit filling
- Fruit smoothie with toast
- French toast
- Cheese or fruit muffin with plain, unsweetened yogurt
- Ham & Egg Cups*
- Cinnamon French Toast*

LUNCH
- Cheddar & Pita Salad*
- Creamy Guacamole* with dippers
- Minestrone soup
- Tofu, Rice & Avocado*
- Pita pizzas with coleslaw
- Cheese omelette with vegetable sticks
- Lentil & Rice Soup*
- Pasta with creamy ham and pea sauce
- Tomato soup with garlic bread
- Pasta, ham, and peas
- Baby's "Baked" Potato*

DINNER

- Salmon or haddock with peas
- Roast meat (or vegetarian alternative) with green beans
- Chicken pot pie with vegetables and mashed potatoes
- Salmon Fingers with Sweet Potato Fries*
- Grilled pork or lamb with Sweet Potato Fries* and broccoli
- Pasta with tomato sauce and meatballs
- Cauliflower & Brown Rice Gratin*
- Veggie Quesadilla*
- Chinese Beef with Noodles*
- Pork and apple stir-fry
- Chicken or vegetable curry with rice
- Pesto pasta with peas and pine nuts
- Creamy Pumpkin Risotto*
- Mini Salmon Cakes*

DESSERT

- Peach Crisps*
- Yogurt and fruit
- Fresh fruit gelatin
- Whipped Ricotta with Cherries*
- Mixed Fruit Compote*
- Fresh or dried fruit salad
- Pancakes
- Cookies and milk
- Strawberries with chocolate drizzle
- Graham crackers with peanut butter
- Tropical Fruit Salad*
- Frozen yogurt
- Rice pudding with raisins
- Oatmeal Cookies*
- Pudding

*in recipe section

FIRST FOODS . . . from 6 months

Introduce foods one at a time as purées. Wait at least 3 to 5 days before offering a new food. Good first foods include rice cereal, sweet potatoes, carrots, butternut squash, and bananas. Supplement purées with single-ingredient iron-fortified cereals. Save commonly allergenic ingredients such as peanuts, tree nuts, eggs, fish, citrus fruits, and wheat for later. As your baby expands his menu options, you can combine tested foods. Try each ingredient, including oil and spices, separately before preparing a recipe.

While babies should not drink cow's milk before 1 year, milk-based foods like yogurt, butter, or cheese can be served to babies over 8 months.

Avoid sugary foods for babies under 1 year. For toddlers, try to keep desserts an occasional treat, and choose desserts that include fruits and whole grains.

Age recommendations for the recipes are offered as a general guide. Babies progress at different rates, so try the recipes you think will work best for your baby.

Portion sizes are infant-size (around 2 tablespoons per serving), unless otherwise noted. Family meals are intended for two adults and two children.

MASHED AVOCADO

Creamy avocados are packed with nutrients and "good" fats.

● 4 servings

Cut **1 avocado** in half and remove the pit. Scoop out flesh and mash with a fork. If you want to thin it out, blend in a bit of breast milk or formula.

Variation *Try blending with banana or sweet potato purée.*

BANANA PURÉE

A very ripe banana will be easier on your baby's digestive system.

● 1 serving

Mash **½ banana** with a fork until as smooth as possible. Add a little formula or breast milk to make a thin purée.

APPLE PURÉE

Apple blends well with rice cereal and is delicious with puréed meat or vegetables.

● 2–3 servings

1 Wash, peel, core, and finely chop **1 apple**. Put the apple in a saucepan with **2 tablespoons water** and bring to a boil. Reduce heat and simmer, partially covered, for 5–8 minutes or until tender.
2 Transfer the apple to a blender or food processor and purée until smooth, adding a little cooking water if necessary.

Variation *Pear, another excellent first food, can be prepared the same way. If the pear is very ripe and soft, simply wash, peel, core, and mash it.*

SWEET POTATO PURÉE

Sweet potatoes and yams are rich in vitamin C and beta-carotene.

- 4–6 servings

1. Peel **1 small sweet potato or yam** and chop into bite-size chunks. Cover with water and bring to a boil, then cook for 10–15 minutes until tender.
2. Drain and transfer to a blender or food processor with a little breast milk or formula, and purée.

GREEN PEA PURÉE

Nutritious, sweet green peas cook readily into a silky-smooth purée.

- 6 servings
- ✳ suitable for freezing

1. Steam **1 cup fresh or frozen peas** until they are bright green and can be mashed easily with a fork.
2. Rinse the peas under cold running water. Transfer the peas to a food processor or blender and process to a smooth purée. Add enough

of the reserved cooking liquid, breast milk, or formula to thin the purée to a consistency your baby can handle.

ZUCCHINI PURÉE

With its mild flavor and tender texture, zucchini is a natural and nutritious first food for your baby.

- 6 servings
- ✳ suitable for freezing

1. Trim **1 medium zucchini** and cut into rounds about 1 inch thick. Steam until tender, about 7 minutes.
2. Rinse the cooked zucchini under cold running water to stop the cooking. Transfer the zucchini to a food processor or blender and process to a smooth purée. Add enough of the reserved cooking liquid, breast milk, or formula to thin the purée to a consistency your baby can handle.

PEACH PURÉE

You also can use a nectarine, plum, or apricot.

- 2 servings
- ✳ suitable for freezing

1. Cut **1 ripe peach** into quarters, removing the pit, and put into a pan with **2 tablespoons water**. Bring to a boil, then simmer 8–10 minutes.
2. Drain the peach. When cool enough to handle, peel off the skin.
3. Transfer the peach to a blender or food processor and purée, adding a little water if necessary.

SQUASH, PARSNIP & APPLE PURÉE

This combo is rich in vitamin C.

- 3–4 servings
- ✳ suitable for freezing

1. Wash, peel, and dice **½ cup butternut squash** (removing any seeds) and **1 small parsnip**. Put in a saucepan and cover with water. Bring to a boil, then reduce heat and simmer mixture 10 minutes.
2. While the vegetables are cooking, wash, peel, core, and dice **1 apple**. Add to the pan and cook another 5 minutes or until tender.
3. Transfer to a blender or processor and blend until puréed, adding a little water if necessary.

BREAKFAST

BANANA & BLUEBERRY SMOOTHIE

This smoothie is full of vital nutrients and provides much-needed energy.

- from 6 months
- 4 servings

1 small banana, sliced
¼ cup blueberries
1 tablespoon apple juice
4 tablespoons breast milk or formula (or cow's milk after 12 months)

Combine all ingredients in a blender or food processor and blend until thick, smooth, and creamy. Pour into cups.

BERRY-CHERRY PURÉE

Fruit purées are among the simplest, most versatile first foods for baby. They are easy to prepare and freeze well, so you can have them on hand for quick meals or for mixing into cereal and meat or vegetable purées.

- from 7 months
- 6 servings
- ✳ suitable for freezing

1 cup fresh or frozen blueberries
1 cup fresh or frozen pitted sweet cherries

1 Combine the blueberries and cherries in a food processor or blender and process to a smooth purée. If desired, to remove the skins, strain the purée through a fine-mesh sieve set over a saucepan, pushing on the solids with a rubber spatula to extract as much flesh and juice as possible. Discard the skins.

2 Place the purée over medium-low heat and cook, stirring often, until heated through and thickened, 4 minutes or so. Remove from the heat and let cool completely before serving.

DATE & VANILLA BREAKFAST YOGURT

This nourishing and energy-boosting blend of protein and slow-release carbohydrates makes an excellent start to the day.

- from 8 months
- 4 servings

¼ cup dried pitted dates, roughly chopped
½ cup water
¼ cup Greek-style yogurt
½ teaspoon vanilla extract
4 tablespoons breast milk or formula (or cow's milk after 12 months)

1 Put the dates and water in a medium saucepan. Bring to a boil and then reduce the heat. Cover and simmer 10 minutes or until dates are soft. Let cool.

2 Put the dates and any remaining water, yogurt, vanilla extract, and milk or formula in a blender or food processor. Blend until smooth and creamy. Spoon into a bowl.

Storage tip *Store any leftovers in an airtight container in the refrigerator for up to 3 days.*

HAM & EGG CUPS

Eggs provide much-needed protein, vitamins D and B, and zinc, but they must be cooked thoroughly to avoid the slight risk of salmonella. These make great finger food for older babies.

- from 12 months, or mash well for babies 9–12 months
- 4 servings

Olive oil, for pan
4 slices lean ham
4 eggs

1 Preheat the oven to 400°F. Lightly oil four cups in a muffin pan and arrange a slice of ham

CINNAMON FRENCH TOAST

This makes a delicious breakfast or finger food. Serve with banana or a favorite fresh fruit to add a nutritional boost.

■ from 12 months
● 1 serving

1 egg, lightly beaten
1 tablespoon breast milk or
   formula (or cow's milk after 12
   months)
Pinch of ground cinnamon
1 teaspoon butter
1 slice brioche or sweet bread

1 Combine egg, milk or formula, and cinnamon in a shallow dish. Melt the butter in a non-stick skillet and swirl to coat the base evenly.
2 Dip both sides of the brioche slice in the egg mixture then allow any excess to drip off.
3 Cook for about 2 minutes on each side or until the egg is set and light golden.

in each one, overlapping the sides to make it fit and form a cup shape.
2 Trim the top of the ham slightly above the top of the pans.
3 Crack an egg into each ham-lined muffin cup, then bake for 10 minutes or until the eggs are set.
4 Remove from the oven and let cool slightly before removing the cups from the pan. Cut ham into small pieces for babies.

Storage tip *Ham cups will keep in the refrigerator for up to 2 days.*

OATMEAL WITH APRICOT PURÉE

An excellent breakfast for young children, oatmeal is known to improve concentration. Instead of apricot purée, try mashed banana or puréed pear or apple.

■ from 8 months
● 2–4 servings (purée serves 4–6)

APRICOT PURÉE
¾ cup unsulphured dried apricots
1¼ cup water

OATMEAL
½ cup oats
½ cup breast milk or formula (or
   cow's milk after 12 months)

1 Place the apricots in a saucepan and cover with water. Bring to a boil, then reduce heat and simmer, covered, for 30 minutes or until the apricots are very tender. Place the apricots and any water left in the pan, in a blender or food processor and purée until smooth, adding more water if necessary.
2 To make the oatmeal, combine oats and milk or formula in a saucepan and bring to a boil, stirring occasionally. Reduce heat and simmer, stirring frequently, for 6 minutes until smooth and creamy.
3 Put the oatmeal into a bowl and stir in a large spoonful of the apricot purée.

LUNCH

SIMPLE HUMMUS

This delicious dip is made with calcium-rich tahini, a paste made from sesame seeds. Chickpeas contain valuable iron and B vitamins.

- from 7–8 months
- 7 servings

1 cup canned chickpeas
1 tablespoon tahini
2 tablespoons extra-virgin olive oil
2 tablespoons water

1 Drain and rinse the chickpeas and put in a food processor or blender with the tahini, olive oil, and water.
2 Process until puréed, scraping down the sides occasionally and stirring to keep the mixture moving. Add a little bit of water if the hummus is too thick.

CREAMY GUACAMOLE

Avocados are a great source of fiber, "good" fats, and vitamin E.

- from 7–8 months
- 6 servings

1 large ripe avocado
½ cup peeled, seeded, and shredded cucumber
¼ teaspoon ground cumin

Add the avocado, cucumber, and cumin to a food processor or blender. Process to a smooth purée, or, depending on baby's age and chewing ability, you can leave the purée a little coarser.

Storage tip *Keep guacamole in the refrigerator in an airtight container for up to 1 day. (Some discoloration may occur during storage.)*

BEET & POTATO SWIRL

Fresh beets are naturally sweet and a good source of folate, potassium, fiber, and disease-preventing antioxidants.

- from 8 months
- 12 servings
- ✳ suitable for freezing

1 bunch beets, about 1 pound total weight, trimmed and scrubbed
1 russet potato, scrubbed

1 Preheat the oven to 375°F. Place the beets in a baking dish and add water to come ½ inch up the sides of the beets. Cover with aluminum foil. Prick the potato in several places with a fork and place on a baking sheet. Place the beets and the potato in the oven and bake until very tender, 45–60 minutes. Remove from the oven and let cool.
2 Peel the beets and the potato and cut into chunks, discarding the skins. Put the potato in a food processor or blender and process to a purée, adding a little water, breast milk, or formula for a smooth consistency. Transfer the potato purée to a bowl.
3 Put the beets in the food processor or blender and process to a purée, again adding a little liquid. Transfer to a separate bowl. To serve, swirl together the potato and beet purées in baby's bowl.

CHEDDAR & PITA SALAD

Young children will enjoy eating this salad as finger food.

- from 12 months
- 1–2 servings

Small pita bread, split in half
1-inch piece of cucumber, peeled
3 cherry tomatoes
3 pitted black olives, quartered
1 ounce cheddar cheese, cut into
    small cubes or shredded

DRESSING (OPTIONAL)
1 tablespoon extra-virgin olive oil
½ teaspoon white wine vinegar

1 Preheat the grill to medium. Split and open the pita bread, then grill until light golden and slightly crisp; let cool. Meanwhile, combine the ingredients for the dressing, if using.

2 Cut the cucumber lengthwise into quarters and scoop out the seeds. Dice into ¼-inch pieces. Chop cherry tomatoes into small pieces.

3 Combine the cucumber and tomatoes in a serving bowl, then add the olives. Pour the dressing over the salad and toss until combined. Break the crisp pita into bite-size pieces and mix into the salad.

4 Mix cheddar into the salad and serve.

BABY'S GREEN BEAN CASSEROLE

With their earthy aromas and soft texture, mushrooms and green beans may appeal to your baby early in his first year of eating. Mushrooms are sometimes overlooked for their healthy qualities, which include a store of the B vitamins, riboflavin and niacin; likewise leeks, which among other powers, aid the balance of cholesterol levels.

- from 8 months
- 12 servings
- ✳ suitable for freezing

A small handful of green beans
    (about 2 ounces), trimmed
2 teaspoons olive oil
1 tablespoon minced leek,
    white parts only
2 ounces white mushrooms,
    brushed clean and finely diced
    (about ¾ cup)
⅓ cup pearl barley
1½ cups low-sodium vegetable
    broth or water
¼ teaspoon dried thyme

1 Steam the green beans until the beans are tender, about 5 minutes. Transfer the beans to a cutting board, chop coarsely, and set aside.

2 In a saucepan over medium-high heat, warm the olive oil. Add the leek and mushrooms and sauté until the mushrooms soften and release their juices, 3–5 minutes. Add the barley and stir to coat with the oil and juices, about 1 minute. Add the broth and thyme and bring to a simmer. Reduce the heat to low, cover, and simmer gently until the barley is tender and most of the liquid is absorbed, 35–40 minutes.

3 Stir the green beans into the barley mixture. Transfer the mixture to a food processor or blender and process to a smooth purée. Depending on your baby's age and chewing ability, you can leave the purée a little coarser, or pulse just a few times for a chunky bean casserole; or add enough broth or water to thin the purée to a consistency your baby can handle. Serve lukewarm or at room temperature.

TURKEY FOR BABY

Turkey is a great first meat for your baby; it's lean and full of nutrients, has a mild flavor, and is easy to digest.

- from 7 months
- 8 servings
- ✳ suitable for freezing

½ pound ground turkey

1 In a frying pan over medium heat, combine the turkey and ¼ cup water. Using a spoon to break up the turkey and stirring constantly, cook until the meat is opaque throughout and no longer pink, about 4 minutes. Remove from the heat and drain the turkey in a fine-mesh sieve set over a bowl, reserving the cooking liquid.

2 Transfer the drained turkey to a food processor or blender and process until finely ground, about 1 minute. With the machine running, add the reserved liquid, 1 tablespoon at a time, until the turkey is smooth and pastelike. Depending on your baby's age and chewing ability, add more of the liquid to thin the purée to a consistency your baby can handle.

ROOT VEGGIE STEW

This is a great stew for babies ready for an array of root vegetables.

- from 7 months
- 16 servings
- ✳ suitable for freezing

1 teaspoon olive oil
2 carrots, peeled and cut into 1-inch chunks
2 yellow potatoes, peeled and cut into 1-inch chunks
1 parsnip, peeled and cut into 1-inch chunks
1½ cups low-sodium vegetable broth or water
Pinch of grated nutmeg

1 In a saucepan over medium-high heat, warm the olive oil. Add the carrots, potatoes, and parsnip chunks and cook, stirring often, until the parsnips and potatoes begin to turn golden, about 5 minutes. Add the broth and nutmeg and bring to a boil. Reduce the heat to medium, cover, and simmer gently until the vegetables are very tender, 25–30 minutes.

2 Transfer the mixture to a food processor or blender and process to a smooth purée. Depending on your baby's age and chewing ability, you can leave the stew a little coarser; or add enough broth or water to thin the purée to a consistency your baby can handle. Serve lukewarm or at room temperature.

LENTIL & RICE SOUP

Lentils and brown rice are a protein-packed pairing, and lentils are also high in folate.

- from 7 months
- 12 servings
- ✳ suitable for freezing

2¾ cups low-sodium vegetable broth or water
⅓ cup brown rice
½ cup red lentils, picked over and rinsed

1 In a saucepan over medium-high heat, bring the broth to a simmer. Add the rice and lentils. Reduce the heat to low, cover, and simmer until the rice is tender, the lentils are soft and mash easily with a spoon, and most of the liquid is absorbed, 30–35 minutes. Remove from the heat and let cool slightly.

2 Transfer the mixture to a food processor or blender and process to a smooth purée. Depending on your baby's chewing ability, you can leave the soup a little coarser; or add enough broth or water to thin the soup to a consistency your baby can handle. Serve lukewarm or at room temperature.

BABY VEGETABLE RISOTTO

Risotto is very simple to make but does require stirring time, which can be relaxing after a hectic day. Purée or mash depending on your baby's age.

- ■ from 8 months
- ● 4 family servings

2 tablespoons olive oil
1 tablespoon butter
½ small onion, diced
4 small zucchini, sliced
1 teaspoon dried oregano
1 cup risotto rice
4 cups low-sodium vegetable broth
   or water
⅓ cup peas
½ cup grated Parmesan cheese

1 Heat the oil and butter in a large heavy-bottomed saucepan. Add the onion and zucchini and cook for 5 minutes or until tender. Add the oregano and rice and cook for 2 minutes, stirring continuously, until the rice is glossy and slightly translucent.

2 Add the water or broth a ladleful at a time, stirring continuously. Wait for the liquid to be absorbed before adding another ladleful. Continue in this way until the rice is tender and creamy but still retains a little bite—it should take about 25 minutes.

3 Add the peas, the last ladleful of water, and all but a few tablespoons of the Parmesan and stir well. Sprinkle with the remaining Parmesan just before serving.

PEA SOUP

Soups are a perfect way to encourage children to eat vegetables. For a thicker soup or purée, decrease the amount of water. When your baby is older, you can make the soup with low-sodium vegetable broth instead of water.

- ■ from 7 months
- ● 4 family servings

1 tablespoon vegetable oil
1 leek, finely sliced
1 stalk celery, finely chopped
1½ cups diced potatoes
4 cups water
1¾ cups frozen garden peas

1 Heat the oil in a large heavy-bottomed saucepan. Add the leek and cook over medium heat for 5 minutes or until softened. Add the celery and potatoes and cook for 5 more minutes.

2 Pour the water over the vegetables and bring to a boil. Cover, reduce the heat, and simmer for 15 minutes. Add the peas and cook for 5 more minutes or until the potatoes are tender.

3 Using an immersion blender or food processor, blend the soup until smooth. For adult servings, season to taste with salt and pepper.

BABY'S "BAKED" POTATO

Here is a baby-friendly version of a comfort-food classic, and a delicious way for the whole family to enjoy creamy potatoes.

- from 9 months
- 4 servings

1 Yukon gold potato, peeled and cut into 1-inch cubes
½ teaspoon unsalted butter, melted
1½ tablespoons plain whole-milk yogurt
2 teaspoons grated Parmesan or Cheddar cheese
1 fresh chive sprig, minced (optional)

1 Bring a small saucepan three-fourths full of water to a boil over high heat. Add the potato, reduce the heat to medium, and cook until very tender, 10–12 minutes. Drain the potato thoroughly in a colander, return to the warm pan, and add the butter.

2 Depending on your baby's age and chewing ability, mash the potato with a potato masher or fork until smooth or leave slightly chunky. Cool slightly, then stir in the yogurt, cheese, and chive, if using, and serve.

TOFU, RICE & AVOCADO

Tofu, brown rice, and ripe avocado are earthy, mild flavors that are rich with healthful oils. These ingredients have the added advantage of being the perfect starter finger foods, letting baby practice her pincer grip and get used to feeding herself.

- from 9 months
- 12 servings

½ cup plain firm tofu, cut into small cubes
½ cup cooked brown rice
½ ripe avocado, cut into small cubes
1 tablespoon finely chopped cilantro

1 In a bowl, combine the tofu, rice, avocado, and cilantro and toss gently to mix. If your baby is interested in picking up the food with her fingers, spread a little on her highchair tray and let her pick up the pieces, helping her as needed.

2 For babies not yet ready for finger foods, transfer the mixture to a food processor or blender and process to a coarse or smooth purée. You can add low-sodium vegetable broth or water to thin the purée to a consistency your baby can handle, if necessary.

Allergy alert *Tofu is packed with protein and calcium, and its mild flavor and soft texture make it a favorite early food with babies. However, if you have food allergies in your family, ask your pediatrician when it's best to introduce tofu or other soy products.*

DINNER

SAVORY BROWN RICE

This nutritious staple is the basis for any number of baby and toddler meals.

- ■ from 9 months
- ● 24 servings
- ✳ suitable for freezing

1 cup brown rice
2 cups low-sodium vegetable broth or water

1 In a medium saucepan over high heat, combine the rice and the broth and bring to a boil. Reduce the heat to low, cover, and simmer gently until the liquid is absorbed and the rice is tender, about 50 minutes. Remove from the heat and let stand, covered, for about 5 minutes.

2 Depending on your baby's age and chewing ability, you can transfer the rice to a food processor or blender, along with ¼ cup water to prevent sticking, and process to a smooth or coarse purée. The rice may still be very sticky, so blend with a few tablespoons of fruit or vegetable purée to smooth it out, if you like.

Storage tip *Refrigerate in an airtight container for up to 3 days, or freeze, covered, for up to 3 months.*

Foods to grow on *Brown rice—a more nutritious choice than white—has had only the outermost hulls removed from the grains, leaving them full of fiber, vitamins, and nutrients. Look for short-grain brown rice, which cooks to a softer texture than long grain.*

BEET, SQUASH & QUINOA

Quinoa is a mild-flavored, grain-like seed that hails from South America and supplies a complete protein. It cooks into soft, round pearls with a pleasant chewiness in the center, making it a nice alternative to rice in vegetable dishes like this one. Look for it in the health-food aisle or in the bulk section of most well-stocked supermarkets.

- ■ from 8 months
- ● 16 servings
- ✳ suitable for freezing

¼ butternut or other winter squash, about 4 ounces, seeded
2–3 baby beets, about 4 ounces total weight, trimmed and scrubbed
½ cup quinoa
2 teaspoons olive oil
1¼ cups low-sodium vegetable broth or water

1 Preheat the oven to 375°F. Put the squash, cut side down, in a shallow baking dish and add water to come ¼ inch up the sides of the squash. Put the beets in another baking dish and add water to come ½ inch up the sides of the beets. Cover each dish tightly with aluminum foil and roast until the squash and beets are very tender, 45–60 minutes.

Continued on next page

Continued from previous page

Remove from the oven and let cool. Scoop out the flesh of the squash and transfer to a food processor or blender, discarding the skin. Process to a smooth purée. Add enough water to thin the purée to a consistency your baby can handle. Transfer to a bowl and set aside. Repeat to peel and purée the beets and set aside.

2 Rinse the quinoa under cold running water and drain well. In a saucepan over medium-high heat, warm the olive oil. Add the quinoa, stir to coat with oil, then add the broth and bring to a boil. Reduce the heat to medium-low, cover, and simmer until the liquid is absorbed and the quinoa is soft, about 20 minutes. Remove from the heat and let stand, covered, for 5 minutes.

3 Fluff the quinoa with a fork and swirl in the vegetable purées. Depending on your baby's age and chewing ability, you can return the mixture to the food processor or blender and process to a coarse or smooth purée.

Storage tip *Refrigerate in an airtight container for up to 3 days, or freeze, covered, for up to 3 months.*

MINI SALMON CAKES

Pair these moist salmon patties with steamed chopped asparagus for a spring dinner. The mini cakes make great grown-up appetizers, too—just double the recipe.

■ from 12 months
● 8 mini cakes

1 slice whole-wheat bread
1 small skinless, boneless salmon fillet, about 10 ounces, finely chopped
1 green onion, white and pale green parts, minced
1 teaspoon fresh lemon juice
1 large egg, lightly beaten
Salt
1 tablespoon canola oil, or as needed

1 In a food processor, process the bread to fine crumbs; you should have about ½ cup. In a bowl, combine the bread crumbs, salmon, green onion, lemon juice, egg, and a little salt. Toss gently just until combined.

2 Divide the salmon mixture into 8 portions and pat each portion into a small cake. Arrange the salmon cakes on a plate, cover with plastic wrap, and refrigerate for 5–10 minutes.

3 In a large frying pan, warm 1 tablespoon oil over medium heat. Add the salmon cakes and cook until golden brown on the first side, about

3 minutes. Turn, adding more oil to the pan if needed to prevent sticking, and cook until the cakes are golden brown on the other side, springy to the touch, and are cooked through in the center, 2–3 minutes longer. Let cool slightly, then serve.

Storage tip *Wrap in plastic wrap and refrigerate for up to 1 day.*

Variation *To make a dipping sauce for the salmon cakes, add to plain whole-milk yogurt a little bit of Dijon mustard, a splash of fresh lemon juice, and some minced green onion or chopped fresh dill.*

LAMB FOR BABY

The lamb chop is a tender and lean cut, with a mild flavor and a particularly high iron content that makes it a good choice for one of baby's first meats. It is also less likely to cause an allergic reaction than chicken or beef. Try mixing the lamb with a fruit purée.

- from 7 months
- 6 servings
- ✳ suitable for freezing

Olive oil for greasing
1 boneless lamb steak or chop, about 6 ounces and 1 inch thick, trimmed

1 Preheat the oven to 400°F. Line a small roasting pan with aluminum foil. Lightly oil a roasting rack and place it in the prepared pan. Place the lamb on the rack. Roast, turning once, until opaque throughout and no longer pink, 12–14 minutes per side. Remove from the oven and let cool.

2 Using a large knife, coarsely chop the lamb, then transfer to a food processor or blender and process for 1 minute. With the machine running, add ¼ cup water. Process until smooth. The texture will be pastelike. Add more water, or breast milk or formula, to thin the purée to a consistency appropriate for your baby.

SALMON FINGERS WITH SWEET POTATO FRIES

This healthy version of fish and chips offers plenty of brain-boosting omega-3 fatty acids. Children need essential fatty acids, provided by salmon, for their rapidly developing brains and nerves. Peas are a perfect accompaniment. For younger babies, mash up this dish.

- from 8 months
- 4 family servings

2 cups fine cornmeal, polenta, or fresh bread crumbs
3 tablespoons freshly grated Parmesan cheese
¾ pound salmon fillet, skinned and sliced into 10 chunky fingers
2 eggs, beaten
Vegetable oil
Pepper (optional)

SWEET POTATO FRIES
1 pound orange-fleshed sweet potatoes, scrubbed and cut into wedges
2 tablespoons olive oil

1 Preheat the oven to 400°F. Pat the sweet potatoes dry with a paper towel. Pour a spoonful of oil into baking pan and warm briefly in oven. Toss the potatoes in the warm oil and bake 30 minutes, turning

Continued on next page

Continued from previous page

halfway through, until tender and golden.

2 Meanwhile, mix together the cornmeal and Parmesan on a plate. Dip each salmon finger into the beaten egg, then roll in the cornmeal and Parmesan mixture until evenly coated.

3 Heat enough oil to coat the base of a large heavy-bottomed skillet. Carefully arrange the salmon fingers in the pan and cook for 6 minutes, turning halfway through, until golden. Drain on paper towels and serve with the sweet potato fries.

Variation *Try using thick fillets of white fish such as cod or haddock in place of the salmon.*

CREAMY PUMPKIN RISOTTO

This simplified version doesn't require constant stirring, so it's easy to make and delicious enough for the whole family; just double the recipe and pass grated Parmesan cheese for the grown-ups.

- from 8 months
- 16 servings
- ✳ suitable for freezing

½ cup Arborio or short-grain rice
1½ cups low-sodium vegetable broth or water
1 teaspoon unsalted butter
½ cup butternut squash purée or canned pumpkin purée
Pinch of grated nutmeg

1 In a saucepan over medium-high heat, combine the rice and broth and bring to a boil. Reduce the heat to low, cover, and simmer gently, stirring occasionally, until the liquid is absorbed and the rice is soft and creamy, about 20 minutes. Remove from the heat and let stand, covered, for 10 minutes.

2 Stir the butter, squash purée, and nutmeg into the rice. Depending on your baby's age and chewing ability, you can transfer the risotto to a food processor or blender and process to a coarse or smooth purée. You can also add broth or water to thin the purée to a consistency your baby can handle, if necessary. Serve lukewarm or at room temperature.

Storage tip *Refrigerate in an airtight container for up to 3 days, or freeze, covered, for up to 3 months.*

CHINESE BEEF WITH NOODLES

Beef is a good source of iron. Serve with a glass of fresh orange juice to enhance its absorption.

- from 12 months
- 4 family servings

2 tablespoons vegetable oil
1 pound lean beef, cut into thin strips
8 ounces medium egg noodles
3 cloves garlic
2 handfuls snap peas, trimmed
1 red bell pepper, seeds removed, cut into thin strips
4 green onions sliced diagonally
6 ounces black bean sauce
2 tablespoons reduced-sodium soy sauce

1 Heat the oil in a wok over medium-high heat. Add the beef and stir-fry 2 minutes. Remove the beef using a slotted spoon; set aside.

2 Meanwhile, bring a large pot of water to a boil. Add the noodles and stir to separate. When noodles are tender, drain and keep warm.

VEGGIE QUESADILLA

For this all-time favorite, chop the spinach and mushrooms finely to ensure that toddlers get a taste of everything in each bite, rather than a big mouthful of spinach or mushroom—which might be off-putting for some young eaters. Serve the quesadillas with plain yogurt and mild salsa for dipping, if you like.

- ■ from 12 months
- ● 1 quesadilla

2 teaspoons olive oil
5 white button or brown cremini mushrooms, brushed clean and finely chopped
½ cup tightly packed baby spinach leaves, finely chopped
Two 8-inch whole-wheat tortillas
⅓ cup shredded Monterey Jack cheese

1 In a frying pan over medium heat, warm 1½ teaspoons of the oil. Add the mushrooms and sauté until they soften, 2–4 minutes. Add the spinach and stir until the leaves are wilted and the pan juices evaporate, 1–2 minutes longer. Transfer the mixture to a plate and wipe the pan clean with a paper towel.

2 Add the remaining ½ teaspoon oil to the pan and warm over medium heat. Place 1 tortilla in the pan and sprinkle evenly with half of the cheese. Top with the spinach-mushroom mixture, spreading it in an even layer almost to the edges of the tortilla. Sprinkle the remaining cheese over the vegetables and top with the second tortilla. Cook, turning once with a wide spatula, until the cheese is melted and the quesadilla is browned on both sides, 1–2 minutes per side.

3 Transfer to a cutting board and let cool slightly before slicing into small wedges.

CAULIFLOWER & BROWN RICE GRATIN

Creamy cauliflower purée and whole-grain brown rice pair up in this savory dish. Cauliflower belongs to the cruciferous family of vegetables, noted for their vitamins, fiber, and disease-fighting phytochemicals. Make sure to let the gratin cool.

- ■ from 9 months
- ● 4 mini gratins
- ✳ suitable for freezing

Unsalted butter for greasing
1 cup cauliflower florets
½ cup grated Parmesan cheese
Pinch of grated nutmeg
1 cup cooked Savory Brown Rice (page 259)
4 tablespoons low-sodium vegetable broth or water

1 Preheat the oven to 375°F. Lightly butter four ½-cup ramekins or custard cups.

Continued on next page

3 Add the garlic, snap peas, and green onions to the wok and stir-fry for 2 minutes, then return the beef to the wok with the black bean and soy sauces; stir-fry for another minute, adding a splash of water if the sauce begins to dry out.

4 Divide the noodles among 4 plates and top with the beef stir-fry.

Variation *You can substitute chicken, pork, tofu, or vegetables of your choice.*

Storage tip *Refrigerate in an airtight container for up to 2 days. Reheat thoroughly.*

Continued from previous page

2 Pour water into a saucepan to a depth of 1 inch. Put the cauliflower in a steamer basket and put the basket in the saucepan. Bring to a boil over high heat. Cover and steam until the cauliflower is tender, 6–8 minutes. Remove from the heat and remove the steamer basket from the saucepan. Transfer the cauliflower to a food processor or blender and process to a smooth purée, adding a little water for a smooth consistency, if necessary. Stir ¼ cup of the cheese and the nutmeg into the cauliflower purée. Set aside.

3 Divide the rice evenly among the prepared ramekins, patting it into the bottoms. Drizzle each with 1 tablespoon of the broth. Spoon the cauliflower purée into each ramekin, dividing it evenly and smoothing the top to cover the rice. Top each ramekin with 1 tablespoon of the remaining cheese.

4 Bake until the tops are golden brown, about 20 minutes. Let cool completely before serving.

HAM & PEA PENNE

Good-quality ham will give the best flavor, but for babies use a reduced-sodium ham (or reduce the amount of salty ham).

- ■ from 12 months
- ● 4 family servings

10 ounces penne
1 tablespoon olive oil
2 large cloves garlic, chopped
¾ cup water
1 cup frozen peas
6 tablespoons heavy cream
4 thick slices of cured ham, cut into bite-size pieces
Pepper (optional)
Freshly grated Parmesan cheese

1 Cook the pasta in a large pot of boiling water, following the instructions on the package. Drain, reserving 2 tablespoons of the cooking water.

2 Meanwhile, heat the olive oil in a large heavy-bottomed skillet and cook the garlic for 30 seconds. Add the water and then the peas and cook over medium-high heat for 2 minutes, or until the peas are cooked and the liquid has reduced.

3 Add the ham to the pan with the cream. Cook over low heat, stirring frequently, until warmed through. Stir in the pasta and the reserved cooking water, if needed, and stir gently until combined. Season with pepper, if using, and serve sprinkled with Parmesan.

Variation *Replace the ham with canned salmon. You could also use fresh-cooked salmon (check for bones) flaked into pieces, or cooked, diced chicken.*

CHICKEN MEATBALLS IN TOMATO SAUCE

This great Italian-inspired dish is delicious with pasta or rice.

- from 12 months
- 4 family servings

CHICKEN MEATBALLS

1 pound ground chicken
3 tablespoons freshly grated
　　Parmesan cheese
1 cup fresh bread crumbs
1 small egg, beaten
Flour, for dusting
Olive oil, for frying

TOMATO SAUCE

1 tablespoon olive oil
1 large garlic clove, crushed
1 teaspoon dried oregano
14-ounce can chopped tomatoes
1 tablespoon tomato paste

1. Combine the chicken, Parmesan, bread crumbs, and egg. Using floured hands, form into 20 small balls.
2. Heat enough oil to just coat a heavy-bottomed skillet and cook the meatballs, in batches if necessary, for 6–8 minutes, turning occasionally, until browned and cooked though. Remove from pan and keep warm.
3. To make the sauce, heat the olive oil in a pan and add the garlic and oregano. Cook for 30 seconds and then add the chopped tomatoes and paste. Cook for 4 minutes over medium-low heat, stirring occasionally.
4. Return the chicken meatballs to the pan; cook for 4 minutes until heated through and the sauce has reduced and thickened.

TURKEY BURGERS WITH PINEAPPLE RELISH

Turkey provides protein and B vitamins and is generally lower in fat than red meat. The relish is rich in vitamin C.

- from 12 months
- 3–4 servings

½ pound lean ground turkey
1 teaspoon dried oregano
1 large garlic clove, crushed
　　(optional)
Olive oil
Mini seeded burger buns or whole-wheat rolls

PINEAPPLE RELISH

¾ cup canned or fresh peeled, finely diced pineapple
1 tablespoon finely chopped mint
1½-inch piece cucumber, peeled, seeded, and finely diced
2 teaspoons lemon juice

1. Combine the ground turkey, oregano, and garlic, if using, in a mixing bowl. Divide the mixture into 3 or 4 portions. Use your hands to roll each portion into a ball, then flatten into a burger patty. Put the burgers on a plate, cover with plastic wrap, and chill for 30 minutes.
2. Preheat the broiler and line the broiler pan with foil.

Meanwhile, mix together the ingredients for the relish and set aside to allow the flavors to mingle.

3. Brush the patties lightly with oil then broil 3–5 minutes on each side, or until cooked through with no trace of pink in the center.
4. Serve in buns topped with a spoonful of the relish. For younger babies, cut burgers into bite-size pieces and serve buns separately.

Storage tip *The patties can be frozen, uncooked, for up to 3 months. Separate the burgers with waxed paper to keep them from sticking together.*

DESSERT

BANANA & MAPLE YOGURT ICE

This is perfect for soothing sore gums. If your bananas aren't very ripe, add maple syrup to sweeten them.

- ■ from 12 months
- ● 2 servings

1 small ripe banana
1 heaping tablespoon Greek-style yogurt
1 teaspoon maple syrup (optional)

1 Peel the banana, wrap it tightly in plastic wrap, and freeze until firm, at least 3 hours—although it can be stored in the freezer until ready to use.
2 Remove the frozen banana from the freezer and unwrap. Let sit for 15 minutes to soften slightly, then break into chunks.
3 Put the banana in a food processor or blender with the yogurt and maple syrup, if using, and blend until thick, smooth, and creamy. Spoon the ice cream into a bowl.

Storage tip *This can be refrigerated in an airtight container for up to 2 days, but it will defrost after an hour and become very soft. The banana can be stored in the freezer for up to 3 months.*

FRUIT SWIRLS

Making your own fruit yogurt means you know exactly what's in it. Frozen fruit—either a single fruit or mixed—counts toward the recommended servings per day of fruits and vegetables.

- ■ from 12 months
- ● 2 servings

4 tablespoons mixed red berries, defrosted if frozen
1 nectarine, pitted and quartered
3–4 tablespoons water
Plain, low-fat yogurt, preferably Greek-style and unsweetened

1 Put the berries, nectarine, and water in a saucepan with a lid. Bring to a simmer, then cook, covered, for 5–7 minutes or until the berries and nectarine soften and begin to break down.
2 Press the cooked fruit through a sieve or food mill to remove any seeds and skin.
3 Spoon a serving of yogurt into a glass or bowl. Add a few spoonfuls of the fruit purée and swirl it into the yogurt for a marbled effect.

TROPICAL FRUIT SALAD

In the wintertime, when local seasonal fruit is limited, look to tropical fruit for bright flavors and soft textures. This colorful fruit salad is a healthy snack for your toddler when he is ready to branch out into more exotic fruits. The firm but soft cubes make perfect finger foods for dipping into vanilla yogurt.

- ■ from 12 months
- ● 8 servings

1 small mango
¼ medium papaya
½ kiwi, peeled and cut into small cubes
½ banana, peeled and cut into small cubes
Whole-milk vanilla yogurt (optional)

1 To prepare the mango, stand it on one of its narrow edges. Using a sharp knife, cut down along each side of the stem end, just grazing the pit. Using a vegetable peeler or paring knife, peel each half, then cut the flesh into small cubes.
2 Peel and seed the papaya and cut into small cubes.
3 In a large bowl, combine the mango, papaya, kiwi, and banana and toss to mix well. Spoon the fruit into a bowl or onto a plate and drizzle with yogurt, if using.

WHIPPED RICOTTA WITH CHERRIES

Naturally sweet and fluffy ricotta cheese is easy to pair with just about any of your baby's favorite fruits. This protein-rich treat is yummy with dark, sweet summer cherries, which are high in beta-carotene and other antioxidants. Fragrant vanilla can encourage the connection between your baby's senses of smell and taste.

- ■ from 9 months
- ● 12 servings

1 cup pitted sweet cherries
½ cup ricotta cheese
½ teaspoon pure nonalcoholic vanilla extract

1 Place the cherries in a food processor or blender and process to a smooth or coarse purée. Depending on baby's age and chewing ability, add a little water for a smoother consistency, if necessary.
2 In a bowl, whisk together the ricotta, cherry purée, and vanilla vigorously until smooth and fluffy. If you like, set aside a bit of the cherry purée before whisking the mixture together to dollop on top of the ricotta.

Storage tip *Refrigerate in an airtight container for up to 2 days.*

OATMEAL COOKIES

These treats are packed with nutritious oats. Serve with milk.

- ■ from 12 months
- ● 12 cookies

½ cup unsalted butter, softened
⅓ cup brown sugar
½ cup self-rising flour
3 tablespoons whole-wheat self-rising flour
1 cup oats

1 Preheat the oven to 350°F. Line two baking sheets with parchment paper.
2 Beat together the butter and sugar in a bowl until light and fluffy. Stir in both types of flour and the oats, then mix well to make a soft dough.
3 Divide dough into 12 pieces. Roll each piece into a ball and arrange on baking sheets, allowing room for the dough to spread. Flatten the top of each ball slightly and bake for 15–20 minutes, or until cookies are just golden but still soft in the center.
4 Let cool for 5 minutes and then transfer to wire racks to cool completely.

MIXED FRUIT COMPOTE

Many children prefer foods with smooth textures. This compote is sieved to remove any offending seeds and skin, resulting in an intensely fruity red sauce.

- from 8 months
- 4–6 servings

7 ounces mixed red fruit such as strawberries, raspberries, and cherries, rinsed, hulled, and pitted, and defrosted if frozen
2 tablespoons apple juice
1 teaspoon cornstarch

1   Purée the fruit in a food processor or blender. Press the purée through a sieve or food mill to remove any seeds or skin.
2   Combine purée, apple juice, and cornstarch in a saucepan and heat gently and briefly, stirring frequently, until thickened.

Variation *Fruit compote is delicious stirred into plain, unsweetened yogurt.*

PEACH CRISPS

This variation on the classic crisp uses whole fruits—perfect if you're just cooking for children since it's easy to make small portions.

- from 12 months
- 2–4 servings

2 peaches, halved and pitted
3 tablespoons all-purpose flour
2 tablespoons unsalted butter
2 tablespoons brown sugar
1 tablespoon oats (optional)

1   Preheat the oven to 350°F. Lightly oil an ovenproof dish and arrange the peach halves in the dish.
2   Put the flour and butter in a bowl and rub together with your fingertips to form coarse crumbs. Stir in the sugar and oats, if using, and mix well.
3   Spoon the topping mixture over the peaches and add 2 tablespoons of water to the dish. Bake for 25 minutes, or until the peaches are tender and the topping is slightly crisp. Let cool before serving.

Variation *Plums, apples, pears, or nectarines make delicious alternatives to peaches. If you have any topping mixture left over, freeze it for future use.*

INTERACTING WITH YOUR GROWING BABY

Creating a loving relationship

Caring for your baby goes well beyond taking care of his basic needs and ensuring he remains safe and well. To thrive, all babies need to form a close, loving, emotional attachment with at least one of their parents, and preferably both.

Building this relationship begins shortly after birth, when a baby first responds to his mother's facial expressions and speech. The trust and confidence that come from bonding will help him attain his full potential as he learns to master essential manipulation, locomotion, and communication skills. In addition to creating this loving bond, parents need to equip their children with important social and emotional skills that will help them negotiate social interactions and participate successfully in the larger community.

Responsiveness

Much of the behavior that draws an infant closer to his parents is instinctive—when he cries, you pick him up; when he coos, you coo back. You can encourage your baby to form a close attachment by being sensitive to his emotional state and by engaging him in ways appropriate to his developmental stage.

Be sensitive to your baby's emotional state. Is he alert enough for stimulating play? According to their temperament, children vary in their baseline level of responsiveness to parents. For this trait there is a continuum of personalities, ranging from active to passive. An active baby is very expressive and gives strong and frequent social signals, such as eye contact, reaching, smiling, and vocalizing. A passive baby exhibits few expressions that reveal

anything about his inner emotions. Most babies fall somewhere in between.

Young babies are more responsive when they're alert, although simply being awake may not mean your baby is ready for stimulation. You don't want to stimulate your baby all the time, or he may not learn how to amuse himself! Also be careful not to stimulate him so much that gets fussy and tunes out. Look for cues that he's ready to play: perhaps when he's lying calmly and quietly in his crib but smiles and moves his arms and legs excitedly as you approach. He'll probably be more alert and willing to be engaged early in the day.

With a little practice, you'll soon learn what stimulation works best for your baby—and when. You'll figure out, for example, that there's no point in showing your young baby a toy while he's feeding, because he's focused entirely on his food; when he's older, however, a toy could help distract him while you spoon some food into his mouth.

Your role

By engaging in appropriate activities, you can help your baby make the most of his skills as he acquires them. Make it fun for him to practice these skills and encourage his efforts, regardless of whether he accomplishes the task at hand. (In other words, praise the process, not the end result.) Your job is to provide the support and environment in which to succeed, not to push your baby to learn.

Try to spend some time every day playing with your baby—and continue to do so as he becomes a toddler and then an older child. This will ensure that you develop a close, loving bond. Not only will you be helping him practice new skills, but you'll also learn much about your growing child through your playtime together.

Your baby will take his lead from you with most things he tries, so be positive and gentle with him, and try to make his environment a happy place to be. Even very young babies pick up on negative feelings. Harsh voices, even when not directed at him, will upset your baby.

The emergence of personality and sociability varies greatly from child to child (see pages 278–279 for key milestones). Do your best not to typecast your child or impose your own choice of temperament on him. Your baby needs to develop his personality and social skills unimpeded by the unrealistic views or expectations of others.

One of your responsibilities as a parent is to set boundaries for your child so that he comes to understand the difference between right and wrong. Key to this is setting the right example—your child will spend more time with you than with anyone else. You need to show him how to play and interact with others by being polite, sharing things, and showing him how to take turns.

How your baby develops

Your baby is unique and different from all other children, and her personality and appearance are like no one else's. But if you look at the big picture, she also has much in common with most other children. Healthy children, for example, have the same body parts, are born roughly the same size and weight, and cry when they're hungry. Children are also remarkably alike in how they mature physically, mentally, and emotionally.

When we talk about growth and development, we're talking about the typical patterns that children follow on their journeys from infancy to adulthood. Growth describes the process of physical enlargement (height, weight, and head size), while development refers to the acquisition of body functions and skills (motor, social, and language), and the successive stages of psychological maturation.

Physical growth

In the first days after birth, your baby will lose weight. The reason for this is simple: More is going out (urine and bowel movements) than is coming in (breast milk or formula), but soon everything changes. In the first 3 to 4 months of life, your baby will grow remarkably rapidly. After that, the rate of growth slows a bit for the rest of the first year and slows down even more between 12 and 24 months. From that point, growth continues at a relatively steady rate until puberty, when your child will go through another huge burst in growth. Growth charts (see pages 275 and 380–383) and graphs tracking changes in height, weight, or head circumference reflect these patterns as your child grows older.

While many predictions and expectations for a child's growth are generally accurate—see the three rules of thumb, below—many healthy children don't

3 rules of thumb about growth

1   Children usually double their birth weight by 5 months of age and triple it by 12 months. Children with lower birth weights typically double and triple faster; those with higher birth weights usually take longer than average.

2   Children usually reach about half their adult height at 24 months. For greater accuracy, measure your child when he's standing up—and standing still! Boys typically will be about 2 inches taller than their doubled 2-year-old height; for girls, subtract 2 inches from their doubled height.

3   Half of a child's head growth occurs in the first year of life; the rest takes years.

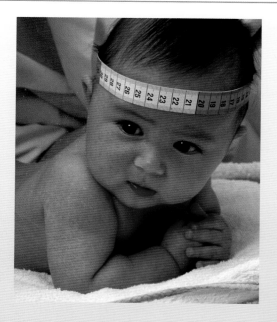

grow precisely according to the typical pattern. The rules are correct, in a broad sense, but they may not apply to your child. Many factors influence how big or small your child is, including genetics. You won't get a good idea of how big your child will grow to be before she's about 2 years old.

Growth charts

Pediatricians use growth charts to track a child's physical growth over time. If your baby is growing normally—which is a reflection of good health—she'll follow the same growth curve (of the many parallel curves on the chart) for weight and height as she gets older. Each time your child visits the pediatrician, her weight and height will be plotted on a growth chart to see that she's growing consistently. It's more important that your child continue to follow a consistent curve than that she measure at a higher or lower percentile.

For example, look at the two growth charts on page 275. The boy whose weight is plotted on the top is growing consistently along the 25th percentile curve. He's healthy because he is growing as he should. The boy whose weight is plotted on the bottom chart has a higher percentile value but isn't growing well. He's "falling off the curve" (meaning he's in a lower percentile with each successive visit), and that's cause for concern. His doctor will need to investigate what's causing this.

Skill acquisition

At birth, your daughter doesn't much resemble an adult. Besides her small size and appearance, she can't take care of herself, can't walk or talk, and certainly can't follow commands. However, you can anticipate that, bit by bit, year by year, she'll acquire new skills so that eventually she'll not only look like, but will also act like, an adult.

Although your baby was born small and helpless, she has the capacity to acquire all the skills of an

Weighing your baby and measuring his height are obvious ways to track growth. So what's going on when your pediatrician measures his head circumference? Taking routine measurements of a baby's head size is one way to track brain growth. Your pediatrician will monitor both your child's head growth and his developmental skills to make sure he's neurologically within the normal range. If a child's head is growing less than expected or is not following a percentile curve consistently, there's a chance that something could be wrong. Conversely, if the head is growing too quickly, there could be too much fluid surrounding the brain (hydrocephalus, see page 367) or another problem.

adult. How she does so depends on her brain and body developing until both are sufficiently mature. Children typically take their first steps at the age of 1 (though the normal range is actually between 10 and 18 months). While you can stand your baby up (support her at the torso; do not hold her up by her hands) and encourage her to walk when she's 6, 7, or 8 months old, she won't be able to do it—no matter how hard she tries—until she's a little bit older and her brain, nerves, and muscles are mature enough to manage walking. Sure, practice can help, but only once the basic maturity is established.

Your baby will appear to have an innate compulsion to try to develop new skills. She'll practice new skills over and over again until she can do them well. In a sense, your baby is driven by an internal mechanism, a standard feature in humans, that tells her she must first learn to walk before she can run and climb, and that she must first utter a few sounds before she can pronounce words and then speak in complete sentences.

When it comes to development, all healthy children are alike in that they share a characteristic pattern and timing for acquiring new skills. But because children are all different, there's a broad range of what's "normal" for developing the ability to perform each new skill. There also are small variations in the orderly sequence of events—some children even skip a skill, such as rolling over or crawling, before going on to more difficult tasks. (Of course, all children eventually will go back and learn to roll or crawl.)

Your pediatrician will carefully observe your baby at office visits and may ask about new skills she's developed. These newly acquired abilities are referred to as milestones. The term comes from the old practice of using rocks or stones to mark each mile along a road. Counting milestones allowed a person to know how far he'd come, and with each passing milestone the traveler knew he was getting closer to his destination. Although milestones in child development are not spaced as equally as stones along a road, you can use these markers to chart out your child's progress as she makes her journey to adulthood.

To get an idea of the usual order in which children learn new skills and when, see pages 278–279. Be sure to pay attention to the range of ages that are considered normal for any new achievement. For each skill, your child may succeed at the average age or earlier or later. As long as your baby is in that normal range, all is fine. It's also important not to assess your baby's developmental health on the basis

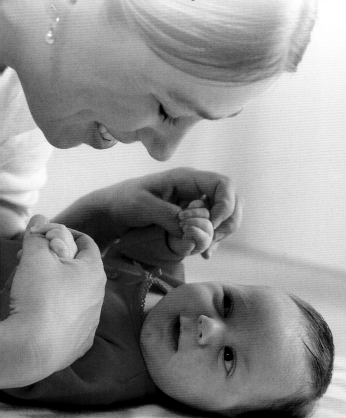

of just one skill. Your pediatrician will look at your child's overall development. If she's late for clapping her hands but on track for everything else, there's probably no need for concern. If you're worried about your baby's development, of course, talk it over with your doctor.

Each of the body's systems and normal functions matures at different times and at different rates. To get an idea of how they develop, read on to learn how vision, teeth, and speech evolve. These examples demonstrate that there is a blueprint for the maturation of every part and function of the human body, and for every developmental skill and milestone. Because some individual children accomplish tasks early, some at an average pace, and others a bit later than average, each child's development is different from every other child's. On the other hand, the ways each child grows and learns new skills are remarkably similar. So all children are very much the same, while at the same time, your child is unique!

Vision

In the first month of life, your newborn sees clearly only objects that are within inches of her face; everything else looks hazy. By about 1 month of age, she'll enjoy focusing on people's faces and will be able to distinguish your face from the faces of others. While you will take pleasure in being the object of your child's gaze, be aware that a light bulb, window, or television screen will give you some stiff competition! Bright lights will likely fascinate her.

While she can see nearby objects, she still has difficulty seeing objects at a distance. By 6 months of age, she'll see you well if you stand several feet away, but her vision probably is only 20/100. These numbers rate her vision compared to the average, normal adult. The first number refers to the distance between the eye chart and the person being tested; the second number is how far away an adult with "normal" vision would have to stand to see the chart exactly as the person being tested. In other words, if your baby has a visual acuity of 20/100, her vision when she's 20 feet from an object is equivalent to the vision of an adult standing 100 feet from the

Growth charts

Growth charts (see pages 380–383) are developed by measuring a large number of healthy children of different ages, known as the "reference group." The range of weights and heights for each age in this group determines the chart. "Normal" weight is defined strictly on a statistical basis: The 50th percentile is calculated by determining the average weight or height of all children in the reference group at each age. The heaviest 3 percent of children at a given age are considered overweight, and the lightest 3 percent are considered underweight.

The percentile value given to a child's weight or height is a way of seeing how that weight compares to all the other boys or girls in the reference group. The percentile value for your son's weight (or height) is the percentage of boys his age who weigh less (or are shorter). So if your 2-year-old son is in the 10th percentile for weight, he is heavier than 10 percent of 2-year-old boys in the reference group. (He is also lighter than 90 percent of the boys.) He is on the small side, but he's still considered normal. Values above the 50th percentile are above average, and those below are below average.

Unfortunately, parents often add inappropriate meaning to these percentiles. A parent whose child measures less than the 50th percentile frequently asks, "Why isn't he bigger?" Growth is not a contest to see who can be the tallest or heaviest, and it's important to remember a higher percentile is no better (or worse) than a lower one. A child can be healthy even if he's below average; keep in mind that half of all children are at or below the 50th percentile.

There is a large genetic component to your child's height and weight. Growth that follows a particular percentile curve (whether an above average, average, or below average curve) indicates that your child is growing according to his genetic potential.

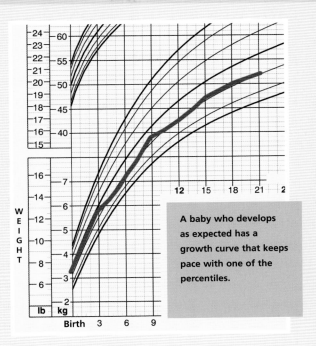

A baby who develops as expected has a growth curve that keeps pace with one of the percentiles.

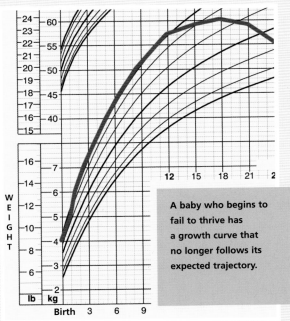

A baby who begins to fail to thrive has a growth curve that no longer follows its expected trajectory.

Denver Scale

Many doctors use the Denver Development Screening Test as a tool for assessing children's progress in reaching milestones—it identifies normal ranges established for children of the same age. By using this chart, your doctor is following your baby's development much like she tracks physical growth on a growth chart. Instead of height, weight, and head circumference, however, this scale compares skills in four categories: gross motor, fine motor-adaptive, language, and personal-social (shown below as an example).

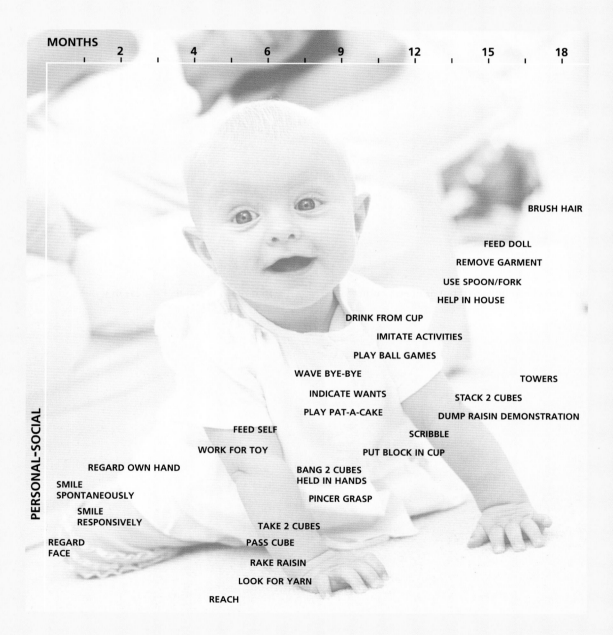

MONTHS

| 2 | 4 | 6 | 9 | 12 | 15 | 18 |

PERSONAL-SOCIAL

BRUSH HAIR

FEED DOLL

REMOVE GARMENT

USE SPOON/FORK

HELP IN HOUSE

DRINK FROM CUP

IMITATE ACTIVITIES

PLAY BALL GAMES

WAVE BYE-BYE

TOWERS

INDICATE WANTS

STACK 2 CUBES

PLAY PAT-A-CAKE

DUMP RAISIN DEMONSTRATION

FEED SELF

SCRIBBLE

WORK FOR TOY

PUT BLOCK IN CUP

REGARD OWN HAND

BANG 2 CUBES HELD IN HANDS

SMILE SPONTANEOUSLY

PINCER GRASP

SMILE RESPONSIVELY

TAKE 2 CUBES

REGARD FACE

PASS CUBE

RAKE RAISIN

LOOK FOR YARN

REACH

THE ACQUISITION OF LANGUAGE SKILLS

	Average age	Early talkers	Late talkers
Babbling (single syllables)	7–8 months	6 months	9–10 months
First words	12–15 months	10–11 months	16–18 months
2-word sentences	20–24 months	18–20 months	24–30 months
3-word sentences	24–26 months	21–24 months	up to 36 months
Follows a command (without you pointing)	15 months	12–14 months	16–17 months
Knows names of body parts	15 months	12–14 months	16–18 months
Counts to 10	26–30 months	24–26 months	30–36 months

same object. Normal adult vision is 20/20. By age 3 or 4, your child's vision will improve to about 20/40; by age 5 or 6, it will be 20/30; and by age 7, it should reach 20/20. Her eyesight will then be as good as (or better than) yours!

Teeth

Your child probably will get her first tooth when she's about 6 months old. But as in every other area of development, this can vary greatly from one child to the next. Some children are even born with an erupted tooth, though this is rare. At the other end of the spectrum, some children don't get a first tooth until they're 12 months or older. Genetics clearly affects how and when teeth erupt; frequently a child who is late getting her teeth has a parent who also was late to get teeth.

The first two teeth to arrive are usually the bottom central incisors, followed by the top four incisors and then the lateral incisors on the bottom. The next teeth to come in are typically the first molars, at about 18 months of age. When the molar erupts, there's a space between the lateral incisor and the first molar because the canine, or "eye" tooth, usually comes in after the first molar. The last of the 20 baby teeth are the second molars, which come in at the outer side of the first molars at about 2½ years of age (see also page 201). Although many

children's teeth follow this pattern and schedule, variations are common and normal.

Speech

A young child's brain is better equipped than an adult's to absorb language. A child possesses not only the built-in equipment for acquiring the ability to communicate with speech but also a compelling drive to do so. Like so many areas in growth and development, there is an orderly sequence of steps that lead from no language at all to fluent speech.

To attain these language skills, a baby must simultaneously master three processes: input, "central processing," and output. She must be able to recognize the difference between speech and other sounds, and must learn to discriminate between the many combinations of sounds that constitute speech. Additionally, she must somehow learn the particular combinations of sounds that represent words and, by intuition, decipher the meaning implied by the speaking person. And finally, once she knows what she wants to say, she must be able to direct her mouth, lips, tongue, and breathing to produce the appropriate sounds.

It may seem an easy task to figure out that "mama" means "mother." But if the loving person who cares for her is "mama," does "mama" mean "mother," "woman," "adult," "caring person," or "tall

Key developmental milestones

0–3 months

- Lifts head when prone
- Moves arms and legs
- Growing ability to follow objects and focus
- Vocalizes sounds (coos)
- Smiles spontaneously and responsively
- Likes to be held and rocked
- Stares at hands

6–9 months

- Rolls from back to stomach
- On back, can lift head up
- Learns to crawl
- Reaches for a toy that's been dropped
- Curious, puts everything in mouth
- Responds to name
- Speaks single consonants ("da-da," "ba-ba")
- Imitates sounds
- May cry when strangers approach
- May cry when parent leaves the room

3–6 months

- Rolls over from stomach to back
- Reaches for and grasps objects
- Sits with support
- Looks at objects in hand
- Grasps object with both hands
- Follows a moving object with eyes
- Laughs aloud
- Makes expressive noises
- Grasps foot and places it in mouth

9–12 months

- Crawls well
- Stands holding onto furniture
- Learns to grasp with thumb and finger
- Puts things in and out of containers
- Interested in pictures
- Drops objects on purpose
- Understands "no"
- Uses "ma-ma" or "da-da"
- Knows meaning of 1–3 words
- Cooperates in games
- Plays peekaboo and pat-a-cake
- Waves bye-bye

12–18 months

- Creeps up stairs
- Walks well alone
- Can stoop to recover an object
- Seats self on chair
- Interested in self-feeding
- Looks at pictures in book
- Scribbles spontaneously
- Uses spoon
- Holds own cup and drinks from it
- Follows one or two directions
- Has 3–5 words
- Will point to five body parts
- Will point to pictures
- Points or vocalizes to make desires known
- Cooperates in dressing

18–24 months

- Runs and jumps
- Uses fingers with skill
- Turns pages of a book
- Walks backward
- Has at least 20 words
- Combines 2 words into phrases
- Verbalizes desires with words
- Uses a spoon well
- Handles a cup well
- Imitates housework
- Removes one piece of clothing

2–3 years

- Ready for toilet training
- Highly mobile—skills are refined
- Uses spoon or fork to feed self
- Throws and kicks a ball
- Disassembles simple objects and puts them back together
- Can do simple puzzles, string beads, and stack toys
- Capable of thinking before acting
- Loves to pretend and to imitate the actions of people she sees
- Engages in creative activities, such as art and using building blocks
- Uses plurals
- Knows 100–300 words

- Uses 2- to 4-word phrases
- Has great difficulty sharing
- Has strong urges and desires; at the same time is developing ability to exert self-control
- Wants to please parents but sometimes has difficulty controlling impulses
- Displays affection, especially for caregiver
- Initiates own play activity and occupies self
- Beginning to be interested in peers

The words for mother and father are remarkably similar in different languages. In English, children call their parents *daddy* and *mommy* and, depending on the family, grandparents may be addressed as *grandpa* or *papa* and *grandma* or *nana*. In French, Italian, and Spanish, the same names are commonly used, but these languages are related. However, in Swahili, *mother* is pronounced *mah-mah*; in Indonesian dialects, father is *bah-pah*, and in Hebrew, *mother* and *father* are *ah-bah* and *ee-mah*. It's as if the words for parents derive from the repetitive first sounds made by infants. Children usually say *da-da* before they say *ma-ma*, because the *da-da* sound is easier for a child to produce.

person with long hair?" Deciphering the meaning of abstract notions, such as colors, shorter and taller, or good and bad, is even more challenging. Yet healthy children do it. Then there are more complicated issues: sentence structure, grammar, tenses, plurals, pronouns, and tasks such as discriminating between different meanings of the same word or words that sound alike but have different meanings.

The beginnings of speech

At first, your child will study you (and the faces of other adults) as you talk and then try to imitate the oral movements that produce the sounds. She'll experiment with sounds in the first months of her life and will be very pleased with herself each time she discovers and succeeds in making a new noise. At 5 to 6 months of age, she'll make sounds known as "raspberries" and may discover how to scream or shriek some sounds. At 7 to 8 months, she may begin repeating a syllable—"da-da-da-da" or "na-na-na-na" (see box at left). Soon words begin to appear.

The range for normal development is wider for speech than for any other developmental skill. Babies who are unusually early talkers say many words well before their first birthdays and speak in full sentences before the age of 2. Late bloomers, who often have a parent or close relative who was also late to speak, may have only a handful of words at 18 months and may not form complex sentences before the age of 3 (see box on page 277). For children who are slow to develop speech, sign language could help them communicate with you and nurture their skills (see page 176).

Playing with your baby

Playing with your baby is wonderful for many reasons. First and foremost, it strengthens the bond of love between the two of you. When you smile adoringly at your baby, he responds and smiles, too. He senses your deep devotion and concern for him. This is essential to his emotional well-being: Feeling loved is a major prerequisite for developing his confidence and sense of self-worth.

Besides being fun, play is also educational. When the two of you play peekaboo or when your baby throws something to the floor and then looks to see where it landed, he's learning about the permanence of objects—that people and objects continue to exist even when they're out his sight. Rolling a ball or passing a small object back and forth with you allows your baby to practice taking turns. Naming games (and reading) teach your baby the meaning of words: "Where is your nose?" "Where is the dog?"

Play also allows your child to practice social skills. Toward the end of your baby's first year,

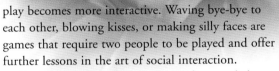

play becomes more interactive. Waving bye-bye to each other, blowing kisses, or making silly faces are games that require two people to be played and offer further lessons in the art of social interaction.

Sharing or taking turns isn't easy for your baby to accept, since children are born with a relatively self-centered and selfish nature. Yet these concepts are central to successfully participating in play. Children usually start learning to share—albeit reluctantly—by the age of 2 or 3.

Your toddler will enjoy pretend play that engages his imagination, such as role-playing games that let him practice social interactions: Your baby can be a chef and you the customer; when you order food, he pretends to cook it and serves it to you. Games also enable him to channel the frustration and anger he keeps within (after being denied having his own way many times each day). If he plays the role of mom or another person who has complete control over

3 types of toys to avoid

1. **Toys with many small pieces** Tiny pieces pose a choking hazard (rule of thumb: if an item fits through a toilet-paper roll, it's a choking hazard). Also, when pieces inevitably get lost, the toy might not be as enjoyable. Always check a toy's age rating.

2. **Toys that are very noisy** A toy drum, xylophone, or anything that makes a loud noise may give you a headache—though your baby probably will love it!

3. **Toys that require batteries** Aside from your child's frustration when a toy stops working, replacing even rechargeable batteries takes time and money. Electronic circuits can easily become damaged, too.

his environment, he might order you around exactly as he perceives he's ordered around. The more often your baby can express his negative feelings through play, the less severe and less frequent his temper tantrums will be.

Play also enables your child to hone locomotive and manipulative skills, and to benefit from exercise. Your baby or toddler probably doesn't need to be told to go exercise; instead, he has a natural desire to be active. If your child is full of energy, take him out to the playground or garden, or a play space in your home where he can move freely. Now his desire to move about can be satisfied in a safe and convenient environment. Let him run around. He'll enjoy the slide, swings, and climbing equipment at the playground; when he's ready to sit still, he can join the fun in the sandpit.

Toys

A toy is age-appropriate for your baby if it's safe (see page 318) and he finds it fun. An enormous number of toys bought for babies are never played with, because toys that may look exciting to grown-ups sometimes aren't so interesting to babies. You'll probably be surprised by which toys your baby finds entertaining. Often very simple toys or household objects are favorites because your child can dream up countless ways to use them. Encourage your child's imaginative play, which is a key way to learn.

Young babies don't need many toys, and even toddlers can make do with a small number of inexpensive playthings. Paper and drawing materials can engage your child from about 15 months throughout his life, while pots and pans can be banged together to make noise, filled with things, and used to carry all sorts of interesting objects.

(see page 318)

<table>
<tr><td>PARENTING**TIP**</td><td>rainy-day play</td></tr>
</table>

Getting outside daily for a walk or playtime at the park is great for both kids and parents. But when it's just too cold or rainy, it is wise to have a backup plan. Scope out ahead of time indoor child-safe spots to play, such as a baby gym, kids' museum, or a kids' area at a mall. Consider saving some special toys for times when you need to stay inside. Or simply improvise toys from safe kitchen items, such as unbreakable cups, bowls, pots, wooden spoons, or cupcake tins.

GREAT TOYS FOR LITTLE ONES

Age	Toys
2–4 months	Rattles; mobiles; brightly colored activity board; books with bold colors
4–7 months	Textured toys; toys that make sounds; baby mirror; baby board or bath books
8–12 months	Stacking toys; bath toys; large building blocks; push-pull toys; "busy boxes" with parts that push, open, and squeak
13–18 months	Lift-out simple puzzles; digging toys; cars, trucks, and trains; board books; shape sorters; dolls; crayons
19 months–2 years	Hammering toy; simple puzzles; toy telephone; musical toys
2–3½ years	Construction toys; dress-up clothes; paints; toy tools; safe household items (such as a dustpan and brush)

Toys that leave more to the imagination—puzzles, building blocks, and shape sorters—are usually enjoyed more than toys with lots of realistic details.

Whether your child is a boy or girl, try not to have preconceptions about what type of toys he or she will like. Offer a variety (see box, opposite page) and see what sticks. It's a mystery why certain toys become favorites and others are rejected outright.

Activities

Between the ages of 9 and 18 months, your baby will happily sit in front of a low-level cabinet in the kitchen and play with pots and pans. In the bath, he'll enjoy pouring water into cups, splashing, and floating boats. There's no end to simple, fun activities you and your baby can enjoy at home.

After 18 months, your toddler will want to help with housework. He can wipe off the table, pick up toys, or, with your help, put the clothes in the washing machine, add the measured detergent, and sort the dried laundry.

Baking and art are nearly universally engrossing to children. When you bake cookies together, your child can shape the dough with his hands or cookie cutters and decorate them with sprinkles or

chocolate bits. Painting at an easel with poster paint, drawing with crayons, and working with clay also are loads of fun. You can play with bubbles, dance to music, and play dress-up. The options are endless.

There's much to enjoy outside the home, too—going to the park, zoo, fire station, or a children's museum. Wherever you are, point out things you see and talk about them with your baby.

You may also be able to choose among special classes for babies: gym, swimming, massage, art, music, dance, and more. Playgroups and toddler classes can be fun for your baby starting at around 10–12 months; before then, they're more about the two of you—or you and other parents—interacting. Classes are optional. Sign your child up for a particular class if you think you both will enjoy it. Be careful about crowding out crucial free-play time with organized activities. Although fun, there's nothing considerable gained in classes that he can't also learn or be exposed to at home.

ORGANIZED CLASS

Main benefits:
- You can enjoy an activity together.
- Your child may get to try equipment you don't have at home, such as a trampoline, a swimming pool, or musical instruments.
- It's a great way for you to meet other parents with children about the same age as your own.

Downsides:
- The money spent on tuition.
- The increased risk that your child could get sick from germs spread child-to-child or via shared play items.
- Your child may have trouble sitting still (especially if she is by nature an active child).

Ways to play

People—particularly parents—and not inanimate toys are the best and most effective playmates for babies. By playing with your baby, you both entertain her and teach her important things, such as language and how things work. Through play, you can help your baby develop all the skills she needs: physical, cognitive, emotional, and social.

However, you'll be most successful if you interact with her in ways that keep pace with her development. Playing peekaboo, for example, will be much more fun for both of you once your baby is around 8 or 9 months old and begins to realize that even when you are hidden from her, you'll soon reappear.

1 month
You can start to play simple games with your baby now. Put her on your lap, with her face

close to yours—no more than 8–12 inches away. Lean toward her and talk happily. Pause and give her a chance to react by smiling, gurgling, wriggling, or moving her mouth back at you. Try doing these things one at a time: smile, stick out your tongue, open and close your mouth exaggeratedly, and giggle. Your baby may start to imitate you!

2 months
While your baby will still enjoy responding to your expressions, now you can try looking together in a mirror. Change the angle of the mirror, but allow her plenty of time to look at her reflection. She'll like watching you sing songs and move her arms and legs in time with the rhythm.

3 months
Coming into contact with brightly colored materials and different textures will be fun for your baby. Stroke her hands with toys or objects—scarves, teething rings, plush animals—that are hard and soft, warm and cool, furry and smooth. Shake a rattle, holding it close to her face; roll her gently on her tummy on a beach ball and play gentle rolling and rocking games.

4 months
Encourage your baby to reach for objects by holding a brightly colored toy or rattle just in front of her. Sing songs or recite

nursery rhymes and accompany them by gently lifting your baby from a lying to supported standing position (hold her torso securely; do not pull her up by her hands).

5 months
Carry your baby around your home as you go about your daily routine and point out familiar items, letting her touch flowers, cushions, and wood furniture to

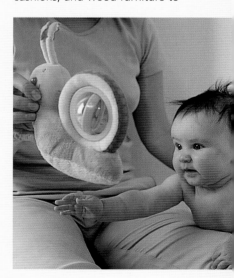

gain a sense of how they feel. She'll enjoy studying faces and objects—and looking at pictures in a book, so this is a good time (if you haven't already started) to begin "reading" board books with large pictures.

6 months

Your baby will enjoy dancing—that is, being held in your arms and moved to a rhythm. She'll also make greater efforts to reach a toy placed out of her grasp.

7 months

Read, sing, and talk to your baby as much as possible. Now is a good time to introduce soft baby blocks and help her build with them while she sits on the floor.

8 months

It will be hard to keep your baby in one place now, but you can try to make it more interesting by stacking different sizes of cushions on the floor and letting her navigate this "obstacle course" in search of soft balls or rattles. She'll also like peekaboo and uncovering hidden items.

9 months

Your baby exhibits great curiosity, and you can stimulate her hearing by playing music and encouraging her to produce noise—even by banging pots and pans. Introduce her to different textures, helping her to "walk" over carpet, hard floors, and upholstered chairs,

and encourage water and sand play. (Never leave a child unattended near water.) Under your supervision, let her smell flowers, citrus fruit, or even a cotton ball (discard afterward) soaked with vanilla extract. Show her brightly colored pictures.

10 months

Your baby will enjoy physical play and will like to climb over you. She'll enjoy experimenting with objects—moving things into and out of each other—so put together a box with socks and a variety of safe objects, such as soft balls and blocks, and let her practice filling and emptying under your supervision.

11 months

Reading together will be more

fun. Your baby will copy the expression on your face, repeat more of the words that she hears, and enjoy linking sounds to pictures. Try to enliven your sessions by making appropriate noises, such as oinking when

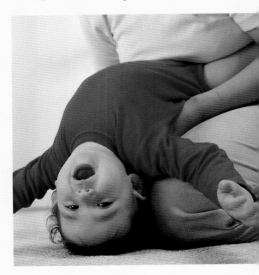

there's a picture of a pig or explaining that water goes "splash." Whatever you do together—giving her a bath, eating, and dressing her—can be turned into a game, and she'll reward you with laughter.

12 months
Your older baby will especially like toys that allow her to do things that you do—toy telephones, dishes, and cutlery, for example. Interacting while she uses them— such as exchanging calls or "eating" together—is fun for both of you and helps build her social and language skills.

13 months
You may find that your toddler starts taking the lead in play, telling you what to do. A favorite game for her might be to throw something and have you fetch it. Messy play will be particularly

enjoyable, and you can introduce your toddler to finger paints.

14 months
Your toddler will love putting small things into and taking bigger things out of empty plastic bowls and other containers. Encourage her to start building with blocks by joining her at her level. Build a tower and then knock it down, or make a bridge for a car to go underneath.

15 months
Your toddler will enjoy chasing games such as hide-and-seek when she can initiate playtime and order you about. It's a good time to engage in activities with commands or actions—"Touch your nose"—that your baby has to follow or to recite rhymes with gestures, such as "The Itsy Bitsy Spider." Finger puppets might make storytelling more fun for

your toddler and develop her eye-hand coordination.

16 months
Help your child learn how the world works by exposing her to different tactile play materials, such as clay, sand, and dirt. Work on simple jigsaw puzzles together, asking her to show you pieces— "Where is the pig?"—before she attempts to place them. This is a good time to begin simple ball games, such as sitting and rolling a ball back and forth.

17 months
Encourage your toddler to collect interesting things when you're out—such as pinecones or leaves—and build on her interest by keeping these treasures in a special place. Use them to talk about past adventures you've shared, and incorporate them into her artwork or a scrapbook.

18 months
Your toddler will be much more accurate at stacking and sorting, at fitting shapes through holes, and at using blocks for building. Making things with clay is fun, and you can ask that she make certain things for you, such as a "cookie."

20 months
Your toddler will be interested in identifying and classifying items: animals, household objects, and vehicles. Using models, blocks, pictures cut from magazines, or puzzle pieces, ask your toddler to sort things into groups—horses,

kitchen equipment, things to ride in, etc.

22 months

Singing and dancing together will be great fun for your toddler. She'll enjoy reading and may want to hear the same story over and over. She'll probably love dressing up, and you can help by playing along. Painting her face and pointing out people's reactions is another activity to enjoy together.

24 months

Your toddler has become much better at working with building blocks and may engage in imaginative play with them, such as building a fort or other enclosure. She'll likely join you in singing songs and repeating nursery rhymes, and particularly will like those with actions, such as "Ring-Around-the-Rosy."

26 months

Your toddler will be interested in pretend play—taking care of her sick teddy bear or putting her baby doll to bed—but may ask you to help, too. Although she won't be interested in playing directly with other children just yet, she may enjoy sharing activities with you at a toddler gym or a swimming class.

28 months

Pretend games can be endlessly developed, from being the mail carrier delivering letters to setting up shop with some pretend food. You can help by constructing a

special place for your toddler to practice imaginative play, such as putting a cloth over a table so that she can "camp out" underneath, or letting her use a large cardboard box as a fire truck or car. When you tell her stories, have her or someone she knows appear as characters in them. Ask her questions about the story.

30 months

Your toddler will be more adept with her hands and will want to help join in housework (which she sees as fun, not a chore). Baking and simple jobs involving water, such as wiping down her high chair or watering plants, will be the most fun for her. You can involve her in simple artwork projects, such as asking her to help decorate cards by coloring or adding glitter or stickers.

32 months

Your toddler will be interested in drawing and in colors, and can now manipulate crayons and paint—making a mess with them will be endlessly attractive. You may be able to interest her in other projects, such as making prints with a potato and poster paints or creating a sticker book.

34 months

Your toddler will enjoy doing simple and easy jobs. She can help with baking—mixing flour, adding raisins, bringing a box from the cupboard, or putting the spoons away. She may enjoy a simple treasure hunt: Show her a picture from a magazine or a

book, for example, and ask her to find something similar. Now is the time to introduce picture books that tell stories. Encourage her to choose which book she wants for a bedtime story.

36 months

Your preschooler is now playing with other children, but anything she does with you will still be the greatest fun. Making music together, dancing, playing catch, helping put away groceries or laundry, baking, and creating art are all opportunities to engage with your child and teach her valuable lessons at the same time. Always keep in mind that children learn best through play.

Reading

Sharing books together is one of the most important activities you and your child can enjoy. Listening to your voice as you read helps your infant gain language skills. He hears and learns not only the sounds and meanings of words but also the way to phrase sentences and the rhythm of speaking. When he's older, after 15–18 months, he can understand what's being read and enjoy the story.

For toddlers and older children, reading holds the key to imagination and is a wonderful educational activity. Making reading an enjoyable part of each day now will ensure that the habit will continue when your child begins to read by himself. There's a strong correlation between being read to (and reading often) and later school success.

Watching TV

Plenty of DVDs and television shows are marketed for very young children, but you may want to tune them out. There may be some modest benefits from these programs, but there are certainly significant disadvantages (see box, right).

The American Academy of Pediatrics recommends that children under the age of 2 watch no TV at all. If you do allow your child to watch some television, experts urge strictly limiting screen time and making sure your child is watching appropriate content. Some suggest limiting TV time for children between the ages of 3 and 7 to no more than 30 minutes a day. If you don't want to adhere to a strict time limit, it might make sense to just put television-watching low on the list of daily activities. If your toddler has already enjoyed outside playtime, imaginative play, reading, and other creative activities, then—and only then—should you consider permitting any screen time.

TELEVISION

Advantages

- Certain educational DVDs and television shows can help early language development and pre-reading skills in children.
- You may sometimes need a brief rest after an exhausting day of running after your baby. Or your baby may just need time to calm down. Watching high-quality, age-appropriate television may provide the break you need. There are many high-quality DVDs for children that your baby will love. However, pay attention to how much TV your child watches and limit how much screen time she's allowed.

Disadvantages

- Watching too much television means there's less time for physical activity, using the imagination, and reading, which are far more important.
- Many of the cartoons and programs on television contain violence and material inappropriate for children. Pay attention to what your child is watching and avoid these.
- Scary scenes seen on television can cause nightmares.
- The more television your child watches, the greater her risk of becoming obese. Children need plenty of opportunities to run around.

Discipline

A newborn is completely unaware of the "right" way to behave. It will take at least 18 years before your child learns to act and think like an adult, but she'll make a great deal of progress in her first 5 years.

Discipline involves teaching your child to follow rules for behavior and in time to want to follow the rules because it makes her feel good, not because of fear of punishment or the need for approval. When you play with your child—sharing things with her and taking turns—you're imparting valuable lessons about interacting with others. She'll emulate much of your social behavior.

Your young child is just learning the rules. Your job is to teach her how to behave well with as little conflict as possible. Whether it's human nature or part of our culture, adults tend to focus on and criticize children's behavior far more often than we think to use praise. Some might argue parents focus on troublesome behavior because children misbehave frequently. But this isn't true. Think about how your child behaves during the day. There may be many moments when she does the right thing and makes the right choice, but these moments often slip by without notice. Positive reinforcement for desirable behavior is far better and more effective than punishment for bad.

Take mealtime, for example. Your baby will throw food on the floor sometimes. You could remind her that "we don't throw food" when she does it, or you could ignore her when she throws food (at times any attention, even negative, reinforces the behavior). Then notice when she doesn't throw her food and tell her how pleased you are with her for eating nicely. Ignoring negative behavior and encouraging positive behavior is highly effective and has the added bonus of nurturing your child's feelings of self-worth. Starting to do this when your child is a baby will help make it a parenting habit.

Going overboard with praise, however, can backfire as your child gets older, because your child may start to think you aren't being honest, may feel pressure to succeed, and may learn to rely on praise for motivation, rather than developing intrinsic motivators—the internal desires to do the right thing because it feels good. An important and valuable technique is to encourage good behavior by commenting positively on your child's efforts—the process—rather than praising the end result. An example would be noticing and commenting on how hard your daughter is working to stack blocks rather than praising her tall tower (the end result).

You and the other adults in your baby's life have the important job of shaping the kind of person she'll become. However, it's important to bear in mind that social and emotional skills, like the many other aspects of her growth and development, are achieved through a programmed, orderly sequence. There's only so much your baby can master at any given age. But the environment in which she's raised strongly influences how she'll act.

A few don'ts to remember:

- *Never lie to your child.* Making up stories to entice her to behave can damage her trust in you.
- *Never hit your child.* Your disapproval is a far more effective tool, and slapping or spanking teaches her that physical domination is a valid way to resolve conflict.
- *Never threaten to leave your child and walk away.* This is extremely distressing to a child, and you almost certainly will have to eat your words if she calls your bluff.

No parent is perfect, and it's likely that you, too, will sometimes make mistakes, say the wrong thing, lose your temper, or handle a situation poorly. Everyone does. Luckily, your baby will forgive your missteps; what matters most is that she feels loved and treasured. Still, you want to try to be the best parent you can, one who approaches discipline as a teaching process.

Why children behave as they do

Adults expect other adults to behave in certain ways

based on social norms and personal experiences. We anticipate that other people will consider our needs and understand the consequences of their actions. We rightly expect that when another adult is told what to do or what not to do, he'll comply.

Children, however, don't behave like adults. It's wrong to apply adult standards of behavior to children. But even the best parent sometimes loses sight of that fact, with unfortunate consequences. Your child will neglect to consider how her actions make you feel not because she's selfish but because she's not yet capable of feeling empathy. If she repeats an unwanted behavior regularly, you may think she's stubborn, purposefully ignoring you, challenging your authority, or misbehaving to upset you. It's far simpler. Your child wants to do what she wants to do, now. Period. Being angry at your young child over an unwanted behavior won't teach her to behave better. In fact, anger-driven responses usually do more harm and leave you feeling guilty and your child confused.

After your child is a year old, she'll start learning what she's allowed to do and how to behave. But even when she knows intellectually what she can't do—run into the street, hit, or bite—it doesn't follow that she can stop herself from doing these deeds. Although what Sigmund Freud called the "superego"—the voice inside each of us that tells us what is wrong or right—is present in toddlers, it's weak and not fully formed. Until your toddler is quite a bit older, there's a basic imbalance between the strong urge to do an undesirable act and the voice of restraint.

When your toddler is upset or excited, for example, she may have a very strong urge to strike out. However, unlike in an adult, the restraining voice telling her not to hit is very faint, and it's no

MORE **ABOUT** | emotional immaturity

Of course parents cherish their children, but they inevitably see characteristics in their children that they don't particularly like. Between the ages of roughly 1 and 3, your child may sometimes be stubborn and entirely self-centered. He only knows what he wants, and he wants it now! Patience—a very handy trait for a parent—is in short supply at this stage of life.

Your child has only a very limited ability to see a situation from your perspective or to consider how his actions make you feel. He has little insight into why he does what he does or why he wants the things he does. Nor does he have much impulse control, so it may seem that he sometimes acts first and thinks about it only afterward. When he has trouble getting you to understand what he wants or when he can't have it, he may have a temper tantrum. Efforts to reason with him are often doomed to fail, because he isn't yet able to look at a problem rationally instead of emotionally.

A true story: A father brought his son, John, to the pediatrician for a checkup. As is typical of young children, John was afraid. He refused to stand on the scale and cried and struggled when the nurse tried to see how tall he was. His father repeatedly told John to do what he was told. John continued not to cooperate.

His father's voice became louder and louder. "Your behavior is atrocious!" yelled his father. To this, John only screamed louder and fought harder. Then his father said, "Stop it! You're acting like a 2-year-old!" This wasn't at all surprising, because John was in fact only 2 years old, and he acted in the only way he was capable of acting. The one who needed to change his behavior was the father, who had to learn that his son was not an adult and couldn't be expected to behave as if he were one.

Anger isn't any use when dealing with a child. It's far more helpful to have patient, realistic expectations and the understanding that your role is to help your child make his way through difficult events.

steps to becoming more patient

1 **Recognize when you've lost patience.** Each time you're unhappy with your own response to your child's actions, take a moment (once you've calmed down) to reflect on the scene in which you just took part. Think about and consider writing in a notebook the answers to these questions: A) What happened? B) What clues were there to alert you that you were about to lose your patience? C) What factors may have shaped your undesirable response? Were you in a hurry to get somewhere? Were you stressed from events in other spheres of your life (perhaps a tough day at work, an argument with your partner, a million things to do, financial stresses, etc.)? Were you not feeling well? Were you tired?

2 **Analyze the event.** Later in the day, perhaps after your child is asleep, revisit your thoughts or review your notes. If you were able to replay the scene, how would you change your actions so that you'd handle it better? The answer may be relatively simple:

- ◆ I was in a rush to get to the birthday party; next time I'll leave myself more time or remind myself that other parents will understand if we're running late.
- ◆ I wasn't in a good mood myself. (I was tired; I was stressed, etc.) If I had recognized this, I might have made allowances for my bad mood. I could have remained silent instead of yelling when he didn't listen to me.
- ◆ He's a very strong-willed child. I'll have to get used to the fact that this is just the way he is. Next time I'll expect him to say "no!" when I ask him to do something.

3 **Notice patterns.** Until we change our behavior, we tend to repeat the same mistakes over and over. As you analyze more examples of your behavior, you'll start recognizing that one of your "bad moments" is like one that occurred before. ("Last week, I lost my temper

when I was in a rush and he wouldn't move quickly. It just happened again.") When you check your notebook that night and review the event, focus especially on what happened early in the scene. Identify clues you can use to warn you that you're about to act poorly. Think of a different approach, one that would have avoided the struggle before it began.

4 **Change the way you respond.** Eventually you'll come to the point when you see you're about to lose patience before it happens. If you can see it coming, you can act differently.

match for the intense desire commanding her to go ahead and hit you. When she's calm, she may be able to verbalize the rule that hitting is wrong. But when she's feeling overwhelming emotions, she can't stop herself, and she won't hear what you have to say. You can tell her over and over again that hitting is wrong, but until she develops a stronger superego, she won't be able to control herself. She'll make noticeable progress by the time she's 2–3 years old, but it will be many more years before she gains adult-like self-control.

It isn't always easy to remember that you're dealing with a child and not an adult. You'll need to be careful to shift gears from your expectations for adults to expectations that are realistic for your child. Try to tailor your expectations for appropriate behavior to your young child's age and level of development.

When your child is 1–2 years old, she probably won't be able to follow many of the rules you'd like her to, and she may not even comprehend instructions. At this age, discipline consists of keeping her safe, setting limits and helping her heed them, and getting through the day with minimal struggles. Separate her from a forbidden object or keep the object out of sight. If she keeps fiddling with the DVD player, move it out of her reach or keep it in a locked cabinet. Distraction often works, too. If your toddler picks up something she shouldn't have, no need to raise your voice—quickly give her a favorite toy and remove the other object. If she's getting into mischief in the kitchen, divert her to a more acceptable activity.

How your child will learn to behave and the ways you'll practice the art of parenting depend on a number of factors.

Your child's temperament

Philosophers have compared the innocence of a child to a blank slate or a pile of moist clay. Supposedly, she can be molded into whatever her parents want her to be. But the concepts of species similarity (that all children are alike) and individual variation (that all children are different) apply here as well. While you will help shape your child, every child starts off with a slightly different temperament

(see page 138). Your baby's temperament determines where the "shaping" process begins. If she's normally shy and clingy, you can encourage her to be more outgoing. However, it's unlikely she'll ever be as gregarious as a child who was more outgoing from birth (assuming this other child is raised in an environment where gregariousness is valued and encouraged).

Your child's innate personality traits also determine how she learns and how best to teach her. For example, if your child is easygoing, it may only take some firmness on your part to quell her protests about brushing her teeth. But if she's determined and stubborn, this approach may be utterly unsuccessful. You'll need to figure out which style of parenting will work best, given your child's unique temperament (see also page 139). Teaching your child is a learning process for you as well as for her; some approaches you try will succeed, and many will fail. When one technique doesn't work, you'll try another, and another, and another until you hit upon something that works for your child.

Parental temperament

Your baby isn't the only one in your family with a unique temperament: You have one, and so does your partner. Are you calm and easygoing, or are you easily upset with your child?

Parents vary tremendously in one aspect of temperament that is central in raising a child: patience. As wonderful as children are, they're guaranteed to try your patience. In her first months of life, your baby may cry for hours, despite your best efforts to calm her; she may spit up all over her new outfit just as you put it on; and invariably she'll soil her diaper just as you have her ready to go out. Later, she may throw her food on the floor, create havoc in your handbag or your CD collection, refuse to go to sleep at night, balk at getting dressed, have a tantrum when you won't buy her candy at the checkout counter, and so on. (Of course, there will be many moments when she's adorable, sweet, well-behaved, and a perfect angel!) No parent is a saint. No one can put up with the constant mischief and rule-challenging that children dish out every

WHEN TO EXPECT BAD BEHAVIOR
- Your child is tired.
- You're tired.
- Your child doesn't feel well.
- You don't feel well.
- You try to rush him.
- You're feeling stressed.
- Your child is hungry.
- Everyone needs you at once.
- Daily routines are disrupted.
- You could use just a few minutes to calm down.
- It's the end of a long day.
- You're in a situation where it's important that he behaves well.
- Lots of people are watching.

day without sometimes getting angry or losing their temper. However, each of us varies in how much we can take before we reach our breaking point.

When you lose your temper, you may say or do things you later wish you hadn't. You may yell at your child. You may call her names or label her unfairly ("You're a troublemaker!"). If you feel as if you might strike your child, put her in a safe place, such as her crib, and leave the room until you've calmed down.

But these kinds of responses aren't effective ways to get your child to behave better. Usually, you just end up feeling bad about your behavior and wishing you hadn't lost control. The more patience you have as a parent, the less often you'll lose your temper and the better parent you'll be.

Your own upbringing

How your parents raised you also has a huge effect on how you parent your child. Interestingly, people usually respond to their children's behavior exactly as their parents did to theirs. It's as if the way we're raised programs us to imitate our parents by default. This can be very helpful: If your parents were patient and loving with you, you'll probably find it easy to be patient and loving with your child.

But if your parents treated you in ways you vowed you would never repeat with your own child—for example, constantly yelling at you—you may be distressed when you find that you're instinctively acting exactly as your parents did many years before. If you're repeating hurtful, ineffective parenting behavior, you'll need to work hard to do otherwise, and you may need additional help from a counselor. Just telling yourself to be more patient or berating yourself after the fact is unlikely to change your temperament. You'll have to work at it long term. The box on page 291 offers helpful advice on learning to be more patient.

Parenting strategies

Chapter 6 discusses different approaches to parenting babies. These same styles apply to raising toddlers. Child-oriented parents believe that the best way to raise their child is to respond immediately to her emotional and physical needs (see page 136). If she's hungry, feed her now; if she's upset, pick her up and calm her. Schedule-based parents, on the other hand, believe that routine is important for their child and try to adhere to set times for activities, such as sleeping. A third, very effective style—flexible parenting—blends the best of these two approaches. Flexible parents appreciate that household routines and guidelines for behavior are good for children, but they also believe that it's important to nurture a loving environment, with occasional exceptions to the rules. They'll take advantage of structured routines while carefully attending to the emotional needs of their child.

Some parents view discipline as a heavily front-loaded process—that it's important to be strict during a child's first years and to deal with bad behavior swiftly before it becomes embedded in a child's behavioral repertoire. They may think that if a child is allowed to get her own way, she'll become "spoiled." This method rarely works in practice. With this approach, children do not develop an intrinsic motivation to behave; they act out of fear of punishment. Parents who subscribe to this approach have unrealistic expectations about

what their child is capable of achieving (see pages 289–290). Strict rules are bound to result in many struggles every day. In this scenario, parenting isn't much fun—and it could be a nightmare.

You're more likely to be successful—and enjoy being a parent—with a flexible approach. This accepts the fact that your child simply isn't capable of acting as an adult in her early years. To work, rules must be appropriate for a child's age and level of development. Rest assured, as she gets older, she'll gradually develop the ability to be less self-centered and to accept rules that infringe on her freedom.

With this approach, your daily goal is to get your toddler to do what has to be done with minimal struggling. Sometimes this requires invoking rules and being firm; other times, it may mean using various strategies to rein in her behavior and teach her limits. As your toddler gets older, her behavior will gradually evolve in step with her psychological development. When she becomes capable of more mature behavior, your expectations will become higher as well. This is a long-term project: You have 18 years to mold her into an adult. You'll get there!

When to be strict

It's very important to choose your battles by deciding ahead of time with your partner on a limited number of age-appropriate nonnegotiable rules, such as always buckling up in the car seat. In daily life, it's smart for parents to ask themselves often whether something, such as a mismatched outfit, really matters before making a big deal out of it. If you hold the line on something that isn't that important, don't be surprised to find it leads to an angry tantrum that has both sides feeling frustrated. If you reprimand her for every tiny infraction, you'll both be miserable—and she'll tune you out.

There are a few situations in which you must have your way. Most important, you need to keep your child safe and not allow her to hurt others. If she's at risk of injuring herself, you must stop her immediately. Similarly, if she's hurting someone else, you need to intervene. It's also unacceptable for her to damage your home or valued possessions.

It's also very important that your child goes to

bed on time and takes naps. Tired children (like tired adults) are cranky and easily upset. If you let your toddler skip a nap or allow her to stay up past bedtime, her behavior is certain to be much worse than usual the next day. It's also necessary to enforce rules that affect her health, such as putting on sun block or brushing her teeth.

You and your partner may agree on a few other rules that will be nonnegotiable. But most of the time, it isn't necessary for the parents to get their way. Keep in mind that you're not spoiling your child by letting her have some control in her life. Making choices and following through, while you're there to support your child, helps build her self-confidence and independence.

Setting limits

Children usually feel most secure and behave best when they know there are limits to their behavior. But where should you set the limits? If you're too strict, you'll face many more struggles. On the other hand, if your boundaries are too lenient, your child will be confused and have no reason to behave well. The ideal solution: Adjust the limits so that it's easy for your child to meet your expectations, and continue to adjust them as she matures. As she grows more capable of following rules, raise your expectations and adjust the limits to accommodate

her new capabilities. When she first learns to walk, she cannot cross a street without holding your hand; some day, of course, she'll need to learn how to cross safely, and you'll need to adjust your rules.

You can begin setting a few reasonable limits when your baby is about 6 months old. Teach her basic limits, focused on her safety, and keep your instructions brief and simple. If she's pulling leaves off a plant, explain gently that the leaves need to stay on the plant. You can guide her finger to gently touch the leaves, if you want, and then move the plant out of reach and redirect her attention. She doesn't understand consequences yet, and scolding her will only confuse and upset her.

Physical barriers can make it easier to enforce some nonnegotiable limits. If your toddler isn't allowed in a kitchen cabinet holding fragile plates, tell her it's off-limits and lock the cabinet door. Keep her off the stairs with safety gates. Move forbidden objects out of view and out of reach.

With experience, you'll figure out which rules your child will follow and which will usually result in a struggle. If your toddler typically brushes her teeth when she's told, it's reasonable to expect her to continue doing it. If she ever balks at brushing, maintain the limit by being firm and insisting that she do it. It's also fine to help motivate her, for example, by making up a teeth-brushing game.

How to get positive results

Use distraction. Most toddlers readily shift their attention from one object to another, more interesting one. If your toddler has hold of something he shouldn't have, prevent a struggle by quickly giving him something else he can safely enjoy. Put the forbidden item away and out of sight. Another option is to physically move your child someplace where there is less temptation.

Try the countdown. This technique is especially helpful if your child has difficulty making the transition from one activity to the other. He may get upset, for example, if he suddenly has to leave the playground, get out of the tub, or go to bed.

Start the process of leaving the playground long before you actually want to leave by giving him several warnings beforehand. As it gets close to the time to leave, help him gather up his sand toys or ask him if he wants to go down the slide one last time. It may help to remind him what's coming next: As you gather toys, tell him what you'll have for lunch once you get home.

You also could try asking him, "Do you want to go home now or do you want to stay another minute?" He'll probably choose the latter, but after you repeat this process a few more times he might be willing to leave without a fight. Your child will feel that

he got what he wanted (to stay longer), and if the process is started early enough, you'll get to leave on time!

With older toddlers, you can try the countdown technique with numbers. Start by announcing, "It will be bedtime in 5 minutes," and hold up five fingers. A few minutes later (your child's sense of time is not as well-tuned as yours), tell him that bedtime will be in 4 minutes. Then 3, 2, and 1 minute. By the end of the countdown, he'll have had several minutes to get used to the impending change.

Make it a game. Try to get your child to do what he should by making it seem fun. For example, to interest him in tidying up, say, "Let's see who can put away the most toys. Ready, set, go!" Or have a race from the living room to the bathroom to see who will arrive first for toothbrushing.

Give choices. Let your child feel he's in control of what happens to him by allowing him to choose among alternatives that are acceptable to you. "Which shirt would you like to wear today—the red one, the blue one, or the one with the panda?" Your child wins by getting to pick for himself, and you win by avoiding a potential struggle. Other variations: "Which do you want to do first: Brush your teeth or get into your pajamas?" "Do you want to get out of the bath now or in another minute?"

Become the tickle monster. This

is a fun alternative to the threat of a logical consequence ("If you don't start getting dressed now, it will be too late go to Tim's house to play"). Tell your child that he must start getting dressed by the count of three or the tickle monster will appear. You, of course, are the monster!

Your child may run to his room and start getting dressed to avoid being tickled. Or he may linger and let you tickle him—keep it gentle and short. (When the tickling is over, he'll probably be much more inclined to go along with your request.) Even if you "have to" tickle him, you win because you avoid raising your voice or punishing. You turn what could be an unpleasant situation into fun for both of you.

Plan ahead. Thinking things through beforehand can go a long way toward preventing struggles. If you make allowances for predictable problem behavior, you can avoid many battles. Here are two examples:

- Every time you are at the grocery store's checkout counter, your toddler wants a candy bar. If you say no, he has a tantrum. Solutions: A) Don't take him shopping with you. B) Decide it's okay to let him have the candy bar if it prevents a miserable scene. You could even share the candy bar, turning a potential conflict into a moment of togetherness.
- It's impossible to get your child dressed in the morning, and you're often late for work. Possible solutions: 1) Get up earlier so that you have more time. 2) Help your child pick out his clothes the night before. 3) Have your partner help you. 4) Change your work hours so you start a little later. 5) Let him wear his PJs to school or day care.

Avoid rushing. Do everything you can to build in extra time for each step of the way, just in case your child decides to resist at some point. If you need to head home immediately, you're more likely to find that your toddler refuses to let you put on his coat or that he's misplaced his shoes—

children have an innate talent for slowing down when their parents are in a hurry! If you steamroll ahead, you'll probably wind up with a tantrum. You might not always have the luxury of time to accommodate your child's refusals, but if you can build this into your schedule, you'll enjoy your time together more.

Think outside the box. Is there a less obvious solution to try? For example, if your toddler is slow to get dressed in the morning, you could let him wear his clothes at night instead of his pajamas. When he wakes in the morning, he'll already be dressed for the day! If your toddler refuses to put on his hat before going out in cold weather, let him go out without his hat but be sure to bring it along. In a few minutes, when his ears are red, you can offer his hat—and he'll probably be grateful to have it.

Be firm. Sometimes simply not giving in and telling your child to do as he's told will achieve the behavior you desire. If this results in tantrums or screaming, try to avoid that particular situation next time or try another technique.

Give in. Sometimes acquiescing is a good choice, but only give in if it won't cause any harm. Never give in while your child is in the middle of a tantrum, for example. (See box, page 298.)

GIVE IN

Letting your child have his way is an option when:

- There's very little consequence if he prevails.
- The consequences for not giving in (a tantrum) are much greater than those for giving in.
- Distraction or other techniques to avoid a struggle don't work.

Only give in at the beginning of a potential struggle, never during the heat of it.

DON'T GIVE IN

Preventing your child from having his way is important when:

- It's a matter of safety, hurting others, ruining valuable possessions, or staying healthy.
- A little firmness is very likely to work.
- Distraction or other techniques to avoid a struggle will work.
- He's already begun to have a tantrum.

If you're likely to succeed, firmness can be a useful tool. This may be all you need to do to have your easygoing child behave well. But if you're unlikely to get anywhere by staying firm, perhaps your limit is too strict. Remember, set and enforce limits when it it's important that you win the battle: when it involves safety, destroying property, getting rest, or being healthy. You want to help your child do well, not set her up for failure.

When to give in

It might be nice if children always listened to and respected adults, but that isn't very realistic. Sometimes it makes sense to give in to your child's wishes, particularly when low expectations are necessary because of your child's age. Other ways to avoid battles over behavior include steering clear of these situations and the parental art of distraction (see page 296).

It's important not to concede to your child if she's throwing a tantrum: If you give in then, your toddler will learn that yelling, kicking, and falling to the floor gets her what she wants. You'd actually be reinforcing the very behavior you want to stop! But if you give in at the first sign of her resistance, before the scene turns into conflict, your child won't feel rewarded for her misbehavior because she hasn't misbehaved yet.

Giving in is an option only when there's no serious consequences to doing so. For example, your child wants to hold your keys, but you're afraid she'll lose them. You've already tried to distract her, but she's focused on holding the keys. You're pretty sure that if you don't find a solution quickly, she'll work herself up into a fit. In this case, it's a reasonable option to give in. If you watch her carefully, she's unlikely to lose your keys or damage them. In fact, she'll probably lose interest in them quickly, and then you can retrieve them. You could even have her "help" you by pressing buttons on the keys to lock or unlock the car, or you could insert the key in the lock on your door and let her try to turn it. You give up very little by letting her have her way, and you can enjoy a happy moment rather than fighting.

Vary your approach

It's surprising how often parents stick with a method that isn't working. If you try one approach (see pages 296–297) and it doesn't give you the results you want, try handling the situation a different way next time. No technique is always successful, but one thing is certain: Repeatedly using a failing technique will continue to be unsuccessful.

Whatever approach you try, it's very important to be consistent. Children may sometimes act like limits and rules are horribly unfair, but in reality they want and need limits. They're most comfortable and secure when they know there are boundaries to their behavior, and they do best when they feel that a specific action on their part will lead to a known response from you. A child would find it terribly confusing if her mother praised her one day for helping to set the table, but the next day screamed at her when she tried to do it again.

Parents often disagree on how best to teach their child. This is normal, but it's important for parents to resolve their differences privately when they don't agree on what should or shouldn't be allowed or on how to handle misbehavior. Parents need to talk through disagreements and come up with a mutually acceptable compromise. It's important to support your partner's actions and decisions involving your child, even if you would have acted in another way. Toddlers are very good at detecting—and exploiting—differences in what each parent will permit. If you tell your child she can't go to the park, she may go straight to her other parent and ask again, hoping for a more favorable response, or she may learn that she's more likely to get what she wants by asking one parent instead of the other. With experience, you'll find it easier to be consistent and maintain a united front.

Tantrums

All kids have tantrums, which help release strong feelings of anger, resentment, and frustration—although the intensity of the tantrum often has nothing to do with the enormity of what is denied. (There is, however, a correlation between the severity of a tantrum and lack of sleep: Tired children have tantrums more often, and their tantrums are much more intense and harder to stop.)

When your child doesn't get her way, she may suddenly start screaming. Some children lie on the floor and beat their fists and feet against the ground. Others bang their heads repeatedly against a wall, throw things, or hit or bite.

The best strategy is to prevent a tantrum from starting. As you learn what sets your child off, you'll get better at avoiding and defusing trigger situations. Sometimes acknowledging her feelings helps: "You're angry because you can't have that toy." You can try distracting her. As your child gets older and develops her sense of humor and imagination, another technique is to fantasize and exaggerate her desire. If your child wants a pool, for example, you can agree and describe together its size, waterfall, slides; the more over-the-top, the better.

But once a tantrum starts, it's too late to give in or try to appease her. At this point the best approach is to ignore her. She'll be too upset to hear anything you have to say anyway. Paying attention—good or bad—will reinforce the behavior. If you're at home, walk away, avoid looking at her, and go on about your business, preferably in another room. If you're worried she might hurt herself, take her to a safer place, but try not to look at or react to her.

If she has a tantrum in a public place and isn't able to calm down quickly, coolly pick her up and leave. Giving her a few minutes to settle down outside or in the car might be enough to allow you to return to what you were doing, but you might need to give up and go home. You might worry that onlookers will think you're a terrible or mean parent. Keep in mind that many of them probably have had similar experiences with their own children. Instead of judging you, they're probably thinking, "I feel so sorry for her. I remember how embarrassed I felt when my son did that."

Discipline

As your child learns to understand actions and consequences, try your best to avoid struggles and to help your child get through difficult moments. Your job is teach your child how to behave and why.

Do your best to minimize raising your voice and using the word "no." The more you bark "No!" the less effective it will be. Reserve these tools for times when it's important that she listen immediately: if she's running into the street, hurting someone, or doing something dangerous. If you do yell and startle her, be sure to swiftly and calmly comfort her and remind her of the rules.

When your child is over the age of 2, she can start to understand consequences. If she is running and shouting in the library, you can tell her she needs to be quiet and walk or else you'll need to leave. If she calms down and behaves, thank her; if she doesn't, follow through and leave.

Positive discipline vs. punishment

It's important to understand the distinction between discipline and punishment. Discipline teaches your child to follow rules and develop self-control. It also teaches that there are logical or natural consequences for behavior. Punishment intentionally inflicts suffering on a child. It builds resentment rather than reinforcing a value or teaching your child limits.

Say you're at the park with your toddler. He wants another child's toy and grabs it. You tell him he cannot take the toy, but he doesn't relent. You can discipline him by calmly telling him to let go of the toy, explaining that he can't use it unless the other boy wants to share. If he continues to resist, you can pick him up and take him to another area to help him calm down. The result: You've reinforced that it isn't acceptable to take something that belongs to another. He's heard the lesson, and you can both move past it and continue to enjoy the park.

Alternatively, you could punish him: You can scold him and tell him that because he isn't playing nicely he's going home—and he can't go to the park tomorrow either. The result: Your child is wailing, you're angry, and the next day your toddler will be confused and angry when you say he can't go to the park. You'll be dealing with a miserable child, with nothing gained for it.

Remember that when children get emotional, they don't listen well. Keep your interaction simple, direct, and brief. Acknowledge your child's feelings: "You're upset you can't play with his toy. That's very frustrating, but it isn't okay to take it." Help him find the words for what he's feeling. Then tell him what he can do: "If the boy doesn't want to share, we can play with a different toy or maybe go on the slide. What would you like to do?"

Consequences When your child is over 2, he's ready to start learning that there are natural and logical consequences in response to his behavior. Logical consequences should be immediate and directly linked to his behavior. Threatening to take away television time won't work. But telling him he needs to pick up his toys before he can watch TV teaches him to finish one activity before starting another. There are also natural consequences. For example, if your child refuses to wear boots in the rain, his feet will get wet. Be consistent: If you don't follow through, he won't learn. And don't apologize. Avoid escalating the situation. It's easy to get carried away: You may start off warning that he won't go to the park if he doesn't stop throwing toys, and before you know it you've taken away park visits for a week. Keep consequences reasonable and appropriate.

Help him be good Childproof your home not only to keep your child safe, but also to make it a child-friendly place to explore. If you're constantly scolding your child for getting into mischief at home, step back and take another look at his environment. Remove anything you don't want him playing with, and lock up or block anything you can't pack away.

Time-outs Time-outs are often misused as punishments. A time-out should be an opportunity to help your child learn to calm down. During a quiet moment explain that when he gets out of control, quiet time will help him feel better. Let him choose a comforting place to go: perhaps a reading corner or his bed with his favorite blanket. Sometimes you could use a time-out, too—it will help him to see you model the same techniques. Time-outs are especially useful when repeated requests for good behavior are ignored, when your toddler loses control of his emotions, and when you need to end inappropriate behavior quickly.

Time-outs should be used sparingly; like all disciplinary techniques, using them too often lessens their impact. Also, time-outs are not meant to last a long time. A good way to determine that the time-out is over is to end it when it has served its purpose: "You can come out of time-out when you're calm."

Encouraging independence and sociability

All parents want to educate their child and enable him to become a functioning adult, capable of living independently and able to interact comfortably with other people. It's a long journey from the needy newborn who's totally reliant on you for his care and nourishment, or from the self-centered, strong-willed toddler who constantly tests the rules of behavior. You both need to make tremendous efforts to reach achievements such as your baby feeling secure when he's out of your sight, learning to take turns, and playing by the rules. It's quite amazing that your baby will come to understand that he isn't the center of the universe; that he's a member of a social network and that to be accepted, he must behave according to its norms and values; and that sometimes he has to put another person's needs

above his own. This startling transformation occurs gradually and predictably as your child matures through successive stages of social and emotional development.

Independence

Beginning at about 10–12 months of age, your baby will begin trying to take more control over his life. It may start with him wanting to hold his own cup or bottle, or to feed himself. When he accomplishes one of these tasks for this first time without your assistance, he'll be very proud. Of course it's faster, easier, and less messy if you pour the juice, put your child's socks on, or insert the key in the lock than to let a 1- or 2-year-old do it, but you should give him the chance to try these things,

3 tips to make it easier to leave

1 **Don't sneak out.** This will make your baby anxious that you'll sneak out again, and he'll worry even more about this possibility whenever he can't see you. Tell him you're leaving before you disappear.

2 **Have a quick departure routine.** Come up with a brief, special good-bye routine, such as three kisses—one for each cheek and one to put in his pocket for later—and say, "See you later, alligator" on your way out. Do the same routine every time you leave. Then leave. Don't linger in hopes of calming him down. You'll more likely prolong the tears.

3 **Remember that the crying typically stops a few minutes after you leave** and resumes when you return. Crying when you return does not mean your child is unhappy to see you—on the contrary, a well-adjusted, loved child recognizes that mom's arms are a safe place to let go of pent-up feelings.

within reason. His own sense of accomplishment, coupled with words of encouragement from you, help instill confidence and reinforce a positive self-image. Praise the process, especially if he does not succeed. ("I'm proud of you—you tried so hard! And keys are so difficult to get into the lock.")

Paradoxically, at the same time that your 1- to 3-year-old seeks more independence, he may be more inclined to cling to you. Being on his own and away from you more—asserting his independence—is wonderful until suddenly it becomes scary; then he needs to be close to you. It's good, when reasonably possible, to accommodate him. Encourage his independence, but be prepared to give reassurance when your child needs to be close to you.

Coping with a clingy baby

It can feel flattering if your baby gets upset when he isn't near you. You're the most important person in his life: He wants only you to hold him or to change his diaper. But this can be tiring and sometimes downright frustrating. Should you stay close to him at all times? Should you make a point of leaving him in someone else's care so he's less focused on you? The answer is simple: If you can conveniently respect his wishes, do so; if you can't, then don't.

Respecting his wishes

If picking your baby up or being the one who always gives him a bath is easier than the alternative—letting him scream—then feel free to do it. You aren't spoiling him. It would only be spoiling if he had a greater capacity to be independent and you continued to cater to him. Unfortunately, always accommodating him can be exhausting.

When you can't accommodate him

There will be times when your arms ache from holding your baby or when you must leave your home without him. After all, you're entitled to take a shower, go to work, or have a few minutes to yourself. And you can't cook meals safely with a baby in one arm. In these situations, it's okay to put him down in a safe place (in his crib or a play yard, or in the care of someone else). He'll probably cry and get upset for a few minutes, but no harm will come to him. As with most tantrums, the better you are at ignoring him, the sooner the crying will end.

Comfort items

From a toddler's point of view, life can be very difficult. A toddler feels he's constantly being told what to do and what not to do. In the span of a few hours, he can be frustrated that he can't get his way, angry at you for not meeting his needs immediately, confused about the conflict between your rules and his urges, guilty when you show disapproval, and anxious about separation when you're momentarily out of his sight. No wonder your child will need a way to calm himself and engender a feeling of safety. He may find relief through attachment to a teddy bear, a blanket, or some other object.

Your child also may be comforted when he twirls his hair, sucks his thumb, or wears the same shirt every day. These are ways he can help himself feel better and generally shouldn't be discouraged.

You also comfort your child by hugging him, smiling at him, and talking to him. Feeling loved by you is the greatest comfort he has. Share your approval and affection liberally.

PARENTING**TIP**	comfort items

Once your baby clearly chooses an object for comfort, such as a blanket, buy a few identical ones just in case your baby's cherished item is lost or ruined. (If there's no replacement, he'll be extremely upset.) Rotate the objects so they all wear out equally—if he loses a worn, faded stuffed puppy, a bright new version won't satisfy him. Alternatively, you could encourage your child to accept a commonplace item as a comfort item, such as a spare cloth diaper or flannel receiving blanket—you'll always have plenty of extras!

other, each playing by himself—called parallel play. True sharing, albeit sometimes begrudging, typically happens after 2½ years. Social skills continue to improve during the later toddler years. Your child will be able to take turns and abide by the rules of a game before he gets to kindergarten. However, he may still get upset when he doesn't win the game.

Convincing your toddler to accept these social demands takes a lot of work. Sometimes the easiest way to deal with children who aren't playing well together is to take your child home. Putting away a toy that isn't being shared might also take care of the problem. But there will be times when it makes sense to cajole and encourage your toddler to share and follow the rules of games. Sometimes you'll need to be firm. It's a learning process. Your pleasure when he behaves in the desired way will encourage him to behave the same way the next time.

How difficult is it to teach a child to take on these social skills? It takes years to refine these abilities—and there are plenty of grown-ups who still don't like to share and who get upset when they don't win!

Soothing fears

At about 2–3 years old, your toddler may suddenly become afraid of dogs, clowns, or the dark. He also could begin suffering more from nightmares.

It's good to acknowledge the reality of your toddler's fear ("I know you're afraid. That can be very scary.") and let him hear you say that you'll protect him from harm. Trying to use logic won't ease your toddler's fears. He won't be able to think about them rationally until he's much older. Such fears go away with time. For the time being, avoid putting your child in situations that he might find frightening (stay away from dogs, don't go to the circus, use a night-light) and comfort him when he is upset.

Sociability

Learning to share and to play well with other children is a seminal achievement. Before the age of 30–36 months, however, your child probably thinks of sharing only as being able to play with someone else's toy (but not sharing his own), and playing together is really two children sitting next to each

Being with others

You may send your toddler to day care or preschool because you need child care while you work, or you may simply want to provide your child with the chance to interact with other kids and have fun. Although a preschool offers many opportunities for your child to learn both socially and academically, the main goal should be to have fun with friends in a safe environment. Academic lessons should be secondary to learning social skills for a toddler.

If your child doesn't attend day care or preschool, he won't necessarily be at a disadvantage. Any skills he might learn outside the home can be accomplished at home with a stay-at-home parent or a good sitter. Instead of playing with other children at school, your child can go to the park or play with neighbors, so he'll still have a chance to learn how to interact with other children his own age. And if your child hasn't mastered all of the simple academic skills taught in preschool, he will likely catch up quickly when he starts kindergarten.

Separation difficulties

The greatest issue facing you and your child when starting day care or preschool is the difficulty of separation. While 2- and 3-year-olds sometimes don't cope well with being apart from Mom (or Dad), some parents also find it very hard to be away from their children. If you're feeling emotional about the separation, do your best to put on a happy face and pretend to be calm. If your child senses that you're upset, he'll grow even more anxious.

Your child's temperament plays an important role. When he's away from his primary caregiver, his anxiety could range from mild to severe. If your child has already had a lot of experience being away from you, he probably won't have much difficulty with separation at preschool. But you don't need to "practice" being separated from each other before starting preschool. There will be time to work through his fears at the start of preschool, and his teachers will be very well practiced in comforting anxious children.

Many preschools have some type of process to help children to get accustomed to being there without their parents. For the first few days or weeks, you might be asked to stay at the edge of the room. After a few days, you might sit outside the room. If your child gets distressed and the teachers can't calm him, you might be asked to leave. If good-byes continue to be tearful after many days of school, be firm and leave quickly when the teacher asks you to (see box page 301). If you're worried that your child is having a very difficult time, ask the staff how he's coping. More often than not, when children make a tremendous fuss when their parents leave, they're happily settled down and playing within a few minutes. In some cases, your child might have an easier time if someone other than a parent drops him off at school.

CHILD CARE

If both parents work, finding high-quality, reliable child care arrangements is key. Your options largely depend on what is available in your area. Research the pros, cons, and costs of different providers and listen to your gut in making the final selection. Start early. Some popular places have waiting lists.

DAY CARE OR PRESCHOOL
Advantages
- The staffing is usually reliable, there are regular hours, and it should be licensed.
- Your child will have lots of playmates and will be exposed to many activities.

Disadvantages
- Your child will be at risk of catching more colds and infections at a younger age.

NANNY OR SITTER
Advantages
- Your child will get one-on-one care; you can determine what you want to happen during the day.
- The helper could perform other useful tasks: errands, cooking, etc.
- You can tailor your helper's working hours to meet your needs.

Disadvantages
- If your helper becomes ill, you're stuck scrambling to make other plans.
- The cost varies and should be considered when deciding.
- A nanny might not share your standards for safety and your approach to child-rearing.
- Young sitters may not be very experienced.

KEEPING YOUR BABY HEALTHY

Parental priorities

Protecting the health and well-being of your baby means creating a safe environment for her; taking her for checkups to monitor her progress, growth, and development; ensuring she's immunized against preventable diseases; ensuring she has good dental care; and recognizing when she's ill or hurt and providing the appropriate care—all in addition to giving plenty of love and attention so that she thrives emotionally, too.

Providing a safe environment

A few easy changes will make your home and yard safe for your child and visiting playmates to explore. Look at your home through your baby's eyes, even getting down on the floor to see it from her eye level: It will help you spot potential problems.

In addition to childproofing your home, you'll need to make your child aware of dangers in and around your home, teaching her about water, electricity, and medicines and other hazardous substances. Your baby will learn about safety from your example. When the opportunity arises, show your baby how you draw away from something hot and say, "Ouch, hot!" or something sharp and say, "Ouch, sharp!" Explain the reason for the danger first and then interest your child in something else. It's important for your baby to see you do the right thing: For example, always look both ways before crossing the street, always wear your seat belt in the car, and always put on your helmet when riding your bike.

It's a balancing act: Ideally, you'll protect your baby from hazards in your home while giving her room and freedom to learn by exploring and trying new things. Although she needs to be watched at all times, give her some space for her own adventures.

By following your example, listening to your simple explanations, and having her own experiences, over time she'll learn how to avoid dangers (see box, right). Bear in mind that it's important to be specific. Warning a young child to simply "be careful" without explaining why won't help her learn to avoid hazards.

Keeping your child healthy

Your child's doctors will help you monitor her health and support you if any problems arise. Weight and growth records, as well as the timing of developmental achievements, give an indication of your baby's well-being.

POTENTIAL DANGERS

- **Roads and traffic** Narrate what's happening as you cross the road, even when your baby is in her stroller. Explain about the walk signals and the traffic light. When she's old enough, ask her to tell you when the walk signal appears and you can cross. Have her join you in looking both ways to check that the road is clear and holds hands as you cross.
- **Strangers** Many outgoing toddlers are happy to talk to anyone. At this age, your baby should be with you constantly when you're out, but it's still worth encouraging her to be cautious of strangers. Teach her to check with you before talking to someone. But don't make her afraid of everyone; strive for a balanced approach.
- **Foods and medicines** Your baby needs to learn that she must consume only food and drink given to her by an adult she knows. Also explain when you give her medicine that it isn't candy and that she should take medicine only from you.

To minimize the risk of future health problems, nurture your child's health as best you can. One example of this is good dental care. By making sure your child's teeth are brushed regularly, you'll not only reduce the risk of cavities in the short term, but you'll also hopefully make it more likely that she'll take good care of her teeth when she's older.

To help your child maintain a healthy weight, encourage her to develop healthy eating habits and get plenty of exercise. Eating and exercise patterns set in childhood are very likely to continue in adulthood.

Childhood vaccinations also are important. The recommended immunization schedule (see page 337) prevents illnesses that may be serious and even life-threatening.

Helping a sick child

Despite your best efforts to keep your child safe and protect her from germs, she'll sometimes be unwell. A wide range of conditions can affect children, from ear infections to head lice. Some specifically affect children, but your child is also especially vulnerable to illnesses that affect all ages. Familiarity with common illnesses will help you figure out what's wrong when your child isn't well, how the illness may affect your child, and how you can treat it.

As a parent, you need to know how to care for your child when something's wrong and recognize when you should seek medical advice. It isn't always easy to tell how sick a child is—particularly a baby, whose symptoms may be less specific and harder to pinpoint than those of older children and adults. Knowing what to look for and understanding your baby's personality and habits will help you decide when she needs medical help.

When your child is ill, you'll need to do what you can to control her symptoms and keep her comfortable. Cuddles and reassurance always help, but you'll also need to make sure she gets necessary fluids and possibly medicine to treat infection or ease discomfort.

You'll need to know how to deal with simple cuts and scrapes, bites, and other common injuries, and you should familiarize yourself with basic first aid measures in case something more serious happens (see also pages 42–43 and 188). You might want to take a first aid course to learn resuscitation techniques for babies and children. Hopefully, you'll never need to put these into action, but you'll feel more confident if you feel prepared.

Safety

Babies are naturally inquisitive. Once they're on the move, they want to explore everything both inside and outside the home. It's impossible to make every situation completely safe for your child, but you can take some simple measures to keep his environment as safe as possible.

Childproofing isn't a one-time project. As your baby grows, you'll need to continuously assess his new skills and interests and make changes to keep him safe. For example, when your child is between 6 and 9 months old, he'll learn to crawl and will soon be able to pull himself up. This opens up a whole new world to him, and you'll have to move objects higher up to ensure they stay out of reach. You'll also need to lower his crib mattress to make sure he doesn't climb out.

On the other hand, some hazards become less of a concern as your child grows. Babies tend to put everything into their mouths: They want to

experience objects fully and learn about them. You'll need to watch carefully for small objects that could be a choking hazard (rule of thumb: an item is a choking hazard if it fits through a toilet-paper tube). But once your child is about 3 or so, this shouldn't be as much of a problem.

Remember that children are individuals in terms of both their personalities and their development. Some children are never interested in putting small objects in their mouths—or in pushing them up their noses or into their ears, for that matter—but others continue to put things in their mouths way past the age of 3. Some children test the boundaries more than others and are more adventurous explorers. Developmental milestones occur at varying ages, and children can suddenly acquire a new skill with little advance warning. To be safe, it's a good idea to try to stay a step ahead of your child's

abilities. Once he can crawl, adjust his environment so that it's safe for a walker.

Constant supervision

It's important to watch over your child at all times. No matter how carefully you maintain your home and try to keep it safe, it will never be completely free of hazards. Keeping your child under constant supervision is the single most important thing you can do to make sure he stays out of danger.

It's also a good idea to familiarize yourself with first aid measures (see pages 42–43 and 188) just in case an accident happens.

Cleanliness

A practical approach to cleanliness will help keep your child safe and healthy. There's no need to be overanxious, but you should take reasonable measures to protect your child from food poisoning, harmful chemicals, and infections. It's impossible to prevent children from getting any infections—and that isn't desirable, anyway, because children build up their immunity when they encounter bacteria and viruses.

Food safety and hygiene

To minimize the risk of food poisoning, you should take some general measures to safeguard the way you store and prepare food, as well as the way you keep your kitchen clean (see also page 231).

Food storage

Foods such as rice and pasta should be kept in sealed containers. Meat and ready-to-eat foods should be stored in the fridge to help prevent bacteria from breeding in them. Wrap raw meat tightly in plastic wrap or place in a covered container and store on the bottom shelf of the refrigerator to ensure that juices from the meat don't drip onto other foods stored below. Keep raw meat separate from other foods during preparation.

Don't keep food out at room temperature for very long. If you cook a dish to serve later, let it cool down until steam has stopped rising from it and then put it straight into the fridge. To cool food as quickly as possible, put it into a shallow dish or cut it into smaller portions.

Leftovers usually keep for up to 3 days in the

If you use a microwave to heat food for your child, be wary of hot spots from uneven heating and remember that food continues to cook even after the microwave stops. Heat food thoroughly and then stir it and let it cool before dabbing a bit on your wrist or sampling it with a spoon to make sure it isn't too hot.

refrigerator. If you open a can of food but don't finish it, refrigerate leftovers in a sealed container or a covered dish (not the can). If you're going to freeze food, do so by the use-by date on the package and ideally on the day you buy it. Prepared meals you plan to serve later should be frozen in portions within 24 hours of preparation. Thaw frozen food in the refrigerator for 24 hours or in the microwave immediately before cooking or serving it.

When you cook defrosted food, make sure it's piping hot all the way through. Don't refreeze already thawed food. Bacteria that cause food poisoning can grow in number while frozen food is thawing and won't die if the food is frozen a second time, so the refrozen food is more likely to have higher levels of potentially dangerous bacteria.

Food preparation

Wash your hands thoroughly before preparing or serving food. It's a good idea to have one cutting board only for raw fish, meat, and poultry and a separate one for cooked foods and vegetables. Thoroughly clean work surfaces and cutting boards. Never use a washcloth that's been used for wiping surfaces to clean your child.

Thoroughly wash utensils and cutting boards as well as your hands after handling chicken and other raw meats, raw fish, and eggs. It's important to dry your hands carefully because many bacteria breed more rapidly in wet or damp environments.

Wipe the tops of jars and cans before opening them. Regularly wash your can opener in the dishwasher or by hand.

Store uncontaminated baby food (food that hasn't already come in contact with your baby's spoon, for example) in the refrigerator for up to 48 hours. Reheat food thoroughly so that it's piping hot through the center—heat kills bacteria—and then let it cool down before serving. To check that the temperature is right for your baby, dab a little bit on the inside of your wrist. If you've reheated food, throw away any leftovers; food shouldn't be reheated more than once.

If you cut yourself while preparing food, be sure to clean the wound and cover it with a bandage. Not only do you not want to bleed on the food, but bacteria can multiply in cuts.

Keep the kitchen clean

Wipe down kitchen surfaces before and after preparing food. Disinfect counters and the sink regularly. Wash cleaning cloths and towels regularly. Alternatively, you can use paper towels.

Healthy habits

You don't need to scrub your home so it's sparkling from top to bottom to keep it safe for your child. A modest, regular housekeeping routine will be fine. Children play happily on the floor at home, and this includes picking up whatever they find on the floor and putting it straight into their mouths. This isn't a problem if the floor is kept reasonably clean.

Wash your hands after changing your baby's diaper; once he's out of diapers, teach him to wash his hands after using the toilet. Be sure to teach your children how to wipe properly—and show girls especially how to wipe from front to back to prevent planting bacteria from the anus near the urinary tract. These normal habits of cleanliness will go a long way toward preventing infection.

Childproofing your home

Accidents at home are very common, especially for children under the age of 4. Young children develop the ability to move around easily long before they understand how to avoid potential dangers. It's your job to both protect your baby from as many hazards as possible and teach her how to keep herself safe when she's older.

The first step to childproofing is simply being observant. Look around each room from your baby's viewpoint for potential dangers. Think about what your baby might be able to reach—not only from the floor, but also from furniture once she's able to pull herself up and climb.

Hiring a childproofing professional to equip your home is not necessary but will be comprehensive and can save you time. If this is an option, weigh the convenience vs. the cost.

General measures
Some safety measures apply to all areas of the home.

Doors
Closing doors can easily trap fingers. Put protectors on doors so they can't slam shut, or set up stoppers so doors remain open.

Stairs
Always keep stairs free of anything that may cause someone to trip.

Install gates at the top and bottom of the stairs. If you position the lower gate three steps from the bottom, your toddler will be able to practice climbing stairs without the risk of a nasty fall.

When buying safety gates, make sure they're fairly easy for you to open and close. If they're difficult to use, you'll be tempted to leave them open when you just need to make a quick trip. Safety gates should meet the ASTM International voluntary safety standards, and the manufacturer should participate in the Juvenile Products Manufacturers Association (JPMA) certification program.

If stair or banister railings are more than 4 inches apart, put up a safety net.

Windows
Install guards to prevent children from climbing out of windows. Locks can keep windows from opening any more than 4 inches. Don't use pressure-mounted window guards, which can break free.

It's also important to keep children away from open windows. Keep furniture away from windows so children can't use the furniture to climb out.

Cords for blinds and drapes are a strangulation risk. Use cord stops or tie them out of reach.

You also can affix stickers to large panes of glass to draw attention to them and reduce the risk of accidents.

Furniture and décor
Make sure your furniture is stable. Look out for furniture your child could pull over on herself if she uses it to pull herself up or tries to climb on it. Use safety latches to keep your child from pulling drawers open. Keep computers and other electronic devices high enough to be inaccessible to a standing

---

PLAY YARDS

Having a play yard for your child is useful when you need a few minutes for yourself, for example, to take a shower. Play yards are more attractive and child-friendly than they were years ago, and some can be used as portable cribs. They're especially helpful when babies start to crawl, and some toddlers happily enjoy a play yard up to the age of 2. If you use a play yard, be sure to provide some toys for your child to amuse himself with, and don't leave him in there for a long time.

5 essentials to keep your baby safe

1 Keep your baby under constant supervision. An accident can happen in a second: Never leave your baby unattended, no matter where she is. Even seemingly benign things can lead to a dangerous situation. You might want to use a play yard for times when you need to leave her for a few minutes, such as to take a shower. Don't leave your baby alone in a car: Cars can heat up inside very quickly even on mild days, and the risk of heatstroke is extremely high. And never leave her with pets or other small children—both are unpredictable.

2 Never let yourself be distracted. It's very easy to lose your concentration mid-task and leave dangerous objects such as scissors within your baby's reach. Even when you're busy or under pressure, keep your baby's safety in mind and take the time to put away potentially dangerous items and lock stair gates securely.

3 Keep forbidden items out of reach. Dangerous objects—such as knives, scissors, and medicines—must be kept well away from little hands. Putting ornamental objects and other treasures out of reach will cut down the number of times you'll need to say "don't" in a day—and lower your stress level.

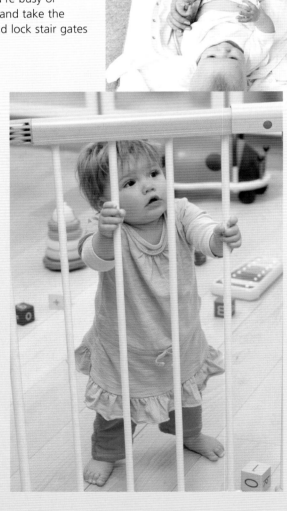

4 Protect against potential dangers. Safety equipment—such as stair gates, window guards, and outlet covers—is essential to keep your baby as safe as possible at home.

5 Teach about dangers. It's never too early to start talking to your child about safety. Your baby won't heed your advice at first, but eventually she'll understand the dangers around her and know how to stay safe.

infant. Make sure heavy lamps can't be pulled down.

Carpets and rugs

Fasten rugs and carpets securely to the floor. Use nonslip pads if needed under area rugs.

Fires and radiators

Install a guard in front of any fireplaces and around radiators. Avoid keeping any objects on the mantel so your child won't be tempted to try to climb up to get them. Keep fireplace tools out of reach.

Trash cans

Small children are fascinated by what's inside trash cans, no matter how unpleasant. Store the trash can in a locked cabinet or out of your child's reach; you also can put a lock on the can's lid. Be careful about what you throw away. Discard potentially hazardous items, such as razor blades, sealed in a bag in a trash can outside. Place recyclable items, such as detergent bottles, in a securely covered container outside.

Plants

Keep plants out of reach. They're easy for children to knock over and can be poisonous. Toxic houseplants include amaryllis, cyclamen, and English ivy. You also need to watch out for pebbles in plant pots, which are a choking hazard. For more information on poisonous plants, see pages 320–321.

Choking and suffocation hazards

Your child can choke on small items with a diameter of 1½ inches or less. Look out for toys that have small parts or tiny pieces that may break off (toys belonging to older siblings could pose a risk), pens and pencils, coins, batteries, anything magnetic that could be swallowed, jewelry, and balloons.

Keep plastic bags out of reach and tie a knot in them for added safety.

Injury hazards

Sharp, fragile, and heavy items can injure your child. Sharp household objects include knives, scissors, tacks, nails, needles, and pins. China, glassware, and lightbulbs break easily and can cause injuries.

Tools that are heavy or have sharp edges are also dangerous, and heavy furniture or decorations can hurt your child. Secure heavy furniture, especially bookshelves, and remove anything dangerous so your child can't get to it.

If your baby wants to draw, give her nontoxic crayons and chubby markers instead of a pen or a pencil.

Fire hazards

Keep matches and lighters well out of reach.

Electrical hazards

Young children are often fascinated with electrical outlets, which are usually positioned at just the right height for them. Babies can easily poke things into the small holes, putting them at risk of electric shock. Install safety plates on all outlets and use protective covers on power strips. Install these well before your child is able to move so that you aren't caught unprepared. Avoid outlet plugs, which are choking hazards.

Keep hair dryers, toasters, and all other electrical equipment well away from your child. Keep lamps

---

BASIC SAFETY EQUIPMENT

A few simple pieces of equipment will help make your house a safer place for your child:

- Stair gates
- Door stoppers/guards
- Window locks/guards
- Outlet covers
- Corner guards for sharp furniture corners
- Locks for drawers and cabinets
- Toilet locks
- Trash can locks
- Bath faucet covers to protect from scalding water and bumps on the head

and nightlights away from curtains to avoid a fire hazard.

Tape down electrical cords or tuck them into inaccessible places behind furniture. Use ties and holders to bundle them and keep them in place.

Water safety

Babies can drown in a very small amount of water. Never leave your baby unsupervised around water, even if it's very shallow. Don't leave liquid in buckets, and be sure to drain the bath right after using it. Never leave your child in the bath alone, not even for a second.

Use a toilet seat lock to keep the toilet securely closed when not in use.

If you have a pool, fountain, water pond, or hot tub, be sure it is inaccessible to your child.

Fire safety

Be sure to have at least one working smoke alarm and carbon-monoxide detector on every floor, ideally placed outside bedrooms. There also should

be alarms on landings and hallway ceilings. Position an alarm near the kitchen rather than in it, where it's more likely to be set off accidentally.

Check smoke alarm and carbon-monoxide detector batteries monthly and replace them at least once a year. Keep a fire extinguisher in the kitchen (out of your child's reach).

Upholstered furniture should be marked as fire-resistant. Make sure your child's bedding and pajamas are flame-retardant.

Keep any candles out of reach and never leave them unattended. Keep a guard in front of any fireplaces, and be sure matches, lighters, and fire starters are out of reach.

Take special care with cigarettes. No one should smoke in a home with a child. If someone in your family does smoke, restrict smoking to outside the house. Don't leave lit cigarettes unattended and be sure cigarettes are always completely extinguished.

Have your heating system regularly serviced.

Have an emergency escape plan in case of fire, with two different routes to escape any room. Practice the plan twice a year and make a copy available to sitters and anyone else caring for your child in your home. Make sure keys for doors and windows are easily accessible. If you have a two-story home, be sure to have a portable emergency escape ladder in an easily accessible location, in case you are unable to access the stairs in the event of a fire. For more help with fire safety, check the website for the U.S. Fire Administration (www.usfa.dhs.gov/campaigns/usfaparents).

5 ways to prevent falls

1 **Use lighting.** Keep areas such as stairs and the path to the bathroom well lit at night.

2 **Avoid leaving objects lying around.**

3 **Secure floor coverings.** Use nonslip backings under rugs and make sure carpets are held down securely.

4 **Dress your child in proper footwear.** Have her wear nonslip socks or slippers or go barefoot.

5 **Clean up messes.** Wipe up spilled drinks and pick up dropped food.

Poisons

Babies and toddlers typically explore the world around them by putting everything they find into their mouths. Parents need to be vigilant: Not only are there choking risks, but many substances around the home—even seemingly harmless ones—are poisonous. Store your alcohol, cleaning products, medicines, lotions, ointments, makeup, perfumes, toothpaste, and mouthwash out of reach.

Take particular care if you have a workshop or garage. These often are stocked with toxic materials and tools, all of which should be kept away from children. To minimize your child's risk of ingesting a toxic substance:

- Ensure that all poisonous substances are stored well out of reach in locked cabinets. Even very small children can find ways to climb up to high cabinets if they are determined.
- Store medicines in a high, locked cabinet.
- Never leave hazardous substances unattended or within reach of your baby. Beware of leaving dangerous materials within reach of your toddler when you're interrupted in the middle of using them (such as by a phone call).
- Don't keep medicine in your purse or bag. If your purse contains makeup or other potentially dangerous items, keep it out of your child's reach. It's a good idea to get in the habit of putting your purse—and those belonging to visitors—beyond your child's reach just in case.
- Avoid buying or storing hazardous substances in colorful containers that could catch your baby's interest.
- Choose the least toxic options when choosing household cleaners and other chemicals for use around the home.
- Buy bottles with childproof tops. However, they should still be kept out of reach because they aren't foolproof.
- Don't store hazardous substances in food containers, such as recycled yogurt tubs or juice bottles. Keep all dangerous liquids and materials in their original containers and make sure they're clearly labeled as poisonous.
- If you throw away unused hazardous materials, follow your city's guidelines for disposal. Minimally, seal them in a bag before disposing in a tightly covered trash can outside.
- Be vigilant when visiting other places; ensure that nothing hazardous is within your child's reach.
- Don't make taking medicine seem like a treat. Children need to understand that medicines are to help them feel better when they're sick and should be taken only from a parent or other trusted adult, such as a medical professional.

Dangerous substances

You might be surprised how many everyday items are hazardous—such as mouthwash, which contains alcohol. If in doubt, keep the substance locked away. Be aware of:

- Alcohol
- Antifreeze
- Bleach and other cleaning materials, such as toilet and oven cleaners
- Paint remover and thinner
- Dishwasher detergent
- Furniture and metal polish
- Glue

- Smoking can damage children's health, even if no one smokes in the same room as a child.
- A child who lives in a house with a smoker is at increased risk of asthma, chest infection, and ear infections. He's also likely to suffer more coughs and colds than a child in a non-smoking home.
- If both parents smoke during pregnancy, their baby's risk for SIDS is eight times higher than if neither parent smokes.
- Smoking is the leading cause of preventable home fire deaths.

- Insect repellents and poisons
- Makeup, perfume, and nail polish remover
- Mothballs
- Medicines, including aspirin, pain killers, and nutritional supplements
- Mouthwash and fluoridated toothpaste
- Gasoline and kerosene
- Weed killer

Kitchen safety

The kitchen will fascinate your baby—there are so many things to explore—but it can be dangerous. As with all areas of the house, never leave your baby alone in the kitchen even for a moment. She'll quickly find her way into all sorts of hazardous places.

Hot foods

Never carry your baby when you're cooking or holding a hot drink. Hot foods and drinks can easily spill and splash. Place anything hot toward the back of work surfaces and away from the edges of tables

to ensure it's well out of reach.

Cabinets, drawers, and work surfaces

Special latches and locks will help protect your baby. Make sure they're fairly easy for you to open, or you'll be tempted to leave drawers and cupboards open to avoid a hassle when working in the kitchen. Use locks on floor-level cupboards and higher ones, too. For added security, keep any hazardous items in cabinets that are well out of reach:

- *Cleaning items,* including detergents and washing materials, are potentially toxic.
- *Plastic wrap* and other dispenser boxes with serrated edges can cause cuts.
- *Plastic bags* may cause suffocation.
- *Refrigerator magnets* present a choking hazard and are particularly dangerous when swallowed; ingesting more than one magnet can lead to serious bowel damage.

Don't let your child sit on work surfaces in the kitchen. Not only might she fall off, but she'll be close to all sorts of hazards.

Appliances

On the stove top, avoid using the front burners—stick to the back as much as possible. Keep pot handles turned to the side. You can install a guard to shield children from pans on the hot stove and keep their curious fingers away from knobs (or get

Why not reserve one kitchen cabinet just for your child? Place objects there that are safe but will keep her amused, such as a wooden spoon, a pan, and a plastic bowl. This will let her have fun with you in the kitchen without taking risks.

separate knob covers). Use an appliance lock to keep the oven door closed.

Keep the oven, grill, and toaster clean to reduce the risk of grease or crumbs catching fire. Keep kitchen towels away from heated appliances. Keep a dry-chemical fire extinguisher in case of a grease fire—water would actually fuel a grease fire.

Use an appliance lock to secure the refrigerator door.

Make sure doors to the dishwasher and the washer and dryer are securely closed at all times. Children can easily get hold of sharp or breakable items in the dishwasher or the detergent inside machines, and they can climb into washers or dryers and pull the door closed behind them.

Keep small kitchen appliances, such as the toaster and coffee maker, away from the edges of counters. Unplug and tuck cords securely out of reach so your child can't pull on them; if the cords are long, consider using wire ties.

Bathroom safety

The bathroom is another dangerous place for babies, but with your vigilance and by following the measures described, you can minimize the main risks of drowning, scalding, and falling.

The door

Keep your bathroom door closed. When your child is old enough to turn a knob and can open the door, use a childproof doorknob cover to keep him from getting into the bathroom—or locking himself in.

The bathtub

Put a nonslip mat in the bottom of the bathtub and another on the floor. Take great care to avoid scalding. If possible, set your water heater so that the water temperature can't exceed 120°F. Test the temperature of bath water with your wrist or use a water thermometer (the temperature should be no more than about 100°F). Put a soft, cushioned guard over bath fixtures so your child can't bump her head or burn herself. Fill the tub with only enough water to cover your baby's legs. Once your baby is able to sit, she can use a seat in the tub.

Never leave a child alone in the tub before she's at least 5 years old. Drain water from the tub as soon as you've finished with it.

The toilet

Keep the toilet closed and locked. Since toddlers can get up onto the toilet seat, remove any dangers that are within the reach of a climber.

Dangerous items

Many things commonly kept in bathrooms need to be stored out of reach. These include:

- *Cleaning materials,* such as tile and toilet scrub and the brush for cleaning the toilet.
- *Electrical appliances*—avoid using these in the bathroom and keep them away from water.
- *Medicines*—keep them in a locked medicine cabinet positioned high on the wall.
- *Makeup* and other beauty products.
- *Mouthwash*—it is toxic to babies if swallowed.
- *Sharp objects,* such as razors and scissors.
- *Choking hazards.*
- *Hazardous trash,* such as used razors and empty mouthwash and detergent bottles. Go without a trash can in the bathroom, if you can.

Bedroom safety

As your baby grows, you'll need to make adjustments to ensure that her bedroom is safe.

The crib

Choose your crib with care to ensure that it meets safety standards (see page 156 for details). Drop-side cribs are prohibited from being sold in the United States; beware of using one given by a friend or relative, as it does not meet current safety standards. Check that the slats are no more than 2⅜ inches apart. Use a firm, tight-fitting mattress; you shouldn't be able to fit more than two fingers between the mattress and the crib sides.

Do not use pillows or blankets in your baby's crib, because they are a suffocation risk. The American Academy of Pediatrics discourages the use of bumper pads because they, too, are a suffocation risk. If you choose to use bumper pads, they should be thin, firm, well secured (knot and cut off ties), and not "pillow-like." Don't let your baby sleep with toys or plush animals in his first year of life; thereafter, use only objects that are safe.

As soon as your baby can push up on hands and knees, lower the mattress so that the rail reaches her chest and remove any mobiles or hanging toys over the crib.

Many parents worry about their babies being cold at night and bundle them up. Overheating is also a danger, however, so it's important to keep your baby's room at a comfortable temperature (between 68°F and 72°F). Keep the crib away from heaters, and use appropriate clothing and bedding. If you think your baby isn't warm enough, dress her in another layer of clothing or put her in a sleep sack—don't use a blanket, because until she's older your baby can't kick it off if she's too hot or the blanket is interfering with her breathing. For more information on safe sleeping, see pages 156–158.

Changing area

Never turn away from your baby on a changing table, not even for a moment. Your baby could very easily roll or tumble off. You may want to use a safety strap for additional reassurance, or use a changing mat on the floor. Make sure everything you need to change her diaper is out of her reach but easily accessible for you.

Toy safety

Choose age-appropriate toys for your baby. Check the age range indicated on the package and consider your child's development. Toys with small parts usually are labeled for age 3 and older, but if your 3- or 4-year-old still puts things in her mouth, continue to avoid these toys. Be mindful that older children's toys may pose a hazard to babies and toddlers—watch for small pieces left lying around.

Toys for children under 3 should be chunky with large pieces. They should be made well and maintained to make sure small pieces can't come loose and cause a choking hazard. Look out for sharp edges and avoid heavy toys that could fall on your child and injure her. Strings on toys should be no longer than 12 inches to avoid risk of strangulation. When buying soft toys, look for ones that are washable.

If you're not sure whether a toy is safe, don't bring it into your home. Secondhand toys can save you money, but always make sure they're clean and in good condition before giving them to your baby. You can check for any recalled toys (or other products) at www.cpsc.gov.

Store toys on shelves or in open containers. These are safest and make it easier to find toys. If you use a toy chest, remove the lid if you can. If you can't, be sure the lid is light, doesn't lock, and won't hurt fingers, and that the chest has ventilation holes in case your child climbs into it.

Pets

Bringing home your baby can be a tough transition time for a pet. After your baby is born, have your partner bring home a baby blanket that's been next to your baby to sniff. Once you're home, try to spend some time one-one-one with your pet, and consider having a friend help out by playing with your pet or taking your dog for walks.

Many pets are child-friendly and tolerate babies patiently. But even the most docile or timid pets can be unpredictable, so it's important to supervise children and pets at all times. Avoid bringing home a new pet for your baby or young toddler. She's too

SAFETY**FIRST**	children's clothes

Make sure sleepwear is snug-fitting and labeled as flame-resistant. Do not dress your baby in clothing with drawstrings, and trim any ribbons longer than 6 inches to reduce the risk of strangulation. If your child walks around in socks, make sure they're nonslip.

young to fully learn how to behave around a pet, and having an animal in your home puts her at risk of injury and presents hygiene issues.

Children under the age of 4 are most at risk of dog bites; as children get older, they learn how to behave around animals. Definitely show your baby how to treat animals early on, but know that it will take time for her to understand and follow your advice. You'll need to teach your child to:

- Be calm and gentle with pets.
- Never disturb a dog or cat when it's asleep or eating.
- Stand still when a dog comes up to her.
- Never approach a dog she doesn't know.
- Never touch dog or cat excrement.
- Wash her hands after playing with a pet.

Some pets become jealous when a new baby joins the family, and they may act out; you may need to give your pet some special attention while it gets used to this new family member.

Keep in mind:

- Keep pets out of your baby's bedroom.
- Make sure your baby can't get into the cat litter.
- Keep pet food away from your baby. If you leave water bowls where she can reach them, be prepared for puddles!
- Remove all dog excrement from the yard.
- Make sure pets are treated to prevent worms and up to date on vaccinations.
- Consider setting up a fenced dog run in your yard to help keep dog waste out of your child's playing area.

BABY WALKERS

Baby walkers are banned in Canada, and in the United States the American Academy of Pediatrics is urging a ban on wheeled walkers. Babies in walkers can reach higher and move faster, meaning they can reach hot stoves, topple over, fall down stairs, or collide with furniture.

Though they help babies move around, walkers don't help babies master walking. In fact, they may interfere with walking because babies build the muscles and skills they need to walk by moving around on the floor and crawling.

Instead of a walker, use a stationary activity center or a play yard.

Safety outside the home

Take care to make the areas outside your home as safe as possible for your child. Always supervise your child outside.

In the yard

If you have a yard, make sure it is secure. Check that fences are well maintained with no gaps. Lock away yard tools when not in use, along with any potentially toxic materials, such as pesticides and fertilizers (see page 315).

Avoid using dangerous equipment, such as power tools and lawn mowers, when your child is outside. Make sure he's safe and secure while you work. If he is outdoors while you work, have someone else supervise him at all times and keep him away from your work area.

Play equipment

When buying an outdoor play set, check that it's been manufactured according to ASTM International standards. You also should carefully check the equipment: It must be sturdy, well made with no sharp edges, and appropriate to the age and development of your child.

If you assemble the equipment yourself, follow the instructions carefully. Position it away from walls or fences and make sure to provide for soft landings with regular play or accidental falls. You can use wood chips or mulched rubber for high sets; sand is an option for playsets under 5 feet high.

Outdoor play structures need to be regularly inspected and carefully maintained. Always supervise children playing on outdoor equipment.

Ride-on toys

Make sure any ride-on toys are the right size for your child. Buying one for him to grow into will put him at greater risk of accidents.

Make sure he always wears his helmet when he rides a tricycle or scooter—even if he's in your yard. A helmet will reduce the risk of a serious head injury if he falls and will teach him good habits for when he rides a bike later.

Pools and ponds

Drowning rates are highest among children ages 1 to 4, and it's the second-leading cause of death for young children in the United States. If you have a pool, pond, hot tub, or fountain, it's important to supervise your child at all times.

Enclose a swimming pool on all four sides with a fence at least 4 feet high, with a self-closing and self-locking gate. Check the fence regularly and remember that it does not provide any guarantee: It easily could be left open or not closed properly. Pool owners must be vigilant at all times.

Don't leave any toys in the pool area: Your child could be tempted to try to get one. Also, it's a good idea to enroll your toddler in swimming lessons; lessons are associated with greatly reduced drowning rates for children under 4.

When not in use, you may want to cover your pool with a rigid screen or cover positioned above the water's surface and secured all the way around. It must be strong enough to bear a child's weight without sagging and must be maintained carefully.

Empty a wading pool whenever it isn't in use and then pack it away or turn it upside down so water can't collect in it and pose a drowning hazard. Do not leave water in containers, such as buckets. A child can drown in even very shallow water.

Poisonous plants

If you have plants, keep them out of your child's reach. Many common houseplants and garden plants are potentially harmful: Some are dangerously toxic if eaten, while others cause skin or eye irritation. Teach your child not to put plants or berries in his mouth or play with plants. It will take some time for him to learn this, so you'll need to supervise him constantly around plants. Do your best to remove any dangerous plants from his environment (see box, right). If you aren't sure whether a plant is safe, take a clipping to a local garden center to find out what it is. Once you know the plant's name, you can call your local poison control center (800-222-1222) to inquire if it is a danger. If your baby does put poisonous leaves or berries into his mouth, remove as much as possible and seek immediate medical attention.

In the driveway

Make sure your child is away from the car and supervised when you drive into or out of your driveway. Check under and around your car before moving it.

Out and about

You and your child will enjoy exploring the world around you. You'll have more fun if you aren't constantly worrying about his safety. If he's walking, make sure he holds your hand at all times or keep him securely strapped into his stroller or carrier.

In the car

To keep your child as safe as possible in the car, remember the following:

♦ Buy a car seat that is appropriate for your baby's age, height, and weight, and make sure it is installed securely and correctly. The seat should face the rear of the car until your child is at least 2 years old or outgrows the seat. Ensure that he stays in the car seat at all times.
♦ Don't let your baby play with window locks or door handles.
♦ If there is an air bag for his seat, switch it off.
♦ Switch on the child locks.
♦ Don't let yourself be distracted by your baby; don't take your eyes off the road. If your child needs you, pull over at the first safe opportunity.
♦ Remove any loose items in the car; they can easily slip or tumble from the area above the back

| SAFETY**FIRST** | poisonous plants |

Common poisonous plants include: azalea, columbine, daffodil (narcissus), daphne, delphinium (larkspur), euphorbia, foxglove, glory lily, hellebore, holly, hydrangea, iris, ivy, Jerusalem cherry, jimsonweed, juniper, laburnum, lantana, laurel, lily-of-the-valley, lobelia, lupine, mistletoe, monkshood, morning glory, mushrooms (some types), nightshade, oleander, pokeweed, privet, rhododendron, rhubarb leaves, sweet pea, tomato plant leaves, wisteria, and yew.

These plants can cause skin irritation: daffodil and daphne (both also poisonous), euphorbia (also poisonous and an eye irritant), helleborus (also poisonous), hyacinth, iris and ivy (both also poisonous), lobelia (also poisonous and an eye irritant, but not the bedding-out varieties), monkshood (also poisonous), nightshade (also poisonous), poinsettia, primula, and tulip.

seat or could fly through the car in the event of a sudden stop or collision.

In stores

Keep your child next to you at all times. If he's riding

in a shopping cart, make sure he's securely buckled in.

At the playground
Stay close by and don't take your eyes off your child for a second. Teach him how to play safely. Don't let him walk in front of or behind swings or twist a swing, because the swing could strike him. Make sure he doesn't climb up a slide that is unsafe for a child of his age. Teach him that at the top, he must wait until the slide is clear before going down. Never slide down with your child in your lap. Check that the play structure is age-appropriate; many parks have structures specifically for toddlers. If the play structure is in full sun, check to make sure that any exposed metal or plastic isn't too hot.

In the sun
Try to keep your baby in the shade as much as you can, particularly around midday. He should wear loose, cool clothes that cover as much of him as possible, as well as a wide-brimmed hat.

Babies can get a sunburn even when they aren't in direct sun, so be sure to cover him up. Once he is 6 months old, you can begin to apply sunscreen with an SPF factor of at least 15 to 30 and reapply it regularly—sunscreen in stick form might be easier to apply to his face than lotion.

Protecting your baby's skin is very important; studies have shown that frequent sun exposure and sunburns in childhood increase the risk of melanomas in adulthood. Babies are particularly at risk of burning because their skin is thinner and more sensitive. Remember to protect your child's skin from everyday sunshine, not just on vacations and beach trips.

While traveling
Visiting new places is a wonderful experience for children of all ages. A few safety precautions will help ensure that all goes well. If you're traveling out of the country, especially to a developing nation, ask your pediatrician about required and recommended vaccinations and whether or not your child needs malaria prophylaxis. Travel vaccines are best given at least a month before departure. You might need to be extra careful about the risk of food poisoning, which can make babies very sick.

Plane travel
Airlines allow babies to sit on a parent's lap until the age of 2, saving the cost of an extra seat. However, the safest place for your baby on an airplane is in his own seat, secured in an Federal Aviation Administration–approved car seat. An older child can use a safety harness.

Bulkhead seats at the front of the plane offer more legroom and have extra oxygen bags for babies who don't have their own seats. But the only storage is in the overhead locker, and sometimes bulkhead seats are right in front of a large video screen.

It's a good idea to check your airline's website or call their customer relations number to review their policies regarding traveling with children. (For more information about air travel and getting through security with a child, see pages 216–217.)

HEALTH**FIRST**	upset tummy

A simple change in diet can affect your child's bowel habits for a while, but when you travel abroad there's also a risk of infection. To minimize the risks:

- *If you think the water may be unsafe to drink, boil it or use bottled water. Decline ice cubes in restaurants.*
- *Give your child only pasteurized dairy products.*
- *Wash fruit with drinkable water and then peel the fruit.*
- *Give your child bottled fruit juice rather than freshly squeezed.*
- *As at home, make sure that all meat and fish are cooked thoroughly.*

Emergency first aid

Despite your best efforts, you probably can't prevent all accidents. You should be able to deal with grazes, cuts, and bites (see pages 340–343) and recognize when urgent medical help is needed. If your child suffers any of the injuries addressed here, call 911 for an ambulance or seek immediate medical attention.

For a list of first-aid supplies to treat injuries, see page 343.

Poisoning

If your child ingests something harmful, or you suspect that she has, or you believe a potential poison has come in contact with her skin or eyes, call 911.

If your child is breathing but unconscious, put her in the recovery position (see pages 42 and 188).

Try to find out what she took, how much, and when so that you can inform the doctor or paramedics. If she vomits, keep a sample (but don't try to make her throw up). Give her only sips of water to drink.

For questions about poisoning, call your local poison control center or the American Association of Poison Control Centers at (800) 222-1222.

Bleeding

For severe bleeding, call 911. Your first objective is to stem the flow of blood. Use disposable gloves, if available, to reduce the risk of cross-infection. Check whether an object is embedded in the wound.

If nothing is embedded, press on the wound with your hand, ideally over a clean pad, and secure with a bandage. If the wound is on an arm or leg, raise the injured limb above the level of the heart.

If you suspect there is something embedded in the wound, be careful not to press on it. Instead, press firmly on either side of the object and build up padding around it before bandaging to avoid putting pressure on the object itself.

Burns and scalds

Babies with burns, even small ones, need medical attention.

If hot water caused the burn, first remove any wet clothing to stop any further skin injury. In these and other types of burns, cool the burned skin as quickly as possible by running cold water over it for at least 10 minutes. Do not apply ice. Cover the injury with a sterile, non-stick dressing, such as a sterile gauze pad or plastic wrap. Hold the dressing in place with a loose bandage. Don't apply any creams. Raise the limb to reduce swelling.

Drowning

If you find your baby in water, immediately lift her out and hold her so her head is lower than her body. This will help prevent water (or vomit) from getting into her lungs. If she's unconscious but still breathing, put her in the recovery position while you call 911. If she isn't breathing, begin resuscitation and call 911. If she has water in her lungs, you'll have to breathe firmly to inflate her lungs.

Electric shock

Call 911 for an ambulance immediately.

Break the contact between your baby and the electrical supply by switching the circuit breaker or unplugging the cord.

If you can't safely turn off the power or break the current, stand on something dry and non-conductive, and use a non-conductive object—such as a wooden broom—to push your baby away from the source of the current or to push the source away from your baby.

Emergency numbers

Keep a list of emergency numbers by all your phones or in another easily accessible place in your home. Include 911, the local poison control center, your child's pediatrician and dentist, and friends and family who can help.

If at any time your baby becomes unconscious, stops breathing, or is choking, start emergency resuscitation (see pages 42–43 and 188).

Doctor visits

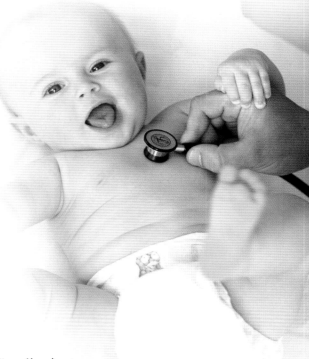

Carefully monitoring your baby's health during her early years is very important for identifying any potential problems as early as possible. She'll be checked over by her doctor and nurses and undergo her first tests in the day or two after birth, and will continue to need regular doctor's visits afterward.

Of course, you'll need a pediatrician you respect and trust to care for your child. Remember, however, that you are vitally important to her well-being. You're with her every day, and you may be the first to notice if something doesn't seem right.

Your child's health team

Your child will need routine visits with her doctor and dentist. Your choices may be limited by your health insurance coverage; check with your insurance company beforehand to see if the medical providers you choose are covered.

There are many reasons to choose only professionals with pediatric experience. Children are not just little adults: They are affected by different diseases, and an ailment in a child may act very differently than the same one in an adult. Medications used in adults may not be safe if given to children, and doses are different. In addition, how an illness or its treatment affects growth and development must be considered. Questions related to your child's behavior and your parenting skills can best be answered by those with pediatric experience. It is highly desirable that your child's doctors be patient and comfortable with children and have a childproof office with child-size furniture, stocked with toys and books. See page 21 for more about the qualities you want in your's child's doctor.

Pediatrician

Many pediatricians provide primary care, covering all aspects of child medicine; others focus on specialty areas, such as cardiac care or cancer. Pediatricians focus exclusively on children and so are experts in children's special medical needs.

Family doctor

A family doctor, or general practitioner, can treat your entire family. If you choose a family doctor, look for one with many young patients.

Dentist

Your child's dentist will help keep her teeth healthy and strong with routine, ongoing care. Many family dentists have a large number of children as patients. Ask your own dentist if he is comfortable with young children. If he is not, seek out a pediatric dentist, who specializes in caring for children. Positive experiences at the dentist in early childhood are very important in setting the stage for a lifetime of good dental care.

Specialists

If you child needs to see a specialist, try to find one who specializes in pediatric care or treats many children. Your child will be more comfortable with medical providers who have a good rapport with children, and you'll be more confident that they have the necessary expertise and knowledge to treat your child.

Checking development

Your child's doctor will conduct screening tests, monitor her weight gain and growth, and assess her development at routine checkups. She'll also provide vaccinations and review other aspects of your child's well-being, providing advice on behavioral challenges or recommending specialists for specific issues.

Every child develops at her own rate, which is determined by the genes she inherits and the environment in which she's raised. Because of this individuality, try not to focus on the exact timing of every developmental milestone. Be aware of the usual age range for achieving key milestones (see page 278) and keep a record of when your child acquires these skills (see page 326), but don't obsess over them. If you have any concerns, bring them up with your doctor.

Your pediatrician will review all aspects of development—posture and movement (gross motor), vision and manual skills (fine motor), hearing and speech, and social behavior and interaction—at routine checkups.

Physical health

Development and physical health are closely related. For example, learning to crawl depends on correctly working muscles and coordination, which both rely on a healthy nervous system. Developmental problems can indicate an underlying medical disorder. Some conditions, such as heart murmurs, can be identified during physical examinations; others may be revealed with blood tests.

Routine checkups

Your child should be seen by her physician at least

MORE ABOUT | hip dysplasia

In some young babies, the hip socket that holds the ball-shaped head of the femur (thigh bone) is too shallow and allows the femoral head to move out of the correct position. It may slip in and out when the baby is examined or, less commonly, stay outside the socket. This condition, known as hip dysplasia, may be present at birth or detected later on. Early diagnosis and treatment are important so that the hip joint will develop properly and the child can learn to walk properly. Without treatment, walking probably will be delayed and the baby may limp and sway from side to side when he walks. The affected leg may appear shorter, and the hip on that side will have a restricted range of movement.

Your pediatrician will check your baby's hips during infancy. If she suspects a problem, she'll order a hip ultrasound. If there's a potential issue, she will refer you to an orthopedic surgeon.

10 times by her second birthday. At these visits, your pediatrician will measure your child's weight gain or growth, check to see whether her hips move normally, listen to her heart and lungs, and examine her from head to toe.

Your pediatrician will ask you about your baby's progress at each assessment, including whether you suspect there are any problems. Your baby's weight, length, and head circumference will be measured at each visit and plotted on a growth chart to make sure she grows steadily. You'll also have the opportunity to ask questions about her health and development and raise any concerns you may have. If you have questions between visits, however, you should call your pediatrician for consultation over the phone or to schedule a visit.

Newborn exam

If you deliver in a hospital, a pediatrician will examine your baby within 24 hours or so of birth. The doctor will first check your baby's overall appearance, and make sure she is healthy and well formed. For example, he will count her fingers and toes, check that her spine appears normal, shine a light in her eyes to detect any signs of a cataract

KEEPING YOUR OWN MEDICAL RECORD

A medical record is an invaluable source of information to help monitor your baby's development. Your pediatrician will track your child's development and overall health in her office records, recording measurements, results of screening tests, and developmental progress so she can see whether your child's development is progressing as expected or if some area of development has slowed, which could indicate a problem. You should keep your own records, including names and contact information for your child's doctors, immunization records, and details about family history, including incidence of allergies, heart disease, diabetes, and other ailments. You also may want to record certain key milestones: It can be a wonderful keepsake for later years. Here's a form to get you started.

First smile _____

Stands with support _____

Sits without support _____

Feeds herself finger foods _____

First words _____

Crawls _____

Says "mama" and "dada" _____

Waves bye-bye _____

Claps _____

Points _____

Takes first steps _____

Drinks from cup with two hands _____

Walks steadily _____

Climbs into a chair _____

Throws a ball _____

Runs _____

Walks upstairs _____

Feeds herself with a spoon _____

Kicks a ball _____

Stays dry during the day _____

Walks up and down stairs confidently _____

(see page 333) and check her mouth for palate irregularities. The doctor will also listen to her heart and lungs, feel her abdomen, and examine her hips for evidence of congenital dislocation (see page 325). If your baby is a boy, the doctor will check that the testes are in the scrotum. Your baby's hearing will be tested (see page 331) before she leaves the hospital.

A nurse will take a small blood sample by pricking your baby's heel. This sample will be tested for several disorders, which may include sickle cell anemia, cystic fibrosis, and hypothyroidism (underactive thyroid gland). Many of these disorders can have serious effects if not identified early. Currently, individual states determine which tests are required. Be sure to find out which conditions your baby is being tested for. Your baby also may be vaccinated against hepatitis B.

2- to 4-week checkup

Your pediatrician will again conduct a complete physical check, examining the hips, listening to the heart, and, if you have a boy, again checking the position of the testes. He may also check eyes for evidence of cataracts and other eye conditions.

He'll ask how often your baby has wet and soiled diapers and how often she's feeding. By 1 month, your baby should be able to follow some objects with her eyes, lift her head briefly when on her stomach, and react to sounds. Topics discussed may include guidance on colic and information about vaccines. She may get her second hepatitis B shot.

2-month checkup

At this visit, your pediatrician will ask about her development, such as whether she's started smiling and tracking with her eyes, how often she cries, and inquire about feedings and sleep.

He'll assess your baby's gross motor development by observing her muscle tone and early head control. To assess her eyesight, he'll watch to see if she follows an object with her eyes when it's moved across her field of vision.

Your doctor will also examine her fully, including reexamining her hips and her heart.

Vaccinations at this visit include diphtheria,

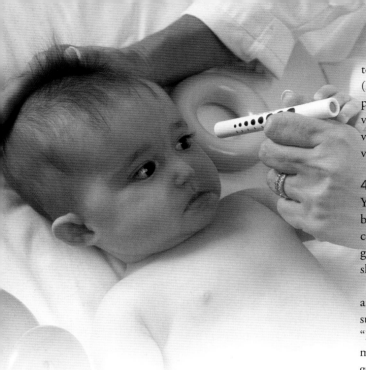

tetanus, and pertussis (DTaP); rotavirus; polio (IPV); haemophilius influenzae type B (Hib); and pneumococcal conjugate (PCV). If the hepatitis B vaccine was not given in the hospital or at the last visit, it will be given now. Possible reactions to the vaccines will be reviewed.

4-month checkup

Your pediatrician will want to know about your baby's social development: Is she smiling and cooing? Does she squeal? He'll want to see if she has good head control, if she reaches for objects, and if she's able to roll from her front to her back yet.

Your doctor may discuss topics such as sleep and an approach to fever and illness. He may also suggest starting your baby on solids (see chapter 10, "Feeding your older baby"). Babies need only breast milk or formula until they're 4–6 months old, but it's good to talk about introducing solids before you start offering them to your baby.

At this visit, she should get a second round of DTaP, rotavirus, IPV, Hib, and PCV shots. If a second dose of hepatitis B vaccine has not yet been given, it will be given now as well.

6-month checkup

Your baby is starting to have more physical self-control. She may be able to sit with support, pick up objects by raking them with her fingers, may roll from back to front and back again, and could be babbling. Babies this age also start reaching for toys and passing them from hand to hand.

If you haven't already started solids, your pediatrician will want to talk about when and how to introduce solid foods. Many doctors will discuss childproofing your home at this visit.

Your baby will get her third round of DTaP, PCV, and

MORE **ABOUT** | heart murmurs

When your pediatrician listens to your child's heart with a stethoscope, she's checking for any abnormal sounds such as turbulent blood flow in the heart. This can indicate a problem with one of the heart valves or another heart abnormality. Some heart problems are found during prenatal tests, but others aren't diagnosed until after birth.

Some congenital heart abnormalities are caused by a problem with the development of the heart during pregnancy. Others occur when changes in the baby's circulatory system that normally take place at or around birth don't occur as they should.

If a murmur is detected, your child will need an appointment with a pediatric cardiologist and may have an echocardiogram, a special ultrasound scan that looks at the heart's structure and functioning.

Not all heart murmurs represent a heart abnormality. Many murmurs of early childhood are considered normal. These are described as innocent murmurs, which require no treatment and usually disappear during the first few years of life.

During a boy's development in the uterus, his testes follow a path of descent from the abdomen, where they're formed, down into the scrotum. Sometimes this descent stops before the testes reach the scrotum and one or both testes remain in the abdomen (known as undescended testes). This is quite a common condition, affecting about 5 percent of boys at birth. It's more common in premature babies because the testes move down into the scrotum during the last months of pregnancy.

In some of these boys the condition will resolve on its own when the testes descend into the scrotum during the first few months of life. Otherwise, treatment will be needed for two main reasons. First, this condition can affect fertility in later life, because the

temperature inside the body is too high for the production of sperm; the lower temperature in the scrotum is ideal. There is also an increased risk of malignancy for testes that remain inside the abdomen. Testes also are brought down for reasons of appearance.

Checking that the testes are in the scrotum is an important part of a baby boy's early checkups.

Sometimes one or both testes will pop up into the groin area during the examination. This is caused by a muscle reflex and the testes are described as being retractile; in this situation, the testes can be guided back into the scrotum. A retractile testis is regarded as normal and requires no treatment, just monitoring to ensure it eventually stays in the scrotum.

rotavirus vaccinations. She also should get a third dose of HepB and IPV either now or sometime between 6 and 18 months. If your child has been getting one of the two types of Hib vaccine, a third dose of vaccine is given at 6 months of age; it is not given if the other type has been used.

9-month checkup

Gross motor skills are developing quickly now—your baby should be able to sit on her own, may stand with support, and could pull herself up to standing. She may be crawling too. Your pediatrician may ask about speech: Around 9 months, most babies repeat syllables (da-da-da), and some may speak a word or two.

Your child may be able to feed herself some finger foods by now. Your pediatrician will check on your baby's progress eating solid foods. Guidance topics may include care of teeth and a discussion on shoes.

12-month checkup

By this milestone visit, your baby may really be on the move, perhaps cruising by holding onto

furniture or even taking early steps. She probably can hold small items between her finger and thumb (known as the pincer grip). She may call her parents "mama" and "dada," and perhaps use a few other words. At mealtime, she may start to use a spoon and hold a cup with both hands. She now can switch from formula to whole cow's milk; if she's breastfeeding, there's no reason to stop now. Guidance topics may include switching from bottles to a cup, further safety issues, and upcoming vaccines. Some pediatricians will test your child for iron deficiency and lead poisoning with a blood test and may also test for exposure to tuberculosis with a skin prick test.

Between 12 and 15 months, she's due to be vaccinated for Hib; measles, mumps, and rubella (MMR); PCV; and varicella. She'll also need hepatitis A vaccination by 23 months.

15-month checkup

By this point, your child should be eating a good variety of food with different textures—ideally three meals a day and two to three healthy snacks (see

(see chapter 10, "Feeding your older baby"). Her growth may be slowing: This is normal, and her appetite will decrease accordingly. She may be able to speak a few words, point to some body parts or pictures, walk, and perhaps climb. Guidance topics may include discussing your child's growing independence and the possibility of picky eating habits. She should get her fourth DTaP shot now.

18-month checkup

Your pediatrician will continue to monitor your toddler's language skills. She should be able to speak a few words and understand simple instructions. She might be scribbling with a crayon, kicking balls, and helping to undress herself. She should be able to walk well on her own and may be starting to run. The topic of toilet training may be introduced.

24-month checkup

By the age of 2, your toddler is probably a confident walker, able to run and even jump. She may scribble circles and stack three to six blocks into a tower.

She may have dozens of words by now, and she should be able to express some of her needs and wishes with a few two-word phrases such as "want milk." She's probably feeding herself reasonably well with a spoon. And she may already be showing signs of readiness for potty training. Guidance topics may include more on potty training, discipline, and managing your child's behavior. You can now switch from full-fat to low-fat dairy products for your child.

Vision and hearing assessments

Normal vision and hearing are crucial to development, and parents may notice problems during everyday activities. However, to be absolutely sure that all is well, certain tests may be carried out routinely at the developmental checks; others are used when problems are suspected.

Vision checks

Beginning in the hospital, your child's eyes will be checked at all doctor's visits for abnormalities, such as glaucoma or cataracts, and for visual problems.

In these early months, visual assessment includes observation to see if she tracks moving objects and

4 times to check your baby's hearing

1 **In the first weeks,** does she sometimes react to sudden noises?

2 **At 4 months,** does she turn toward your voice?

3 **At 7 months,** does she react to quiet noises?

4 **At around 9 months,** has she started making babbling sounds?

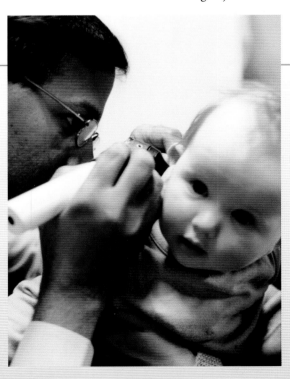

reaches for objects placed before her. In addition, your doctor will check to see that her eyes look straight ahead; he'll make sure that both eyes work cooperatively and that she does not have a "lazy" eye. By the time she's 3, she may be asked to identify letters or pictures on an examination chart.

Your baby should be able to track objects moving in front of her face by 3 months. If you suspect she has a vision problem—for example, if she can't keep steady eye contact—talk to your doctor. If there's reason to suspect she has a vision problem, she'll be referred to a pediatric ophthalmologist.

Hearing checks

Your baby's hearing will first be checked right after birth. You should monitor your baby's hearing as well (see box, opposite page).

Newborn tests

These tests are used to check hearing in newborns:

- *Otoacoustic emissions (OAE)* Soft earphones placed over your baby's ears emit clicking sounds into each ear. A tiny probe in the ear canal should pick up vibrations in the cochlea if it's functioning normally. This is the most common test used for newborn hearing screening.
- *Automated auditory brainstem response* Again, earphones placed over the ears emit clicks. These noises trigger impulses in the ear that are carried to the brain, where they trigger electrical responses. These responses are recorded and analyzed by a computer.

Usually, the OAE test is done first. In children in whom a normal response is obtained, no further testing is done. But if your newborn doesn't show an appropriate response, it will be repeated. Any persistent abnormality in hearing is confirmed with the more accurate ABR test. Finally, children with an abnormal result using the ABR test will be referred to an audiologist for further evaluation.

If your child doesn't seem to respond to sounds, has not started saying repetitive syllables by 10 months, or is slow to develop speech, talk to your doctor. Audiologists have sensitive tests to evaluate hearing in infants and toddlers. It is not until age 3 to 3½ that your child will be able to cooperate with routine hearing screens in your pediatrician's office.

Plagiocephaly

Your pediatrician will also monitor your baby for flattened head syndrome, or plagiocephaly, which occurs when a baby constantly holds his head turned to one side when lying down and develops a misshapen skull. When a head-turning preference persists, the muscles on one side of his neck may adjust to the situation by shortening and tightening. This adds to the problem, making it uncomfortable for your child to turn to the non-preferred direction.

Your pediatrician may teach you some exercises to do with your child to reduce muscle tightness, or she may refer you to a physical therapist to stretch his muscles. Studies show that if your baby is left alone, the shape of his head most likely will improve as he gets older and spends less time flat on his back. His head will also look rounder once he grows a full head of hair.

In more extreme cases, your pediatrician may recommend a custom-molded helmet. A helmet will encourage rounding out of flattened areas. Helmets need to be replaced as your child's head grows, are expensive (and sometimes not covered by insurance), and need to be worn around the clock for months. Only use one if advised by your pediatrician.

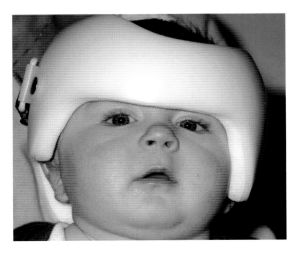

Developmental concerns

If your child doesn't seem to be developing as he should, it is likely that you will be the first to suspect it. The typical ages when babies achieve different milestones are found on page 276.

Remember that there isn't a single age, but a range of ages, that's normal for each skill. Even if your child achieves a skill later than average, as long as it was acquired within the normal ranges, your child has reached that milestone on time.

But you shouldn't hesitate to talk to your pediatrician if you suspect your child has any developmental issues. Your baby probably is fine, but by speaking up early you can save yourself a lot of worrying. And if something is amiss, you can begin assessing what's wrong and finding out what can be done to treat it.

If your child needs specialized care, your pediatrician will help you develop a team of professionals to help.

Common developmental problems
Developmental delays may affect only one specific area or may be more general (this is known as global delay). Chapter 13 covers many of the longer-lasting problems in more detail.

Motor development
Babies typically make major advances in gross motor development in the first year; yet it is still normal to begin walking as late as 18 months of age. If you or your pediatrician suspect a problem, the first step is to determine if the delay is in motor skills only or encompasses other spheres of development as well. An isolated motor delay can be due to muscle diseases, hypotonia (see page 334), or even cerebral palsy (see page 378). Your baby may be referred to a specialist, such as a child neurologist, for a full assessment. Usually parents get advice on encouraging their child's development, and the child gets help in the form of therapy.

Speech and language
Speech development may be delayed for a number of reasons. The most common cause of speech delay is familial delay—in quite a few families, normal speech development simply starts later than usual as a rule. But a hearing impairment must always be considered, because normal speech does not develop in a child without hearing.

Sometimes language is delayed because of a more general developmental problem, such as mental retardation or autism (see Chapter 13).

Other speech disorders do not involve delay in speech onset; instead they affect various aspects of comprehension or expression. The most frequently seen problem is one of speech clarity: A child has normal speech content but has difficulty pronouncing certain words.

In such cases, assessment by a speech therapist and possibly a developmental pediatrician is needed. If hearing impairment is suspected, hearing tests will be necessary.

Social development and interaction
As with all other areas of development, children vary in when they develop social skills and how well they communicate at any particular age. Communication problems may relate to delays in speech and language development. Or a child who prefers to play alone may be shy or may just enjoy working alone. But in a few cases, problems with communication and social skills will be part of a more generalized disorder, such as autism.

Vision and hearing problems
Healthy development—particularly fine motor and language development—relies heavily on normal visual and hearing skills, so it's very important that problems in these areas are diagnosed early and treated appropriately. Routine examination, as well as testing in the early years, can reveal several eye

disorders and visual problems, as well as detecting many types of hearing impairment.

Cataract

A cataract is a clouding in the lens of the eye that prevents light from reaching the retina, where vision sensors are located. Although more common in the elderly, cataracts can be present at birth (congenital cataracts) or develop during childhood. One or both eyes may be affected.

How cataracts affect vision depends on their size and position in the lens. If they are large and central, their effects will be more noticeable than if they are small and lie away from the center of the visual path.

Cataracts may be discovered during a physical exam or may be diagnosed when other signs of poor vision in one or both eyes become apparent.

Surgery may be needed to remove the cataract if its effect on vision is significant.

Farsightedness (hyperopia)

Children who are farsighted are able to see things better far away than close up. It's a common condition that may be identified when your child's vision is assessed with an eye chart, or you may notice your child has difficulty with near vision. If he struggles when looking at picture books or squints, consult your pediatrician. Children with hyperopia often need glasses, although many will outgrow hyperopia by adulthood.

Nearsightedness (myopia)

Myopia is less common than farsightedness, but some young children are able to see things better close up than far away. Your child may have difficulty reading faraway signs or seeing the blackboard at school. Myopia may also be detected using the eye chart. Referral to an eye doctor is advised, and if required, glasses will be prescribed.

Crossed eyes (strabismus)

This occurs when the eyes aren't aligned correctly and appear to look in different directions. Crossed eyes can have various causes; at times it is due to

an imbalance in the many muscles involved in eye alignment, but more often it results because one eye doesn't see as well as the other, perhaps because of hyperopia or a cataract. Crossed eyes are common in newborns, but this usually resolves on its own by 2 to 3 months of age. If they don't disappear, your child may need to see an ophthalmologist. Treatment depends on the underlying cause and can include a patch or glasses, or, less commonly, surgery to better align muscles controlling eye movement.

Astigmatism

The cornea at the front of the eye has a smooth curve that helps bend light rays from objects in the field of vision to meet on the retina at the back of the eye and form an image. If the curve of the cornea isn't the correct shape, light rays don't meet on the retina as they should, and the resulting image is blurred. If you suspect impaired vision or your pediatrician detects it at a routine checkup,

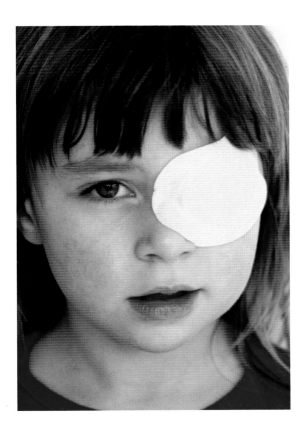

your child should see a pediatric ophthalmologist. Astigmatism may resolve as your child gets older. In the meantime, glasses may improve visual acuity.

Lazy eye (amblyopia)

Lazy eye, more properly known as amblyopia, can develop in young children if for any reason, such as farsightedness or astigmatism that's worse in one eye than the other, each eye sees a slightly different image. Blurred images result, which the brain finds undesirable. For the sake of clear vision, the brain reacts by ignoring one of the two images. If this is allowed to continue long enough, the brain areas that process visual impulses from the ignored eye will not develop and will not learn to see. The eyeball may be perfectly normal, but vision is lost because visual data from the affected eye are not interpreted by the brain. Early treatment can prevent amblyopia and includes relieving the cause of the blurred images; it may be treated by using glasses or wearing a patch over the stronger eye so the weaker eye is forced to work harder.

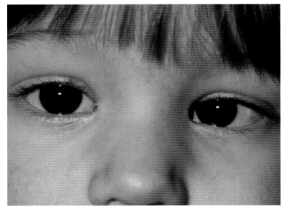

Toddler with amblyopia, or lazy eye.

MORE**ABOUT** | hypotonia

Low muscle tone, known as hypotonia, occurs in conditions such as Down syndrome, cerebral palsy, and muscular dystrophy, but it also can occur in otherwise normal, healthy infants (benign hypotonia). Children affected with hypotonia have muscles that are slow to begin muscle contraction, contract very slowly in response to a stimulus, and cannot maintain a contraction for as long as other children. They're sometimes described as "floppy" and may be unable to maintain any position for very long, such as holding up their heads or holding out their arms. They are prone to walking late and may shuffle on their bottoms for longer than usual. Physical therapy may help. Benign hypotonia improves as your child gets older.

Conductive hearing impairment

This type of hearing loss is caused by problems in the ear canal or middle ear, where the tiny bones called ossicles lie. The most common cause is otitis media, or middle-ear infection (see pages 344–345). In such cases, the hearing impairment is usually brief. Occasionally, however, the fluid in the middle ear persists and mild-to-moderate hearing impairment can continue for weeks. If your child has trouble hearing, your pediatrician will want to examine your child's ear and may suggest a tympanogram to get an idea of how much middle ear fluid, if any, is present. If your child is old enough to cooperate, a hearing test can also be performed. For persistent abnormalities, your child may be referred to a specialist. Treatment often consists of watchful waiting, as improvement is often seen without intervention, but at times it is best to give antibiotics for infection or to remove persistent fluid through surgery (placing tiny tubes through the eardrum to equalize pressure).

Sensorineural hearing impairment

A problem in the cochlea or with the auditory nerve that carries messages from the ear to the brain can cause sensorineural hearing impairment, an uncommon type of hearing loss that may be present at birth or develop during the first months of life. While no cause for the hearing loss can be found in many cases, sometimes it is the result of an infection in utero or the inheritance of a mutated gene. Unfortunately, it is a permanent condition.

Hearing aids or a cochlear implant can help. Children with sensorineural hearing loss may need special assistance at school. They may learn to speak, but speech skills probably will be delayed. Using simple sign language in the early years can help children learn to communicate.

Growth and weight gain

The rate at which young children grow and gain weight is an important indicator of their overall well-being (see also page 275).

Your pediatrician will track your child's weight gain, along with his height and head circumference, to check that he follows a normal, steady curve. Growth charts are different for boys and girls (see charts on pages 380–383).

Weight gain can falter occasionally—a short illness, for example, can temporarily slow growth—but overall it should rise steadily. If your baby's weight gain falls off significantly, your pediatrician may be concerned and consider whether an underlying medical condition is present. More commonly, it's linked to eating problems.

A thorough assessment of diet and feeding routines, developmental progress, and physical health is needed to identify the cause of growth faltering.

If you have any concerns about your child's growth, talk to your pediatrician right away.

Monitoring weight also helps identify children who may be gaining weight too rapidly. Obesity rates are increasing dramatically among all age groups in the United States, including young children. Heavy infants and children who gain weight rapidly during the first 2 years of life are at greater risk of being obese later in life. It's important to help your child establish healthy eating and activity habits early in life. Talk to your pediatrician for advice.

More about developmental problems
There is much more information about developmental problems and how parents can deal with them in the next chapter (Chapter 13, "Addressing health issues").

Vaccinations

Health experts recommend children receive more than a dozen vaccinations by the age of 6. Many are available as combination shots. Talk with your pediatrician about which vaccines your child will receive and when, and the possible side effects.

Why vaccinate your baby?

There are two key reasons to be sure your baby is vaccinated: to protect your baby from potentially serious diseases, and to protect other children.

Vaccines have spared children more illness and prevented more disability and death than any other discovery in the history of medicine. Don't assume that vaccines are no longer necessary because many of these childhood diseases are now uncommon. Whenever a vaccine is shunned, usually due to unfounded claims that it is harmful to children, large outbreaks of disease have resulted. An example of this phenomenon occurred in England over 30 years ago, when fear over the safety of the pertussis vaccine resulted in over a hundred thousand cases of whooping cough and many deaths.

It's important that as many children as possible get their childhood vaccinations. A small percentage of children cannot be vaccinated due to medical reasons. If enough of the population is vaccinated, these few vulnerable children are fairly well protected because there aren't enough unvaccinated children left to spread the infection. This is known as herd immunity. If vaccination rates decline, more children are left unprotected and uncommon diseases appear more frequently. There are currently outbreaks of pertussis (whooping cough) and measles in American communities with lower vaccination rates.

Some parents worry about the safety of vaccines. While no medical procedure is completely risk-free, the benefits of vaccination (protecting your child from serious diseases) far, far exceed the slim chance of a bad reaction to a vaccine. And it is absolutely clear that vaccines do not cause autism (see box, page 338).

What do these immunizations protect against?

Hepatitis B This viral disease attacks the liver, causing an acute hepatitis (liver infection). While most affected children and adults recover fully, hepatitis B is occasionally fatal, and a significant proportion of individuals become chronically infected and remain contagious. Chronic infection can result in cirrhosis and liver cancer. It can be passed from mother to baby during delivery, and older children and adults may acquire it from contact with blood or sexual contact.

The newborn dose of vaccine is given to prevent the spread of infection from a chronically infected but asymptomatic mother to her newborn during delivery. It's important to vaccinate babies, because more than half of people who are chronically infected with hepatitis B have no symptoms. While an adult who becomes infected has less than a 10 percent chance of becoming persistently infected, 90 percent of children with hepatitis B will develop lifelong disease.

Rotavirus Rotavirus is highly contagious and can cause severe vomiting, diarrhea, and dehydration. Nearly every child is infected with rotavirus in his first 2 years of life, and many have more than one bout of disease. The virus is spread on fingers and through contact with feces. The vaccine is given orally.

Diphtheria Now rare in developed countries, this bacterial infection affects the throat and can obstruct breathing. In addition, a toxin released by the bacteria can damage the heart. It's shared through coughing and sneezing. Diphtheria vaccine is usually given in the combination DTaP shot (diphtheria, tetanus, and pertussis) and requires a booster every 10 years.

Tetanus Tetanus, or lockjaw, is caused when bacteria from soil or feces infect a wound and release a toxic substance into the bloodstream. This toxin causes severe, painful muscle spasms throughout the body. Spasms of throat, chest, and jaw muscles can make swallowing and breathing difficult. Tetanus vaccine is included in the DTaP. After receiving the childhood series, the vaccine is given every 10 years. A "tetanus" booster also includes diphtheria vaccine and sometimes pertussis vaccine. Parents and adults surrounding a newborn should receive DTaP (unless they have had it recently) to protect the baby.

Pertussis This highly contagious bacterial illness, also known as whooping cough, causes bouts of coughing so severe that a child often may turn blue. The disease can be deadly in infants and young children. Vaccination has helped make whooping cough less common, but the bacteria still circulates in the United States. The vaccine is also included in the DTaP.

Polio The polio virus has become very rare in developed countries since the vaccine was introduced in the 1950s. The highly contagious virus, spread by contact with infected feces or saliva, can damage the nervous system, resulting in paralysis. There is no risk of contracting polio from inactivated poliovirus (IPV).

Haemophilus influenzae type B This bacterium can cause serious diseases including bacterial meningitis, a potentially deadly infection of the outer layers of the brain and spinal cord. It can also cause pneumonia; sepsis (infection in the blood); and epiglottitis, a life-threatening inflammation of the flap of cartilage that lies behind the tongue (see page 349). The Hib vaccine is given in two or three doses, depending on the vaccine given (there are two different versions of the vaccine), plus a booster.

Meningococcal disease This bacterium also can cause the life-threatening conditions of meningitis (see page 348) and sepsis. It's spread by respiratory and throat secretions during close contact, such as coughing or kissing. The meningococcal conjugate vaccine (MCV4) is routinely recommended for 11- to 18-year-olds, but high-risk children may receive the vaccine as young as 9 months of age. Planning for a

vaccine for U.S. infants is under way.

Measles Measles causes fever, a rash, and cold-type symptoms. In some cases it can cause serious and potentially life-threatening complications, including encephalitis or brain infection (see page 355). The vaccine is part of the measles, mumps, and rubella shot (MMR).

Mumps Mumps causes swelling of the salivary glands and can lead to meningitis and hearing loss.

THE SCHEDULE

Newborn	Hepatitis B (HepB)*
1–2 months	HepB
2 months	Diphtheria, tetanus, and pertussis (DTaP); rotavirus; polio (IPV); haemophilius influenzae type B (Hib); pneumococcal conjugate (PCV)
4 months	DTaP; rotavirus; IPV; Hib; PCV
6 months	DTaP; rotavirus; PCV; Hib**
6–18 months	HepB; IPV
12–15 months	Hib; measles, mumps, rubella (MMR); PCV; varicella
12–23 months	Hepatitis A (HepA), 2 doses
15–18 months	DTaP
4–6 years	DTaP; IPV; MMR, varicella

* If HepB is not given at birth, an alternative schedule (2 months, 4 months, and 6 months) may be used.
** A third dose of Hib at 6 months may or may not be given, depending on type of Hib vaccine used.

Rubella (German measles) Rubella symptoms tend to be mild, but serious complications, especially damage to an unborn child, can occur (see also page 356).

Pneumococcal disease The pneumococcus is a common cause of pneumonia (see page 347), meningitis (see page 348), and ear infections. The pneumococcal conjugate vaccine (PCV) protects against the most important strains of this bacterium.

Influenza Children over 6 months of age and their caregivers should be vaccinated against the flu every year, before the December-to-May flu season. Flu virus is very contagious and can cause ear infections, pneumonia, and even death.

Varicella Varicella, or chicken pox, causes a blister-like skin rash that is very itchy. Secondary bacterial infections of the skin, lung, and bloodstream can result in life-threatening illness. Chicken pox is especially severe in children being treated for cancer and those with weakened immune function.

Hepatitis A The hepatitis A virus causes liver disease. It's highly contagious and spread through feces, or via contaminated food or water. While infants with hepatitis A are often symptomless, they may spread infection to parents and other family members. Older children and adults typically recover after 2 to 3 weeks, but a number of fatal cases occur yearly.

Why babies aren't vaccinated

Your baby may not receive all of these vaccinations on time if she is more than mildly ill when she's due for a shot. But it is perfectly safe to vaccinate children who have head colds or minor illnesses.

Possible side effects

All vaccinations have possible side effects. Usually any problems are minor; serious complications such as severe allergic reactions are extremely rare. Your child might have swelling or redness at the site of the injection, fussiness, or a fever that night. Some vaccinations, such as measles and rubella, are live virus vaccines and can cause a mild form of the illness they protect against, giving about 1 in 10 vaccine recipients a fever and a rash in about a week.

Remember, the risk of serious complications following immunizations is much, much lower than the risks associated with the diseases themselves.

Travel vaccinations

Children may need vaccinations when traveling abroad. However, some vaccinations are not recommended for or given to very young children. Talk with your pediatrician well before your trip.

MORE ABOUT | mmr vaccination

Some parents have worried about possible complications associated with the measles, mumps, and rubella vaccine—particularly autism (see page 375) and inflammatory bowel disease. These links were suggested in a now-discredited paper published by a British doctor in 1998, which looked at only 12 children with autism and inflammatory bowel disease. After this study, MMR vaccination rates fell dramatically. The incidence of measles rose, which is very worrisome in light of the serious and potentially life-threatening complications it can cause.

The 1998 study has since been described as fraudulent by a British medical journal, and Britain has revoked the medical license of the study's lead author. Since 1998, more than 20 studies addressing this issue have, without exception, found no relationship between MMR and autism.

While your rational side may realize that MMR does not cause autism, your emotional side may still be concerned. It's worth remembering that the MMR vaccine has been given to millions of children around the world. The protection this vaccine offers against three potentially serious and sometimes life-threatening illnesses is a major benefit for your child.

When your baby is unwell

It's normal to feel anxious and worry when your baby is sick. Becoming more familiar with the signs of common childhood illnesses and simple ways you can ease symptoms will make you more confident in caring for your baby and knowing when she needs medical help.

Fevers

Normal body temperature is around 98.6°F in adults, but is roughly 1 degree higher in infants and toddlers. Whether well or sick with a fever, your child's temperature can vary over the course of a day, with the highest temperatures late in the evening and lowest ones a few hours before breakfast. A raised temperature or fever is a sign that your child's immune system is working to get rid of an infection.

Despite centuries of incorrectly thinking about fever as the source of illness, we now know that fever itself is not the enemy. As it turns out, fever is part of our body's defense against infection and serves a number of useful functions, including "turning on" our immune system. Though it may be hard to believe, fever is actually good for your sick child!

There is no correlation between the height of fever and the severity of a child's illness. But because of misinformation, there often is a correlation between the height of fever and a parent's panic. In fact, most 105°F fevers are caused by mild, viral illnesses, while many children who are critically ill with life-threatening infections may have little or no fever. The best way to judge if your child has a serious infection (as opposed to a "regular" illness) is by observing his behavior, not his temperature.

Measuring body temperature

You can use a digital thermometer orally, rectally, or under your child's armpit. And otic thermometers can take your child's temperature in her ear.

Rectal temperatures are most accurate—otic thermometers automatically convert the temperature in the ear to an "equivalent" rectal temperature by using a mathematical formula.

Treating a fever

Fevers often are associated with shivering, headaches, and other signs of illness. They're common during childhood illnesses and usually short-lived. They're rarely serious. If your baby has a fever she may be flushed and feel hot to the touch.

♦ Make sure she drinks plenty of liquids.
♦ Don't use too many blankets or clothes. If she is having chills, wrap her in a blanket. Otherwise dress her lightly.
♦ Don't overheat the room; be guided by whether you feel comfortable in normal indoor clothing.
♦ Give her medication to relieve her symptoms if she is uncomfortable, not just to bring down her fever (see box, below).

Repeatedly checking your child's temperature serves no purpose other than to heighten your worrying. Yet this is exactly what most parents do. Instead, consider her behavior and activity level when trying to assess how sick she might be.

Fever in a newborn or young infant is more

MORE ABOUT | children's medications

To treat fever and pain in children, pediatricians usually recommend children's preparations of acetaminophen or ibuprofen, which can be bought over the counter. As with all medicines, it's very important to read the label carefully and give only the recommended dosages. Do not give drugs containing aspirin to children under the age of 12 because of the small but significant risk of Reye's syndrome, a serious condition that affects the brain and liver.

concerning. If your baby is younger than 3 months and has a rectal temperature at or above 100.4°F or higher, seek medical help right away.

Giving medicines

Babies usually aren't very enthusiastic about taking medicine. You'll need time, patience, and ideally a helper to hold your baby while you administer her medicine. Be as relaxed as possible: If you're anxious, your child will feel anxious as well.

Oral medicine

You can give liquid medicine with a measuring spoon, but a syringe is usually easier with a young or unwilling child and allows more accurate measurement of the dose. Prop up your baby or have her sit so that her head is higher than her body. Have a favorite drink ready for right afterward—but avoid actually mixing the medicine with food or drinks because, if everything isn't finished, she may not get the full dose. You may be able to crush tablets and dissolve them in water, or mix the crushed tablet with a bit of applesauce. A number of pharmacies now offer multiple flavors that can be added to your child's prescription medicine to improve its taste. Check with your pediatrician or pharmacist. It might be easier to give your child her medicine before she eats, but check the medication instructions first.

Ear drops

Sit or lay your baby next to you with her head resting on its side on your knee. Pull her ear upward and back slightly to straighten the ear canal and allow the drops to fall straight in. Keep

---

HEALTHFIRST	seeking medical advice

By far the best and most accurate way to judge the severity of illness is by considering your child's behavior, not how high her fever is. For example, if your fussy child has periods when she seems almost back to normal in behavior and activity, even if this occurs after acetaminophen or ibuprofen has been given, it is likely that nothing serious is going on.

Consult her doctor if your baby:

- *Seems sleepier than normal and is lethargic during times she's usually alert and active*
- *Seems floppier than usual*
- *Is very fussy, without periods of better behavior and activity, or is not consolable or very difficult to console*
- *Has a cry that sounds different from her typical cry*
- *Is drinking less than half of what she usually does*
- *Is passing less urine than usual*
- *Is vomiting or passing blood in her stools*
- *Has a temperature that persists for more than 48 to 72 hours*
- *Has a severe, persistent, or mucousy-sounding cough*
- *Seems to be having trouble breathing*
- *Has one or more purplish-red spots (see pages 348–349)*
- *Looks very sick to you*
- *Is in a high-risk category and has a fever: Call if she is 3 months of age or younger, has cancer or an immune deficiency, or takes medications that weaken the immune system*

---

her head on its side for a few minutes to prevent the drops from trickling out again. When she returns to the upright position, wipe away all leftover drops exiting from her ear.

Eye drops

Lay your baby across your knee on her back and support her head in the crook of your arm. Gently pull her bottom eyelid down so that the drops can fall as they should between the eyeball and the lower lid. You'll probably need a helper so that you can hold your child still and open up her eye, or try swaddling her in a blanket to keep her arms out of the way.

Cuts and scrapes

It's important to stop any bleeding and prevent

infection from entering the wound. Wash your hands thoroughly first. Rinse the wound under cold running water to remove any dirt. Clean it with wipes or swabs, using a new one every time you wipe across the area. Start with the wound itself and then clean the surrounding skin to avoid introducing bacteria into the wound. Pat dry and apply antibiotic ointment. Apply an adhesive bandage over small cuts; for larger wounds, tape the dressing in place.

Bruises

When small blood vessels are damaged—often from being bumped or banged hard—and allow blood to leak out into the surrounding tissues, you'll see a bruise. Treat bruises by controlling any swelling and relieving discomfort.

Bruising can develop quickly. Applying a cold compress or an ice pack will help reduce any swelling. If you don't have a cold pack, you can put ice in a bag, soak a cloth in cold water and wring it out, or even use a bag of frozen vegetables; always wrap the cold pack in something like a clean hand towel or wash cloth, so the ice is not directly on the skin. Hold the compress over the area for 5 to 10 minutes. Bruises can appear gradually over a period of days if the blood leaks out of the blood vessels slowly. It can take up to 2 weeks for a bruise to disappear completely. At the other extreme, when hit on the forehead, your child may quickly develop an egg-shaped bruise that will disappear within minutes when ice is applied.

Animal bites

Wash an animal bite carefully with soap and water and pat dry. Apply antibiotic ointment, then cover the injury with an adhesive bandage or sterile dressing. Be sure to contact your child's doctor because he might need antibiotics, a tetanus booster, or other treatment. Acetaminophen or ibuprofen can help relieve pain.

If the wound is bleeding, apply firm pressure with a clean cloth or sterile dressing and raise the injured

MORE **ABOUT** | febrile convulsions

Convulsions are relatively common in childhood and can occur when body temperature rises rapidly. About 2 in 100 children are affected between the ages of 6 months and 5 years. Febrile convulsions often run in families and feature stiffening and then jerking of the body.

If your baby has these symptoms, you should:

- ◆ *Lay her on her side, ideally with her head lower than the rest of her body.*
- ◆ *Let the convulsion run its course—don't try to hold her still or restrain her.*
- ◆ *Call 911 if the convulsion lasts more than 5 minutes. Otherwise, seek urgent medical advice once the convulsion has stopped. A doctor should check your child and try to find the underlying cause of the raised temperature. This assessment may include blood and urine tests, as well as an examination of your child's ears, throat, and chest.*

In most cases, febrile convulsions are caused by a viral illness that requires no treatment other than typical measures to bring down a fever (see page 339). However, sometimes they're caused by a bacterial infection that must be treated with antibiotics.

Your doctor will give you advice on dealing with a fever and a convulsion in case they happen again. (Up to 40 percent of children who have a convulsion will have another one in the future.)

The risk of another seizure usually ends as the child gets older. However, a few children who have prolonged, more severe fits or have convulsions that occur more than once during the same illness may be more likely to develop epilepsy.

limb. If the wound is very deep or big, or if it continues to bleed, stitches (sutures) may be needed, so seek medical help.

Cat scratches

Carefully wash scratches from cats and apply antibiotic ointment.

Burns

Quickly remove wet clothing if the burn is from hot water. For all burns, apply cool compresses (not ice) and loosely cover the burn with sterile gauze or dressing. Acetaminophen or ibuprofen can ease pain. (For more about burn first aid, see page 323.) If the burn covers a large area— or if your child has blisters, swelling, fever, or faintness—seek urgent medical help.

For a sunburn, apply aloe gel or moisturizing cream and give her plenty of cool fluids. Apply cool compresses and give acetaminophen or ibuprofen for relief of pain. (For ways to protect your baby from the sun, see page 322.)

Stings

If a stinger is embedded in your child's skin, try

to remove it by scraping across the area or using tweezers. An ice pack can relieve discomfort and swelling. If your child shows signs of an allergic reaction such as hives, trouble breathing, or vomiting—symptoms will usually appear within minutes of the bite—call 911.

Splinters

Any foreign object in the skin should be removed promptly to avoid infection. Wash the area around the splinter with soap and water. Sterilize a needle and tweezers by running them under boiling water or holding them in the flame of a match for a second, then wipe with a sterile pad or alcohol. If the end of the splinter is sticking out of the skin, grab hold of it with the tweezers and pull it out firmly but gently, in the same direction as it

MORE**ABOUT**   anaphylaxis

Anaphylaxis is a severe allergic reaction to an insect sting or a particular food, such as peanuts (see page 377). Such reactions are relatively uncommon, but if your child has anaphylaxis he'll need immediate medical help—it can be life-threatening.

Symptoms appear within minutes of exposure and may include breathing difficulties and wheeziness; swelling of the face, neck, lips, and around the eyes; abdominal pain, nausea, and vomiting; and redness of the skin (hives). A child may become unconscious (see pages 42–43 and 188 for emergency first aid).

If you think your child may be having an

anaphylactic reaction, call 911. While you wait for help, sit him up to help his breathing. Talk to him reassuringly to calm him as much as possible.

Children who have had severe allergic reactions and are known to be at risk of anaphylaxis are usually prescribed epinephrine. A special pen device called an epinephrine auto-injector swiftly delivers the drug into the bloodstream.

If your child is at risk of anaphylaxis, make sure you and all other caregivers have access to and know how to use the auto-injector.

entered the skin. If the splinter is completely embedded, use the needle to gently scrape away the overlying skin so you can grab hold of it. Make sure no pieces are left in the skin, then clean the area. If the splinter is too deep to remove or becomes red, swollen, or sore, take your child to a doctor.

Foreign objects

When curious young children get hold of small objects, there's a good chance they'll put them in their mouths, in their ears, or up their noses.

If your baby swallows an object, call your pediatrician for advice. Most objects, once they reach the stomach, will be passed uneventfully in the stool after a few days. Persistent coughing or drooling may signal an object caught in the esophagus or in the wind pipe (trachea). Also seek help if your child swallows magnets, batteries, or any poisons.

If your child puts something into her ear, check whether the object is visible. Try tilting her head to see whether it falls out. If it remains stuck, bring her to a doctor. Don't try to remove it: It's easy to push it farther in and damage the delicate structures inside the ear.

If something becomes stuck in your child's nose, teach her to blow air out through her nose with her mouth closed. Compress and hold the opposite nostril closed and have her blow hard through the nostril on the side of the foreign object. If this doesn't succeed in ejecting the object, consult a doctor.

If your child is prescribed a drug, it's important to ask the following questions. Your pediatrician or pharmacist can advise you.
- *What is the drug for?*
- *How much should be given, how often, and for how long?*
- *When should it be taken? Should it be taken with food?*
- *What are the possible side effects?*

Be sure the doctor prescribing the medicine is aware of any other drugs your child is taking and of any other health conditions.

At home, always:
- *Read the label carefully. Check the name of the drug, the dosage, and the use-by date.*
- *Measure medication carefully with a syringe or measuring spoon, as directed by your doctor.*
- *Finish courses of antibiotics, which usually are prescribed for a certain number of days, even if symptoms disappear.*
- *Keep medication in a cool, dry place away from sunlight, unless advised to keep it refrigerated. Always keep medicines out of reach of your child.*

YOUR FIRST-AID KIT

You can buy a first-aid kit and add to it, or assemble your own. Keep the kit safely out of your child's reach. Be sure to replace items that have expired. Your kit should include:
- Thermometer
- Acetaminophen or ibuprofen
- Diphenhydramine (Benadryl) for allergic reactions
- Calamine lotion
- Antiseptic wipes
- Antibiotic ointment
- Scissors
- Adhesive and elastic bandages
- Adhesive tape
- Sterile gauze
- Syringe or measuring spoon for dosing medicine
- Disposable gloves

Childhood illnesses

Although no parent wants his or her child to get sick, it's inevitable and part of the human experience to sometimes fall ill. Most of the childhood ailments described here are common enough that a number will be experienced by your child. A few, such as meningitis and epiglottitis, are unusual, but it's good to be aware of the warning signs so you will know that your child needs medical help. To reduce your child's risk of illness, practice—and teach—good handwashing habits and don't share drinking glasses or utensils. Be sure your child is up to date on vaccinations.

Colds

Viral infections commonly cause colds and sniffles in early childhood. Thousands of different viruses cause these upper respiratory infections. Your child will begin picking up these viruses shortly after birth when she starts to come into contact with infections that her immune system hasn't encountered before. Cold viruses are often shared through coughs and sneezes, and when children touch their noses and then touch another child. Toys picked up by your child that were previously held by or in the mouth of another child also can spread germs. And contrary to popular belief, going outside without a coat or with wet hair won't cause your child to catch a cold.

Symptoms

When your child has a cold, she may have a runny or blocked nose, sneezing, and sometimes a fever. Other symptoms include a sore throat, a cough that's often worse at night, poor appetite, lethargy, and fatigue. Colds usually last about a week.

Children with colds may develop other illnesses, such as chest and ear infections. These may result from so-called secondary bacterial infections, when bacteria normally found in or on the body take advantage of weakened local defenses caused by the viral attack. Even a simple cold can be associated with a high temperature in children.

Treatment

You can relieve your child's symptoms and help keep her comfortable by making sure she gets plenty of fluids and giving her acetaminophen or ibuprofen to temporarily relieve aches and pains. Saline nose drops, a humidifier, or inhaling steam from a nearby hot shower can relieve stuffiness and congestion. Don't give over-the-counter cough or cold medicine to children under 4, unless recommended by your child's doctor. Consult a doctor if she:

- Is very lethargic
- Isn't drinking
- Has a persistent cough or brings up a lot of mucus
- Is having breathing difficulties or is wheezy
- Is pulling on her ear
- Is very sick and you are worried

Of course, you should seek medical advice if you have any other concerns.

Ear infections

Acute infections of the middle ear (otitis media) are common and can be caused by both bacteria and viruses. Many children have repeated episodes

because their Eustachian tube, which connects the middle ear cavity with the back part of the nose, is short and positioned horizontally rather than at an angle. Luckily, as she grows your child will develop a stiffer and more angled Eustachian tube, and she will get far fewer ear infections.

To understand how ear infections occur and why fluid sometimes accumulates in the middle ear cavity, it helps to learn more about the anatomy of the middle ear. There are three sections of the ear that allow us to hear: the external, middle, and inner ear. The external ear consists of skin-covered structures: the earlobe and the ear canal. The middle ear consists of the eardrum and the three ossicles (tiny bones) that transmit sound vibrations from the eardrum to the inner ear, where the hearing apparatus is located. The middle ear cavity is normally filled with air. The Eustachian tube opens and closes to allow middle ear pressure to adjust so that it is equal to pressure outside the body.

When a child has a head cold and stuffy nose, the Eustachian tube can sometimes become obstructed or stuck in the closed position. Two problems can result from this. First, harmless bacteria normally living in the nose can ascend the Eustachian tube and cause infection in the middle ear. The cells lining the middle ear cavity secrete mucus when infection is present, and pus fills the middle ear. The pressure of the increasingly large amount of thick fluid against the eardrum causes the pain of an ear infection. Second, in a middle ear that does not have infection (or at the end of an infection that is being cleaned up), the lining cells will sense low middle-ear pressure (the Eustachian tube is unable to open and pressure cannot be equalized). In response to the low pressure, the cells secrete a clear, watery fluid, called serous fluid. This fluid accumulates and persists in the middle ear until, at the end of the cold, the Eustachian tube regains its function and opens again. The fluid is removed, and the middle-ear cavity is again filled with air. When pus or fluid fills the middle ear, the fluid lessens the eardrum's mobility, dampening the sound vibrations and perhaps decreasing hearing.

Symptoms

Symptoms of a head cold are usually present, including a runny nose, sniffles, a cough, and perhaps a fever. Your child may pull on her ear due to pain. She may not have much of an appetite. Young children who may not be able to explain ear pain may just seem miserable.

A very inflamed eardrum occasionally may rupture—meaning pressure has caused a tiny hole to open—allowing fluid to drain to the outside. The perforation should eventually heal.

Diagnosis and treatment

Your doctor will examine your baby's ears to look for redness and bulging of the eardrum. Medication can relieve pain and bring down fever. Depending on many factors (such as your child's age, the severity of symptoms, and the personal preference of parents and doctor), antibiotics may or may not be prescribed for the infection. Because the condition at times can clear up without treatment, watchful waiting is sometimes an option.

If your child has recurring ear infections, her doctor may recommend surgically inserting ear tubes. In a number of children, the Eustachian tube continues to malfunction even after the cold is all better, and serous fluid remains in the middle ear for weeks or even months. This is especially likely to occur in children who get frequent ear infections. Your doctor will usually give middle-ear fluid a chance to go away by itself. But under some circumstances, such as a significant hearing loss, fluid present continuously for more than 3 months, or frequent ear infections in an infant or younger toddler, surgery may be helpful. During surgery, "tubes" (formally known as pressurizing tubes; one per ear) usually are inserted. Occasionally the adenoids are removed as well, to prevent obstruction of the nasal end of the Eustachian tube. A tube straddles the eardrum and allows air to freely pass through it, keeping middle-ear pressure the same as pressure outside the body. The tube bypasses the need for the Eustachian tube to open and close. Now that middle-ear pressure is normal, the lining cells stop secreting fluid. Hearing quickly improves, and in many children, because low middle-ear pressure is one of the factors favoring middle-ear infection, ear infections become much less frequent.

Bronchiolitis

An inflammation of the small airways in the lungs (the bronchioles), bronchiolitis is usually caused by a virus called RSV (respiratory syncytial virus). The disease mainly occurs in the first 2 years of life and usually is mild. However, it can cause breathing problems and require hospitalization.

Symptoms

Cold symptoms usually develop first and may be followed 2 to 3 days later by a dry cough. Your child may become short of breath and wheezy. Shortness of breath may interfere with feeding. If your baby develops breathing difficulties, seek medical advice.

Diagnosis and treatment

Your doctor will examine your baby by listening to her chest and may take a sample of nasal secretions with a swab to test for the presence of RSV. Except in milder cases, a chest X-ray may be ordered.

Babies with mild symptoms usually can be cared for by their parents at home. Acetaminophen may be given for aches and pains. Encourage fluids. A humidifier may also help relieve the symptoms.

Children who are hospitalized are usually treated with oxygen and drugs to widen the airway. Bronchodilator drugs are given through a nebulizer, which delivers the airborne medication through a mask. Children also may be given fluids intravenously if they are not drinking well.

Most children recover within a few days, although some may be more prone to coughing and wheezing in the future.

Sore throats and tonsillitis

A viral or, more rarely, a bacterial infection can cause inflammation of the throat (pharyngitis), or the tonsils (tonsillitis) that lie at the back of the mouth.

Symptoms

Your child may have a sore throat, lethargy, fever, headache, stomachache, vomiting, and swollen glands in the neck. The back of the throat will appear red, and the tonsils may be red, enlarged, and sometimes dotted with small patches of pus.

Treatment

Most sore throats and episodes of tonsillitis are caused by viruses and supportive treatment is all that is needed. If strep throat is suspected, a throat swab will be taken, and if the test is positive for strep, antibiotics are prescribed as well.

Sore throats and tonsillitis, whether viral or strep throat, usually go away within a few days.

Croup

In this common condition, a viral infection affects the larynx (the voice box) and the trachea (windpipe) just below it. Several viruses can cause croup, which is more common in autumn but occurs throughout the year. Children under the age of 3 are usually the most severely affected.

Symptoms

Croup often starts with a low-grade fever and cold-type symptoms, such as a runny nose and sniffles, followed by the main symptoms: a barking cough, noisy breathing (particularly when inhaling), and hoarseness. These symptoms tend to be worse at night. If severe, inflammation can cause narrowing of the trachea and breathing difficulties.

Treatment

If your child's symptoms are mild, you can care for her at home by making sure she has plenty of fluids and treating aches and pains with acetaminophen or ibuprofen. Sitting in the bathroom for a few minutes breathing in steam (sit outside of the hot shower) often relieves sudden bouts of coughing, which characteristically occur at midnight. Alternatively, having your child breathe in cold nighttime air also relieves the croupy cough. A humidifier can also help ease symptoms. Consult your doctor if her breathing is labored, she draws her chest in when she breathes, or she makes a loud noise when breathing in. Children who are hospitalized with croup may be given IV fluids, medication to reduce airway swelling, and perhaps oxygen.

Influenza

More often known as the flu, this viral illness is highly contagious. Infants tend to have the most severe cases of influenza among all children. Annual flu vaccination offers protection against flu viruses and is recommended for all children. You can further protect your child by being sure you and all other household members get the vaccine as well.

Symptoms

Symptoms, which develop within a couple of days of exposure, are similar to those of a cold but more severe. If your child has the flu, she may have a fever, chills, a runny nose, a dry cough, and perhaps sneezing. She may have a sore throat and swollen glands, and she probably will have muscle aches and little appetite.

Flu may be complicated by a bacterial infection, such as pneumonia or otitis (ear infection). Babies and young children are particularly vulnerable to these so-called secondary infections.

Treatment

Acetaminophen or ibuprofen can relieve aches and pains. It is important to allow her to rest and to ensure that she has plenty of fluids to keep her well hydrated. Antiviral drugs (Tamiflu, Relenza) may also be prescribed.

Symptoms should ease after a few days. Seek medical advice if your baby is very young and develops a fever; symptoms persist for more than a few days; she has breathing difficulties or wheezing, earache, discharge from the ear, or a bad cough; or you are worried.

Lung infections

This covers a number of conditions including bronchitis—in which the upper airways of the lungs become inflamed—and pneumonia, which affects tissue deep within the lungs.

Bronchitis can be caused by both bacterial and viral infections and affects children of all ages. Infection is spread through coughs and sneezes.

Pneumonia is more serious. It is also caused by many different pathogens. Pneumonia affects all ages, but very young children and those with long-term illnesses are especially at risk.

Symptoms

Bronchitis is usually marked by cold-type symptoms and a mucousy cough, which may be worse during the night. Your child also may wheeze.

Children with pneumonia may start with a cold and then become sicker, with a worsening cough and fever. Breathing may become rapid or labored.

Seek prompt medical attention if your baby has a persistent or severe cough or breathing difficulties.

Diagnosis and treatment

Lung infections usually are diagnosed by listening to the chest through a stethoscope, and sometimes with a chest X-ray. Antibiotics may be prescribed and in more severe cases, can be given intravenously in the hospital. At home, you may give your child medicine to relieve pain, along with plenty of fluids.

The amount of illness accompanying pneumonia ranges from mild ("walking pneumonia") to quite serious. Hospitalization is sometimes necessary, but most cases can be treated at home.

The worst symptoms of both pneumonia and bronchitis should pass in a few days, but the cough may persist for a week or two.

Whooping cough

Pertussis, or whooping cough, is a respiratory infection caused by the bacterium *Bordetella pertussis*. Infection of the airways may affect the tissue of the lungs. Although most children recover fully, whooping cough is dangerous for infants and small children, and can be life-threatening.

Whooping cough vaccination doesn't guarantee 100 percent protection, but it does greatly reduce the risk of contracting the disease. Vaccinated children who get whooping cough have much less severe illnesses.

Symptoms

Children with whooping cough usually have cold-type symptoms for a week before developing the characteristic cough, which occurs in long bouts, with whooping noises at the end of an inhalation. The cough may be so severe that an affected child turns blue during a coughing fit.

The force of coughing can cause vomiting, and tiny blood vessels in the conjunctiva (the whites of the eyes) may burst, causing small red spots. Infants with pertussis may stop breathing for short periods and may not produce the whooping sound.

Bouts of coughing can go on for up to 6 weeks, and coughing can continue for months.

Treatment

Many children can be cared for at home. But children who have severe bouts of coughing and babies who have episodes of apnea need to be hospitalized for monitoring and treatment.

Antibiotics reduce contagiousness, but care is primarily supportive. Anyone who has had contact with a child who has whooping cough also should receive antibiotics.

Meningitis

Meningitis is inflammation of the membranes that surround the brain and spinal cord (the meninges). The most common causes are viral and bacterial infections. Viral meningitis tends to be milder. With bacterial meningitis, symptoms are more severe and come on rapidly.

Symptoms

Babies with meningitis may have these signs:

- Fever
- Vomiting
- Less alertness than usual
- Poor feeding
- Floppiness and drowsiness
- Bulging of the anterior fontanelle in infants
- Stiff neck (can't move head up and down) in toddlers and older children
- Seizures and loss of consciousness

Children with meningitis also may be lethargic and have a headache and sensitivity to light.

In bacterial meningitis (or serious bloodstream infections), a rash first appears as tiny, flat purplish spots; it then spreads to form purplish-red patches that may appear anywhere on the body (see box, opposite page).

If you suspect meningitis for any reason or see a rash of flat, purplish spots, seek immediate medical attention.

Although children with viral meningitis usually recover over a few days, meningitis is a potentially life-threatening condition requiring urgent treatment. Some children recover fully, but others sustain long-term problems, such as hearing loss, epilepsy, or other neurological deficits.

Diagnosis

The doctor probably will carry out a lumbar (low back) puncture, removing fluid from the space surrounding the spinal cord. Cultures of blood and

Meningitis symptoms can be vague and difficult to identify in babies, so it's important to be alert for any signs that your child may be unwell. If you don't see any sign of a rash, that doesn't mean you can rule out bacterial meningitis—in many cases there is no rash, or the rash develops late in the course of the disease.

To check whether a rash is cause for concern, press a clear glass firmly over any pinprick-sized, flat red spots or large purple marks to see if they fade or turn white under pressure. If the spots and rash remain visible through the glass and do not fade, seek immediate medical attention.

No matter the results of the glass test, seek advice immediately if you have any concerns. No one will fault you for being cautious.

spinal fluid will help identify any bacterial infection.

Treatment

Bacterial meningitis requires immediate treatment with intravenous antibiotics. Intravenous fluids and other supportive measures may be needed. Children with viral meningitis usually need only simple measures to relieve symptoms and provide fluids.

Epiglottitis

This is a very serious condition in which the epiglottis (the flap of tissue at the back of the tongue that covers and protects the trachea when we are passing food or liquids into our esophagus) becomes inflamed and swollen due to infection with the Haemophilus influenzae type B bacterium. Epiglottitis has become much less common since the introduction of the Hib vaccine.

Swelling of the epiglottis and the surrounding tissues limits the flow of air into the trachea and down into the lungs. The infection also passes into the bloodstream (this is called sepsis), causing the affected child to become very ill. Children between the ages of 1 and 6 are particularly at risk.

Symptoms

A child with epiglottitis will have a high temperature and feel poorly. A very painful throat makes it impossible to swallow, causing drooling. Breathing is noisy, and the child will soon have difficulty breathing; she'll need to keep her mouth open to breathe and sit very still. If your child has these symptoms, she needs immediate medical attention.

Treatment

A doctor will start treatment to ensure an open airway immediately when epiglottitis is suspected. The first step is intubation: inserting a tube through the mouth and into the trachea. This is followed by intravenous antibiotics. Once treatment has begun, children usually recover fully within a few days. Anyone who has close contact with a child with epiglottitis should receive antibiotics as a precaution.

Conjunctivitis or pinkeye

Inflammation of the conjunctiva—the tissue that covers the eyeball and lines the eyelid—is common, particularly in the first weeks after birth. Viruses, bacteria, and allergies can cause conjunctivitis, which usually heals without medication.

Symptoms

Your child may have red, itchy, or painful eyes with thick, yellow-green discharge.

Treatment

Clean away the sticky discharge with a cotton ball dipped in water; use a fresh cotton ball for each eye.

Consult your pediatrician to decide how to treat conjunctivitis. If it's caused by a bacterial infection, your child may need antibiotic eye drops or ointment. Conjunctivitis can also be caused by viruses (in which case drops are not needed) or by allergies (such as to pollen or cats). Your doctor might also be able to suggest treatment consisting of oral medication or eye drops to ease the discomfort of conjunctivitis caused by allergies or a virus.

Infectious conjunctivitis is easily passed on to others. Causative bacteria and viruses are spread on fingers and inanimate objects, such as toys and computers that were touched by a contagious child. Don't share towels or pillows used by the affected child. Keep children with viral conjunctivitis at home and away from school and friends until the infection clears up. Children with bacterial conjunctivitis are considered no longer infectious when they have been treated with antibiotic eye drops for 24 hours. Allergic conjunctivitis is not contagious.

Urinary tract infections

Urinary tract infections (UTIs), which are relatively common in childhood, may affect the bladder (cystitis) or kidneys (pyelonephritis). Most UTIs occur in girls and result from fecal bacteria ascending the urethra (which connects the bladder to the outside world). Poor wiping technique after going to the bathroom is often a contributing factor. Some children, however, have a "plumbing" problem in the urinary tract that makes them more prone to infections (see *Vesico-ureteral reflux,* opposite page). It's very important to treat pyelonephritis as soon as possible to prevent damage to the kidneys.

Symptoms

Symptoms tend to vary according to the age of the child. Babies will seem generally unwell, with a fever and possibly a tummy ache. They may vomit, have diarrhea, and have no appetite.

Older children will have the same nonspecific symptoms as with any infectious illness—fever, lethargy, poor appetite, vomiting, and diarrhea. If they're talking, they also may describe more specific symptoms, such as urinating more frequently than usual, painful urination, abdominal pain, and pain in the small of the back with kidney involvement. A child who is toilet trained may have daytime accidents or start to wet the bed again.

While symptoms such as burning and frequent urination are common in both cystitis and pyelonephritis, generalized symptoms such as fever are mild in cystitis and more prominent in pyelonephritis.

Diagnosis and treatment

When symptoms suggest a UTI, or when your young infant has no symptoms other than a fever, your doctor will obtain a urine specimen from your child. Urinalysis, usually done in the office, can quickly give valuable clues to the presence of a UTI. To prove infection, a urine culture is performed.

Antibiotic treatment of cystitis usually is started before results of the urine culture are available if symptoms and urinalysis suggest an infection. When the diagnosis is uncertain, however, it is often prudent to withhold antibiotic treatment until culture results are available.

Pyelonephritis, if suspected, is treated immediately and may require intravenous antibiotics in the hospital.

SIGNS OF DEHYDRATION

Young children can easily become dehydrated when they're sick. Signs of dehydration include:

- Urinating less than usual
- Sunken eyes
- Dry skin
- Dry mouth
- Lethargy
- Breathing more rapidly than usual
- Less alert than usual or drowsy

Gastroenteritis and food poisoning

Upset stomachs with vomiting and diarrhea are common for all ages, but babies and young children get them often due to poor hygiene and their habit of putting everything in their mouths. They are particularly at risk of becoming dehydrated because their fluid losses are proportionately larger, and when sick they often drink much less than usual. Gastroenteritis may be caused by a variety of bacteria and viruses, but viruses cause the vast majority. The most common cause of infectious gastroenteritis in children is rotavirus, which is especially common in winter. Bacterial infections occur less frequently. Gastroenteritis from "food poisoning"—caused by bacteria or toxins in the food, not poison—results from poor hygienic practices when handling foods (see pages 231 and 309–310).

Symptoms

Your child will have crampy abdominal pain, vomiting, and diarrhea, perhaps accompanied by fever or listlessness. Watch for signs of dehydration (see box, opposite page).

Blood in stools usually indicates a bacterial infection and is often accompanied by abdominal pain.

Treatment

The most important part of the treatment of gastroenteritis is to make sure your child doesn't become dehydrated. Your doctor may recommend oral electrolyte solutions, but fluids containing salt and sugar—such as ginger ale or sports drinks—usually suffice. Giving sips or small amounts (½ ounce at a time) of fluids every few minutes is more successful than having your child ingest larger amounts, which are

COLLECTING URINE SAMPLES

A urine sample can be collected from a young child by catching a specimen in a clean cup when the diaper is removed, or by securing a plastic bag over the genitalia with adhesive tape and waiting until the child passes urine. The area should first be cleaned carefully to remove skin bacteria that could contaminate the urine culture. Doctors may also obtain bladder urine by catheterization. This method has a lower chance of contamination by skin bacteria, and you don't need to wait until your child voids. However, there is some discomfort involved.

Older children can be asked to give a midstream sample of urine.

MORE **ABOUT** | **vesico-ureteral reflux (vur)**

Veisco-ureteral reflux, or VUR, results from an abnormality in the development of the urinary tract. The ureters are tubes that lead from the kidneys to the bladder. They usually meet the bladder at a defined angle that acts as a valve, preventing urine in the bladder from flowing back up the ureters. With VUR, this valve does not function properly. The condition often runs in families. It may be very mild, with urine flowing up into the lower part of the ureters when the bladder contracts to expel urine, or it may be severe and cause urine to flow all the way back into the kidneys. Removing bacteria that reach the bladder by urinating them out is a major defense against UTI. However, in a child with VUR, the refluxed urine is not voided and remains in the bladder, allowing bacteria to remain there as well. Thus VUR raises a child's chance of getting a UTI. More severe grades of VUR may permit bladder bacteria to reach the kidneys.

Mild degrees of VUR usually resolve with time. Children with higher grades are often given daily antibiotics to prevent further infection, but ultimately they may need repair of the valve.

Children with a diagnosed urinary tract infection are sometimes examined for evidence of reflux. This can include an ultrasound scan or X-rays.

often vomited. Once she's no longer vomiting and can keep liquids in, she can have food and drink as normal.

You should contact your doctor if:

- Your child is drinking poorly or throwing up whatever fluids are ingested
- Your baby shows any signs of dehydration
- There is blood in the stool
- Your baby looks very ill

Children who become dehydrated may need to be hospitalized and receive intravenous fluids. But in most cases of gastroenteritis, the illness is short-lived and resolves on its own.

Don't watch and wait for the signs of dehydration. If your baby has an upset stomach, make sure she has plenty of fluids right away.

Constipation

Some babies pass stools every day; others, particularly breastfed infants, may not have a bowel movement for a few days. Passing normal stools without discomfort after a long interval is normal, but if your baby passes hard stools infrequently and seems to be in discomfort or pain when she does, she may be constipated.

Brief periods of constipation may follow an infectious illness, such as gastroenteritis. Children may also avoid passing stool if they have a small, painful tear in the skin near the anus (an anal fissure), which can be caused by passing a large, hard stool. In these cases, children should resume normal bowel movements after a few days of healing.

However, constipation at times persists. Sometimes with toddlers it's related to anxiety about potty training or problems at home or in preschool. Not uncommonly, a toilet-trained child, ignoring the urge to defecate when rushing off to school or to the playground, becomes constipated because he just doesn't take the time to sit and have a bowel movement. Occasionally there's an underlying medical condition causing constipation.

Symptoms

A constipated child may feel pain when trying to pass a stool. She may complain of pain just before moving her bowels. Within a few days, her rectum can become overfull so that the wall is stretched. Eventually, she may lose the urge to pass motions and instead may involuntarily soil herself. Drops of red blood when passing a stool may signal a fissure.

Diagnosis and treatment

If your baby appears to be constipated, seek medical advice promptly so that the problem can be addressed early. Your pediatrician may examine your baby's abdomen before recommending treatment.

For mild constipation, increasing fluids and fiber in the diet will solve the problem. If that's not enough, your doctor may prescribe a laxative that draws fluid into the bowel and softens the stool, or a mild stimulant laxative that increases the contractions of the bowel wall, helping to move its contents along.

More severe constipation requires more intensive treatment, which may include suppositories, stool softening laxatives, stimulant laxatives, and special fluids to increase the water content of the stools. Laxatives may be continued for some time until the child returns to a regular pattern of defecation. Increasing fiber in your child's diet may help to avoid another episode of constipation.

Mild cases of constipation usually are resolved over a few days or a week or two. If ongoing constipation has caused the rectum to become distended for some time, it will take a while for the rectum to return to its usual size and for the child to regain the urge to have bowel movements. Chronic constipation and soiling can be very upsetting for children, who'll need plenty of encouragement and support during treatment.

Chicken pox

The varicella zoster virus causes the characteristic chicken pox rash and accompanying illness.

Symptoms

The red spots, which soon develop into small blisters, tend to appear first on the torso before spreading to the arms and legs. They're accompanied by mild fever. Spots appear in waves for about 5 days and crust over within a few days. In mild cases, there may be only a handful of spots, but there will be over a hundred in typical cases.

Usually, the biggest problem is itchiness of the skin. Rarely, chicken pox can lead to complications including bacterial infection of the skin or invasion of the brain by the chicken pox virus (encephalitis).

Diagnosis and treatment

The appearance of the rash usually makes diagnosis easy. Calamine and other anti-itching ointments, or acetaminophen and ibuprofen, can relieve discomfort. Aspirin should not be given. Children with impaired immunity are at particular risk for severe chicken pox and may be given an intravenous antiviral drug. A doctor should always be consulted when small babies or children with impaired immunity are exposed to chicken pox, no matter how small the exposure. Also seek help if your child seems quite sick.

Most children with chicken pox get through the worst of it in 5 to 7 days, but it may take 2 to 3 weeks before spots are gone. Chicken pox rarely recurs, but the virus can collect in nerve cells and later in life reappear as a rash known as shingles.

Once all the spots have crusted over, the infected child is no longer contagious.

Abdominal pain

One of the most common and most nonspecific symptoms your child may complain about is abdominal pain. There are hundreds of causes of abdominal pain, ranging from minor, such as constipation, to quite serious. When your child complains of abdominal pain, the first step in evaluating it is to observe your child. Does he look sick to you?

Symptoms

Abdominal pain in a sick child is most often infectious in nature. Gastroenteritis or strep throat are common causes. However, you should also consider surgical conditions, such as appendicitis.

In non-surgical conditions:
- Your child may or may not have a fever

- Vomiting is common; vomited material may be yellow, brown, or the color of food eaten—should not be green
- Diarrhea is common
- Abdominal pain is located around the umbilicus, and is crampy (comes and goes)
- Pain is mild to moderate
- Your child walks normally
In surgical conditions:
- Your child may or may not have a fever
- Vomiting is common; vomited material can be any color; green suggests a surgical condition
- Usually no diarrhea
- In appendicitis, pain starts around the umbilicus but becomes localized in the lower abdomen on the right side
- Pain is constant and severe
- Your child walks bent over; it's painful to jump up and down

If your child is very sick, not keeping fluids in, has severe pain, or any of the symptoms of a surgical condition noted above, call your doctor.

If your child has abdominal pain but looks well, the list of possible causes is enormous. Only a few common conditions will be discussed.

Diagnosis and treatment

Constipation Constipation is one of the most common causes of abdominal pain in children; for more information, see page 352.

Lactose intolerance Lactose intolerance refers to the discomfort resulting from drinking milk or eating dairy products when a child has lost the ability to break down milk sugar (lactose). Abdominal pain is the most common symptom, but diarrhea, vomiting, and gassiness may also occur. Often lactose intolerance occurs following a stomach virus. Cells lining the small intestine can be damaged by the infection and the enzyme (lactase) that breaks down lactose is temporarily in short supply. In a few days, the intestine repairs itself and the lactose intolerance is gone.

Another group of children get lactose intolerance as they grow older because their intestinal cells stop producing or make only a little of the enzyme.

Usually, this trait is inherited from parents. The treatment of lactose intolerance is to avoid lactose-containing foods. Lactose is found almost exclusively in milk and dairy products. Lactose-free products are widely available: soy formulas, lactose-free milk, ice cream without lactose, etc. There are also enzyme-containing chewable pills that can be taken before ingesting lactose to help avoid abdominal symptoms.

Stomach acid problems If stomach acid reaches the lower esophagus, pain may result. Too much stomach acid (and a bacterium called *Helicobacter pylori*) can also injure stomach cells. The pain in these ailments is typically a burning pain, located in the upper abdomen, which may spread upward toward the chest. Often the pain occurs during or right after a feeding, and sometimes wakes the child up during the night. His appetite is often lessened. Consult your doctor if symptoms like these appear in your child. Treatment consists of antacids or medication to lower stomach acid. Chronic symptoms may be caused by Helicobacter; this is treated with antibiotics and acid-lowering medication.

Urinary tract infection See section on page 350. Pain is usually lower, in the central abdomen, and accompanied by pain or burning on urinating.

Anxiety and stress Toddlers who have a new sibling, a mean classmate at school, or a parent away on a trip may manifest abdominal pain caused by stress or anxiety. Some children learn that when they say their stomach hurts, they get attention from their parents.

Children with such "functional" pain usually get pain at unusual times (just before going to school, for example). The pain is centrally located, dull, and doesn't last long. It doesn't usually occur when a child is having fun. The diagnosis of abdominal pain from stress or anxiety is only reached after considering other medical conditions, such as those above. Treatment consists of trying to lower stress and anxiety, if its source can be identified. For the child who uses abdominal pain to get attention, give

him a hug and a quick rub of his tummy, and send him back to play.

Fifth disease

Fifth disease, caused by a parvovirus, can occur at any time of year but is especially common in the spring. The virus is often passed through secretions, such as in sneezes and coughs.

Symptoms

The illness begins with symptoms typical of a head cold. These symptoms disappear, and a week or so later the child develops red cheeks (it's sometimes known as "slapped cheek disease") and may have a very slight fever or none at all. A rash appears on the trunk, arms, and thighs. The rash is only occasionally itchy, appears redder after a hot bath or running around, and usually fades in a few days, but can last for up to 6 weeks. Rare complications can include joint pain and inflammation. If a woman acquires Fifth disease while pregnant, infection can spread to the unborn baby.

Treatment

Symptoms are mild, and no specific treatment is required. Children usually aren't contagious once the rash appears, so they can continue to go to school.

Hand, foot, and mouth disease

This illness, characterized by small red pimples and pimple-blisters in the mouth and on the hands and feet, can occur at any age, but it most commonly affects infants and toddlers. It is not the same as foot and mouth disease in livestock.

Symptoms

Affected children tend to start by feeling poorly, possibly with a fever, for a day or two. This is followed by a sore throat and then small spots in the mouth, including on the tongue. These spots soon develop into painful ulcers. Spots develop on the hands and feet and sometimes on the legs, buttocks, and other areas of the body. The spots look similar to chicken pox but are smaller in size. They tend to be sore rather than itchy and can last for a week or so.

Treatment

Acetaminophen or ibuprofen can reduce general aches and pains, and can ease discomfort from the sores. Cool drinks and sucking on ice pops can help too. Encourage your baby to drink even though she may find it uncomfortable for a few days. It's usually a mild illness. The biggest problem for children with the disease tends to be the sore mouth, which can cause discomfort when eating and swallowing.

The disease is infectious, particularly while the fever, spots, and ulcers are present. It can be spread on fingers and through saliva and feces, so it's important to keep up good hand-washing habits to minimize the spread.

Measles

This viral disease has become much less common thanks to the measles vaccination. However, outbreaks have increased as vaccination rates have fallen (see page 338).

Measles can be a very serious illness. Children who are sick feel miserable, and a small but significant number of children develop life-threatening complications: In about 1 in 1,000 cases, infection of the brain (encephalitis) occurs. Other possible complications include pneumonia and diarrhea. Ear infections are common.

Symptoms

The illness starts with a fever and cold-type symptoms, including sniffles, a cough, and sometimes conjunctivitis. After 3 days or so, the rash appears first on the face, and then behind the ears and down the rest of the body. The rash begins as groups of spots, but after 3 days or so the spots join together to form a blotchy rash.

Treatment

Children with measles can take acetaminophen or ibuprofen to alleviate aches and pains and should get plenty of fluids. An ear infection or pneumonia may require antibiotics.

A child with measles is infectious from before the rash appears until the fifth day of the rash.

Mumps

Mumps is usually a mild illness. In typical cases, children may have a fever lasting 3 days or so and the characteristic swelling of one or both parotid glands, located along the jaw just in front of the ears. Mumps can sometimes cause hearing problems. Before the wide use of mumps vaccine, mumps was the most common cause of acquired sensorineural hearing loss in children.

On rare occasions, the mumps virus causes meningitis (see page 348), or infection of the brain itself (encephalitis). It also can cause inflammation of the testes, but this tends to affect teenage boys and adults rather than young children. It also can cause joint inflammation (arthritis).

Mumps has become less common due to widespread MMR vaccination. However, mumps outbreaks have risen as vaccination rates have fallen (see page 338). Mumps tends to occur in winter and spring and is spread through secretions, such as coughs and sneezes.

Symptoms

Mumps is characterized by swollen salivary glands. This may start on one side, but usually the other side becomes swollen within a few days. The swollen glands, which persist for 5 to 10 days, may be painful and cause an earache or discomfort swallowing. The disease is infectious for a week after the parotid glands become swollen.

Treatment

If swallowing is painful, provide your child with plenty of fluids and soft foods. Avoid orange and other citrus juices. Ibuprofen or acetaminophen can ease pain. Alert your doctor if you think your child has mumps. If you child becomes seriously ill, has a headache with a stiff neck, swollen testicles, abdominal pain, or persistent earache, seek medical attention.

Roseola infantum

This common viral illness causes a rash and a high fever. It's particularly common between the ages of 6 months and 2 years.

Symptoms

The first symptoms can include a high fever, a dry cough, and swollen glands in the neck. Some children have mild diarrhea. A rash of tiny spots develops on the face and trunk a few days later, just as the fever breaks. Although still uncommon, febrile convulsions (see page 341) occur more often in roseola than in most other viral illnesses.

Treatment

Roseola is diagnosed when the typical rash is seen following a febrile illness. For aches and pains, give acetaminophen or ibuprofen and make sure she gets adequate fluids. The fever lasts 3 to 4 days, and the child is considered contagious until 1 to 2 days after the appearance of the rash.

Rubella

Also known as German measles, this viral illness is usually mild and may pass unnoticed. It's of greatest concern to pregnant women because it can seriously harm unborn babies. The infection is passed in secretions through sneezes and coughs.

Symptoms

A rash of tiny pink spots develops on the face and trunk before moving down the body; it lasts for up to 5 days. An infected child can have swollen lymph nodes and a mild fever, but no other particular signs of illness. Rare symptoms include inflammation of the joints (arthritis) and brain (encephalitis).

Rubella is usually a mild childhood illness. The primary reason we vaccinate children against it is to prevent pregnant women from catching rubella and spreading it to the fetus.

Treatment

No specific treatment is required other than to lessen discomfort with acetaminophen or ibuprofen.

Pinworms

This infestation is common in childhood and particularly in preschool children. Pinworms live in the digestive system. During the night, females work their way down to the end of the bowel and lay their eggs in the area around the anus. The eggs are picked up on the fingers when scratching and then ingested or passed on to others.

Pinworms spread easily. Strict hygiene measures are necessary to eradicate them permanently.

Symptoms

Pinworms can cause intense itching at night or early in the morning around the anus and sometimes in the genital area. However, they sometimes cause no symptoms and may go unnoticed for some time. The tiny, thread-like worms might be visible around the anus.

Treatment

Once the diagnosis has been confirmed, your pediatrician may prescribe antiworm medication for the entire family. Trim nails short to prevent scratching. Try to keep children from sucking their thumb or biting their nails. Frequent and thorough hand-washing is critical to ending an infestation.

Even with medication and good hygiene, pinworms occasionally may persist. If the problem continues, consult your pediatrician for advice.

Head lice

A head louse is a tiny insect that lives on the scalp and feeds on blood. Lice are easily spread from one child to another in schools and child care settings.

Symptoms

The scalp may be intensely itchy. You may see adult lice on the scalp or eggs, known as nits, on the hairs. Nits stick to the hair and so move away from the scalp as the hairs grow.

Diagnosis

The presence of head lice is diagnosed by seeing the adult louse moving quickly through the hair or discovering the nits. A nit looks like a flake of dandruff, but unlike dandruff, it is glued to the hair and cannot be flicked away with your finger.

Treatment

Lice can become resistant to certain drugs, so treatment recommendations vary. Ask your pediatrician for advice on a medicated lotion or rinse to treat lice. Use a fine-tooth comb to comb out lice.

Head lice can be transmitted by brushes, combs, towels, and hats, as well as by close contact. To halt an infestation, inspect all family members regularly. Wash bedding, clothing, and stuffed toys in hot water (or dry clean), and thoroughly vacuum cloth-covered furniture and carpets.

Impetigo

This common skin condition is usually caused by staphylococcal ("staph") bacteria and is very contagious. Impetigo is especially prevalent in early childhood and tends to develop in areas of skin that are already irritated, such as by eczema (see below), cuts, scrapes, and insect bites.

Symptoms

Impetigo typically is characterized by superficial sores, red pimples, or blisters of the skin. The small blisters can leak and leave honey-colored crusted areas.

Diagnosis and treatment

Impetigo is usually diagnosed by examining the skin lesions. Your pediatrician may take a sample with a swab to identify the bacteria. Antibiotic ointment can be used to treat mild cases, or your child may be prescribed an oral antibiotic.

Impetigo spreads by direct contact with skin lesions or via fingers of the infected child who has touched the sores or his nose. Infected children should stay away from other children until the sores have completely dried or until more than 24 hours of antibiotic treatment has been given. Towels and linens should be washed thoroughly to prevent spreading the infection.

Eczema

Eczema, also known as atopic dermatitis, is a common, chronic illness characterized by rough, reddened, itchy skin. Fortunately, the symptoms usually are easy to treat, and the condition typically becomes milder as children grow older.

Eczema and allergies often occur in the same child. The eczema often appears during the first year of life and is especially common when family members have allergic conditions such as hay fever—and children with eczema are more likely to develop these allergies as well. In such children, eczema may be precipitated by eating certain foods to which they are unknowingly allergic.

Symptoms

Eczema causes red, dry patches of skin, which can become quite itchy. Scratching makes it worse—scratched areas become weepy and form crusts, and repeated scratching can cause the skin to thicken.

Eczema affects children differently as they grow older. For infants, it's typically found on the face, neck, and scalp; older children tend to have patches in joint creases.

Patches of eczema can become infected after scratching when bacteria enter damaged skin. Rarely, eczematous skin becomes infected with herpes or chicken pox virus, which can become quite serious.

An environment of dry air, frequent bathing or swimming, and food allergies may exacerbate eczema.

Treatment

Keep nails trimmed short and avoid substances that can irritate the skin, such as harsh soaps. Dress your child in soft clothing. Nonsoap cleansers and emollients can soothe skin. Give baths infrequently. If your home or apartment is dry inside in winter due to heating, using a humidifier can be helpful.

Besides good skin care, moisturizing lotions, such as hand creams, are very helpful. Apply to dry areas right after baths and up to three times a day. Hydrocortisone cream is also very effective, but should be used sparingly and according to a doctor's instructions. Newer topical medications are sometimes used in the more stubborn cases. Oral antihistamines may be recommended to relieve itching; if your child develops a bacterial infection, oral or topical antibiotics may be needed.

Seborrheic dermatitis

The skin inflammation of seborrheic dermatitis (seborrhea) tends to begin on the scalp (where it's known as cradle cap) and may spread to the face and skin creases—the neck, the armpits, the groin area, behind the ears, and at the tops of the legs. Seborrheic dermatitis affects young babies but often doesn't cause any itching or discomfort. Cradle cap is used to describe the scaly, thick yellow crusts on the scalp; elsewhere, seborrheic dermatitis causes reddened skin.

Treatment

Treatment of seborrhea is mostly cosmetic, but older children especially may be treated to relieve itching. For treatment, massage a mild oil, such as baby or olive oil, over the scales and the entire scalp. Then vigorously shampoo your child's hair, massage the scalp, and rinse thoroughly. You can also use a soft brush to help remove scales. Cradle cap eventually goes away on its own.

SEEING THE DOCTOR

Mild or short-term illness

Even when your child isn't seriously ill, it can be difficult to absorb everything your pediatrician says during your child's appointment. It's a good idea to bring a pen, paper, and a list of questions to ask. These may include:

◆ What is the diagnosis?

◆ How long is the illness likely to last?
◆ What is the prescribed treatment and what can I do to alleviate the symptoms?
◆ When should I return or call for advice (for example, if symptoms persist for 48 hours)?
◆ Can my child go to daycare or school?

Severe or long-term illness

If you suspect that your child has a severe or acute illness, or one that is lasting a long time, you'll want to fully understand your doctor's diagnosis and recommended treatment, which may include a complex explanation that may raise more questions than it answers. It's a good idea to bring your partner, a friend, or a relative to help you remember what your doctor has to say and to think of questions to ask. Bring a pen and paper for notes, too.

Before an appointment, think about what worries you and write down your questions. It can be very frustrating to leave a long-awaited appointment only to realize you forgot to ask something important.

If your child is being treated at the hospital, note the names of any doctors or specialists who see him. Ask about follow-up care and find out when and how your pediatrician will be informed. Request copies of any letters sent to your pediatrician.

If you receive upsetting news and want someone to take the time to talk with you about it, you may want to ask to meet with a counselor who can provide support, give you a chance to openly discuss your concerns, and help you find ongoing resources and support.

Caring for your child in the hospital

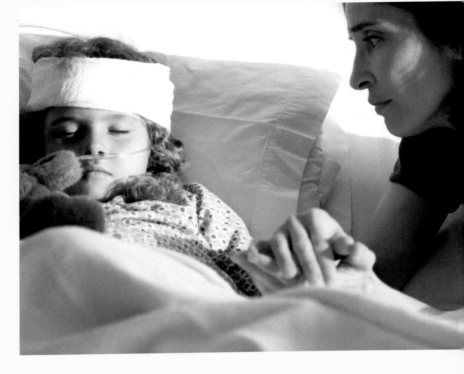

Few events cause parents more anxiety than when their child is diagnosed with a serious illness. It's distressing enough when you have to bring your child to the doctor for a relatively minor ailment. But the anxiety is heightened if your child needs to be hospitalized. Fortunately, most children who are hospitalized aren't critically ill. They might be hospitalized because:

◆ Outpatient treatment hasn't been successful.
◆ Treatment requires special equipment, personnel, or supervision.
◆ Careful observation is needed in case of complications or worsening of her condition.
◆ Outpatient treatment would require too great an effort for the parents.

Children who are hospitalized are often released within a few days. It's uncommon for a child to face a long hospitalization, but it may occur with a serious problem such as an accident or trauma, a surgical emergency, or cancer.

Regardless of the reason for your child's hospitalization, you will have worries and fears about the outcome, and that's natural.

You may feel you have little control over his illness and what's happening at the hospital. You might find the hospital setting uncomfortable yourself, increasing your anxiety. You're being asked to trust nurses, aides, technicians, and doctors you've never met before. And most likely you have limited knowledge to judge whether their advice is sound and appropriate for your child.

Your child probably feels afraid and anxious too (and he may feel quite sick, as well). Away from the security of familiar surroundings he might feel terrified. He'll certainly be aware of your anxiety and

COMMON REASONS FOR HOSPITALIZATION

◆ Respiratory illnesses such as moderate or severe cases of asthma, croup, bronchiolitis, and pneumonia. Oxygen, intravenous medications, fluids, and close observation may be needed.
◆ Dehydration due to a stomach virus, requiring intravenous fluids.
◆ Moderate or severe infections, requiring intravenous antibiotics and observation.
◆ A convulsion from which a child hasn't completely recovered.

apprehension, which can intensify his own anxiety. Strangers keep examining and treating him, and some of what they do is scary and unpleasant. Just being examined may feel like torture, plus there may be the pain of blood tests, intravenous insertion, and other medical procedures. Even placing a mask over his face to supply oxygen or inhaled respiratory treatments may make him feel as if he's being smothered.

What you can do to help your child

Although you may feel powerless to help your child get well sooner, there is much important work for you to do. You are your child's link to what is familiar and constant. You can provide tremendous support just by being there with him. If at all possible, a parent or other familiar adult should stay with your child at all times, including during painful procedures, and stay in his room overnight. You may not be able to heal him, but you have a vital role in his care: to comfort your child and reassure him that he'll soon be well.

Here are some tips:

- Try not to show your child how worried you are. If you're visibly upset, you won't be effective at soothing and calming your child.
- Hold him and try to distract and comfort him during painful procedures.
- Let the doctors and nurses do their jobs. Cooperate as much as you can.

- You know your child best. If you have an idea on how to make him more comfortable, let the hospital staff know. Your suggestions will be very helpful, but remember that your doctor and nurses have had much more experience dealing with sick children than most parents do.
- Educate yourself about your child's illness and his treatment plan. Ask questions of your doctors and nurses until you understand what is happening. Have them explain any unfamiliar terms you don't understand. Try to avoid turning to the Internet to research your child's condition, because you may get misleading or unnecessarily alarming information (for more information, see page 66).
- Bring some of the objects from home that may comfort your child: his blanket or teddy bear, his favorite book or DVD. If he's allowed to eat, have his favorite foods from home on hand.
- If your child is well enough, keep him occupied with activities such as coloring, simple games, or puzzles, or read to him.
- Try to stick to your child's daily routines as much as possible.
- Reassure him often that he'll be well soon and can then go home.
- When discharged, give your child a chance to "come to grips" with his hospital experience. One way to do

this is to get a toy doctor kit and pretend he is the doctor and you or a teddy bear is the patient. Ask him how the patient feels about being sick. This kind of role-playing can help him process his experience.

- Another technique is to encourage him to draw pictures of what it was like to be in the hospital. You also can read a book about going to the doctor or the hospital. Or you can make up a story about another child who was sick enough to go the hospital and experienced trials and tribulations similar to his. Of course, the story should end happily with the child getting all better and going home, where his parents loved him forever and ever!

For more about the emotional difficulties you and your child may have in the hospital, or to learn more about dealing with a disabled child, see Chapter 4 and Chapter 13.

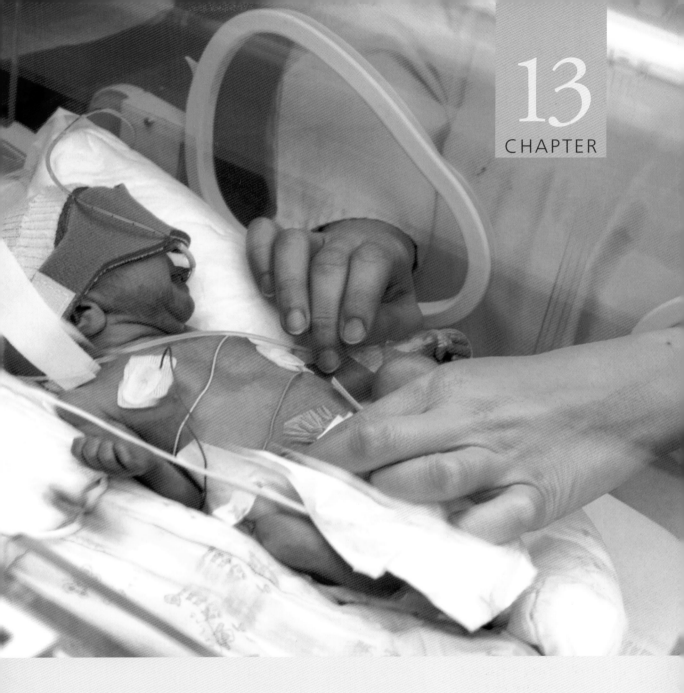

ADDRESSING
HEALTH ISSUES

Birth injuries

The majority of birth-related injuries occur during vaginal deliveries, but caesarean deliveries have risks, too.

Cephalhematoma

During a vaginal delivery, uterine contractions can force a baby's head against his mother's pelvic bones, resulting in bleeding and bruising within the scalp. A raised, soft lump results, caused by blood collecting in the soft tissues. Cephalhematomas usually occur on one or both sides of the back of the head but don't cross the midline. Gradually, they shrink and disappear completely. They sometimes contribute to jaundice (see opposite page) because the hematoma is full of red blood cells that need to be destroyed. Occasionally babies are left with a remnant, a small hard bump on the skull.

Forceps marks

After a forceps-assisted delivery, a baby may be bruised where the forceps were applied. These black-and-blue marks corresponding to where pressure from the forceps was applied gradually fade and disappear in a few days. After they disappear, however, at about 1 week of age, you may feel a peanut-size hard lump just below the skin of your newborn's cheek. This is an injury to the fatty layer of skin, caused by the forceps; it will slowly shrink and disappear.

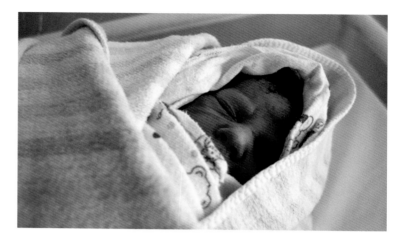

Occasionally, the pressure from the forceps damages the facial nerve controlling the mouth muscles so that when a baby cries, the shape of his mouth is uneven. Most of these injuries heal within a few weeks.

Clavicle fracture

During a vaginal delivery, a very large baby is at increased risk of fracturing his collarbone. This is usually diagnosed the day after delivery when the skin over the clavicle appears swollen or bruised. The injury is usually harmless and heals without treatment, but a newborn with a clavicle fracture may hesitate to raise his arms above his head, although he'll move them normally otherwise. On rare occasions during a difficult delivery, nerves from a baby's spinal cord to his upper arm can be injured as they pass from the area beneath the clavicle to the upper arm. An infant injured this way won't be able to move his arm or shoulder well, and his arm may lie limply at his side. Luckily, many such injuries heal in a matter of weeks.

Deviated septum

When large amounts of downward pressure are exerted on a baby's nose in utero or during delivery, the nasal septum, which divides the right and left sides of the nose, can be pushed off-track. At birth, the nose will look crooked (the alignment of the bottom part of the nose will be off-center), and one nostril will be larger than the other. When detected, a deviated septum can be correctly realigned relatively easily while the baby is still in the hospital.

Minor problems at birth

The delivery or the growth of a baby can result in some conditions that are generally short lived.

Polycythemia and hypoglycemia

A high red blood cell count (polycythemia) and low blood sugar (hypoglycemia) occur primarily in very large infants (especially those whose mothers had gestational diabetes) and in very small ones.

Polycythemia may be suspected if your baby's skin color is very reddish. It is diagnosed with a blood test. Your doctor may encourage your baby to take extra fluids, draw off blood and replace it with IV fluids, or do nothing and allow the condition to correct itself over time.

Symptoms of hypoglycemia include shakiness, pale color, rapid breathing, and lethargy. In most hospitals, blood sugar level can be quickly tested by pricking a baby's heel, placing 1 or 2 drops of blood on a reagent strip, and reading the value either manually or with a glucose meter. Infants who are hypoglycemic are given glucose orally (in sugar water or formula) to quickly raise their blood glucose levels; if that's unsuccessful, the next step is to give intravenous fluids containing glucose. Once feedings are established, most hypoglycemic infants are able to maintain their blood sugar normally.

Transient tachypnea

Shortly after birth, some babies begin to breathe rapidly because they haven't yet completely cleared amniotic fluid from their lungs. Infants born by caesarean section are more likely to develop tachypnea because they have little time to prepare for their births. Most infants with transient tachypnea require only close observation and perhaps extra oxygen; the problem resolves on its own within a day or so in the majority of cases.

Jaundice

Babies with neonatal jaundice develop yellowing on their skin and in the whites of their eyes in the first few days of life. It's a fairly common condition caused by a high blood level of bilirubin, a waste product created from the breakdown of red blood cells (RBCs).

Everyone produces bilirubin daily as old red blood cells are destroyed and replaced with new ones. In adults and older children, the liver efficiently removes bilirubin from the bloodstream and secretes it into the bile; in utero, bilirubin is carried across the placenta and removed by the mother's liver. In most full-term newborns, the liver's removal function takes 3 or 4 days to mature, and it takes even longer with premature babies.

For the few days that the liver is still maturing, bilirubin accumulates in the bloodstream. If it reaches a high enough level, it can cause jaundice.

Jaundice is most common in newborns with cephalhematomas or other bruises from delivery (the hematomas and bruises contain RBCs that the body will break down), in babies who don't have the same blood type as their mothers (maternal antibodies destroy some of the baby's RBCs; see box on maternal antibodies on page 95), and babies who are born prematurely (due to reduced excretion of bilirubin by the premature liver).

Jaundice usually doesn't need to be treated. Bilirubin is harmful only in very high concentrations, but your pediatrician will monitor your baby to make sure it drops to a safe, normal level. Bilirubin levels usually peak 3 or 4 days after birth, so if your baby is discharged early from the hospital, you may need to see a doctor in the next day or two to check for jaundice.

If jaundice requires treatment, babies are usually given light treatments, called phototherapy, (see page 364) that help them eliminate excess bilirubin.

Phototherapy

Exposure to light was introduced as a treatment for jaundice long before anyone understood why it works. An observant nurse in the 1950s noticed that babies whose cribs were near the windows and exposed to sunlight were less jaundiced than babies kept farther from the windows. Later, tests with blood samples confirmed the observed connection. Phototherapy lights were designed to emit the same frequencies of light as sunlight.

We now know that this approach works by energizing bilirubin molecules in the skin and superficial blood vessels. This extra energy causes a small structural change in the bilirubin molecule, now allowing it to be easily excreted in urine. Phototherapy doesn't cure jaundice, but it does keep the bilirubin level in a safe range until a baby's liver matures.

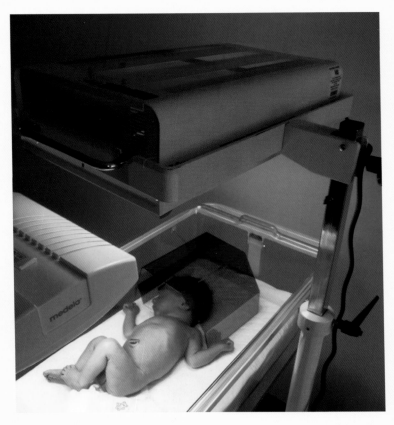

Phototherapy is effective only where the light rays reach the skin; for maximum effectiveness, as much skin as possible should be exposed to the light. When babies are placed under phototherapy lights—or "bili lights"—they are undressed and placed in a heated incubator to keep warm.

Soft shields over the baby's eyes protect them from the light. Research done on animals has shown that sustained use of phototherapy can injure an animal's unprotected eyes, but there have been no reports of human infants suffering eye injuries related to bili lights.

While a baby is under phototherapy, it's impossible to visually assess how jaundiced he is. Because phototherapy removes bilirubin in the areas exposed to light, a baby can look much less jaundiced on the outside even when the level of bilirubin inside his body is still high.

The more time a newborn spends under phototherapy lamps, the better the therapy works. If your baby is treated under bili lights, the hospital staff may want to limit the amount of time he's out of the incubator for holding and feeding. Even if you can't hold your baby in your arms as much as you'd like, you should be able to sit by his side and insert your hands through the incubator portholes so you can touch and talk to your baby while he is being treated.

Formula-fed babies can be fed while remaining in the incubator (see page 91); if you are breastfeeding, return your baby to the incubator quickly after the feeding is done.

Abnormalities at birth

Given the extraordinary complexity of the human body, the complicated process of growing from a one-cell fertilized egg into an organism with billions of cells, and the hundreds of errors that can occur along the way, it's remarkable how many babies are born healthy and without any abnormalities.

Fortunately, when physical abnormalities do occur, they're usually minor. Here are some of the most common yet relatively minor abnormalities.

Finger and toe problems

Most abnormalities of fingers and toes are inherited. These include having a second toe that's taller than the big toe, a fifth toe that curves in, two toes joined together at their bases but separated farther toward the ends, and extra fingers or toes.

Extra digits range in complexity: An extra toe or finger might be a small bullet-shaped object, just a centimeter or two long, with no nail or internal bones, hanging from the side of the little toe or pinky by a very thin stalk, or it might be a fully developed sixth finger or toe.

Extra digits don't cause any health concerns, but many parents elect to have them removed for cosmetic reasons. An extra digit on a thin stalk may be tied off with suture material or removed by a surgeon at the hospital or perhaps in a clinic after discharge; removing a complete extra finger or toe would require surgery in the hospital.

Skin tags

Skin tags are pimple-size areas of extra skin that most often appear near the "button" of the earlobe but can occur anywhere. Usually, the only concern is for appearance. On some rare occasions, they're a clue to an underlying problem, particularly if they are over the lower spine or occur in association with an abnormal earlobe.

Hip dislocation

If your pediatrician hears a click or feels a clunk when she examines your newborn's hips, your baby may have a shallow hip socket. Some babies just need monitoring, but others need a harness to promote hip joint development (see page 325).

Clubfoot

This foot deformity may affect one or both feet and usually is apparent at birth. An affected foot turns downward and inward: It's held straight and flexed downward at the ankle, and tilted sideways so that the big toe side of the foot is raised and the little toe side is down. Babies are at higher risk of clubfoot if a parent or sibling also had one.

The cause of this deformity is often unknown, but sometimes it's because the foot was held fixed in this position in the womb, without room to move to another position. It can also be the result of rare diseases of the muscles or nerves, which affect other joints as well as the ankle and foot.

Treatment begins shortly after birth. Conservative treatment, which can be very effective, involves gently setting the foot in a position as close to normal as possible and holding it there in a plaster cast. After a week, the cast is removed, the foot is manipulated even closer to the normal position, and a new cast is applied. This is repeated weekly for about 3 months, and then a final cast is used to keep the foot in its final orientation for another 2 to 3 months. In cases that are more difficult to treat, surgery is also an option.

Most babies born with a clubfoot have a very good chance of developing full function and having a foot that looks nearly normal, whether treated by casts or surgery.

Undescended testicle

When one testicle is undescended (not yet present in the scrotal sac) at the time of a baby's birth, it most likely will settle in its normal position within a few months. (See box on testicular descent on page 329.)

It's very unusual for neither

testicle to be in place, except in small, premature babies. If neither is evident, more testing will be needed. In rare cases, this may suggest that a child is a female with masculine external genitalia. A blood test analyzing the baby's chromosomes will determine whether the child is genetically a male or female.

Hydrocele

A hydrocele is a small amount of tissue fluid surrounding one or both testicles. One testicle will seem larger than the other because it's surrounded by fluid. Most small and medium-size hydroceles disappear within the first months of life. Hydroceles that don't disappear or are large may persist and often are associated with an inguinal hernia (see page 101). Minor surgery may be needed.

Heart murmurs and malformations

Your pediatrician may report to you that he hears a heart murmur when listening to your baby's heart with a stethoscope. Murmurs occur when blood flow through an area within the heart or a major blood vessel is more turbulent (not as smooth) than usual. Murmurs detected on the first day of life are often temporary and may be gone the next day—they're not a concern. Some heart murmurs, however, indicate a structural problem in the heart. The most common cause of a significant murmur in a newborn is a ventricular

septal defect (VSD). The left and right ventricles are supposed to be completely separated by a muscular wall called the septum. But with a VSD, a small hole in the wall allows blood from the left ventricle to flow into the right ventricle. This type of murmur is typically detected after a baby is 2 or 3 days old. Usually the opening closes as the heart grows. But if a child is showing signs of heart failure, it can often be corrected with surgery.

Besides the presence of a heart murmur, symptoms of a heart problem may include blueness of the lips (not the hands and feet, which are normally purplish-blue in healthy newborns), rapid breathing, paleness, and poor feeding. If your pediatrician suspects a structural cardiac defect, your baby will need to be seen by a pediatric cardiologist and undergo tests such as an ECG (electrocardiogram), an echocardiogram (sonogram of the heart), and perhaps a chest X-ray.

Cleft lip and palate

Cleft lips and palates vary in extent from just a small notch in the lip to an opening in the roof of the mouth all the way to the nose. About 1 in 2,500 people is born with a cleft palate. A cleft can make feeding very difficult for a newborn because it interferes with generating the negative pressure needed to suck successfully. A temporary solution is to provide bottle feedings with a very large nipple. A plastic device can also be fitted to

artificially close off the opening.

Cleft lips and palates are usually repaired surgically during infancy. Subsequent surgeries and speech therapy may be needed. In general, children with a repaired cleft palate are more prone to ear infections and often require speech therapy.

Sacral dimples

These are small puckerings or indentations of the skin over the lower spine, appearing just above the crease between the buttocks. Most sacral dimples are normal and nothing to worry about, particularly if the skin isn't broken and there's no opening to underlying tissue. If there's a small tuft of hair or a skin tag in the area, or if the bottom of the dimple isn't easy to see, there's a chance that the spinal column—the bones surrounding the spinal cord—may not have formed properly, and the baby may have a form of spina bifida (see pages 378–379).

An opening or sinus tract leading from the skin to the area around the spine can result in a serious spinal infection caused by bacteria from the skin. Other potential problems with spina bifida include benign fatty tumors (which can press on the spinal cord) and injury to the lower spinal cord and nerves leading to the pelvic area and legs.

While sacral dimples are common, and spina bifida or sinus tracts are relatively rare, if there is sufficient suspicion, your pediatrician probably will want to conduct tests such as a sonogram or MRI (magnetic resonance imaging) scan.

Hydrocephalus

The brain and spinal cord are normally surrounded by a protective, water-like liquid called spinal fluid. This fluid is produced in a small number of cavities in the brain, called ventricles, and travels to the area between the brain and skull and between the spinal cord and surrounding vertebrae. Our bodies constantly produce spinal fluid while cells lining the outer brain remove it at an equal rate, so the volume of spinal fluid remains constant.

A blockage in any of the passageways within the brain causes fluid to accumulate in the ventricles upstream from the blockage. Hydrocephalus develops as the ventricles become distended with excess fluid, which then puts pressure on the surrounding brain tissue. Hydrocephalus affects an estimated 1 in 500 children.

Spinal fluid blockage can occur in premature infants with bleeding in the ventricles—blood clots may block the path that spinal fluid usually follows out of the ventricle.

Hydrocephalus also can be caused by a problem in the formation of the ventricles or passageways while the baby was in the womb, scarring after a brain infection in utero, or a tumor in the brain compressing the ventricle or spinal fluid passageways.

Hydrocephalus may also result when too much spinal fluid is produced or when the body fails to properly reabsorb spinal fluid. An injury to the cells lining the brain following meningitis (see page 348) can cause an imbalance between the production and removal of spinal fluid, resulting in an elevated volume of fluid and increased pressure in the ventricles.

As hydrocephalus advances, the increased volume of spinal fluid causes the skull to rapidly enlarge. An abnormally large head circumference (see page 273) may indicate hydrocephalus. If the skull can't expand quickly enough and pressure increases within the skull, the anterior fontanel on the top of a baby's head may bulge upward, and the baby may vomit and become lethargic.

Another sign of pressure on the brain is called sunsetting: The baby's eyes are fixed downward so that only the top part of the iris (the colored part of the eye) is visible above the lower eyelid, resembling the setting sun as it drops below the horizon.

If hydrocephalus develops slowly and symptoms aren't severe, spinal fluid can be removed with a spinal tap (lumbar puncture) to reduce pressure. Premature babies with hydrocephalus caused by bleeding in the ventricles often need repeated taps to remove fluid while the blood clots are reabsorbed by the body.

Sometimes spinal fluid is diverted with a shunt, a long plastic tube inserted into one of the cerebral ventricles and connected to a catheter that usually ends in the abdominal cavity. Some shunts include a pressure-sensitive valve to control the flow of fluid. When spinal fluid reaches the abdominal cavity, it is readily reabsorbed.

Using a shunt has risks, significantly mechanical failure and infection. One alternative is surgery to enlarge the opening in the brain to allow spinal fluid to flow out more easily.

Special challenges

Few deliveries go exactly as expected, but in the end most parents welcome a healthy baby into the world. So if you learn that something is wrong with your baby, you may feel devastated. Such news is often unexpected and shocking. Pregnancy and childbirth are a highly emotional time even in the best of circumstances. Discovering that your baby may be in trouble is tremendously distressing—even when the difficulty is relatively minor.

Complications during delivery can injure babies or cause temporary medical problems. Rarely, babies may be born with a deformity or serious problem. Many of these don't require long-term care. But a few conditions have lifelong implications for how your child will grow and develop and how you'll parent him.

Routine babycare is already exhausting, but as the parent of a child with special needs, you also may need to give your child medications, learn to use and monitor special equipment, make extra visits to medical specialists, and bring your baby to frequent physical, occupational, or speech therapy

sessions. You'll need to work with your pediatrician, specialists, therapists, and your insurance company to get the services your child needs, and you'll want to research and stay up to date on the latest therapies and treatments. If your toddler has limited mobility, you'll have to take on the physical burden of lifting and carrying him.

It's normal to have very mixed emotions. As much as you love your baby, if you're like most parents, you'll sometimes, at some level, resent him and his disability. You'll probably feel moments of sadness, anger, and guilt.

You may feel sad that your child isn't perfectly healthy and needs to live his life with this disability. It's normal to sometimes feel sorry for yourself, too, that you're unable to live the kind of life you had envisioned. Caring for your baby can be difficult and frustrating, and you might feel angry sometimes: "Why me? What did I do to deserve this?" And then, naturally, you may feel guilt. You might scold yourself for feeling sad or resentful.

Raising a child with special needs is generally very stressful for everyone in the family. Be sure to seek out support services. A great many nonprofit organizations offer resources and support for families affected by disabilities. Often, tapping into a community of people who understand what you're going through can make a tremendous difference.

Medical care

Seek out doctors and therapists who are kind, caring, and familiar with your child's medical condition. Knowledgeable specialists are an important part of your child's medical team, but keep in mind that specialists tend to look at only one part of a child. Your pediatrician will play a prominent role. Not only will she tend to your child's general medical needs (from vaccines to treating head colds), but she also may coordinate your child's care. She'll be the one responsible for his overall health and well-being. Make sure you keep your pediatrician informed about decisions and recommendations made by specialists, and feel free to ask her opinion: "Do you agree with the plan? What do you think should be done next? Should we get another opinion?"

Many people may help care for your child. But you will always be the most valuable member of his medical team. No one will know as much about your child's history, ongoing care, and future needs as you do. To be most effective, try to stay organized. Use a calendar to keep track of appointments and remind yourself of future needs. Keep medical paperwork organized and accessible. Digital tools online or on your mobile phone can help you stay on top of everything.

Educate yourself about the coverage your health insurance is supposed to provide. If your insurer denies coverage for treatments or supplies, you may need to appeal the decision. Your child's doctors may be able to help. Keep a written log of your phone calls, including date, time, and the name of anyone you speak to, and a file of all correspondence.

Education

In the United States, public schools try to include children with special needs in regular classrooms as much as possible. Under the Individuals with Disabilities Education Act (IDEA), all children are entitled to a free and appropriate education, in a regular classroom as much as possible. IDEA provides services for children from birth to the age of 18 or 21.

Early intervention programs are available to children from birth to age 3 and include an

DOES EARLY INTERVENTION WORK?

Early intervention programs are a relatively recent phenomenon. They're designed to take advantage of what's known as "plasticity" in young brains: Studies show that providing extra stimulation and instruction to young animals results in large gains in brain function. Plasticity refers to the brain's ability to change in response to environmental stimulation. Just how long and how much this can occur is still being researched, but plasticity is greatest in young children—meaning, in short, that they have a much greater capacity to learn.

The goal of early intervention programs is to make the most of this time when children have such extraordinary potential to learn. It's hoped that these programs can help children who begin life at a disadvantage.

The most widely studied early intervention program is the Head Start Program for low-income (not disabled) preschool children, which is run by the U.S. Department of Health and Human Services. Researchers have demonstrated substantial gains in cognitive and social skills compared to similar children not involved in the program when the children reach kindergarten. The difference became less pronounced several years later, however.

Early intervention also is linked to improved outcomes for autistic children with hearing loss, and has led to modest developmental gains for premature infants. It's unclear, however, whether extra practice in motor, language, and cognitive skills is of much benefit to children with other disabilities. In children who have disabilities due to cerebral palsy or developmental delays (not prematurity), preliminary research results support early intervention, but the gains are modest—and they're less significant for more severely disabled infants. Experts are still studying these programs and trying to find out which children benefit most from early intervention and whether any gains are short or long term.

Daily care aids

There are a wide range of products available that can help make looking after a special needs baby easier. Some may be provided by your healthcare providers, and some may be covered by insurance.

Bath supports
Special seats can help keep children secure in the bathtub. Overlays and hoists also can help reduce back strain for parents—bathing even small children in a full-size tub can be difficult and uncomfortable.

Potties
Secure backrests, trainer seats, and supports for arms and feet provide additional support and safety. Mobile potty chairs, which can be wheeled over a toilet or used with a separate commode, are especially useful if your bathroom is small.

Cribs
A crib with an adjustable mattress height makes it easier to settle children comfortably in bed. There are models that are specially adapted to accommodate babies and older children with special needs.

Play equipment
Well-chosen toys can help children improve their balance, coordination, and manipulative skills, and there are products that provide additional support or ensure a soft play area. Adaptive toys may have special switches or joysticks. There are also dolls with wheelchairs, Down syndrome, etc.

Special clothing
Choose clothing with large front fastenings, elastic waistbands, stretchy fabrics, and loose styles. Buy shoes with Velcro fastenings.

Strollers
You can find strollers with adjustable seats, supportive seating, and a backrest with head support, along with specially adapted double strollers.

Car seats
Seats with special restraints, swivel mechanisms, and head and foot supports can make transporting your child easier. There are also special car seats for children with hip dysplasia.

Individualized Family Service Plan to coordinate and guide services for both the child and the entire family. Once children reach the age of 3, an Individualized Education Program, or IEP, will guide their education. The IEP sets out goals and support services needed to help the child reach those goals.

Sleep

Children with developmental delays, cerebral palsy, and many other disabilities are more likely to have sleep problems. You can take some steps to help your child sleep better at night, but sometimes the problem is a medical issue.

For many children, a big part of the problem is simply poor sleep habits. Children usually sleep best when they have a set bedtime each night, preceded by a consistent routine for preparing for bed. Ideally, they go to sleep on their own in a dark, quiet room without aids such as being rocked to sleep or drinking from a bottle (see pages 161–163).

However, if your special needs child gets upset at bedtime or sleeps poorly, consider what effects your child's medical issues may have. For example, discomfort from gastroesophageal reflux (see page 171), which is more common in children with cerebral palsy and similar disorders, can interfere with sleep. If your child has sleep problems, consult your pediatrician.

Discipline

There's no reason to approach discipline (see pages 289–300) for a special needs child any differently than you would for any other child. Be sure to base your expectations for his behavior on his temperament and developmental level (see pages 289–290). Just as it isn't appropriate to expect that a 2-year-old be as well behaved as an older child, it's unfair to demand more of a special needs child than he's developmentally capable of doing. You'll both be better served if you can find a way to avoid repetitive, frequent struggles.

While your child's particular condition shouldn't affect your overall approach to discipline, there are some factors that will influence how you put this approach into action.

Guilt

When you upset your child by denying him what he wants, you might feel guilty—even if you know your response was the right one to teach him good behavior or to keep him safe. It's human nature to second-guess how you handle these situations: No parents want to upset their child. If you become angry or raise your voice, if you lose your patience, or if you simply say "no," even your child's momentary unhappiness can break your heart.

All parents feel this way. But as the parent of a child with special needs or developmental delay, you might feel especially awful. These episodes can stir up deeply held sadness for your child and his condition. Being strict and upsetting your child may seem unfair, since your child has to deal with so much more hardship than most children.

You may have to remind yourself that your child needs to learn how to behave appropriately for his developmental level. Disappointing him may be hard on you, but neglecting to teach him these important lessons—in essence, not helping him become what he's capable of—would be a tremendous disservice to him.

Giving in

It makes sense to choose your battles, and sometimes that means letting your child have his way. The guiding principles for when to give in (see page 298) are the same for your developmentally challenged child as for every other child. Consistency is key.

For important issues, you must be firm. Your child shouldn't be allowed to do anything that could harm him or hurt others, he shouldn't damage or destroy valuable objects, and he should take naps as needed and go to bed on time. These rules are appropriate for all children. You may also insist that your child take his medications and participate in therapeutic and medical treatment.

While it's very important that you prevail on these issues, it's best to avoid confrontation when possible. It may be fairly easy to get your child to take his medications, but what do you do if he refuses to cooperate at speech therapy? The answer is complex, but no different for your child than for a child without a disability. There are many possible strategies: Be consistent with your expectations, make it a game, give a time-out, use rewards, or admit that this session just isn't going to work out and go home. And always make sure your child gets to bed on time and has his nap, for like everyone else, his behavior will most likely deteriorate when he's tired. But if his resistance recurs regularly, work with the therapist to try a different, more enjoyable, approach to therapy.

For all other matters of discipline, two guidelines apply:

◆ If in the past your child has cooperated with your requests for good behavior in particular situations, continue to expect him to behave well in those situations.

◆ If he repeatedly fails to behave as you'd like him to in certain situations, take a step back and reconsider. Perhaps you need to lower your expectations for his behavior or try another approach (see pages 296–297).

Remember that children described as having special needs cover a very broad spectrum of capabilities. Children with more limited physical disabilities, such as hearing or vision loss, may be developmentally like their peers in most other ways. At the other end of the spectrum, some severely challenged children may remain, developmentally, infants. Be careful to adjust your expectations to your child's developmental ability. If your child is severely delayed, revise your expectations accordingly. If your child is developmentally on track aside from a hearing or vision problem, you can expect much the same behavior you would for other children his age.

Independence

You might feel very protective of your child. He's been through so much in his short life, and you don't want him to face any more difficulties. You may worry that his particular challenges may put him at risk for injuries and accidents. And you might be concerned that as he grows, he'll see that he isn't just like the other children around him. You may want to shield him from disappointment and frustration for fear that failure to do what the children around him can do will erode his self-confidence.

These fears and concerns are typical. You might discourage him from taking risks or participating in activities with even a hint of danger. You may not let him go on a swing for fear he'd fall off, or you may not let him try riding a tricycle because he lacks physical coordination. You might hold him back from trying something new because you're afraid he won't succeed. It's very difficult to quiet these anxieties. But it's important, for both of you, that you give him a chance to try.

You may be used to providing much of the daily care for your child, perhaps helping him with feeding and dressing. While it's faster and easier for you to do everything for him, your child needs a chance to try to do some of these tasks for himself.

Children with disabilities possess many of the same innate psychological needs as other children. Like all children, your child has a natural need to take control of the world around him. When he first succeeds in accomplishing something by himself, he'll most likely be delighted. Your sharing in his happiness will give him an added boost.

Failure is not unique to a special needs child: All children want to do more and learn new skills, and often they don't succeed. You can help make failure a positive experience with comforting words: "I know that climbing those stairs is difficult to do. And you tried so hard. I'm proud of you!" By giving your child a chance to try new challenges and do more for himself, you're giving him a chance to succeed and feel good about himself. He may require special equipment or extra precautions, but he'll still enjoying riding a tricycle as much as, or perhaps more than, anyone else. It's important to give him opportunities to enjoy life and accomplish personal growth—all according to his ability. Encourage your child to get involved in activities with other children, perhaps modifying the rules of a game or taking extra safety precautions if necessary. Your child will be happier and feel much better about himself if he's treated as much as is reasonably possible like a child without disabilities.

Love

You weren't planning to have a child with a disability when you imagined your future life. But your child is a special person, and you'll love him just as other parents love their children. Your love won't cure his disability, but it will make all you do for him even more worthwhile. No matter his limitations, your child is unique, he is wonderful, and he is your precious child.

ways to help you cope

1   **Rally support.** Your family can be an enormous help. They can assist you physically (by taking care of your child) and emotionally (by validating your complicated feelings and showing you that they care about you and your child). Some families find great comfort through prayer or through support groups.

2   **Make time for yourself.** Let someone you trust look after your baby while you do something for you—take a nap, take a shower, sit down and eat, or just get out of the house and go for a walk. It's normal to be grouchy and more prone to anger and frustration when you're tired and stressed. A little time away, ideally on a regular basis, is refreshing. When you return to duty, you'll feel more patient and happier.

3   **Work on your relationship with your partner.** With a special needs baby, both parents usually focus most of their energy on their child. You have so many time-consuming things to do, tending to your relationship can fall to the bottom of the priority list. Make an effort to regularly spend time alone together. Sharing your worries and feelings about your baby will strengthen the bond between you, and your lives will be much more enjoyable if you work together to care for your baby and each other. Listening empathetically to your partner's feelings is a wonderful way to be supportive. And you'll feel better, too, when you know your partner understands your emotions and stresses.

4   **Contact organizations.** Finding other parents who have similar concerns and experiences also will aid you. No matter what disability or medical problem your baby has, there is probably a national organization that provides educational resources, advice, and information to prepare you for what lies ahead. Many have networking programs and supportive online forums, and some may sponsor support groups in your community. Also check to see if there are any government services for which your family is eligible.

5   **Investigate.** Learn as much as you can about your baby's condition so you can confidently take charge of your child's care. Knowing what you need to do and how you will do it will silence many of your self-doubts.

6   **Get counseling.** Don't hesitate to seek help if you find yourself struggling with your emotions. Look for support groups in your community, seek professional counseling, or consult with religious advisors. It's important to take care of your emotional well-being.

Lifelong conditions

It's impossible to describe for you here every illness or disease that could have lifelong implications for a newborn—and thankfully, most of these are very rare. Here are a few of the more common conditions, how they can affect a child's health and development, and how they might be treated.

Hearing impairment

Hearing impairment can be present at birth (congenital) or develop later in childhood (acquired). Premature infants have a higher rate of hearing problems. Causes of congenital hearing loss include in utero viral infections and inherited forms of hearing loss. An acquired hearing problem can be caused by prematurity and its complications, medications, meningitis, or uncommon diseases of the middle and inner ear. Early detection and intervention—hearing aids, speech and language therapy, special programs, and sometimes cochlear implants—have greatly improved speech and language development for infants with hearing loss (see page 334).

Visual impairment

Vision damage can be caused by inherited diseases, glaucoma, congenital cataracts (see page 333), amblyopia (see page 334), damage to the area of the brain responsible for interpreting visual input, trauma, or prematurity.

Brain-based vision loss can occur if an eye isn't exposed to visual stimuli in the first month or two of life—for instance, due to a congenital cataract. The area of the brain that converts signals from that eye into visual images won't fully develop, and vision from that eye may remain poor. Vision loss can also occur if the eyes aren't aligned properly (as in amblyopia), resulting in a blurred image. The brain tries to create a clearer visual image by ignoring the image from one eye. If this continues, the suppressed eye can have permanent vision loss.

A large iris, tearing, and redness in the white of the eye can indicate glaucoma—increased fluid pressure in an eyeball. (The most common cause of excessive tearing is a blocked tear duct, which is a benign condition; see page 29 for more details.) Severe glaucoma can cause vision loss. Treatment can involve medicated eye drops and surgery.

Developmental delay

The term "developmental delay" encompasses a wide variety of conditions. Though they have different causes and symptoms, all have a similar result: slow progress reaching developmental milestones. Temporary developmental delays that are caused by environmental factors or illness are usually considered normal variations in development.

Developmental delay, as used here, refers to persistent delays in at least two, if not all four, spheres of development: gross motor, fine motor, personal-social, and language.

Note that a developmental delay is not the same as an intellectual disability—having an intelligence quotient (IQ) below 70 (compared to the average of 100) along with significant difficulty managing daily living skills, including communicating.

There's a long list of things that can cause a developmental delay, including inherited conditions, disorders of brain formation and growth, congenital infections, environmental toxins, brain injuries, oxygen deprivation, and meningitis. Yet many times a reason for a child's developmental delay is unknown.

A small head circumference at birth, poor head growth, and seizures or abnormalities in the neurological exam may be signs of a developmental delay, but some children show none of these signs.

Autism

Autism is a developmental disorder that primarily affects language and social interactions. Children with autism typically lack the ability to form bonds and interact with other people in the usual way. They may also struggle with verbal communication, have delayed development of speech abilities, and lack some of the skills required for normal interactive conversations.

Children with autism often have few, if any, delays in gross and fine motor skills, and many are very intelligent. There is a range of severity among children with autism, from profound to relatively mild impairment (Asperger's syndrome). Children with Asperger's syndrome have near-normal language and vocabulary, although they do not use language in the usual manner. They still lack social awareness and basic interactive skills, and exhibit behavioral rigidity.

Our knowledge of what causes autism is rudimentary. Autism may be a final common pathway of several disorders. We do know that there are some genetic predispositions for autism and that, in many cases, development of autism begins before birth or shortly after.

myths about autism

1 **Autism has increased in the past few decades.** More children are classified as having autism today than 30 years ago. Studies have shown much of the apparent increase is because doctors are more familiar with it and recognize it more often, and because the definition of autism has expanded. Years ago, only "classic" or "full-blown" cases of autism were formally diagnosed, but today we talk of an autistic spectrum of disease that includes variations and milder cases. A recent study demonstrated that as the number of diagnosed autism cases steadily increased in the past two decades, diagnoses of somewhat similar conditions decreased. Children who in the past might have been given a different diagnosis are today counted as having autism.

2 **The MMR vaccine causes autism.** In 1998, Dr. Andrew Wakefield published a report in the *Lancet* medical journal that started an international uproar—the misinformation heard 'round the world. Dr. Wakefield stated in his conclusions, "We did not prove an association between measles, mumps, and rubella vaccine [MMR] and the syndrome described . . . Further investigations are needed to examine this syndrome and its possible relation to this vaccine." Since then, more than 20 scientific studies have examined the connection between autism and MMR; all have shown that there is no relationship between MMR and autism. And in 2010, the *Lancet* retracted the discredited report. (See page 338 for more on the controversy.) It's clear that a diagnosis of autism soon after vaccination is a coincidence, not a cause-and-effect relationship. Regardless, some parents continue to view the MMR vaccine with suspicion, either requesting to receive the individual vaccines separately or not at all. Again, there is no scientific basis for these beliefs. Lower vaccination rates are causing several childhood diseases to become more common. Many of these, including measles, can have very serious effects (see page 355).

3 **Thimerosal (ethyl mercury) in vaccines causes autism.** No evidence has ever been presented that the mercury preservative in vaccines has harmed children. Thimerosal has been phased out of children's vaccines in the United States since 1999 as a precaution; today, vaccines for children under age 6 contain no or only trace amounts of thimerosal. There has been no decline in autism cases.

It's difficult to diagnose autism in infants because until they grow older, children don't have sophisticated interpersonal interactions and language skills. These usually aren't evident until the age of 15–18 months, so autism is usually diagnosed after this age. Early diagnosis and intense individual behavioral therapy can help autistic children improve their social and communication skills.

Attachment disorder

Reactive attachment disorder occurs when infants—typically neglected, abused, or orphaned—don't bond with a parent or caregiver and fail to establish a loving, caring attachment. In turn, these children are unable to form healthy relationships.

Most parents respond when their infant cries, praise him when he accomplishes a new skill, and shower him with love. As a result, their child learns that his basic needs will be met and that he is loved; these interactions form the basis of his ability to regard himself as a good person, to trust, and to have the capacity to care for others.

If deprived of these basic responses, a child may not develop the ability to care about and accept caring from other people. It's as if the infant says to himself, "If no one cares about me, then I won't care about anyone. If no one praises me for my accomplishments and encourages me to learn new skills, then I won't."

Parents are likely to see the effects of an attachment disorder if they adopt or foster children who suffered from early social isolation. Treatment involves plenty of love, psychological counseling, parental education, and activities designed to address developmental deficits.

Impaired bonding

A few conditions affecting the mother or infant can impair infant-parent bonding.

Postpartum depression is one of the most common maternal causes of impaired social relationships. Postpartum depression often leaves a mother both physically and emotionally spent, unable to lovingly respond to her newborn. If the family is intact, her partner or other relatives may need to step in to provide the infant with love and stimulation while the mother receives treatment. If you suspect that you may be suffering from postpartum depression, contact your doctor immediately—for the sake of you and your baby.

Premature infants and children with serious or chronic medical conditions may also suffer a degree of social isolation during long hospitalizations. However, this can be avoided by frequent contact with parents during such ordeals, and relieved by parental attention and caring behaviors.

Another instance of poor bonding may occur when an infant is born with a physical deformity or a poor prognosis for normal development. When faced with such a child, it is common for parents to mourn the loss of the newborn they were expecting. Most develop a strong attachment to their child despite the medical problems, but some reject the child and avoid forming bonds with him.

Heart disease

Heart disease may be congenital or acquired. Congenital defects are caused by abnormalities in the formation of the heart structures during fetal development. Acquired disease may result from viral infection of the heart muscle (myocarditis), bacterial infection of the heart valves (endocarditis), rheumatic fever (a complication of strep throat), inherited diseases of metabolism or connective tissue (Marfan syndrome), toxins, or poisons. There are also cardiac diseases of unknown origin, such as Kawasaki disease.

Many congenital defects can be improved or even repaired with surgery. In severe cases, a heart transplant may be recommended. Medication may increase the heart's efficiency when its pumping function is suboptimal. Children with certain abnormalities may need antibiotics before undergoing dental work to prevent heart valve infection. Good nutrition is key.

Children with acquired diseases and those who can't be fully healed with surgery can suffer lifelong disability. The most significant problem for children with chronic heart disease is the inability to meet the body's need

Severe food allergies

Severe food allergies are a serious condition that will affect your daily life and that of your child. If your child has a peanut or other food allergy that causes a severe allergic reaction, there is an ever-present possibility of accidental exposure and a life-threatening allergic reaction, called anaphylaxis. In addition to peanuts, common food allergies include tree nuts, dairy, eggs, soy, wheat, fish, and shellfish.

The number of children with peanut allergies has increased markedly in the past two decades, but no one knows exactly why. One popular hypothesis has been that early exposure to peanuts contributes to developing an allergy. This has led many families to hold off on giving their children peanuts until the age of 2 or 3. However, recent studies show no benefit to delayed exposure to peanuts. It's a good idea to talk with your pediatrician about the latest research and your family's medical history before deciding if and when to expose your child to peanuts.

Anaphylaxis can occur moments after ingesting peanuts or another food allergen. Symptoms can include swelling of the mouth, lips, and throat; shortness of breath; wheezing; abdominal pain and vomiting; rash (hives); pale appearance; and low blood pressure (shock). Seek medical help immediately if your child appears to be having an anaphylactic reaction.

Anaphylaxis can be treated with injections of epinephrine and sometimes antihistamines, but the best "treatment" is to prevent exposure to the allergy-causing food. This is no small task when a child is very young.

Carefully read food product labels to make sure they don't contain the allergy-causing food. Even if foods such as peanuts aren't listed as an ingredient, you need to be cautious because products can be contaminated with small remnants from other products manufactured at the same plant. There's also the chance that manufacturers of food products you've long known to be safe for your child can change ingredients without warning and add the allergy-causing food to the recipe.

Eating out is also a challenge. Carry with you some food you know that your child can safely eat. When you order, carefully question your server about the food and its preparation or ask to speak to the chef directly. Remnants of foods such as peanuts can linger on kitchen tools such as serving spoons and ice cream scoops.

Social gatherings aren't easy, either. At playdates or preschool, your child might be unwittingly exposed to allergy-causing foods in another child's lunch or snack.

Treats at birthday parties might contain peanuts, for example. The ever-present risk of accidental ingestion may make it hard for you to let your child out of your sight for long, and it can make even the most relaxed parent very anxious.

Children with a peanut or other serious allergy should have injectable epinephrine with them at all times and wear a medical-alert tag or bracelet. Be sure to talk to your child's teachers and parents of her friends about your child's peanut allergy. Some schools have a no-peanuts policy, and others may be willing to enact one. Provide a written emergency plan and epinephrine to your child's school. Also constantly check, ask, and remind your child, her playmates, and their parents to minimize chances of exposure.

A very helpful resource for parents of food-allergic children is the Food Allergy and Anaphylaxis Network (www.foodallergy.org).

for oxygen. Many such children do fine when at rest but are easily winded and exhausted. For small infants, the work of sucking on a bottle or the breast during a feeding can cause them to sweat and become short of breath. This can lead to an early end to the feeding and poor caloric intake. Treatment for nonsurgical heart diseases varies with the severity and type of disease, but often consists of enhanced nutrition and medication to allow the heart to adjust to the extra demands placed on it.

Down syndrome

Down syndrome is caused by an error in cell division early in the life of the tiny fetus. The typical facial and physical characteristics and associated medical problems derive from an extra copy of chromosome 21 in each cell.

Parents of children with Down syndrome sometimes learn their child has this condition in the second or third trimester, but many don't learn of the diagnosis until after delivery. Clues to Down syndrome at birth include very floppy muscle tone and a "scruffy" neck with excessive, loose skin at the back of the neck. Newborns don't yet show some of the typical facial features, including eyes that slant upward and outward, an extra fold of skin on the eyelids, and a face that appears flattened.

Children with Down syndrome may have a host of medical problems. Newborns are at risk for congenital heart defects, which may require surgery, and intestinal blockage. In childhood, they're at higher risk of ear infections and hypothyroidism (underactive thyroid).

Children with Down syndrome generally are slower to reach development milestones and have varying degrees of learning disability and cognitive impairment.

Cerebral palsy (CP)

Cerebral palsy is a disorder of motor skills caused by damage to the areas of the brain that control movement of the muscles. It sometimes includes learning disabilities or even mental retardation, although many children have perfectly normal intelligence and only impaired muscle control. Cerebral palsy may be caused by complications from prematurity, difficulties during labor and delivery that deprive the baby's brain of oxygen, meningitis (see page 348), or head trauma. Most often, though, the cause is unknown and probably is related to errors or accidents in brain development during fetal life.

Signs of CP usually don't appear until a baby is at least 5 to 6 months old. The first signs are delays in reaching motor milestones and tight muscle tone. The most common form of CP is spastic cerebral palsy, characterized by stiff muscles. Spastic CP can affect the arm and leg on one side of the body, both legs, or the whole body, causing the head to be held to one side and the wrists to be held in a bent position.

Children with cerebral palsy are likely to have several related medical problems, which can include muscle stiffness and weakness, gastroesophageal reflux disease (see page 171), difficulty swallowing and eating, clumsiness, and seizures. They may also have neurological difficulties, including intellectual and learning disabilities.

While cerebral palsy can't be cured, it also doesn't progress or become more severe. Treatment involves minimizing reflux symptoms, ensuring adequate nutrition, and encouraging motor skills with physical therapy, occasional injections of botulinum toxin to relieve muscle tightness and contractions, and use of devices such as braces to improve walking skills.

Spina bifida

This condition includes a broad range of abnormalities in the formation of the back of the spinal column, involving the bones or vertebrae that surround and protect the spinal cord as well as overlying skin and soft tissues. It develops in the first month of pregnancy when the neural tube doesn't close completely. The abnormality usually is located at the lower end of the spine.

The mildest cases, called spina bifida occulta, may be diagnosed only when an X-ray of the abdomen or pelvis taken for unrelated reasons reveals that vertebrae in the lower spine don't fully surround the spinal cord.

In the most severe cases, known as myelomeningocele, the lower spine isn't covered by skin. Without skin, soft tissues, and vertebrae to protect the spinal cord, the cord's lower end protrudes through the opening. Damaged nerves may cause some degree of paralysis and incontinence. Also, a significant number of cases have associated hydrocephalus (see page 367).

There are many variations in spina bifida, such as a sinus tract connecting the spine to the skin (see page 366), between these two extremes.

A skin abnormality over the lower part of the spinal column can be an early sign of spina bifida. Sacral dimples (see page 366), tufts of hair, or skin tags in this area may signal an abnormality in deeper tissues and vertebrae.

Spina bifida occulta requires no treatment and usually has no complications. Sinus tracts and other soft tissue abnormalities near the lower end of the spinal cord can be corrected surgically. If a newborn has myelomeningocele, he's first tested to see whether hydrocephalus is developing. Surgery is used to close the spinal defect and to treat hydrocephalus if present.

Even when spinal defects are surgically repaired, nerves have already been damaged. New research in myelomeningocele has shown that closing the spinal defect during fetal life (fetal surgery while still in the womb) can lessen the degree of or even prevent nerve damage.

Cystic fibrosis (CF)

This inherited, progressive disease primarily affects the lungs and gastrointestinal tract. It takes many forms, but it always involves abnormally thick mucous secretions in the lungs, pancreas, and other organs.

In the lungs, the thick secretions clog the small air conduits called bronchioles, leading to repeated cycles of infection and inflammation. Over time, the cumulative damage to the lungs becomes severe, and lung function declines. When thick secretions block pancreatic ducts, digestive enzymes can't reach the intestines, and digestion is impaired. The trapped enzymes also damage pancreatic cells.

There are many ways CF might become evident. In the newborn period, symptoms may include intestinal obstruction from a mass of thick mucus and feces (meconium). This syndrome, called meconium ileus, is unique to cystic fibrosis but relatively uncommon in affected children. Most often, a previously healthy infant or toddler has recurrent episodes of pneumonia and wheezing that leads to a diagnosis of CF. For some children, CF is diagnosed when poor digestive function causes poor weight gain and diarrhea. Other possible symptoms of CF include a chronic cough, recurrent sinus infections, nasal polyps, vomiting, and persistent diarrhea. Keep in mind that many of these symptoms, including wheezing, sinus infections, and nasal polyps, are common in otherwise healthy children who do not have cystic fibrosis.

Some states screen newborns for CF. Without screening, most children are diagnosed by the age of 2. Once suspected clinically, cystic fibrosis is confirmed by a sweat test or a blood test.

Lung function gradually worsens throughout childhood. Although pulmonary disease causes the most difficulty for children with CF, the abnormal secretions cause many other complications, such as sinusitis, nasal polyps, dehydration, and pancreatic or liver damage.

Children with CF usually are treated with outpatient care from a team of doctors, nutritionists, and other therapists at one of 110 accredited cystic fibrosis care centers in the United States and, when necessary, in a hospital. The life expectancy for a child with this chronic disease in the United States is in the mid-30s—a tremendous improvement in the past few decades.

Advances in treatment and better nutrition have greatly improved and extended the lives of children with CF. Pneumonia is aggressively treated with antibiotics. On a daily basis, rigorous chest physiotherapy helps clear air passageways. Inhaled medication also can help. Pancreatic enzyme pills aid digestion.

GROWTH CHARTS—BOYS

Birth to 24 months: Boys
Length-for-age and Weight-for-age percentiles

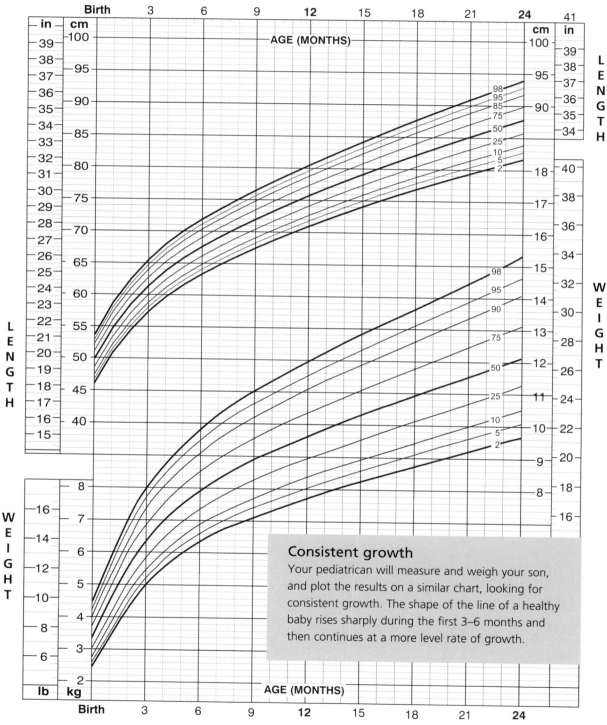

Consistent growth

Your pediatrican will measure and weigh your son, and plot the results on a similar chart, looking for consistent growth. The shape of the line of a healthy baby rises sharply during the first 3–6 months and then continues at a more level rate of growth.

2 to 5 years: Boys
Stature-for-age and Weight-for-age percentiles

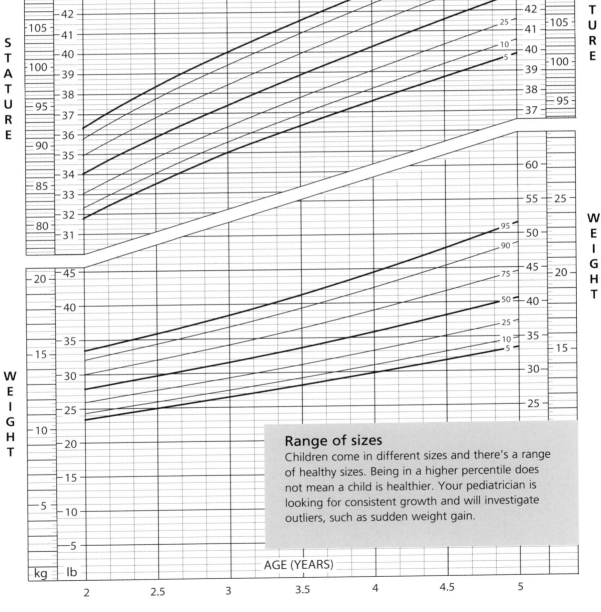

Range of sizes
Children come in different sizes and there's a range of healthy sizes. Being in a higher percentile does not mean a child is healthier. Your pediatrician is looking for consistent growth and will investigate outliers, such as sudden weight gain.

GROWTH CHARTS—GIRLS

Birth to 24 months: Girls
Length-for-age and Weight-for-age percentiles

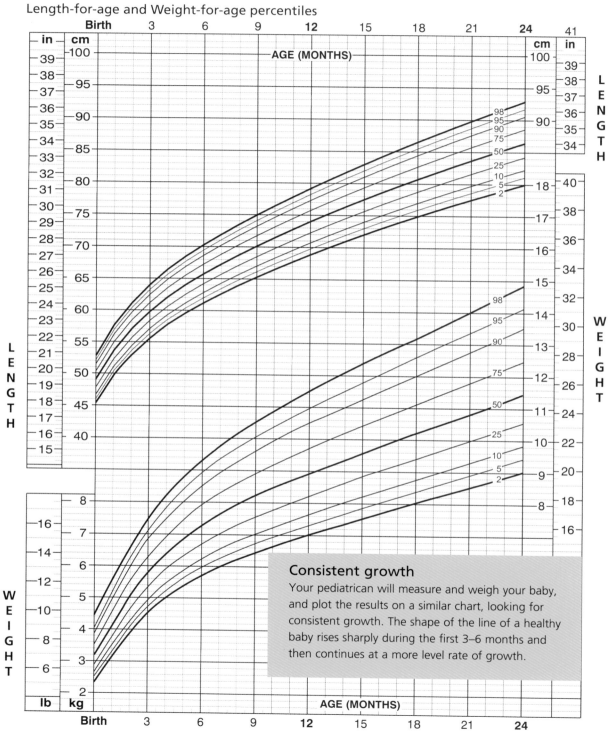

Consistent growth

Your pediatrican will measure and weigh your baby, and plot the results on a similar chart, looking for consistent growth. The shape of the line of a healthy baby rises sharply during the first 3–6 months and then continues at a more level rate of growth.

2 to 5 years: Girls
Stature-for-age and Weight-for-age percentiles

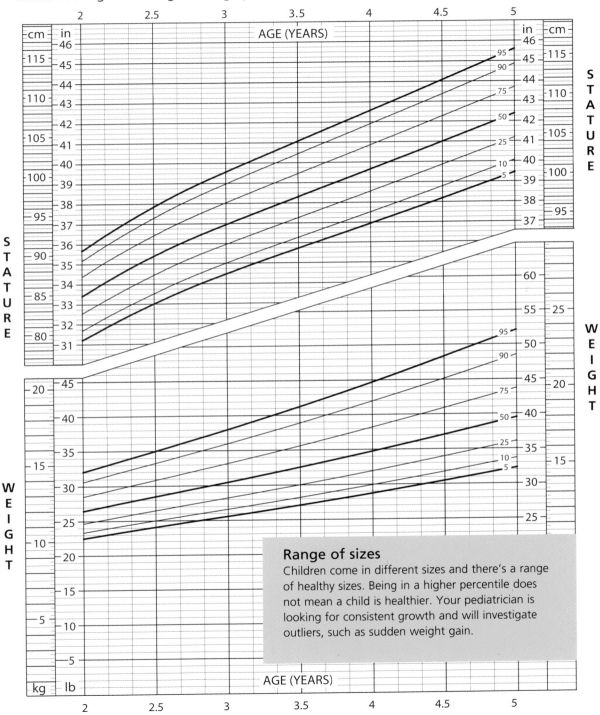

Range of sizes
Children come in different sizes and there's a range of healthy sizes. Being in a higher percentile does not mean a child is healthier. Your pediatrician is looking for consistent growth and will investigate outliers, such as sudden weight gain.

Index

Acknowledgments

Weldon Owen would like to thank Karen Ansel, MS, RD; Marianna Monaco; Macie Schreibman, Cathleen Small; Marisa Solís; Darienne Hosley Stewart; and Mary Zhang for their editorial assistance, and Simonne Waud, John Casey, and Emily Cook at Carroll & Brown.

Carroll & Brown would like to thank Brackley Proofreading Services, Jeseama Owen for make-up, and Amanda Williams for illustrations.

Picture credits

Front Jacket: Camera Press/Eltern
p9 Photolibrary.com; p10 Mothercare; p12–15 Mothercare; p21 Photolibrary.com; p25 Photolibrary.com; p27 (top left) Scott Camazine/ Science Photo Library; (top right) Lea Paterson/ Science Photo Library; (bottom left) Dr P. Marazzi/ Science Photo Library; (bottom right) Science Photo Library; p46 Photolibrary.com; p48 image courtesy of JoJo Maman Bebe; p56 Photolibrary. com; p58 Photolibrary.com; p60 BabyBjorn; p61 Photolibrary.com; p65 Photolibrary.com; p67 Photolibrary.com; p72 Photolibrary.com; p74-75 Angela Spain/Mother & Baby Picture Library; p76 Indira Flack/Mother & Baby Picture Library; p79 Photolibrary.com; p87 Photolibrary.com; p89 Photolibrary.com; p94 Photolibrary.com; p97 Tiny Traveller image courtesy of Bettacare Ltd; p98 Tracy Dominey/Science Photo Library; p118 Photolibrary.com; p121 Photolibrary.com; p124 Photolibrary.com; p126 Photolibrary.com; p128 Photolibrary.com; p130 Photolibrary.com; p155 Photolibrary.com; p169 Photolibrary.com; p172 Photolibrary.com; p176 Leigh Schindler; p179 Photolibrary.com; p196 Photolibrary.com; p197 (bottom) Photolibrary.com; p201 Photolibrary. com; p210 Photolibrary.com; p213 Photolibrary. com; p215 Photolibrary.com; p219 BabyBjorn; p220 BabyBjorn; p221 Photolibrary.com; p238 Photolibrary.com; p239 Photolibrary.com; p272 BSIP, Villareal/Science Photo Library; p280 Photolibrary.com; p281 Photolibrary.com; p286 Photolibrary.com; p287 Photolibrary.com; p292 Photolibrary.com; p295 Photolibrary.com; p296 Photolibrary.com; p303 Photolibrary.com; p312 Photolibrary.com; p319 Photolibrary.com; p321 Photolibrary.com; p324 Ian Hooton/Science Photo Library; p328 Photolibrary.com; p330 Annabella Bluesky/Science Photo Library; p331 Dr P. Marazzi/ Science Photo Library; p333 Paul Whitehill/Science Photo Library; p334 Dr P. Marazzi/Science Photo Library; p335 Dr P. Marazzi/Science Photo Library; p349 (top) Gustoimages/Science Photo Library; p361 AJ Photo/Science Photo Library; p362 Photolibrary.com; p364 Gustoimages/Science Photo Library; p368 LA LA/Science Photo Library; p370 (top) Bath Support image courtesy of Homecraft Rolyan Ltd; (middle) Buggie image courtesy of Amilly International Ltd; (bottom) Photolibrary. com; p380–383 Centers for Disease Control and Prevention (www.cdc.gov/growthcharts/).

Recipe credits

The following recipes appearing on pages 251–268 originally appeared in *The Baby and Toddler Cookbook,* by Karen Ansel, MS, RD, and Charity Ferreira, © 2010 Weldon Owen Inc.: Green Pea Purée; Zucchini Purée; Berry-Cherry Purée; Creamy Guacamole; Beet & Potato Swirl; Baby's Green Bean Casserole; Turkey for Baby; Root Veggie Stew; Red Lentil & Rice Soup; Baby's "Baked" Potato; Tofu, Rice & Avocado; Savory Brown Rice; Beet, Squash & Quinoa; Mini Salmon Cakes; Lamb for Baby; Creamy Pumpkin Risotto; Veggie Quesadilla; Cauliflower & Brown Rice Gratin; Tropical Fruit Salad; Whipped Ricotta with Cherries.